S0-CFG-514

SharePoint 2007 Development Recipes

A Problem-Solution Approach

Mark E. Gerow

SharePoint 2007 Development Recipes: A Problem-Solution Approach

Copyright © 2008 by Mark E. Gerow

All rights reserved. No part of this work may be reproduced or transmitted in any form or by any means, electronic or mechanical, including photocopying, recording, or by any information storage or retrieval system, without the prior written permission of the copyright owner and the publisher.

ISBN-13 (pbk): 978-1-4302-0961-4

ISBN-13 (electronic): 978-1-4302-0962-1

Printed and bound in the United States of America 9 8 7 6 5 4 3 2 1

Trademarked names may appear in this book. Rather than use a trademark symbol with every occurrence of a trademarked name, we use the names only in an editorial fashion and to the benefit of the trademark owner, with no intention of infringement of the trademark.

Lead Editor: Tony Campbell
Technical Reviewer: Seth Bates
Editorial Board: Clay Andres, Steve Anglin, Ewan Buckingham, Tony Campbell, Gary Cornell,
    Jonathan Gennick, Kevin Goff, Matthew Moodie, Joseph Ottinger, Jeffrey Pepper, Frank Pohlmann,
    Ben Renow-Clarke, Dominic Shakeshaft, Matt Wade, Tom Welsh
Project Manager: Richard Dal Porto
Copy Editor: Sharon Wilkey
Associate Production Director: Kari Brooks-Copony
Production Editor: Katie Stence
Compositor: Susan Glinert
Proofreader: Liz Welch
Indexer: Julie Grady
Artist: April Milne
Cover Designer: Kurt Krames
Manufacturing Director: Tom Debolski

Distributed to the book trade worldwide by Springer-Verlag New York, Inc., 233 Spring Street, 6th Floor, New York, NY 10013. Phone 1-800-SPRINGER, fax 201-348-4505, e-mail orders-ny@springer-sbm.com, or visit http://www.springeronline.com.

For information on translations, please contact Apress directly at 2855 Telegraph Avenue, Suite 600, Berkeley, CA 94705. Phone 510-549-5930, fax 510-549-5939, e-mail info@apress.com, or visit http://www.apress.com.

Apress and friends of ED books may be purchased in bulk for academic, corporate, or promotional use. eBook versions and licenses are also available for most titles. For more information, reference our Special Bulk Sales—eBook Licensing web page at http://www.apress.com/info/bulksales.

The information in this book is distributed on an "as is" basis, without warranty. Although every precaution has been taken in the preparation of this work, neither the author(s) nor Apress shall have any liability to any person or entity with respect to any loss or damage caused or alleged to be caused directly or indirectly by the information contained in this work.

The source code for this book is available to readers at http://www.apress.com. You may need to answer questions pertaining to this book in order to successfully download the code.

Contents at a Glance

About the Author ix

About the Technical Reviewer xi

Introduction xiii

CHAPTER 1   Site Management 1

CHAPTER 2   Working with Users 79

CHAPTER 3   Working with Lists 145

CHAPTER 4   Working with Web Parts 207

CHAPTER 5   Working with Event Handlers 337

CHAPTER 6   Working with Templates and Other XML Files 377

CHAPTER 7   Modifying Pages with JavaScript 427

CHAPTER 8   Advanced Dishes 443

INDEX 483

Contents

About the Author ix

About the Technical Reviewer xi

Introduction xiii

■CHAPTER 1   **Site Management** 1

Recipe 1-1. Creating a Site Collection by Using the Object Model. 1

Recipe 1-2. Creating a Site Collection by Using Web Services 10

Recipe 1-3. Creating a Site (or Web) by Using the Object Model. 21

Recipe 1-4. Creating a Site (or Web) by Using a Web Service 28

Recipe 1-5. Adding and Modifying Properties of a Site. 38

Recipe 1-6. Adding a Web Part by Using the Object Model 46

Recipe 1-7. Adding a Web Part by Using a .dwp or .webpart File 55

Recipe 1-8. Calculating Storage for all Document Libraries in
            a Site. 64

Recipe 1-9. Creating a Script to Back Up All Site Collections
            by Using STSADM 73

■CHAPTER 2   **Working with Users** 79

Recipe 2-1. Obtaining and Displaying Users of a Site. 79

Recipe 2-2. Adding Users to a Site by Using the Object Model 90

Recipe 2-3. Adding Users and Groups to a Site by Using the
            Web Services 97

Recipe 2-4. Adding Groups to a Site by Using the Object Model 105

Recipe 2-5. Adding Roles to a Web Site by Using the Object Model . . . 112

Recipe 2-6. Adding Roles to a Web Site by Using the Web Services. . . 121

Recipe 2-7. Adding Users to Active Directory. 132

■**CHAPTER 3** **Working with Lists** 145

Recipe 3-1. Creating a List by Using the Object Model 145
Recipe 3-2. Creating a List by Using Web Services 156
Recipe 3-3. Updating a List by Using the Object Model 167
Recipe 3-4. Updating a List by Using Web Services 180
Recipe 3-5. Adding a Document to a Document Library
by Using the Object Model 191
Recipe 3-6. Adding a Document to a Document Library
by Using Web Services 197

■**CHAPTER 4** **Working with Web Parts** 207

Recipe 4-1. Creating a Simple RSS Feed Web Part 208
Recipe 4-2. Creating an XML Web Part 219
Recipe 4-3. Creating a SQL Web Part 238
Recipe 4-4. Creating a Page Viewer Web Part 250
Recipe 4-5. Creating a Connectable Page Viewer Web Part 261
Recipe 4-6. Reading Web-Part Parameters from the Querystring 273
Recipe 4-7. Using the SmartPart to Expose a .NET User Control 285
Recipe 4-8. Creating a ZoneTab Web Part 298
Recipe 4-9. Creating a Web Part to Edit SPWeb Properties 316

■**CHAPTER 5** **Working with Event Handlers** 337

Why Create an Event Handler? 337
When to Use an Event Handler Rather Than a Workflow? 338
Event Handler Enhancements in SharePoint 2007 338
Recipe 5-1. Updating List Fields When Adding a Document
to a Document Library 339
Recipe 5-2. Sending an Email When a Task Is Completed 349
Recipe 5-3. Preventing Deletion by Using an Event Handler 357
Recipe 5-4. Creating a Calculated Field by Using an Event Handler . . . 364

■**CHAPTER 6** **Working with Templates and Other XML Files** 377

Recipe 6-1. Adding a PDF Image to Docicon.xml 377
Recipe 6-2. Adding Custom Menus by Using a Feature 381
Recipe 6-3. Adding Web Parts Through Onet.xml 402
Recipe 6-4. Adding an ExecuteUrl Directive to Onet.xml 409

CHAPTER 7   Modifying Pages with JavaScript 427

Recipe 7-1. Hiding the QuickLaunch Menu 427
Recipe 7-2. Opening List Items in a New Window.................. 435

CHAPTER 8   Advanced Dishes 443

Recipe 8-1. Customizing the STSADM Command.................. 443
Recipe 8-2. Crawling a Database Table by Using a BDC Schema..... 452
Recipe 8-3. Creating a Custom MOSS Search Page 471

INDEX 483

About the Author

MARK GEROW works for Fenwick & West LLP in Mountain View, California, where he directs the application development team and is responsible for defining and implementing the firm's intranet and extranet strategies using SharePoint technologies. He is the author of *Creating Client Extranets with SharePoint 2003* (Apress), as well as numerous articles on a variety of aspects of SharePoint application development for ASP Today Online, *Advisor Guide to Microsoft SharePoint*, Law.com, and *Peer to Peer—The Quarterly Magazine of ILTA*. Mark has 25 years of experience in all aspects of business and commercial software development and project management.

About the Technical Reviewer

SETH BATES is the managing solutions architect for DataLan Corporation, a Microsoft Gold Certified Partner specializing in information-worker solutions, located in White Plains, New York. He coauthored *SharePoint 2007 User's Guide: Learning Microsoft's Collaboration and Productivity Platform* and *SharePoint 2003 User's Guide*, both published by Apress. He also performed the technical editing of the Apress books *Advanced SharePoint Services Solutions* and *Microsoft SharePoint: Building Office 2003 Solutions*, and wrote an article titled "SharePoint Web Part Development" in the April 2005 edition of *Dr. Dobb's Journal*. Seth has helped numerous organizations, including Fortune 500 companies, successfully adopt the SharePoint platform and has spoken at SharePoint industry conferences. With more than 10 years of experience engineering business solutions, primarily using Microsoft technologies, Seth brings a broad mix of expertise in all phases of the software engineering life cycle to his work.

Introduction

Welcome to *SharePoint 2007 Development Recipes: A Problem-Solution Approach*! What you're about to read is the result of an idea thread that's been rolling around in my head for several years—the need for a practical guide that empowers and enables developers to leverage the full potential of SharePoint in the enterprise.

Note Thanks to Microsoft, just about every book on SharePoint 2007 starts out with a note defining the term. That's because *SharePoint* can refer to two distinct but closely related products. The first, Windows SharePoint Services (or WSS) is a part of the Windows 2003 operating system (although it must be downloaded and installed separately). WSS, which is free of charge, provides all the core services that you expect, such as security, list management, and web-part support. It's possible to build very sophisticated solutions just using WSS. The second product is Microsoft Office SharePoint Server (MOSS), which builds on top of WSS, is not free, and provides such features as the Business Data Catalog (BDC), Records Management, Enterprise Search, and much more. MOSS takes WSS to new levels in terms of supporting enterprise use of the Office components. Most of the recipes in this book will work equally well in either environment. I will note where a recipe is applicable to only one of the two, or where some changes need to be made depending on the environment.

Early on in my work with SharePoint 2001, I came to view it more as a platform than a product. Since that time, SharePoint has grown tremendously in scope. With SharePoint 2003, we saw the development of robust .NET and web services APIs, as well as a fully thought-out templating model. Just when I thought I understood SharePoint pretty well, the 2007 version was released.

One admittedly crude way of gauging functionality is to look at the number of class library namespaces (for example, `Microsoft.SharePoint.Administration`) in the API. In SharePoint 2003 there were about 15 libraries in the WSS object model. That number has grown to 35 in the current version! Here are just a few of the major new or significantly enhanced features in SharePoint (both WSS and MOSS):

- .NET 2.0 web-part support

- Auditing

- Business Data Catalog (BDC)

- Content types

- Event receivers

- Forms-based authentication

- Features and solutions

- Master pages

- RSS

- Search

- Workflow

...and a thousand others.

■**Note** For a complete list of SharePoint namespaces, classes, methods, and properties, refer to the SharePoint 2007 SDK at http://msdn.microsoft.com/en-us/library/ms550992.aspx.

If nothing else, SharePoint is a great platform for developers who love to learn new programming constructs, objects, and tools (if you don't *love* to learn, you're in for a rough ride with SharePoint). The reward, however, is equally great. In my 25 years of building software, I have never worked with a platform that is as broad and deep, has such a well-developed API, or is as malleable as SharePoint. I'm no apologist for Microsoft, but I must say they *get* developers, and SharePoint is a case in point.

But you didn't buy this book to hear me wax poetic about a product or the company that produced it. You bought this book to get real work done real soon. Let me say a few words about how this book is organized and then we'll get to the meat of it.

Is This a "Beginner" or "Advanced" Book?

One question that always comes up when discussing a book is the audience: specifically, whether a book is for beginning, intermediate, or advanced readers. To me, this is the wrong question. The *right* question is, "Will the book provide information that you don't already possess, or provide information that you already have but in a more accessible form?" In my experience, people who write computer applications tend to be very bright, so it's not a question of intelligence. But SharePoint is such a broad and deep technology that it's quite possible to be a master of some topics and a novice at others. For example, you might be an expert at creating web parts or BDC schemas yet never have looked into creating event handlers or workflow.

Like a cookbook, *SharePoint 2007 Development Recipes* assumes a certain level of proficiency on the part of the reader. I'll assume you know how to create the basic .NET project types: console, ASP.NET, and ASP.NET web service. That being the case, I won't do a lot of setup for the recipes, just launch in to where the coding begins.

In addition, although we'll cover the basics of deploying a web part, feature, or solution, that's not the focus here. There are many great books and articles that can help you do those things. So the emphasis, again, will be on the cooking rather than the preparation.

Which leads me to another point: this book is much less about theory than practice. Not that understanding the underlying theory of a software platform isn't valuable; it is. It's just that my bias is toward getting things done rather than figuring out how many angels can dance on the head of any particular pin. If you want to know why Microsoft wants you to use SharePoint for human-centric workflows and BizTalk for machine-centric workflows, ask Microsoft. If you want a set of guidelines for when to use a list event receiver, and when to use a workflow to accomplish a given task, or how to add a web part to 1,000 sites programmatically, you've come to the right place.

At the end of the day, this book is designed to be used as a desk reference by those developing applications on top of the SharePoint 2007 platform. It's organized much like a cookbook, with recipes grouped by purpose (administration, webs, lists, web parts, and so forth). Although you can pick just the recipes that meet your immediate needs, browsing through other sections will provide you with lots of ideas for new approaches, techniques, and applications. Of course, a book like this, on a platform as extensive as SharePoint, can never be all-encompassing. What you'll find here are my favorites: recipes that have proven useful in my experience, and that as a whole expose a large part of what's possible with SharePoint. If I hear from one reader that a recipe in this book enabled them to meet a deadline because they could "steal" some code, tweak it a bit, and get what they needed working quickly, I'll feel I've done my job.

How This Book Is Organized

Each recipe is presented by using a common structure that's designed to provide you with a complete set of conceptual tools, as well as working source code, to implement and build on that recipe to make it your own. Specifically, each recipe has the following components:

Recipe Type

The recipe tells you right up front what will be cooked up—a console application, web service, web application, event handler, web part, or script.

Ingredients

Provides a list of all key libraries, classes, and web services that the recipe relies on. Ingredients are further broken down into assembly references (that is, those you need to add to your Visual Studio project), class library references that need to be referenced with `using` or `Imports` statements, web services references, or individual classes used.

Special Considerations

Gives pointers and alerts you to issues you need to be aware of to correctly use the recipe and understand why certain design decisions were made.

Process Flow

The process flow includes a graphical representation of key recipe processes, as well as a supporting narrative describing those steps. This helps clarify the logic behind the core elements of the recipe.

Recipe Code

Ultimately, this book is about building working solutions. With that in mind, each recipe provides complete, working code in both C# and VB.NET. Recipes range from .NET console applications to web applications to web services. The emphasis is on demonstrating the core SharePoint programming constructs rather than creating fancy user interfaces—which I leave to you.

To Run

This is where you get to "taste" the fruits of your labor. In this section, you'll find exactly what you need to run the application you've just built, including any steps to add web parts, create Internet Information Services virtual directories, set properties, and the like.

Variations

Here I'll provide suggestions for alterations to the recipe that you may want to consider. Of course, the real fun is when you make these recipes your own by creating the variations that are uniquely yours!

Related Recipes

If there are other recipes in the book that share similarities or may be of particular interest in relationship to the currently described recipe, I'll note them in this section.

Have Fun with It!

Finally, the term *recipe* has been used intentionally, as I hope you will take what you find here and make it your own by adding your own dashes of code and flourishes of genius.

Consider what you find in these pages a starting point, not the final word.

Happy coding!

CHAPTER 1

■■■

Site Management

The recipes in this chapter focus on automating tasks related to managing site collections and sites. You might be thinking that SharePoint 2007 (either Microsoft Office SharePoint Server or Windows SharePoint Services 3.0) already provides some pretty nifty ways to manage sites through the user interface (UI). For example, it's easy to add a web part and configure it on a web-part page. And backing up a site collection by using STSADM is pretty straightforward.

But what if, instead of a single site, we're talking about 1,000 sites that all need the same web part added? You could, of course, create a Feature and deploy it to your web application, but that doesn't put the web part on the page. And what if you want to make the same change to one or more property settings on a web part for all those 1,000 sites? And what if that change differs based on some other information on the site? You get the picture.

So the first set of recipes in this chapter shows you how to create site collections and sites, as well as enables you to manage web parts programmatically, making it feasible to customize large numbers of sites. There are also recipes to help you calculate storage for a given list or for a site (you can already get the storage for an entire site collection).

Finally, this chapter provides a recipe to enable you to take control of the backup process, making it easier to backup and recover individual site collections when needed.

Let's dig in…

Recipe 1-1. Creating a Site Collection by Using the Object Model

Programmatically generating site collections has many advantages in terms of promoting consistency of organization. For example, you may want to make sure that the naming of new site collections follows a corporate standard and that these collections are created by using a particular path. You may also want to ensure that a specific account is assigned to the site collection administrators group. The following recipe shows you how to accomplish these programming goals by using the object model and a .NET console application. The functionality is similar to that found in the STSADM -O CREATESITE command, with one twist—this recipe will prompt the user for missing parameters. However, you can build on this recipe to expand its functionality as needed.

Recipe Type: .NET Console Application

Ingredients

■**Note** Assembly references are made by right-clicking the project name in the Solution Explorer and then choosing the Add Reference option. Class Library references are added by placing C# `using` or Visual Basic (VB) `Imports` statements for the specified library at the top of a module, class, or code-behind file.

Assembly References

- Windows SharePoint Services .NET assembly

Class Library References

- `Microsoft.SharePoint` library

- `Microsoft.SharePoint.Administration` library

Special Considerations

- SharePoint requires that site collections be created by accounts that have sufficient privileges. The following recipe is designed to be used in a .NET console application, and can be run either manually or via the Windows Task Scheduler. Console applications are particularly useful in combination with the Windows Task Scheduler application, enabling you to create processes that run against SharePoint at predefined intervals.

- Although this recipe essentially duplicates what is available through the `STSADM -O` `CREATESITE` command, it opens up many possibilities for customizations (such as prompting the user for missing parameters).

- Because of security restrictions that SharePoint imposes on ASP.NET web applications and services, members of the `Microsoft.SharePoint.Administration` library are best used through console or Windows applications, where the security context is directly inherited from the user. The limitation is that these applications must be run from a front-end web server that is part of the SharePoint farm. This is appropriate for administrative tools, but not convenient if you want to make this functionality available to end users. In a related recipe using the SharePoint web service, you'll see how to build an ASP.NET web application to add new site collections.

Process Flow

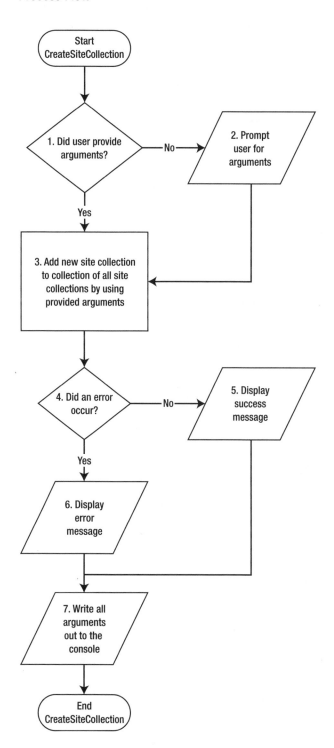

1. The first step is to determine whether the user passed in the necessary arguments to this process. If so, they will be used when calling the SPSiteCollection.Add() method. If not, you need to get that information from the user now.

2. Prompt the user for the necessary data by using the WriteLine() and Read() methods.

3. Using the supplied inputs, call the SPSiteCollection.Add() method to add the new site collection.

4. If the SPSiteCollection.Add() method throws an exception, go to step 6; otherwise go to step 5.

5. Display a success message to the console. Go to step 7.

6. Display an error message, including a description of the exception thrown, to the console.

7. Write all parameters back to the console so the user can see exactly what was received and acted on by the application.

■**Note** The SPSiteCollection object is poorly named, in that it really refers to a collection of site collections. This naming is a continuation of the semantic confusion of earlier versions of SharePoint, where the terms *site* and *site collection* were (and still are) used interchangeably in some contexts, while the terms *site* and *web* are used to mean the same thing in others.

Recipe—VB (See CreateSiteCollectionConsole-VB, File Module1.vb)

```vb
Imports Microsoft.SharePoint
Imports Microsoft.SharePoint.Administration
Module Module1
    Sub Main (ByVal args() As String)
        'Steps 1-2: If no arguments have been passed,
        'prompt user to enter them now
        If args.Length = 0 Then
            ReDim args(7)
            args = GetParams(args)
        End If
        'Add the new site collection using the provided arguments
        AddSiteCollection(args)
    End Function
    Private Function AddSiteCollection(ByVal args() As String) As Integer
        Try
            'Get a handle to the root site on server
            Dim arrSitePath As String() = args(0).Split("/")
            Dim strServerPath As String = arrSitePath(0) & "//" & _
            arrSitePath(2)
            Dim site As New SPSite(strServerPath)
            'Get the list of site collections for the web application
```

```vb
            Dim siteCollection As SPSiteCollection = _
                site.WebApplication.Sites
            'Step 3: Add the site collection
            'args(0) = Site url
            'args(1) = Title
            'args(2) = Description
            'args(3) = Web template
            'args(4) = Owner login
            'args(5) = Owner name
            'args(6) = Owner email
            siteCollection.Add( _
                args(0), _
                args(1), _
                args(2), _
                1033, _
                args(3), _
                args(4), _
                args(5), _
                args(6))
            'Step 5: Confirm site collection information
            Console.WriteLine()
            Console.WriteLine("Site collection '" & args(0) & _
                "' successfully created.")
            Console.WriteLine()
            DisplayParams(args)
            'Release memory used by SPSite object
            site.Dispose()
            Return 0
        Catch ex As Exception
            'Step 6: If error occurs, display parameters and error message
            Console.WriteLine()
            Console.WriteLine("** ERROR OCCURRED **")
            Console.WriteLine()
            Console.WriteLine(ex.Message)
            Console.WriteLine()
            DisplayParams(args)
            Console.WriteLine()
        End Try
    End Sub
    Private Sub DisplayParams(ByVal args)
        Try
            'Step 7: Display parameters to console
            Console.WriteLine("Site url: " & args(0))
            Console.WriteLine("Title: " & args(1))
            Console.WriteLine("Description: " & args(2))
            Console.WriteLine("Template name: " & args(3))
            Console.WriteLine("Owner login: " & args(4))
```

```vb
            Console.WriteLine("Owner name: " & args(5))
            Console.WriteLine("Owner email: " & args(6))
        Catch ex As Exception
            'If error occurred, display the error message
            Console.WriteLine()
            Console.WriteLine(ex.Message)
            Console.WriteLine()
        End Try
    End Sub
    Private Function GetParams(ByRef args() As String) As String()
        Try
            'Step 2: Get parameters from user
            Console.WriteLine()
            Console.Write("Site url: ")
            args(0) = Console.ReadLine()
            Console.Write("Title: ")
            args(1) = Console.ReadLine()
            Console.Write("Description: ")
            args(2) = Console.ReadLine()
            Console.Write("Template name: ")
            args(3) = Console.ReadLine()
            Console.Write("Owner login: ")
            args(4) = Console.ReadLine()
            Console.Write("Owner name: ")
            args(5) = Console.ReadLine()
            Console.Write("Owner email: ")
            args(6) = Console.ReadLine()
        Catch ex As Exception
            'If an error occurred, display the error message
            Console.WriteLine()
            Console.WriteLine(ex.Message)
            Console.WriteLine()
        End Try
        Return args
    End Function
End Module
```

___

■**Tip** Whenever you create a new SPSite object or reference an SPWeb object, you should call their Dispose()
methods when done, to avoid leaving discarded copies in memory and the associated "memory leak." The
reason that you need to explicitly Dispose() of these objects is that SPSite and SPWeb are thin wrappers
around unmanaged code, and thus are not automatically handled by the .NET garbage-collection routines.
See the Microsoft article at http://msdn2.microsoft.com/en-us/library/aa973248.aspx for
more information.

___

Recipe—C# (See CreateSiteCollectionConsole-CS, File Program.cs)

```csharp
using Microsoft.SharePoint;
using Microsoft.SharePoint.Administration;
using System;
class Module1 {
    static void Main(string[] args) {
        // Steps 1-2: If no arguments have been passed,
        // prompt user to enter them now
        if ((args.Length == 0)) {
            args = new string[7];
            args = GetParams(ref args);
        }
        // Add the new site collection using the provided arguments
        AddSiteCollection(args);
    }
    private static int AddSiteCollection(string[] args) {
        try {
            // Get a handle to the root site on server
            string[] arrSitePath = args[0].Split('/');
            string strServerPath = (arrSitePath[0]
                + ("//" + arrSitePath[2]));
            SPSite site = new SPSite(strServerPath);
            // Get the list of site collections for the web
            // application
            SPSiteCollection siteCollection =
                site.WebApplication.Sites;
            // Step 3: Add the site collection
            // args(0) = Site url
            // args(1) = Title
            // args(2) = Description
            // args(3) = Web template
            // args(4) = Owner login
            // args(5) = Owner name
            // args(6) = Owner email
            siteCollection.Add(args[0], args[1], args[2], 1033,
                args[3], args[4], args[5], args[6]);
            // Step 5: Confirm site collection information
            Console.WriteLine();
            Console.WriteLine(("Site collection \'"
                    + (args[0] + "\' successfully created.")));
            Console.WriteLine();
            DisplayParams(args);
            // Release memory used by SPSite object
            site.Dispose();
            return 0;
        }
```

```
            catch (Exception ex) {
                // Step 6: If error occurs, display parameters and error message
                Console.WriteLine();
                Console.WriteLine("** ERROR OCCURRED **");
                Console.WriteLine();
                Console.WriteLine(ex.Message);
                Console.WriteLine();
                DisplayParams(args);
                Console.WriteLine();
                return -1;
            }
        }
        private static void DisplayParams(string[] args) {
            try {
                // Step 7: Display parameters to console
                Console.WriteLine(("Site url: " + args[0]));
                Console.WriteLine(("Title: " + args[1]));
                Console.WriteLine(("Description: " + args[2]));
                Console.WriteLine(("Template name: " + args[3]));
                Console.WriteLine(("Owner login: " + args[4]));
                Console.WriteLine(("Owner name: " + args[5]));
                Console.WriteLine(("Owner email: " + args[6]));
            }
            catch (Exception ex) {
                // If error occurred, display the error message
                Console.WriteLine();
                Console.WriteLine(ex.Message);
                Console.WriteLine();
            }
        }
        private static string[] GetParams(ref string[] args) {
            try {
                // Step 2: Get parameters from user
                Console.WriteLine();
                Console.Write("Site url: ");
                args[0] = Console.ReadLine();
                Console.Write("Title: ");
                args[1] = Console.ReadLine();
                Console.Write("Description: ");
                args[2] = Console.ReadLine();
```

```
            Console.Write("Template name: ");
            args[3] = Console.ReadLine();
            Console.Write("Owner login: ");
            args[4] = Console.ReadLine();
            Console.Write("Owner name: ");
            args[5] = Console.ReadLine();
            Console.Write("Owner email: ");
            args[6] = Console.ReadLine();
        }
        catch (Exception ex) {
            // If an error occurred, display the error message
            Console.WriteLine();
            Console.WriteLine(ex.Message);
            Console.WriteLine();
        }
        return args;
    }
}
```

To Run

This console application would typically be either run interactively from a command window or called from a command script. Figure 1-1 shows it being run interactively.

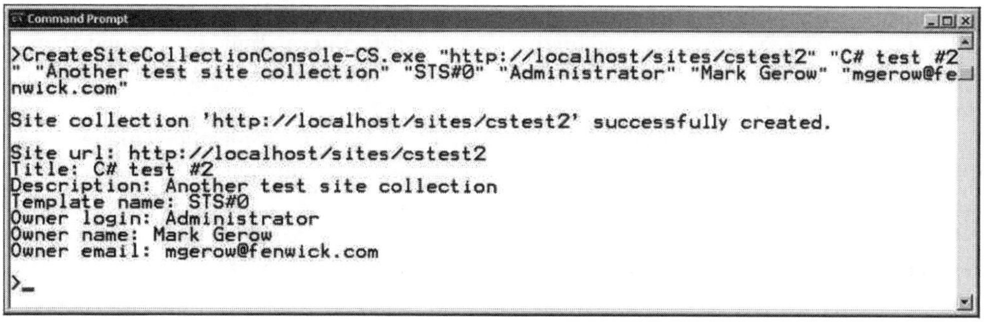

Figure 1-1. *Running the CreateSiteCollectionConsole application*

In the preceding example, I passed all the needed parameters on the command line and so was not prompted to enter them. If I'd entered only the command CreateSiteCollectionConsole-CS.exe, the program would have prompted me to enter the missing data.

Variations

- Use a console app as in the preceding example, but instead of using the SharePoint object model classes, shell out (that is, run a separate command file) to the STSADM -O CREATESITE command. Although this may be less work initially, it makes input validation and error trapping more difficult.

- Use a web application that shells out to the preceding application. This sidesteps Share-Point's security restriction on ASP.NET applications, but again makes error trapping next to impossible. You'll see in a related recipe how to use the SharePoint web services in combination with an ASP.NET application as a better alternative to this variation.

- Use a .NET Windows application instead of a console application. This enables you to create a more elegant UI, but remember that the application can run only on a front-end web server in your SharePoint farm.

Recipe 1-2. Creating a Site Collection by Using Web Services

As you saw in the previous recipe, it's a straightforward matter to create a new site collection by using the object model. Why then would you ever need to use the SharePoint web service alternative? The answer to this highlights one of the key benefits of using the SharePoint web services, namely, portability.

Although the object model exposes virtually all the features and functions of SharePoint, it must be used by .NET programs that execute on a SharePoint front-end web server. This is not true of the web services, which may be called from any computer that has sufficient privileges to connect to the SharePoint web site. This means that by using SharePoint web services (or custom web services you create based on the object model), you can build distributed Share-Point solutions in which some of the components may reside anywhere in the world that an Internet connection is available.

We also saw that SharePoint's security restrictions on ASP.NET applications made calling the SPSiteCollection.Add() method from an ASP.NET application impractical. The web service equivalent does not have that limitation.

The following recipe provides similar functionality to that available in the object model version, but uses the SharePoint web service instead.

■**Note** The account you use to access the Admin web service must be a member of the Farm Administrators group in the Central Administration site.

Recipe Type: ASP.NET Web Application

Ingredients

Web Services

- `http://Virtual_Server_Name:[central admin port]/_vti_adm/Admin.asmx`

- `http://Virtual Server Name:[web app port]/_vti_bin/Sites.asmx`

■**Note** Web services references are added by right-clicking on the project name in the Solution Explorer window and choosing the Add Web Reference option.

The preceding two URLs represent the logical locations for SharePoint web services. To make these web services available, use the Visual Studio Add Web Reference option. In the following code, I've named the references `AdminService` and `SitesService`, respectively.

Special Considerations

- The most important thing to keep in mind with SharePoint web services (as with any web service) is that they are web pages that you call programmatically. And, like many web pages, they require the calling process to authenticate before responding. With a web service, this authentication must be explicit, so it's important to always set the `Credential` property of the object instance of the service before calling any method that will return data. Not doing so, in my experience, is the number one cause of errors when using SharePoint web services.

- In the following code, I'm using the `System.Net.CredentialCache.DefaultCredentials` property to assign the credentials of the current user (assuming the ASP.NET application is impersonating the logged-in user). This means that if the current user doesn't have *Farm Administrator* permissions, that user won't be able to add a site collection and the add operation will fail. If you want to force all requests to run under a specific account, you can use the `System.Net.NetworkCredential()` method instead to create a credential for a specific user login (for example, a service account) that you know will have sufficient permissions.

■**Note** This is an ASP.NET recipe, but SharePoint web services may be called from any .NET application, including Console, WinForm, Windows Service, Web Application, or Web Service.

Process Flow

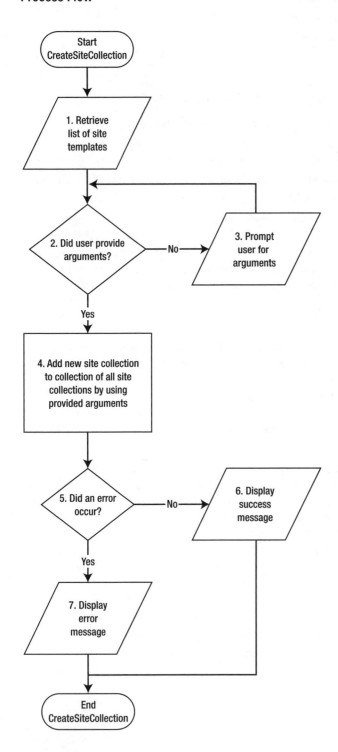

1. Retrieve the list of available site templates.

2. Verify that the user filled in all fields on the web page.

3. If one or more required fields are missing, prompt the user to provide missing data before proceeding.

4. Call the SharePoint web service to add the new site collection.

5. Trap any errors.

6. If no errors occurred while adding the new site collection, display a success message.

7. If an error did occur, display an error message.

Recipe—ASPX (See Project CreateSiteCollectionWebService-VB, File Default.aspx)

■**Note** The following is the ASPX code for the VB version of this recipe. Other than minor changes to the %@Page language and code file attributes, this code is identical to the C# version.

```
<%@ Page Language="VB" AutoEventWireup="false" CodeFile="Default.aspx.vb"
        Inherits="_Default" %>
<!DOCTYPE html PUBLIC "-//W3C//DTD XHTML 1.0 Transitional//EN"
        "http://www.w3.org/TR/xhtml1/DTD/xhtml1-transitional.dtd">
<html xmlns="http://www.w3.org/1999/xhtml" >
<head runat="server">
    <title>Untitled Page</title>
</head>
<body>
    <form method="post" id="form1" runat="server">
    <div>
        <table>
            <tr>
                <td style="width: 163px">
                    Site collection path:</td>
                <td style="width: 100px">
                    <asp:TextBox ID="txtSiteCollPath" runat="server">
                        http://localhost/sites</asp:TextBox></td>
                <td style="width: 169px">
                    </td>
            </tr>
            <tr>
                <td style="width: 163px">
                    Template:</td>
```

```
                <td style="width: 100px">
                    <asp:DropDownList ID="ddlTemplate" runat="server">
                    </asp:DropDownList></td>
                <td style="width: 169px">
                </td>
            </tr>
            <tr>
                <td style="width: 163px">
                    Site name:</td>
                <td style="width: 100px">
                    <asp:TextBox ID="txtSiteName" runat="server"></asp:TextBox></td>
                <td style="width: 169px">
                </td>
            </tr>
            <tr>
                <td style="width: 163px">
                    Site owner login:</td>
                <td style="width: 100px">
                    <asp:TextBox ID="txtOwnerLogin" runat="server"></asp:TextBox>
                 </td>
                <td style="width: 169px">
                </td>
            </tr>
            <tr>
                <td style="width: 163px">
                    Owner name:</td>
                <td style="width: 100px">
                    <asp:TextBox ID="txtOwnerName" runat="server"></asp:TextBox>
                </td>
                <td style="width: 169px">
                </td>
            </tr>
            <tr>
                <td style="width: 163px">
                    Site owner email:</td>
                <td style="width: 100px">
                    <asp:TextBox ID="txtOwnerEmail" runat="server"></asp:TextBox>
                </td>
                <td style="width: 169px">
                </td>
            </tr>
            <tr>
                <td style="width: 163px">
                    Title:</td>
                <td style="width: 100px">
                    <asp:TextBox ID="txtTitle" runat="server"></asp:TextBox></td>
                <td style="width: 169px">
                </td>
```

```
            </tr>
            <tr>
                <td style="width: 163px">
                    Description:</td>
                <td style="width: 100px">
                    <asp:TextBox ID="txtDescription" runat="server" Rows="5"
                        TextMode="MultiLine" Width="350px"></asp:TextBox></td>
                <td style="width: 169px">
                </td>
            </tr>
            <tr>
                <td style="width: 163px">
                </td>
                <td style="width: 100px">
                     </td>
                <td style="width: 169px">
                </td>
            </tr>
            <tr>
                <td style="width: 163px">
                </td>
                <td style="width: 100px">
                    <asp:Button ID="cmdCreateNewSiteCollection" runat="server"
                        Text="Create New Site Collection" /></td>
                <td style="width: 169px">
                </td>
            </tr>
            <tr>
                <td style="width: 163px">
                </td>
                <td style="width: 100px">
                     </td>
                <td style="width: 169px">
                </td>
            </tr>
            <tr>
                <td align="center" colspan="3">
                    <asp:Label ID="lblMessage" runat="server" ForeColor="Red">
                    </asp:Label>
                </td>
            </tr>
        </table>

    </div>
    </form>
</body>
</html>
```

Recipe—VB (See CreateSiteCollectionWebService-VB, Class Default.aspx.vb)

```vb
Partial Class _Default
    Inherits System.Web.UI.Page
    Protected Sub Page_Load(ByVal sender As Object, _
        ByVal e As System.EventArgs) Handles Me.Load
        Try
            'Step 1: Get list of templates for the selected web application
            Dim objSites As New SitesService.Sites
            objSites.Credentials = _
                System.Net.CredentialCache.DefaultCredentials
            Dim arrTemplates() As SitesService.Template
            Dim templateCount As Integer = __
                objSites.GetSiteTemplates(1033, arrTemplates)
            Dim i As Integer
            Dim listItem As ListItem
            ddlTemplate.Items.Clear()
            For i = 0 To arrTemplates.Length - 1
                'Don't include hidden templates,
                'which are not intended for interactive use
                If Not arrTemplates(i).IsHidden Then
                    listItem = New ListItem(arrTemplates(i).Title, __
                        arrTemplates(i).Name)
                    ddlTemplate.Items.Add(listItem)
                End If
            Next
            ddlTemplate.Enabled = True
            lblMessage.Text = ""
        Catch ex As Exception
            lblMessage.Text = ex.Message
        End Try
    End Sub
    Protected Sub cmdCreateNewSiteCollection_Click(ByVal sender As Object, _
ByVal e As System.EventArgs) Handles cmdCreateNewSiteCollection.Click
        Try
            'Step 2: Make sure all necessary data is provided
            If txtSiteCollPath.Text > "" _
                And txtSiteName.Text > "" _
                And txtTitle.Text > "" _
                And txtDescription.Text > "" _
                And ddlTemplate.SelectedValue > "" _
                And txtOwnerLogin.Text > "" _
                And txtOwnerName.Text > "" _
                And txtOwnerEmail.Text > "" Then
                'Step 4: Add new site collection
                Dim objAdmin As New AdminService.Admin
                objAdmin.Credentials = _
                    System.Net.CredentialCache.DefaultCredentials
```

```
                objAdmin.CreateSite( _
                    txtSiteCollPath.Text & "/" & txtSiteName.Text, _
                    txtTitle.Text, _
                    txtDescription.Text, _
                    1033, _
                    ddlTemplate.SelectedValue, _
                    txtOwnerLogin.Text, _
                    txtOwnerName.Text, _
                    txtOwnerEmail.Text, _
                    "", "")
                'Step 6: Display success message
                lblMessage.Text = "Successfully added new site"
                lblMessage.Visible = True
            Else
                'Step 3: Prompt user to enter all data
                lblMessage.Text = "Please fill in all fields"
                lblMessage.Visible = True
            End If
        Catch ex As Exception
            'Step 7: Display error message
            lblMessage.Text = ex.Message
            lblMessage.Visible = True
        End Try
    End Sub
End Class
```

Recipe—C# (See CreateSiteCollectionWebService-CS, Class Default.aspx.cs)

```csharp
using System;
using System.Data;
using System.Configuration;
using System.Web;
using System.Web.Security;
using System.Web.UI;
using System.Web.UI.WebControls;
using System.Web.UI.WebControls.WebParts;
using System.Web.UI.HtmlControls;
public partial class _Default : System.Web.UI.Page {
    protected void Page_Load(object sender, System.EventArgs e) {
        try {
            if (!IsPostBack)
            {
                // Step 1: Get list of templates for the selected
                // web application
                SitesService.Sites objSites =
                  new SitesService.Sites();
                objSites.Credentials =
                    System.Net.CredentialCache.DefaultCredentials;
```

```csharp
                SitesService.Template[] arrTemplates;
                uint langId = (uint)1033;
                uint templateCount =
                    objSites.GetSiteTemplates(langId, out arrTemplates);
                int i;
                ListItem listItem;
                ddlTemplate.Items.Clear();
                for (i = 0; (i <= (arrTemplates.Length - 1)); i++)
                {
                    // Don't include hidden templates, which are
                    // not intended for interactive use
                    if (!arrTemplates[i].IsHidden)
                    {
                        listItem = new ListItem(arrTemplates[i].Title,
                            arrTemplates[i].Name);
                        ddlTemplate.Items.Add(listItem);
                    }
                }
                ddlTemplate.Enabled = true;
                lblMessage.Text = "";
            }
        }
        catch (Exception ex) {
            lblMessage.Text = ex.Message;
        }
    }
    protected void cmdCreateNewSiteCollection_Click1(object sender,
        EventArgs e)
    {
        try
        {
            // Step 2: Make sure all necessary data is provided
            if (txtSiteCollPath.Text != ""
                && txtSiteName.Text != ""
                && txtTitle.Text != ""
                && txtDescription.Text != ""
                && ddlTemplate.SelectedValue != ""
                && txtOwnerLogin.Text != ""
                && txtOwnerName.Text != ""
                && txtOwnerEmail.Text != "")
```

```
        {
            // Step 4: Add new site collection
            AdminService.Admin objAdmin = new AdminService.Admin();
            objAdmin.Credentials =
                System.Net.CredentialCache.DefaultCredentials;
            objAdmin.CreateSite((txtSiteCollPath.Text + ("/" +
                txtSiteName.Text)),
                txtTitle.Text,
                txtDescription.Text,
                1033,
                ddlTemplate.SelectedValue,
                txtOwnerLogin.Text,
                txtOwnerName.Text,
                txtOwnerEmail.Text,
                "", "");
            // Step 6: Display success message
            lblMessage.Text = "Successfully added new site";
            lblMessage.Visible = true;
        }
        else
        {
            // Step 3: Prompt user to enter all data
            lblMessage.Text = "Please fill in all fields";
            lblMessage.Visible = true;
        }
    }
    catch (Exception ex)
    {
        // Step 7: Display error message
        lblMessage.Text = ex.Message;
        lblMessage.Visible = true;
    }
    }
}
```

To Run

The application is run from a web browser. When the ASP.NET web form first loads, the drop-down list of templates is populated. After all fields have been filled in, you click the Create New Site Collection button. A simple validation check ensures that data has been entered for all fields. Figure 1-2 shows the recipe in action.

After processing is complete (or has thrown an exception), the message label at the bottom of the page is set and the page is refreshed.

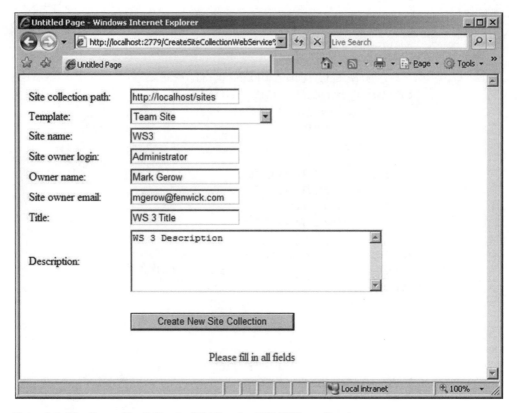

Figure 1-2. *The CreateSiteCollectionWebService ASP.NET application*

Variations

- In this simple example, all fields were required, with validation running in the event handler for the Create New Site Collection button. An alternative is to add client-side validation by using validator controls.

- Provide the option of opening up the new site in the same or a new browser window.

- Allow the user to create a range of site collections (for example, WS1–WS99) through a single page.

- Provide a series of checkboxes to enable the user to indicate which web parts to place on the home page of the root web site.

Recipe 1-3. Creating a Site (or Web) by Using the Object Model

Having the ability to create sites programmatically is a great time-saver that opens the door to creating automated workflows around site provisioning. Although Microsoft provided lots of options in terms of tailoring site definitions through Features, and provides the `<ExecuteUrl>` directive in `Onet.xml` that enables you to automatically run an ASP.NET page immediately after a site is created, nothing beats having direct, complete control when it comes to provisioning new sites.

This recipe shows you how to provision a new site by using the SharePoint object model. As you've already learned, applications that use the object model must execute on a front-end web server in the SharePoint farm, and must execute under the credentials of an account with sufficient permissions. For that reason, provisioning sites by using the object model works best when using a .NET console or Windows Forms application. The following recipe demonstrates how to create a .NET console application that provisions a site.

Recipe Type: ASP.NET Console Application

Ingredients

Assembly References

- Windows SharePoint Services

Class Library References

- `Microsoft.SharePoint` library

Special Considerations

- Although this recipe essentially duplicates what is available through the `STSADM -O CREATEWEB` command, it opens up many possibilities for customizations (such as prompting the user for missing parameters).

- If you're somewhat new to SharePoint, it's easy to get confused about the distinction between a *site collection*, *site*, and *web*, especially because Microsoft doesn't use the latter two terms consistently in its object model or documentation. Sometimes *site collection* and *site* are used to mean the same thing, and other times *site* and *web* are used synonymously. The `SPSite` class represents a collection of `SPWeb` objects. When you provision a new site collection (as in the two earlier recipes), it automatically includes one web that is designated as the *root web* and is accessed via the `SPSite.RootWeb` property. Thus site collections always have at least one child web. The choice of terminology is unfortunate, but it seems like we're stuck with it!

Process Flow

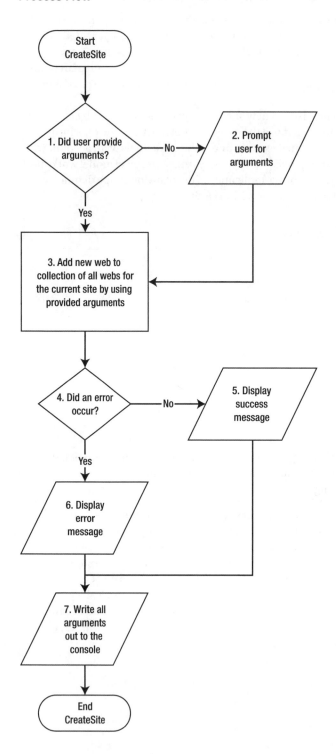

1. Make sure that all necessary information is provided by the user. This information may be provided on the command line that calls the program, or may be entered in response to prompts that the program displays.

2. If arguments weren't provided from the command line, prompt the user to enter necessary data at the console.

3. Call the `SPSite.AllWebs.Add()` method to add the new site (web).

4. Determine whether an error occurs.

5. If no error occurs, display the success message.

6. Otherwise, if an error occurs, display the error message to the console.

7. Write out all the arguments that were used to provision the new site (web) to the console window.

Recipe—VB (See Project CreateSiteConsole-VB, File Module1.vb)

```vb
Imports Microsoft.SharePoint
Imports System
Module Module1
    Sub Main(ByVal args() As String)
        ' Steps 1-2: If no arguments have been passed, prompt user to
        ' enter them now
        If (args.Length = 0) Then
            args = New String((7) - 1) {}
            args = GetParams(args)
        End If
        ' Add the new site (web) using the provided arguments
        AddSite(args)
    End Sub
    Private Function AddSite(ByVal args() As String) As Integer
        Try
            ' Get a handle to the site collection to which the
            ' new site will be added.
            Dim strSitePath As String = args(0)
            Dim site As SPSite = New SPSite(strSitePath)
            ' Add the new site (web)
            ' ----------------------
            ' Step 3: Add the site collection
            ' args(0) = Site collection url
            ' args(1) = Site (web) url
            ' args(2) = Title
            ' args(3) = Description
            ' args(4) = Template
```

```vb
            Dim web as SPweb = site.AllWebs.Add(args(1), _
                args(2), _
                args(3), _
                CType(1033, UInteger), _
                args(4), _
                False, _
                False)
            ' Step 5: Confirm site (web) information
            Console.WriteLine()
            Console.WriteLine(("Site '" _
                + (args(0) & args(1) + "' successfully created.")))
            Console.WriteLine()
            DisplayParams(args)
            ' Release memory used by SPSite and SPWeb objects
            web.Dispose()
            site.Dispose()
            Return 0
        Catch ex As Exception
            ' Step 6: If error occurs, display parameters and
            ' Error message
            Console.WriteLine()
            Console.WriteLine("** ERROR OCCURRED **")
            Console.WriteLine()
            Console.WriteLine(ex.Message)
            Console.WriteLine()
            DisplayParams(args)
            Console.WriteLine()
            Return -1
        End Try
    End Function
    Private Shared Sub DisplayParams(ByVal args() As String)
        Try
            ' Step 7: Display parameters to console
            Console.WriteLine("Site collection url: " + args(0))
            Console.WriteLine("Site (web): " + args(1))
            Console.WriteLine("Title: " + args(2))
            Console.WriteLine("Description: " + args(3))
            Console.WriteLine("Template: " + args(4))
        Catch ex As Exception
            ' If error occurred, display the error message
            Console.WriteLine()
            Console.WriteLine(ex.Message)
            Console.WriteLine()
        End Try
    End Sub
```

```
    Private Shared Function GetParams(ByRef args() As String) As String()
        Try
            ' Step 2: Get parameters from user
            Console.WriteLine()
            Console.Write("Site collection url: ")
            args(0) = Console.ReadLine
            Console.Write("Site (web): ")
            args(1) = Console.ReadLine
            Console.Write("Title: ")
            args(2) = Console.ReadLine
            Console.Write("Description: ")
            args(3) = Console.ReadLine
            Console.Write("Template: ")
            args(4) = Console.ReadLine
        Catch ex As Exception
            ' If an error occurred, display the error message
            Console.WriteLine()
            Console.WriteLine(ex.Message)
            Console.WriteLine()
        End Try
        Return args
    End Function
End Class
```

Recipe—C# (See Project CreateSiteConsole-CS, File Program.cs)

```
using Microsoft.SharePoint;
using System;
using System.Collections.Generic;
using System.Text;
class Module1
{
    static void Main(string[] args)
    {
        // Steps 1-2: If no arguments have been passed,
        // prompt user to enter them now
        if ((args.Length == 0))
        {
            args = new string[7];
            args = GetParams(ref args);
        }
        // Add the new site (web) using the provided arguments
        AddSite(args);
    }
```

```csharp
private static int AddSite(string[] args)
{
    try
    {
        // Get a handle to the site collection to which the
        // new site will be added.
        string strSitePath = args[0];
        SPSite site = new SPSite(strSitePath);
        // Add the new site (web)
        // ----------------------
        // Step 3: Add the site collection
        // args(0) = Site collection url
        // args(1) = Site (web) url
        // args(2) = Title
        // args(3) = Description
        // args(4) = Template
        SPWeb web = site.AllWebs.Add(
            args[1],
            args[2],
            args[3],
            (uint)1033,
            args[4],
            false,
            false);
        // Step 5: Confirm site (web) information
        Console.WriteLine();
        Console.WriteLine("Site \'" + args[0]+args[1]
        + "\' successfully created.");
        Console.WriteLine();
        DisplayParams(args);
        // Release memory used by SPSite, SPWeb objects
        web.Dispose();
        site.Dispose();

        return 0;
    }
    catch (Exception ex)
    {
        // Step 6: If error occurs, display parameters and error message
        Console.WriteLine();
        Console.WriteLine("** ERROR OCCURRED **");
        Console.WriteLine();
        Console.WriteLine(ex.Message);
        Console.WriteLine();
        DisplayParams(args);
        Console.WriteLine();
        return -1;
    }
```

```csharp
        }
        private static void DisplayParams(string[] args)
        {
            try
            {
                // Step 7: Display parameters to console
                Console.WriteLine(("Site collection url: " + args[0]));
                Console.WriteLine(("Site (web): " + args[1]));
                Console.WriteLine(("Title: " + args[2]));
                Console.WriteLine(("Description: " + args[3]));
                Console.WriteLine(("Template: " + args[4]));
            }
            catch (Exception ex)
            {
                // If error occurred, display the error message
                Console.WriteLine();
                Console.WriteLine(ex.Message);
                Console.WriteLine();
            }
        }
        private static string[] GetParams(ref string[] args)
        {
            try
            {
                // Step 2: Get parameters from user
                Console.WriteLine();
                Console.Write("Site collection url: ");
                args[0] = Console.ReadLine();
                Console.Write("Site (web): ");
                args[1] = Console.ReadLine();
                Console.Write("Title: ");
                args[2] = Console.ReadLine();
                Console.Write("Description: ");
                args[3] = Console.ReadLine();
                Console.Write("Template: ");
                args[4] = Console.ReadLine();
            }
            catch (Exception ex)
            {
                // If an error occurred, display the error message
                Console.WriteLine();
                Console.WriteLine(ex.Message);
                Console.WriteLine();
            }
            return args;
        }
}
```

To Run

This console application is typically either run interactively from a command window or called from a command script. Figure 1-3 shows it being run interactively.

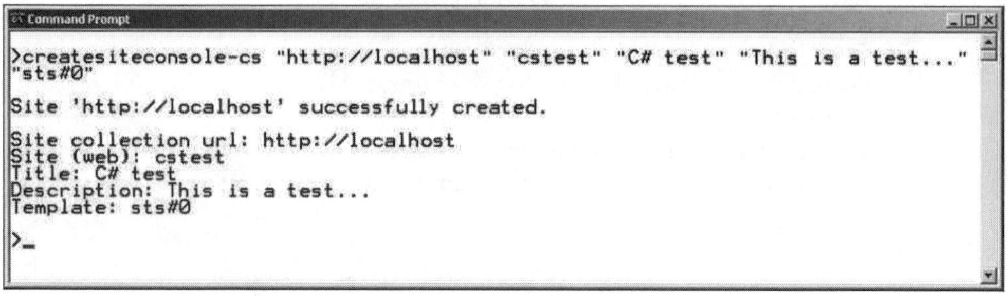

Figure 1-3. *Running the CreateSiteConsole application*

In the preceding example, I passed all the needed parameters on the command line, and so was not prompted to enter them. If I'd entered only the command CreateSiteConsole-CS.exe, the program would have prompted me to enter the missing data.

Variations

- Use a console app as in the preceding example, but instead of using the SharePoint object model classes, shell out (that is, run a separate command file) to the STSADM –O CREATEWEB command. Although this may be less work initially, it makes input validation and error trapping more difficult.

- Use a web application that shells out to the preceding application. This sidesteps Share-Point's security restriction on ASP.NET applications, but again makes error trapping next to impossible. You'll see in a related recipe how to use SharePoint web services in combination with an ASP.NET application as a better alternative to this variation.

- Use a .NET Windows application instead of a console application. This enables you to create a more elegant UI, but remember that the application can run on only a front-end web server in your SharePoint farm.

Recipe 1-4. Creating a Site (or Web) by Using a Web Service

As you saw in the previous recipe, having the ability to create sites programmatically is very useful. Although Microsoft provided lots of options in terms of tailoring site definitions through Features, and provides the <ExecuteUrl> directive in Onet.xml that enables you to automatically run an ASP.NET page immediately after a site is created, nothing beats having direct, complete control when it comes to provisioning new sites.

The previous recipe demonstrated how to create a site by using the object model; this one shows you how to accomplish the same thing by using a custom ASP.NET web service. Substituting a web service for an object model call enables this variant to run on any Internet Information Services (IIS) web server anywhere in the world that has the ability to connect to our SharePoint server farm.

Unfortunately, Microsoft left out a *CreateWeb* web service, so we'll need to build our own ASP.NET web service here. We'll then install our web service in the same location that Microsoft places the standard SharePoint web services, and call it from an ASP.NET web form.

Recipe Type: ASP.NET Web Application

Ingredients

Assembly References

- Windows SharePoint Services

Class Library References

- `Microsoft.SharePoint` library

Web Services References

- `http://Virtual Server Name:[web app port]/_vti_bin/Sites.asmx`

Special Considerations

- For consistency with Microsoft's convention of calling web services at `http://<server name>/<path>/_vti_bin/<web service>`, we'll create a virtual directory in IIS under that path and point to our custom web service.

■**Note** For an explanation of how to set up a virtual directory in IIS, see Recipe 6-2 in Chapter 6.

- To avoid any problems with user security, we'll use the `SPSecurity.RunWithElevatedPrivileges()` method to ensure that the web service can add the requested web site. If you want to restrict who can call the web service, you can either add declarative security to the `Web.config` file of the service, or set Windows permissions on the folder containing the web service application.

- The front-end ASP.NET application is very similar to that contained in Recipe 1-2, so I won't discuss it in detail here.

Process Flow: Web Service

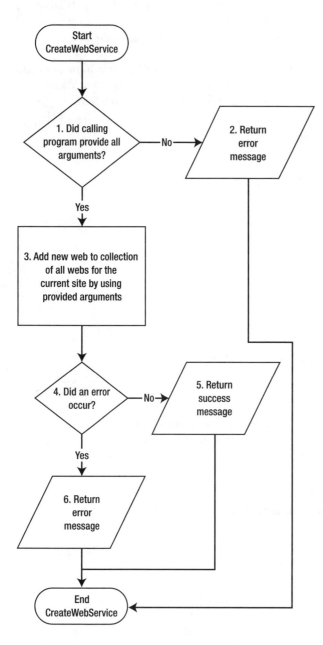

1. Make sure that all necessary information is provided by the user. This information may be provided on the command line that calls the program, or may be entered in response to prompts that the program displays.

2. If necessary arguments weren't provided, return an error.

3. Call the `SPSite.AllWebs.Add()` method to add the new site (web).

4. Determine whether an error occurs.

5. If no error occurs, return a success message.

6. Otherwise, if an error occurs, return the error message to the calling program.

Recipe—VB: Web Service (See Project CreateWebService-VB, Class Service.vb)

```vb
Imports System.Web
Imports System.Web.Services
Imports System.Web.Services.Protocols
Imports Microsoft.SharePoint
Imports Microsoft.SharePoint.WebControls
<WebService(Namespace:="http://tempuri.org/")> _
<WebServiceBinding(ConformsTo:=WsiProfiles.BasicProfile1_1)> _
<Global.Microsoft.VisualBasic.CompilerServices.DesignerGenerated()> _
Public Class Service
    Inherits System.Web.Services.WebService
    Private _retVal As String = ""
    Private _siteUrl As String = ""
    Private _webName As String = ""
    Private _title As String = ""
    Private _description As String = ""
    Private _webTemplate As String = ""
    <WebMethod()> _
    Public Function CreateWeb( _
        ByVal strSiteUrl As String, _
        ByVal strWebName As String, _
        ByVal strTitle As String, _
        ByVal strDescription As String, _
        ByVal strWebTemplate As String _
        ) As String
        _siteUrl = strSiteUrl
        _webName = strWebName
        _title = strTitle
        _description = strDescription
        _webTemplate = strWebTemplate
        'Step 1: Verify that all arguments have been passed
        If _siteUrl > "" _
            And _webName > "" _
            And _title > "" _
            And _description > "" _
            And _webTemplate > "" Then
            'Run with permissions of collection administrator
            SPSecurity.RunWithElevatedPrivileges(AddressOf myCreateWeb)
            Return _retVal
```

```vb
            Else
                '2. If some arguments are missing, return error message
                Return "Missing arguments"
            End If
        End Function
        Public Sub myCreateWeb()
            'Step 4: Trap error, if any
            Try
                Dim site As New SPSite(_siteUrl)
                'Step 3: Add the new site to collection
                Dim web As SPWeb = _
                site.AllWebs.Add(_webName, _title, _description, _
                    CType(1033, UInteger), _webTemplate, False, False)
                'Step 5: Return success message
                retVal = "Successfully added new site"

                'Release memory used by SPSite, SPWeb objects
                web.Dispose()
                site.Dispose()
            Catch ex As Exception
                'Step 6: Return error message
                _retVal = ex.Message
            End Try
        End Sub
    End Class
End Class
```

Recipe—VB: Web Form (See Project CreateWeb-VB, Class Default.aspx.vb)

```vb
Partial Class _Default
    Inherits System.Web.UI.Page
    Protected Sub Page_Load(ByVal sender As Object, _
        ByVal e As System.EventArgs) Handles Me.Load
        Try
            If Not IsPostBack Then
                'Step 1: Get list of templates for the selected
                'web application
                Dim objSites As New SitesService.Sites
                objSites.Credentials = _
                    System.Net.CredentialCache.DefaultCredentials
                Dim arrTemplates() As SitesService.Template
                Dim templateCount As Integer = _
                    objSites.GetSiteTemplates(1033, arrTemplates)
                Dim i As Integer
                Dim listItem As ListItem
                ddlTemplate.Items.Clear()
```

```
            For i = 0 To arrTemplates.Length - 1
                'Don't include hidden templates,
                'which are not intended for interactive use
                If Not arrTemplates(i).IsHidden Then
                    listItem = New ListItem(arrTemplates(i).Title, _
                        arrTemplates(i).Name)
                    ddlTemplate.Items.Add(listItem)
                End If
            Next
            ddlTemplate.Enabled = True
            lblMessage.Text = ""
        End If
    Catch ex As Exception
        lblMessage.Text = ex.Message
    End Try
End Sub
Protected Sub cmdCreateWeb_Click(ByVal sender As Object, _
    ByVal e As System.EventArgs) Handles cmdCreateWeb.Click
    Try
        'Step 2: Make sure all necessary data is provided
        If txtSiteCollPath.Text > "" _
            And txtWebName.Text > "" _
            And txtTitle.Text > "" _
            And txtDescription.Text > "" _
            And ddlTemplate.SelectedValue > "" Then
            'Step 4: Add new site collection
            Dim objCreateWebService As New CreateWebService_VB.Service
            objCreateWebService.Credentials = _
                System.Net.CredentialCache.DefaultCredentials
            objCreateWebService.CreateWeb( _
                txtSiteCollPath.Text, _
                txtWebName.Text, _
                txtTitle.Text, _
                txtDescription.Text, _
                ddlTemplate.SelectedValue)
            'Step 6: Display success message
            lblMessage.Text = "Successfully added new site '" & _
                txtWebName.Text & "'"
            lblMessage.Visible = True
        Else
            'Step 3: Prompt user to enter all data
            lblMessage.Text = "Please fill in all fields"
            lblMessage.Visible = True
        End If
```

```vb
        Catch ex As Exception
            'Step 7: Display error message
            lblMessage.Text = ex.Message
            lblMessage.Visible = True
        End Try
    End Sub
End Class
```

Recipe—C#: Web Service (See Project CreateWebService-CS, Class Service.cs)

```csharp
using System.Web;
using System.Web.Services;
using System.Web.Services.Protocols;
using Microsoft.SharePoint;
using Microsoft.SharePoint.WebControls;
[WebService(Namespace = "http://tempuri.org/")]
[WebServiceBinding(ConformsTo = WsiProfiles.BasicProfile1_1)]
public class Service : System.Web.Services.WebService
{
    private string _retVal = "";
    private string _siteUrl = "";
    private string _webName = "";
    private string _title = "";
    private string _description = "";
    private string _webTemplate;
    [WebMethod]
    public string CreateWeb(string strSiteUrl, string strWebName,
        string strTitle, string strDescription, string strWebTemplate)
    {
        _siteUrl = strSiteUrl;
        _webName = strWebName;
        _title = strTitle;
        _description = strDescription;
        _webTemplate = strWebTemplate;
        // Step 1: Verify that all arguments have been passed
        if (_siteUrl != ""
            && _webName != ""
            && _title != ""
            && _description != ""
            && _webTemplate != "")
        {
            // Run with permissions of collection administrator
            SPSecurity.RunWithElevatedPrivileges(myCreateWeb);
            return _retVal;
        }
```

```
        else
        {
            // 2. If some arguments are missing, return error message
            return "Missing arguments";
        }
    }
    private void myCreateWeb()
    {
        // Step 4: Trap error, if any
        try
        {
            SPSite site = new SPSite(_siteUrl);

            // Step 3: Add the new site to collection
            SPWeb web =
                site.AllWebs.Add(_webName, _title, _description,
                ((System.UInt32)(1033)), _webTemplate, false, false);
            // Step 5: Return success message
            _retVal = "Successfully added new site";
            // Release memory used by SPSite, SPWeb objects
            web.Dispose();
            site.Dispose();
        }
        catch (System.Exception ex)
        {
            // Step 6: Return error message
            _retVal = ex.Message;
        }
    }
}
```

Recipe—C#: Web Form (See Project CreateWeb-CS, Class Default.aspx.cs)

```
using System;
using System.Data;
using System.Configuration;
using System.Web;
using System.Web.Security;
using System.Web.UI;
using System.Web.UI.WebControls;
using System.Web.UI.WebControls.WebParts;
using System.Web.UI.HtmlControls;
public partial class _Default : System.Web.UI.Page {
    protected void Page_Load(object sender, System.EventArgs e) {
```

```
        try {
            if (!IsPostBack) {
                // Step 1: Get list of templates for the
                // selected web application
                SitesService.Sites objSites = new SitesService.Sites();
                objSites.Credentials =
                    System.Net.CredentialCache.DefaultCredentials;
                SitesService.Template[] arrTemplates;
                uint templateCount = objSites.GetSiteTemplates(1033,
                    out arrTemplates);
                int i;
                ListItem listItem;
                ddlTemplate.Items.Clear();
                for (i = 0; (i <= (arrTemplates.Length - 1)); i++)
                {
                    // Don't include hidden templates, which are not
                    // intended for interactive use
                    if (!arrTemplates[i].IsHidden) {
                        listItem = new ListItem(arrTemplates[i].Title,
                            arrTemplates[i].Name);
                        ddlTemplate.Items.Add(listItem);
                    }
                }
                ddlTemplate.Enabled = true;
                lblMessage.Text = "";
            }
        }
        catch (Exception ex) {
            lblMessage.Text = ex.Message;
        }
    }
    protected void cmdCreateWeb_Click1(object sender, EventArgs e)
    {
        try
        {
            // Step 2: Make sure all necessary data is provided
            if (txtSiteCollPath.Text != ""
                && txtWebName.Text != ""
                && txtTitle.Text != ""
                && txtDescription.Text != ""
                && ddlTemplate.SelectedValue != "")
```

```
        {
            // Step 4: Add new site collection
            CreateWebService_CS.Service objCreateWebService
                = new CreateWebService_CS.Service();
            objCreateWebService.Credentials
                = System.Net.CredentialCache.DefaultCredentials;
            objCreateWebService.CreateWeb(
                txtSiteCollPath.Text,
                txtWebName.Text,
                txtTitle.Text,
                txtDescription.Text,
                ddlTemplate.SelectedValue);
            // Step 6: Display success message
            lblMessage.Text =
                ("Successfully added new site \'" + txtWebName.Text + "\'");
            lblMessage.Visible = true;
        }
        else
        {
            // Step 3: Prompt user to enter all data
            lblMessage.Text = "Please fill in all fields";
            lblMessage.Visible = true;
        }
    }
    catch (Exception ex)
    {
        // Step 7: Display error message
        lblMessage.Text = ex.Message;
        lblMessage.Visible = true;
    }
    }
}
```

To Run

On the form load event, a call is made to the http://localhost/_vti_bin/sites.asmx web service to obtain a list of templates available on this web application. As with the web application that creates a new site collection, we prompt the user for the necessary parameters, verify that all data has been provided, and then call our web service. Figure 1-4 shows the CreateWeb application in a browser.

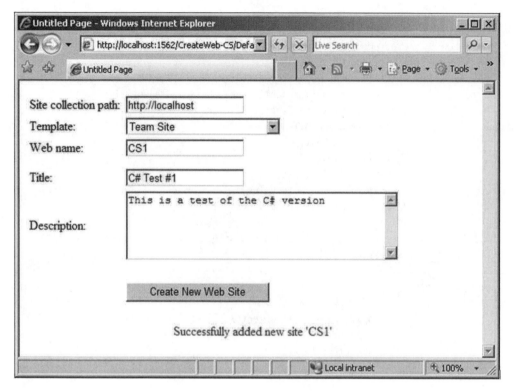

Figure 1-4. *The CreateWeb ASP.NET application running in a browser*

Variations

- I could have combined the logic in the ASP.NET web form and web service so that only one application is required. The value of creating a web service is that it can be called from any number of applications, including ASP.NET, .NET console, and .NET Windows Forms applications. You'll definitely find it comes in handy!

Recipe 1-5. Adding and Modifying Properties of a Site

Did you know that you can assign custom properties to sites? Each site has a *property bag* that holds key/value pairs (like the .NET config AppSettings collection). This collection of properties was undoubtedly designed for use by Microsoft's programmers, but it is exposed for general use.

You can use this to store any string data that you need to assign to a given site. For example, you might want to associate a customer ID with an extranet, so that you can look up the customer information to present on the site when viewed by users. Or you may want to set a flag that determines whether a particular extranet site should be billed to the customer.

In this recipe, you'll create a simple ASP.NET application that you can use to create, edit, and save values to a site's property collection.

Recipe Type: ASP.NET Web Application

Ingredients

Assembly References

- Windows SharePoint Services

Class Library References

- `Microsoft.SharePoint` library

Special Considerations

- Because SharePoint uses the `SPWeb.Properties` collection to store internal data, you need to be careful to avoid naming conflicts with the properties that SharePoint creates. One simple technique is to use a unique prefix for each variable you create. For example, in this recipe I prefixed my variables with `mg_`.

- As noted in the code, you must set the `SPWeb.AllowUnsafeUpdates` property to `true` to enable the program to save the updates to the property collection. Otherwise, an error will be thrown.

- And speaking of updates, be sure to call the `SPWeb.Properties.Update()` method after you've modified the properties, or your changes won't be saved.

Preparation

1. Create a new VB or C# ASP.NET web application.

2. Add a reference to the Windows SharePoint Services .NET assembly.

Process Flow

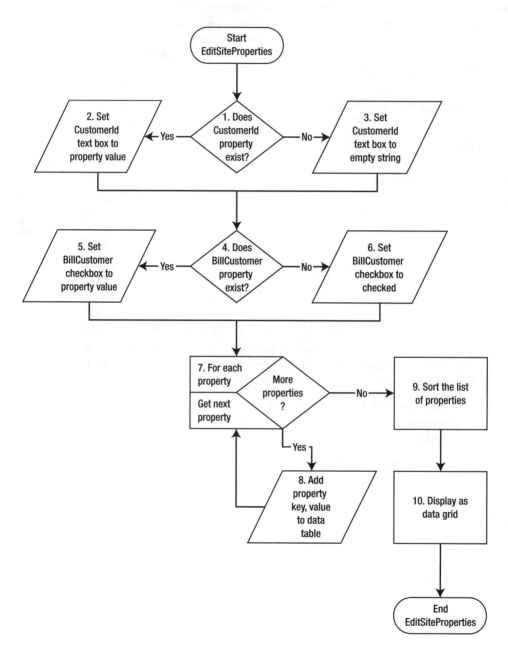

1. Check to see whether a property named CustomerId already exists for this site.

2. If it does, read its value and assign it to the txtCustomerId.Text property.

3. If not, set the value of txtCustomerId.Text to an empty string.

4. Check whether a property named `BillCustomer` already exists for this site.

5. If yes, assign its value to the `cbBillCustomer` checkbox.

6. If not, set the value of `cbBillCustomer.Checked` to true.

7. Loop through the list of properties in the current site.

8. Add a property key name and value to the data table.

9. Assign the data table to a data view and sort by key.

10. Refresh the grid view on the page to display the most current values.

Recipe—VB (See Project EditProperties-VB, Class Default.aspx.vb)

```vb
Imports System
Imports System.Data
Imports System.Configuration
Imports System.Web
Imports System.Web.Security
Imports System.Web.UI
Imports System.Web.UI.WebControls
Imports System.Web.UI.WebControls.WebParts
Imports System.Web.UI.HtmlControls
Imports Microsoft.SharePoint
Imports System.Collections
Public Class _Default
    Inherits System.Web.UI.Page
    ' Hard-coded to save/retrieve properties of root site collection
    Private site As New SPSite("http://localhost")
    Protected Sub Page_Load(ByVal sender As Object, _
        ByVal e As EventArgs) Handles Me.Load
        If Not IsPostBack Then
            Dim web As SPWeb = site.RootWeb
            ' Step 1: Determine whether a value exists for customer id key
            If web.Properties.ContainsKey("mg_CustomerId") Then
                ' Step 2: Initialize to stored value
                txtCustomerId.Text = web.Properties("mg_CustomerId").ToString
            Else
                ' Step 3: Otherwise set to empty string
                txtCustomerId.Text = ""
            End If
            ' Step 4: Determine whether a value exists for bill flag
            If web.Properties.ContainsKey("mg_BillCustomer") Then
                ' Step 5: Initialize to stored value
                cbBillCustomer.Checked = _
                    (web.Properties("mg_BillCustomer").ToString.ToLower = _
                    "true")
```

```vbnet
        Else
            ' Step 6: Otherwise set default value
            cbBillCustomer.Checked = True
        End If
        ' Display list of key/value pairs
        refreshPropertyList()
        ' Release memory used by SPSite, SPWeb objects
        web.Dispose()
        site.Dispose()
    End If
End Sub
Protected Sub refreshPropertyList()
    Dim web As SPWeb = site.RootWeb
    Dim dtProperties As DataTable = New DataTable("PropertyList")
    Dim dvProperties As DataView = New DataView
    Dim drProperty As DataRow
    dtProperties.Columns.Add("Key")
    dtProperties.Columns.Add("Value")
    ' Step through list of properties, adding
    ' key/value pairs to data table.
    For Each key As Object In web.Properties.Keys
        drProperty = dtProperties.NewRow
        drProperty("Key") = key.ToString
        drProperty("Value") = web.Properties(key.ToString)
        dtProperties.Rows.Add(drProperty)
        dtProperties.AcceptChanges()
    Next
    ' Sort the list and display
    dvProperties.Table = dtProperties
    dvProperties.Sort = "Key"
    gvPropertyList.DataSource = dvProperties
    gvPropertyList.DataBind()
End Sub
Protected Sub cmdSave_Click(ByVal sender As Object, _
ByVal e As EventArgs) Handles cmdSave.Click
    Dim web As SPWeb = site.RootWeb
    ' Error will occur if AllowUnsafeUpdates property
    ' not set prior to update
    web.AllowUnsafeUpdates = True
    web.Properties("mg_CustomerId") = txtCustomerId.Text
    web.Properties("mg_BillCustomer") = cbBillCustomer.Checked.ToString
    web.Properties.Update()
    ' Redisplay list to reflect changes
    refreshPropertyList()
End Sub
End Class
```

Recipe—C# (See Project EditSiteProperties, Class Default.aspx.cs)

```csharp
using System;
using System.Data;
using System.Configuration;
using System.Web;
using System.Web.Security;
using System.Web.UI;
using System.Web.UI.WebControls;
using System.Web.UI.WebControls.WebParts;
using System.Web.UI.HtmlControls;
using Microsoft.SharePoint;
using Microsoft.SharePoint.WebControls;
using System.Collections;
public partial class _Default : System.Web.UI.Page
{
    // Hard-coded to save/retrieve properties of root site collection
    SPSite site = new SPSite("http://localhost");
    protected void Page_Load(object sender, EventArgs e)
    {
     if (!IsPostBack)
        {
            SPWeb web = site.RootWeb;
            // Step 1: Determine whether a value exists for customer id key
            if (web.Properties.ContainsKey("mg_CustomerId"))
            {
                // Step 2: Initialize to stored value
                txtCustomerId.Text =
                    web.Properties["mg_CustomerId"].ToString();
            }
            else
            {
               .// Step 3: Otherwise set to empty string
                txtCustomerId.Text = "";
            }
            // Step 4: Determine whether a value exists for bill flag
            if (web.Properties.ContainsKey("mg_BillCustomer"))
            {
                // Step 5: Initialize to stored value
                cbBillCustomer.Checked =
                    (web.Properties["mg_BillCustomer"].ToString().ToLower()
                        == "true");
            }
            else
            {
                // Step 6: Otherwise set default value
                cbBillCustomer.Checked = true;
            }
```

```
            // Display list of key/value pairs
            refreshPropertyList();
            // Release memory used by SPSite, SPWeb objects
            web.Dispose();
            site.Dispose();
        }
    }
    protected void refreshPropertyList()
    {
        SPWeb web = site.RootWeb;
        DataTable dtProperties = new DataTable("PropertyList");
        DataView dvProperties = new DataView();
        DataRow drProperty;
        dtProperties.Columns.Add("Key");
        dtProperties.Columns.Add("Value");
        // Step through list of properties, adding
        // key/value pairs to data table.
        foreach (object key in web.Properties.Keys)
        {
            drProperty = dtProperties.NewRow();
            drProperty["Key"] = key.ToString();
            drProperty["Value"] = web.Properties[key.ToString()];
            dtProperties.Rows.Add(drProperty);
            dtProperties.AcceptChanges();
        }
        // Sort the list and display
        dvProperties.Table = dtProperties;
        dvProperties.Sort = "Key";
        gvPropertyList.DataSource = dvProperties;
        gvPropertyList.DataBind();
    }
    protected void cmdSave_Click(object sender, EventArgs e)
    {
        SPWeb web = site.RootWeb;
        // Error will occur if AllowUnsafeUpdates property
        // not set prior to update
        web.AllowUnsafeUpdates = true;
        web.Properties["mg_CustomerId"] = txtCustomerId.Text;
        web.Properties["mg_BillCustomer"] =
            cbBillCustomer.Checked.ToString();
        web.Properties.Update();
        // Redisplay list to reflect changes
        refreshPropertyList();
    }
}
```

To Run

Press F5 to start the project if you're in Visual Studio, or simply enter the URL of the page in the browser location field. When you first run the application, the Customer Id field will be empty and the Bill Customer checkbox will be selected. Try changing values in either of those fields and click the Save Changes button. You will note that the two additional properties, mg_billcustomer and mg_customerid (substitute your own prefix if desired), will be added to the list of site properties displayed in the table. Figure 1-5 shows EditSiteProperties running in a browser.

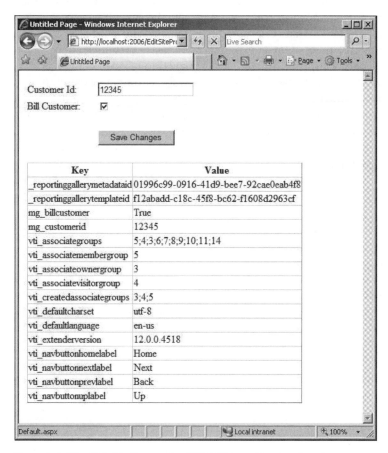

Figure 1-5. *The EditSiteProperties ASP.NET application in a browser*

Variations

- Instead of creating an ASP.NET web application, use an ASP.NET 2.0 web part to edit and display the properties for a site. In this case, rather than explicitly referencing the site and web, use the SPControl.GetContextWeb(context) method to return the site of the page containing the current instance of the web part.

Recipe 1-6. Adding a Web Part by Using the Object Model

It's not uncommon for a SharePoint installation to have hundreds or thousands of sites and subsites. Let's say you are responsible for one of these installations. You have just created the coolest web part, one that needs to be added to each and every site on your server! One approach would be to open each web site, switch to edit-page mode, add the web part, set any properties required, save your changes, and move on to the second of 2,000 sites. Not a very appealing prospect!

An alternative is to write a bit of ASP 2.0 code to programmatically iterate through all the sites on your server, open the `Default.aspx` web-part page, add the new web part, set its properties, and move on. Now that's what I call smart SharePoint administration!

In this recipe, you'll create a program to do two things: 1) add a new content editor web part and 2) add a web part of any type. The reason for going through each of these is to see both scenarios; at times you'll know the class you want to inherit from (for example, the `ContentEditorWebPart` class), which gives you access to the web-part-specific properties, and at other times you'll just know it's some type of web part, in which case all you can assume are the properties and methods inherited from the parent `WebPart` class.

Recipe Type: .NET Console Application

Ingredients

Assembly References

- Windows SharePoint Services

- `System.Web` assembly

Class Library References

- `Microsoft.SharePoint` library

- `System.Web` class library

Preparation

1. Create a new .NET console project.

2. Add a reference to the Windows SharePoint Services .NET assembly.

3. Add a reference to the `System.Web` .NET assembly.

Process Flow: AddWebPart()

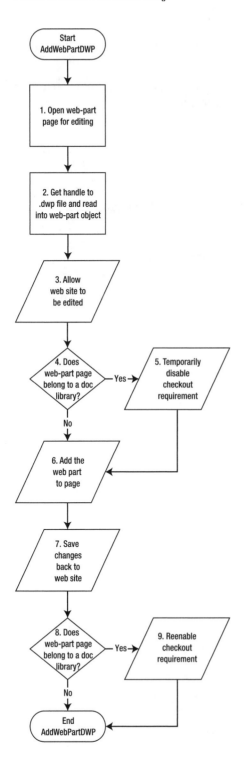

1. Create an SPSite object that points to the web site containing the web-part page.

2. Set AllowUnsafeUpdates to true to enable programmatic updates to the site.

3. Check to see whether the page belongs to a document library that might require the page to be checked out before editing.

4. If the page is stored in a document library, temporarily disable the requirement that documents be checked out to avoid an error during processing.

5. Add the new web part.

6. Save changes back to the web site.

7. Determine whether the web-part page is stored in a document library.

8. If the page is stored in a document library, reset the required checkout flag to its original value.

Recipe—VB (See Project AddWebPartOM-VB, Module Module1.vb)

```vb
Imports Microsoft.SharePoint
Imports Microsoft.SharePoint.WebControls
Imports Microsoft.SharePoint.WebPartPages
Imports System.Web
Imports System.Web.UI.WebControls
Imports System.Xml
Module Module1
    Sub Main()
        'Example 1:
        'Add an instance of a SharePoint "ContentEditorWebPart", which
        'is a descendent of the generic .NET 2.0 WebPart class
        Dim oCEwp As New _
            Microsoft.SharePoint.WebPartPages.ContentEditorWebPart
        oCEwp = AddContentEditorWebPart( _
            "Hello World!", _
            "Hello World web part", _
            "http://localhost", _
            "", _
            "Pages", _
            "Default.aspx", _
            "Right", _
            0, _
            WebParts.PersonalizationScope.Shared _
            )
        'Example 2:
        'Add a PageViewer web part
        Dim oPVwp As New Microsoft.SharePoint.WebPartPages.PageViewerWebPart
        oPVwp.SourceType = PathPattern.URL
        oPVwp.ContentLink = "http://www.fenwick.com"
```

```vbnet
    oPVwp = AddWebPart( _
        oPVwp, _
        "Hello World web part", _
        "http://localhost", _
        "", _
        "Pages", _
        "Default.aspx", _
         "Top", _
        0, _
        WebParts.PersonalizationScope.Shared _
        )
End Sub
Private Function AddContentEditorWebPart( _
        ByVal strContent As String, _
        ByVal strTitle As String, _
        ByVal strSiteUrl As String, _
        ByVal strWebName As String, _
        ByVal strDocLibName As String, _
        ByVal strPage As String, _
        ByVal strZone As String, _
        ByVal numOrder As Integer, _
        ByVal pScope As _
            System.Web.UI.WebControls.WebParts.PersonalizationScope _
    ) As Microsoft.SharePoint.WebPartPages.ContentEditorWebPart
    Try
        'Create an empty content editor web part.
        Dim cewp As New _
            Microsoft.SharePoint.WebPartPages.ContentEditorWebPart
        'Create an xml element object and transfer the content
        'into the web part.
        Dim xmlDoc As New XmlDocument
        Dim xmlElem As System.Xml.XmlElement = _
            xmlDoc.CreateElement("xmlElem")
        xmlElem.InnerText = strContent
        cewp.Content = xmlElem
        'Call generic method to add the web part
        cewp = AddWebPart( _
            cewp, _
            strTitle, _
            strSiteUrl, _
            strWebName, _
            strDocLibName, _
            strPage, _
            strZone, _
            numOrder, _
            UI.WebControls.WebParts.PersonalizationScope.Shared _
            )
        Return cewp
```

```
        Catch ex As Exception
            Throw New Exception("AddContentEditorWebPart() error: " & _
                ex.Message)
        End Try
    End Function
    Private Function AddWebPart( _
            ByVal oWebPart As Web.UI.WebControls.WebParts.WebPart, _
            ByVal strTitle As String, _
            ByVal strSiteUrl As String, _
            ByVal strWebName As String, _
            ByVal strDocLibName As String, _
            ByVal strPage As String, _
            ByVal strZone As String, _
            ByVal numOrder As Integer, _
            ByVal pScope As _
                System.Web.UI.WebControls.WebParts.PersonalizationScope _
        ) As Web.UI.WebControls.WebParts.WebPart
        Try
            'Get handles to site, web, and page to which
            'web part will be added.
            Dim site As New SPSite(strSiteUrl)
            Dim web As SPWeb = site.OpenWeb(strWebName)
            'Enable update of page
            web.AllowUnsafeUpdates = True
            Dim webParts As SPLimitedWebPartManager
            If strDocLibName > "" Then
                webParts = web.GetLimitedWebPartManager( _
                    strDocLibName & "/" & strPage, pScope)
            Else
                webParts = web.GetLimitedWebPartManager(strPage, pScope)
            End If
            'If web part page is in a document library,
            'disable checkout requirement
            'for duration of update
            Dim list As SPList
            Dim origForceCheckoutValue As Boolean
            If strDocLibName > "" Then
                list = web.Lists(strDocLibName)
                origForceCheckoutValue = list.ForceCheckout
                list.ForceCheckout = False
                list.Update()
            End If
            'Add the web part
            oWebPart.Title = strTitle
            webParts.AddWebPart(oWebPart, strZone, numOrder)
```

```
            'Save changes back to the SharePoint database
            webParts.SaveChanges(oWebPart)
            web.Update()
            'If necessary, restore ForceCheckout setting
            If strDocLibName > "" Then
                list.ForceCheckout = origForceCheckoutValue
                list.Update()
            End If
            ' Release memory used by SPSite, SPWeb objects
            web.Dispose()
            site.Dispose()
            Return oWebPart
        Catch ex As Exception
            Throw New Exception("AddWebPart() error: " & ex.Message)
        End Try
    End Function
End Module
```

Recipe—C# (See Project AddWebPartOM-CS, File Program.cs)

```csharp
using Microsoft.SharePoint;
using Microsoft.SharePoint.WebControls;
using Microsoft.SharePoint.WebPartPages;
using System;
using System.Web;
using System.Web.UI.WebControls.WebParts;
using System.Web.UI.WebControls;
using System.Xml;
class Module1
{
    static void Main()
    {
        // Example 1:
        // Add an instance of a SharePoint "ContentEditorWebPart", which
        // is a descendent of the generic .NET 2.0 WebPart class
        Microsoft.SharePoint.WebPartPages.ContentEditorWebPart oCEwp
            = new Microsoft.SharePoint.WebPartPages.ContentEditorWebPart();
        oCEwp = AddContentEditorWebPart(
            "Hello World!",
            "Hello World web part",
            "http://localhost",
            "BBB",
            "",
            "Default.aspx",
            "Right",
            0,
            System.Web.UI.WebControls.WebParts.PersonalizationScope.Shared);
```

```
    // Example 2:
    // Add a PageViewer web part
    Microsoft.SharePoint.WebPartPages.PageViewerWebPart oPVwp
        = new Microsoft.SharePoint.WebPartPages.PageViewerWebPart();
    oPVwp.SourceType = PathPattern.URL;
    oPVwp.ContentLink = "http://www.yahoo.com";
    oPVwp = (Microsoft.SharePoint.WebPartPages.PageViewerWebPart)
    AddWebPart(
        oPVwp,
        "Hello World web part",
        "http://localhost",
        "BBB",
        "",
        "Default.aspx",
        "Left",
        0,
        System.Web.UI.WebControls.WebParts.PersonalizationScope.Shared);
}
private static Microsoft.SharePoint.WebPartPages.ContentEditorWebPart
AddContentEditorWebPart(
    string strContent,
    string strTitle,
    string strSiteUrl,
    string strWebName,
    string strDocLibName,
    string strPage,
    string strZone,
    int numOrder,
    System.Web.UI.WebControls.WebParts.PersonalizationScope pScope)
{

    try
    {
        // Create an empty content editor web part.
        Microsoft.SharePoint.WebPartPages.ContentEditorWebPart cewp
            = new Microsoft.SharePoint.WebPartPages.ContentEditorWebPart();
        // Create an xml element object and transfer the content
        //into the web part.
        XmlDocument xmlDoc = new XmlDocument();
        System.Xml.XmlElement xmlElem = xmlDoc.CreateElement("xmlElem");
        xmlElem.InnerText = strContent;
        cewp.Content = xmlElem;
        // Call generic method to add the web part
        cewp = (Microsoft.SharePoint.WebPartPages.ContentEditorWebPart)
```

```
        AddWebPart (
            cewp,
            strTitle,
            strSiteUrl,
            strWebName,
            strDocLibName,
            strPage,
            strZone,
            numOrder,
            System.Web.UI.WebControls.WebParts.PersonalizationScope.Shared);
        return cewp;
    }
    catch (Exception ex)
    {
        throw new Exception(
            "AddContentEditorWebPart() error: " + ex.Message);
    }
}
private static System.Web.UI.WebControls.WebParts.WebPart
AddWebPart(
    System.Web.UI.WebControls.WebParts.WebPart oWebPart,
    string strTitle,
    string strSiteUrl,
    string strWebName,
    string strDocLibName,
    string strPage,
    string strZone,
    int numOrder,
    System.Web.UI.WebControls.WebParts.PersonalizationScope pScope)
{
    try
    {
        // Get handles to site, web, and page to which
        // web part will be added.
        SPSite site = new SPSite(strSiteUrl);
        SPWeb web = site.OpenWeb(strWebName);
        // Enable update of page
        web.AllowUnsafeUpdates = true;
        SPLimitedWebPartManager webParts;
        if ((strDocLibName != ""))
        {
            webParts =
                web.GetLimitedWebPartManager(
                    strDocLibName + "/" + strPage, pScope);
        }
```

```
            else
            {
                webParts =
                    web.GetLimitedWebPartManager(strPage, pScope);
            }
            // If web part page is in a document library,
            // disable checkout requirement
            // for duration of update
            SPList list = null;
            bool origForceCheckoutValue = false;
            if ((strDocLibName != ""))
            {
                list = web.Lists[strDocLibName];
                origForceCheckoutValue = list.ForceCheckout;
                list.ForceCheckout = false;
                list.Update();
            }
            // Add the web part
            oWebPart.Title = strTitle;
            webParts.AddWebPart(oWebPart, strZone, numOrder);
            // Save changes back to the SharePoint database
            webParts.SaveChanges(oWebPart);
            web.Update();
            // If necessary, restore ForceCheckout setting
            if ((strDocLibName != ""))
            {
                list.ForceCheckout = origForceCheckoutValue;
                list.Update();
            }
            // Release memory used by SPSite, SPWeb objects
            web.Dispose();
            site.Dispose();
            return oWebPart;
        }
        catch (Exception ex)
        {
            throw new Exception(
                "AddWebPart() error: " + ex.Message);
        }
    }
}
```

To Run

This recipe has no UI. Simply run the program within Visual Studio or at the command prompt. When the program has successfully completed running, you can verify results by opening the target web-part page in a browser to see two web parts added.

Variations

- In this example, we added a simple Content Editor web part. However, you can add any standard SharePoint or custom web part by using this technique. If you are adding a custom web part, be sure to include a reference to the custom web-part assembly (.dll) in the project.

- Also note that in this example we used a console application, which presents fewer security complications than an ASP.NET application. However, you can use an ASP.NET application to add web parts as well, but you may need to impersonate the system account to perform certain operations, because of SharePoint's security policies that determine the permissions provided to a standard ASP.NET application.

Related Recipes

- Recipe 1-7

Recipe 1-7. Adding a Web Part by Using a .dwp or .webpart File

The preceding recipe showed you how to add a web part to a page programmatically. That's particularly helpful if you need to customize a web part based on some metadata on a large number of pages. By adding the web part programmatically, you can examine characteristics of the web site or page and adjust the properties of the web part accordingly.

On the other hand, you might have a web part to add to multiple sites that doesn't need any customization; it just needs to be added as is. In that case, the easiest approach is to add the web part to a single page, configure its properties as desired, and then export the web part to a .dwp (2003 format) or .webpart (2007 format) web-part definition file. You can then create a program to read in the definition file and add the web part by using that definition programmatically.

Another advantage of this approach is that you don't need to include a reference to custom web-part assemblies as you did with the object model approach. Not having to include a reference could be helpful if you don't have easy access to the assembly .dll.

Recipe Type: .NET Console Application

Ingredients

Assembly References

- Windows SharePoint Services assembly

Class Library References

- System.Web library

- System.Xml library

- System.Web.UI.WebControls.WebParts.WebPart class

Special Considerations

- Remember that the XmlReader will be looking for the .dwp file in the same directory as the .exe unless you provide a fully qualified path.

- As with Recipe 1-6, the recipe to add a web part by using the object model, we need to check to see whether the web-part page is stored in a document library, and to turn off the checkout requirement if so. In such a case, we'll reinstate the checkout requirement after the web part has been added.

Preparation

1. Create a new .NET console application.

2. Add references to the following:

   - Windows SharePoint Services

   - System.Web

   - System.Xml

Process Flow: AddWebPartDWP

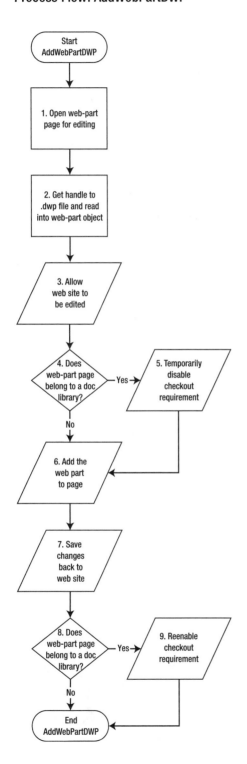

1. Open the web-part page for editing.

2. Read in the definition of the web part from the `.dwp` file created during export.

3. Set the web site to allow programmatic changes.

4. Check to see whether the web-part page is stored in a document library.

5. If so, temporarily disable the requirement that documents be checked out to edit in that library.

6. Add the web part created in step 2 to the page.

7. Save updates to the SharePoint database.

8. Determine whether the web-part page is stored in a document library.

9. If the page is stored in a document library, restore the document library settings determining whether checkout is required.

Recipe—VB (See Project AddWebPartDWP-VB, Module Module1.vb)

```vb
Imports System.Xml
Imports System.Web
Imports System.Web.UI.WebControls
Imports Microsoft.SharePoint
Imports Microsoft.SharePoint.WebControls
Imports Microsoft.SharePoint.WebPartPages
Module Module1
    Sub Main(ByVal args() As String)
        If args.Length < 6 Then
            GetArgs(args)
        End If
        Console.WriteLine( _
        AddWebPartDWP( _
          args(0), _
          args(1), _
          args(2), _
          args(3), _
          WebParts.PersonalizationScope.Shared, _
          args(4), _
          args(5)))
        Console.WriteLine()
        Console.WriteLine("Press any key to continue...")
        Console.Read()
    End Sub
    Private Sub GetArgs(ByRef args() As String)
        ReDim args(5)
        Console.WriteLine()
        Console.Write("Site Url: ")
```

```vbnet
        args(0) = Console.ReadLine()
        Console.Write("Web Name: ")
        args(1) = Console.ReadLine
        Console.Write("Doclib containing page (leave blank for none): ")
        args(2) = Console.ReadLine
        Console.Write("Page Name: ")
        args(3) = Console.ReadLine
        Console.Write("Path to DWP: ")
        args(4) = Console.ReadLine
        Console.Write("Zone: ")
        args(5) = Console.ReadLine
        Console.WriteLine()
End Sub
Public Function AddWebPartDWP( _
        ByVal strSiteUrl As String, _
        ByVal strWebName As String, _
        ByVal strDocLibName As String, _
        ByVal strPage As String, _
        ByVal pScope As _
            System.Web.UI.WebControls.WebParts.PersonalizationScope, _
        ByVal strDWPPath As String, _
        ByVal strZone As String _
        ) As String
        Try
            'Get handle to site and web to be edited
            Dim site As New SPSite(strSiteUrl)
            Dim web As SPWeb = site.OpenWeb(strWebName)
            Dim wp As WebPart
            'Step 1: Get handle to web part page to
            ' contain new web part
            Dim webParts As SPLimitedWebPartManager
            If strDocLibName > "" Then
                webParts = _
                    web.GetLimitedWebPartManager( __
                        strDocLibName & "/" & strPage, pScope)
            Else
                webParts = _
                    web.GetLimitedWebPartManager(strPage, pScope)
            End If
            'Step 2: get handle to .DWP file and import definition
            Dim reader As XmlReader = XmlReader.Create(strDWPPath)
            wp = webParts.ImportWebPart(reader, "")
            'Step 3: allow website to be edited
            web.AllowUnsafeUpdates = True
            'Steps 4-5: If web-part page is in a document library,
            'disable checkout requirement for duration of update
            Dim list As SPList
```

```vb
                Dim origForceCheckoutValue As Boolean
                If strDocLibName > "" Then
                    list = web.Lists(strDocLibName)
                    origForceCheckoutValue = list.ForceCheckout
                    list.ForceCheckout = False
                    list.Update()
                End If
                'Step 6: Add the web part
                webParts.AddWebPart(wp, strZone, 0)
                'Step 7: Save changes back to SharePoint database
                webParts.SaveChanges(wp)
                web.Update()
                'Steps 8-9: If necessary, restore ForceCheckout setting
                If strDocLibName > "" Then
                    list.ForceCheckout = origForceCheckoutValue
                    list.Update()
                End If
                ' Release memory used by SPSite, SPWeb objects
                web.Dispose()
                site.Dispose()
                Return "Successfully added '" & strDWPPath & "'"
            Catch ex As Exception
                Return ex.Message
            End Try
        End Function
    End Module
```

Recipe—C# (See Project AddWebPartDWP-CS, File Program.cs)

```csharp
using System.Xml;
using System.Web;
using System.Web.UI.WebControls;
using System.Web.UI.WebControls.WebParts;
using Microsoft.SharePoint;
using Microsoft.SharePoint.WebControls;
using Microsoft.SharePoint.WebPartPages;
using System.IO;
using System;
class Module1
{
    static void Main(string[] args)
    {
        if ((args.Length < 6))
        {
            GetArgs(ref args);
        }
        Console.WriteLine(
```

```csharp
        AddWebPartDWP(
            args[0],
            args[1],
            args[2],
            args[3],
            PersonalizationScope.Shared,
            args[4],
            args[5]));
    Console.WriteLine();
    Console.WriteLine("Press any key to continue...");
    Console.Read();
}
private static void GetArgs(ref string[] args)
{
    args = new string[6];
    Console.WriteLine();
    Console.Write("Site Url: ");
    args[0] = Console.ReadLine();
    Console.Write("Web Name: ");
    args[1] = Console.ReadLine();
    Console.Write("Doclib containing page (leave blank for none): ");
    args[2] = Console.ReadLine();
    Console.Write("Page Name: ");
    args[3] = Console.ReadLine();
    Console.Write("Path to DWP: ");
    args[4] = Console.ReadLine();
    Console.Write("Zone: ");
    args[5] = Console.ReadLine();
    Console.WriteLine();
}
public static string AddWebPartDWP(
    string strSiteUrl,
    string strWebName,
    string strDocLibName,
    string strPage,
    System.Web.UI.WebControls.WebParts.PersonalizationScope pScope,
    string strDWPPath,
    string strZone)
{
    try
    {
        // Get handle to site and web to be edited
        SPSite site = new SPSite(strSiteUrl);
        SPWeb web = site.OpenWeb(strWebName);
        System.Web.UI.WebControls.WebParts.WebPart wp;
        // Step 1: Get handle to web part page to contain new web part
        SPLimitedWebPartManager webParts;
```

```
    if ((strDocLibName != ""))
    {
        webParts
            = web.GetLimitedWebPartManager(strDocLibName +
                "/" +strPage, pScope);
    }
    else
    {
        webParts =
            web.GetLimitedWebPartManager(strPage, pScope);
    }
    // Step 2: get handle to .DWP file and import definition
    XmlReader reader = XmlReader.Create(strDWPPath);
    string strErrMsg;
    wp = webParts.ImportWebPart(reader, out strErrMsg);
    // Step 3: allow web site to be edited
    web.AllowUnsafeUpdates = true;
    SPList list = null;
    bool origForceCheckoutValue = false;
    if (strDocLibName != "")
    {
        list = web.Lists[strDocLibName];
        origForceCheckoutValue = list.ForceCheckout;
        list.ForceCheckout = false;
        list.Update();
    }
    // Step 6: Add the web part
    webParts.AddWebPart(wp, strZone, 0);
    // Step 7: Save changes back to SharePoint database
    webParts.SaveChanges(wp);
    web.Update();
    // Steps 8-9: If necessary, restore ForceCheckout setting
    if (strDocLibName != "")
    {
        list.ForceCheckout = origForceCheckoutValue;
        list.Update();
    }
    // Release memory used by SPSite, SPWeb objects
    web.Dispose();
    site.Dispose();
    return ("Successfully added \'" + strDWPPath + "\'");
}
catch (Exception ex)
{
    return ex.Message;
}
    }
  }
}
```

To Run

First, add a web part to a SharePoint page and customize the web part as desired. Then export the web part to a `.dwp` file. The following listing shows part of the `.dwp` for the `ContentEditor` web part I used in my example:

```
<?xml version="1.0" encoding="utf-8"?>
<WebPart xmlns:xsi="http://www.w3.org/2001/XMLSchema-instance" ➥
    xmlns:xsd="http://www.w3.org/2001/XMLSchema" ➥
    xmlns="http://schemas.microsoft.com/WebPart/v2">
  <Title>This web part was added using it's .WEBPART file</Title>
      ... ...
  <TypeName>Microsoft.SharePoint.WebPartPages.ContentEditorWebPart</TypeName>
  <ContentLink xmlns="http://schemas.microsoft.com/WebPart/v2/ContentEditor" />
  <Content xmlns="http://schemas.microsoft.com/WebPart/v2/ContentEditor">
      <![CDATA[<FONT size=4>Now is the time for all <STRONG>
      <FONT size=5>good </FONT></STRONG>
SharePoint developers to learn new ways to
programmatically add web parts to a page....</FONT>]]>
  </Content>
  <PartStorage xmlns="http://schemas.microsoft.com/WebPart/v2/ContentEditor" />
</WebPart>
```

Next, run the application in Visual Studio or at the command prompt. Unless you enter all parameters, you'll be prompted to enter the parameters at the console. Enter parameters as appropriate for your environment, keeping in mind that the location of the `.dwp` file will be relative to the location of the executable. Figure 1-6 shows the `AddWebPartDWP` application after it has been run successfully.

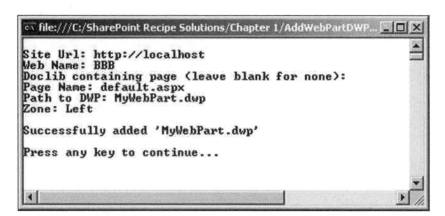

```
Site Url: http://localhost
Web Name: BBB
Doclib containing page (leave blank for none):
Page Name: default.aspx
Path to DWP: MyWebPart.dwp
Zone: Left

Successfully added 'MyWebPart.dwp'

Press any key to continue...
```

Figure 1-6. *Successful execution of the AddWebPartDWP application*

After the program has run successfully, you can navigate to (or refresh) the target page to see the web part that has been added. Figure 1-7 shows the resulting web-part page with the added web part.

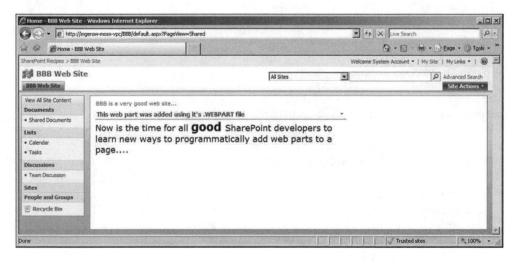

Figure 1-7. *Web-part page displaying the added web part*

Recipe 1-8. Calculating Storage for all Document Libraries in a Site

Surprisingly, there's no convenient way to determine the storage required by a document library without a bit of programming. This recipe displays a list of all document libraries in a given web site, providing the total storage required.

Recipe Type: .NET Web Application

Ingredients

Assembly References

- System.Text library

- Windows SharePoint Services assembly

Class Library References

- Microsoft.SharePoint library

Special Considerations

- This recipe does not take into account versioning. The recipe will need to be modified to include document versions if that's a requirement.

Preparation

1. Create a new ASP.NET web application project in Visual Studio.

2. Add a reference to the Windows SharePoint Services assembly.

3. At the top of the code-behind for Default.aspx (assuming you use that for your web page), add using (C#) or Imports (VB.NET) statements for System.Text, Microsoft. SharePoint, and Microsoft.SharePoint.WebControls.

4. Add a new Extensible Stylesheet Language Transformations (XSLT) file to your project. In the following example, I called it Recipes.xsl. The file should contain the following XSLT code:

```
<?xml version="1.0" encoding="utf-8"?>
<xsl:stylesheet version="1.0" xmlns:xsl="http://www.w3.org/1999/XSL/Transform">
   <xsl:output method="html"/>
   <xsl:template match="/">
      <table>
         <tr>
            <td width="5%">
               <strong>
                  <u>ID</u>
               </strong>
            </td>
            <td width="45%">
               <strong>
                  <u>File Name</u>
               </strong>
            </td>
            <td align="right" width="10%">
               <strong>
                  <u>Size</u>
               </strong>
            </td>
```

```
                <td/>
            </tr>
            <xsl:for-each select="DocumentElement/ListItems">
                <tr>
                    <td>
                        <xsl:value-of select="ID"/>
                    </td>
                    <td>
                        <xsl:value-of select="FileName"/>
                    </td>
                    <td align="right">
                        <xsl:value-of select="format-number(FileSize,' #,###')"/>
                    </td>
                    <td/>
                </tr>
            </xsl:for-each>
            <tr>
                <td/>
                <td/>
                <td align="right">---------------</td>
                <td/>
            </tr>
            <tr>
                <td/>
                <td align="center">Total Bytes:</td>
                <td align="right">
                    <xsl:value-of select= ➥
                        "format-number(sum( ➥
                            DocumentElement/ListItems/FileSize),'#,###')"/>
                </td>
                <td/>
            </tr>
        </table>
    </xsl:template>
</xsl:stylesheet>
```

Process Flow

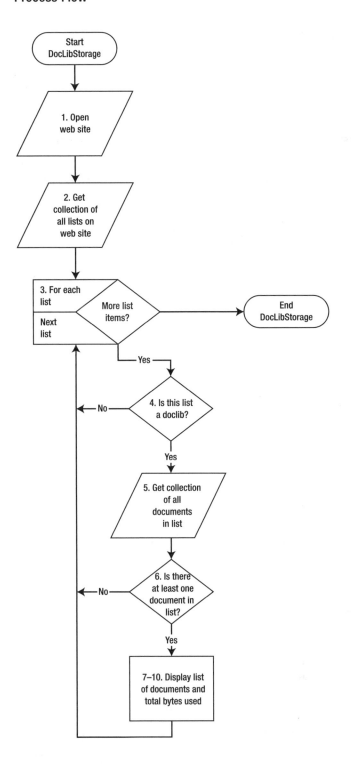

1. Create an SPWeb object representing the web site containing the lists for which you want to calculate storage.

2. Return a list of all lists in the web site.

3. Iterate through the list of lists.

4. Only process lists of type DocumentLibrary.

5. Obtain a list of all documents in the list as a data table.

6. Verify that there's at least one document in the list; otherwise, move on to the next list.

7. Format the list of documents to include only the ID, filename, and number of bytes used. Then write out the list by obtaining an XML representation of the data and formatting it by using an XSLT.

Recipe—VB (See Project DocLibStorage-VB, Class Default.aspx.vb)

```vb
Imports System
Imports System.Data
Imports System.Configuration
Imports System.Web
Imports System.Web.Security
Imports System.Web.UI
Imports System.Web.UI.WebControls
Imports System.Web.UI.WebControls.WebParts
Imports System.Web.UI.HtmlControls
Imports Microsoft.SharePoint
Imports Microsoft.SharePoint.WebControls
Imports System.Text
Partial Public Class _Default
    Inherits System.Web.UI.Page
    Protected Sub Page_Load(ByVal sender As Object, ByVal e As EventArgs) _
Handles Me.Load
        'Step 1: Open site collection and web site
        ' for which we want to report on list storage
        Dim site As New SPSite("http://localhost")
        Dim web As SPWeb = site.RootWeb
        'Step 2: Get collection of all lists
        Dim lists As SPListCollection = web.Lists
        'Step 3: Iterate through all lists, finding
        ' those which are document libraries
        Dim dtListItems As DataTable
        For Each list As SPList In lists
            'Step 4: Is this a document library?
```

```vbnet
            If list.BaseTemplate = SPListTemplateType.DocumentLibrary Then
                'Step 5: Get list of all documents in library
                dtListItems = list.Items.GetDataTable()
                'Step 6: Is there at least one document in
                ' the library?
                If dtListItems IsNot Nothing Then
                    'Step 7: Add heading
                    Dim lbl As New Label()
                    lbl.Text = "<h1>" + list.Title + "</h1>"
                    Me.Controls.Add(lbl)
                    'Step 8: Select just the desired columns
                    dtListItems = FormatTable(dtListItems)
                    'Step 9: Create XML representation of document list
                    Dim sb As New StringBuilder()
                    Dim sw As New System.IO.StringWriter(sb)
                    dtListItems.WriteXml(sw)
                    'Step 10: Format XML using XSLT
                    Dim xmlListItems As New Xml()
                    xmlListItems.DocumentContent = sb.ToString()
                    xmlListItems.TransformSource = "Recipes.xsl"
                    Me.Controls.Add(xmlListItems)
                End If
            End If
        Next
        web.Dispose()
        site.Dispose()
    End Sub
    Private Function FormatTable(ByVal dtListItems As DataTable) As DataTable
        Dim dtMyList As New DataTable("ListItems")
        dtMyList.Columns.Add("ID")
        dtMyList.Columns.Add("FileName")
        dtMyList.Columns.Add("FileSize")
        For Each drListItem As DataRow In dtListItems.Rows
            Dim drMyListItem As DataRow = dtMyList.NewRow()
            drMyListItem("ID") = drListItem("ID")
            drMyListItem("FileName") = drListItem("LinkFileName")
            drMyListItem("FileSize") = drListItem("FileSizeDisplay")
            dtMyList.Rows.Add(drMyListItem)
            dtMyList.AcceptChanges()
        Next
        Return dtMyList
    End Function
End Class
```

Recipe—C# (See Project DocLibStorage-CS, Class Default.aspx.cs)

```csharp
using System;
using System.Data;
using System.Configuration;
using System.Web;
using System.Web.Security;
using System.Web.UI;
using System.Web.UI.WebControls;
using System.Web.UI.WebControls.WebParts;
using System.Web.UI.HtmlControls;
using Microsoft.SharePoint;
using Microsoft.SharePoint.WebControls;
using System.Text;
public partial class _Default : System.Web.UI.Page
{
    protected void Page_Load(object sender, EventArgs e)
    {
        //Step 1: Open site collection and web site
        // for which we want to report on list storage
        SPSite site = new SPSite("http://localhost");
        SPWeb web = site.RootWeb;
        //Step 2: Get collection of all lists
        SPListCollection lists = web.Lists;
        //Step 3: Iterate through all lists, finding
        // those which are document libraries
        DataTable dtListItems;
        foreach (SPList list in lists)
        {
            //Step 4: Is this a document library?
            if (list.BaseTemplate == SPListTemplateType.DocumentLibrary)
            {
                //Step 5: Get list of all documents in library
                dtListItems = list.Items.GetDataTable();
                //Step 6: Is there at least one document in
                //  the library?
                if (dtListItems != null)
                {
                    //Step 7: Add heading
                    Label lbl = new Label();
                    lbl.Text = "<h1>" + list.Title + "</h1>";
                    this.Controls.Add(lbl);
```

```
                    //Step 8: Select just the desired columns
                    dtListItems = FormatTable(dtListItems);
                    //Step 9: Create XML representation of document list
                    StringBuilder sb = new StringBuilder();
                    System.IO.StringWriter sw
                        = new System.IO.StringWriter(sb);
                    dtListItems.WriteXml(sw);
                    //Step 10: Format XML using XSLT
                    Xml xmlListItems = new Xml();
                    xmlListItems.DocumentContent = sb.ToString();
                    xmlListItems.TransformSource = "Recipes.xsl";
                    this.Controls.Add(xmlListItems);
                }
            }
        }
        web.Dispose();
        site.Dispose();
    }
    private DataTable FormatTable(DataTable dtListItems)
    {
        DataTable dtMyList = new DataTable("ListItems");
        dtMyList.Columns.Add("ID");
        dtMyList.Columns.Add("FileName");
        dtMyList.Columns.Add("FileSize");
        foreach (DataRow drListItem in dtListItems.Rows)
        {
            DataRow drMyListItem = dtMyList.NewRow();
            drMyListItem["ID"] = drListItem["ID"];
            drMyListItem["FileName"] = drListItem["LinkFileName"];
            drMyListItem["FileSize"] = drListItem["FileSizeDisplay"];
            dtMyList.Rows.Add(drMyListItem);
            dtMyList.AcceptChanges();
        }
        return dtMyList;
    }
}
```

To Run

Either run the application from within Visual Studio, or open a browser and navigate to the application page. You should see output similar to the following, including sections for each document library in the target website. Figure 1-8 shows the resulting storage report in a browser.

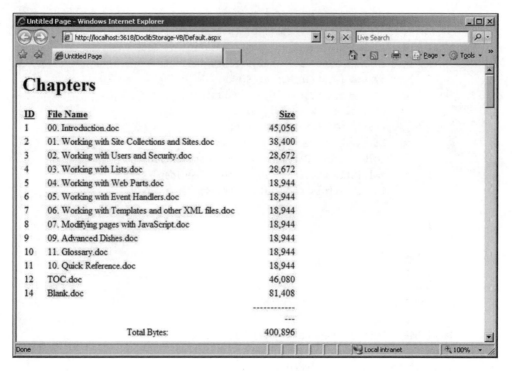

Figure 1-8. *DocLibStorage report displayed in a browser*

Variations

- In our version, we did not take into account the possibility of multiple document versions. You may want to add this.

- Because the output is formatted by using an XSLT, you can easily modify that output by making changes to the XSLT. Note that if you decide to include more or different columns from the document list data table, you will need to modify the XSLT to reference those nodes in the resulting XML.

Recipe 1-9. Creating a Script to Back Up All Site Collections by Using STSADM

SharePoint backup and disaster recovery should be a multilayered affair, ranging from full Structured Query Language (SQL) database and file system backups to recover from catastrophic server failure, all the way to the humble yet important Recycle Bin. Along this continuum is the ability to recover a single site collection to its original or a new server. This can be accomplished by using the STSADM BACKUP and RESTORE commands.

This recipe shows you how to automate the process of backing up all site collections on a given SharePoint farm automatically by using a command script, which can be run from the Windows Task Scheduler or manually as needed.

Recipe Type: Windows Command Script (.vbs)

Ingredients

- Scripting.FileSystemObject class

- WScript.Shell class

- MSXML2.DOMDocument class

Special Considerations

- The STSADM BACKUP command can consume a large amount of server resources, so it should generally be run off-peak. In addition, the following script can open a large number of scripting sessions, one for each site collection. For that reason, the script includes the ability to insert a delay between each call to the STSADM BACKUP command to throttle back the number of concurrent sessions. The actual number of seconds' delay needed will depend on many factors, including the speed of your server, average size of site collections, and amount of server memory.

Preparation

1. Create a new text file named Backup.vbs.

Process Flow

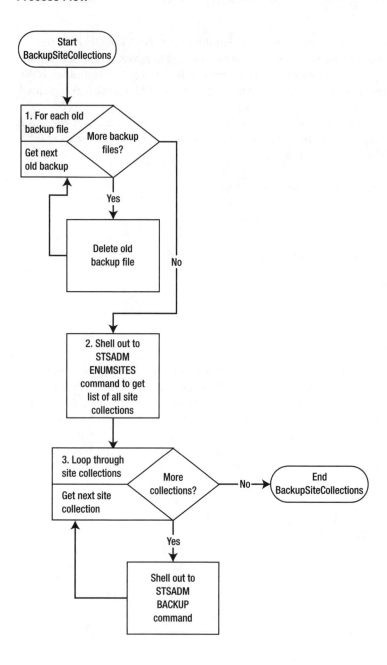

1. Get a list of all preexisting files in the backup folder and loop through the list to delete each file.

2. Call the STSADM ENUMSITES command to return an XML document containing a list of all site collections on the local server.

3. Loop through each node (that is, site collection) in the returned XML document, and again shell out, this time to the STSADM BACKUP command, to write a site collection backup to the target backup folder.

Recipe—VBScript

```
' ----------------------------------------------------------------
' Purpose:    Back up all SharePoint site collections on server
' By:         Mark Gerow
' Date:       1/3/08
' ----------------------------------------------------------------
Option Explicit
' Set the path to the STSADM utility
Const STSADM_PATH = _
 "C:\Program Files\Common Files\Microsoft Shared\ ➥
      web server extensions\12\BIN\stsadm"
' Set the path to where you want the backups made
Const BACKUP_PATH = "C:\SharePoint_Backups\"
' Define needed variables
Dim objFso, objFolder, objFiles, objFile, objShell
Dim objExec, strResult, objXml, objSc, objUrl
Dim strUrl, strFileName, strCmd
' Step 1: OPTIONAL: Delete any preexisting backups
Set objFso = CreateObject("Scripting.FileSystemObject")
Set objFolder = objFso.GetFolder(BACKUP_PATH)
Set objFiles = objFolder.Files
For Each objFile in objFiles
  objFile.Delete(True)
Next
' Step 2: Retrieve all site collections in XML format.
Set objShell = CreateObject("WScript.Shell")
Set objExec = objShell.Exec(STSADM_PATH & " -O ENUMSITES -URL http://localhost/")
strResult = objExec.StdOut.ReadAll
' Load XML in DOM document so it can be processed.
```

```
Set objXml = CreateObject("MSXML2.DOMDocument")
objXml.LoadXML(strResult)
' Step 3: Loop through each site collection and call
' stsadm.exe to make a backup.
For Each objSc in objXml.DocumentElement.ChildNodes
    strUrl = objSc.Attributes.GetNamedItem("Url").Text
    strFileName = BACKUP_PATH & _
        Replace(Replace(strUrl,"/","_"),":","") & ".bak"
    strCmd = STSADM_PATH & " -O BACKUP -URL """ & _
        strUrl + """ -FILENAME """ + strFileName + """"
     ' For testing, display pop-up for each collection backed up
     WScript.Echo "Backing up site collection " & _
          strUrl & " to file " & _
          strFileName & " using the following command " & _
          strCmd
     WScript.Echo

     objShell.Exec(strCmd)

      ' Optional, if there will be many site collections, may want
      ' to insert a delay to avoid overloading server memory
     GoSleep(3)
Next
' This function can be used to insert a delay in the processing
' to avoid overloading server memory if there are many
' site collections to be backed up.
Function GoSleep(seconds)
    Dim startTime, endTime, nowTime, dummy
     startTime = DateAdd("s",0,Now)
     endTime = DateAdd("s",seconds,Now)
     nowTime = DateAdd("s",0,Now)
     While endTime > nowTime
         ' Need some commands in while loop to
         ' ensure it actually executes
         nowTime = DateAdd("s",0,Now)
         dummy = Time
     Wend
End Function
```

To Run

Open a command window, navigate to the folder containing the Backup.vbs file, and type the following command:

```
CSCRIPT Backup.vbs
```

Figure 1-9 shows a command window after the preceding command has been entered.

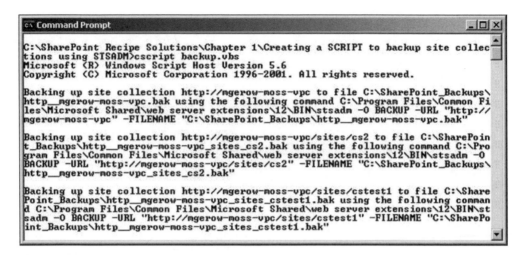

Figure 1-9. *The Backup.vbs command running in a command window*

Assuming the script is set to write backup files to C:\SharePoint_Backups, you should find one or more .bak files in that folder after the script runs. Figure 1-10 shows a directory listing of backup files.

Name ▲	Size	Type	Date Modified	Attributes
http__mgerow-moss-vpc.bak	25,845 KB	BAK File	1/3/2008 1:04 PM	A
http__mgerow-moss-vpc_sites_cs2.bak	625 KB	BAK File	1/3/2008 1:04 PM	A
http__mgerow-moss-vpc_sites_cstest1.bak	632 KB	BAK File	1/3/2008 1:04 PM	A
http__mgerow-moss-vpc_sites_cstest2.bak	632 KB	BAK File	1/3/2008 1:04 PM	A
http__mgerow-moss-vpc_sites_s1.bak	624 KB	BAK File	1/3/2008 1:04 PM	A
http__mgerow-moss-vpc_sites_s2.bak	624 KB	BAK File	1/3/2008 1:04 PM	A
http__mgerow-moss-vpc_sites_s3.bak	624 KB	BAK File	1/3/2008 1:04 PM	A
http__mgerow-moss-vpc_sites_s4.bak	624 KB	BAK File	1/3/2008 1:04 PM	A
http__mgerow-moss-vpc_sites_s5.bak	624 KB	BAK File	1/3/2008 1:04 PM	A
http__mgerow-moss-vpc_sites_td1.bak	625 KB	BAK File	1/3/2008 1:04 PM	A
http__mgerow-moss-vpc_sites_td2.bak	625 KB	BAK File	1/3/2008 1:04 PM	A
http__mgerow-moss-vpc_sites_td3.bak	625 KB	BAK File	1/3/2008 1:04 PM	A
http__mgerow-moss-vpc_sites_td4.bak	625 KB	BAK File	1/3/2008 1:04 PM	A
http__mgerow-moss-vpc_sites_td5.bak	625 KB	BAK File	1/3/2008 1:04 PM	A
http__mgerow-moss-vpc_sites_td6.bak	625 KB	BAK File	1/3/2008 1:05 PM	A
http__mgerow-moss-vpc_sites_ts1.bak	625 KB	BAK File	1/3/2008 1:05 PM	A
http__mgerow-moss-vpc_sites_ts7.bak	625 KB	BAK File	1/3/2008 1:05 PM	A

21 objects (Disk free space: 2.10 GB)   36.9 MB   My Computer

Figure 1-10. *Resulting backup files*

Variations

- This recipe could alternatively be written as a .NET console application, but given that it will still shell out to the STSADM command, there's little value in the additional overhead of the managed code.

- As an alternative, you could use the Microsoft.SharePoint.Administration SPSiteCollection.Backup() method to perform the same operation in a .NET application. This may be preferable if you want to provide the end user a user interface from which to select the site collection or collections to back up.

CHAPTER 2

■ ■ ■

Working with Users

One of the compelling reasons for using the SharePoint platform as a basis for your intranet and extranet web applications is its built-in security model. This model provides a rich set of tools for securing objects (web applications, site collections, sites, lists, folders, and items) and assigning permissions on those objects to users.

This group of recipes focuses on automating tasks around users and user permissions. You'll find recipes to add users, groups, and roles by using both the object model and web services, because there are advantages to both.

Finally, you'll see recipes for working with Active Directory (AD). The reason for including AD is that there will be times when you need to add, edit, or delete the underlying user accounts, rather than just their assigned permissions in SharePoint. In that case, assuming you're using Windows authentication, you'll need recipes for accessing AD directly.

Recipe 2-1. Obtaining and Displaying Users of a Site

It's often useful to know who has access to a site. You might need to produce a report showing who has access across multiple sites, or might want a count of users in each site group on a site—and the ability to obtain this information is a huge benefit in any company subject to legal or industrial compliance requirements. Of course the built-in SharePoint UI can help with this, but if you're managing a large number of sites, going to each site's user administration page to tally or list users can be tedious to say the least.

In this recipe, you'll see how to enumerate the users who are members of site groups as well as those who are given explicit permissions on a site. You'll also see how to identify Active Directory groups that are given permissions to a site.

Recipe Type: ASP.NET Web Application

Ingredients

Assembly References

- Windows SharePoint Services assembly

Class Library References

- Microsoft.SharePoint library

Classes Used

- SPGroup class

- SPUser class

- SPUser.Roles collection

- SPWeb.SiteGroups collection

- SPWeb.Users collection

Special Considerations

- The Microsoft Windows SharePoint Services (WSS) SDK, as well as IntelliSense in Visual Studio, will inform you that the SPUser.Roles collection is *obsolete*. However, the Roles collection is still the simplest way to obtain user role information, requiring less code, so I generally use it instead.

Preparation

1. Create a new ASP.NET web application.

2. Add a reference to the Windows SharePoint Services library.

3. Add Imports or using directives to the top of the code-behind file for Default.aspx (assuming you're using this as your application web page) to the following:

   - Microsoft.SharePoint
   - System.Collections

Process Flow: GetAllSiteUsers

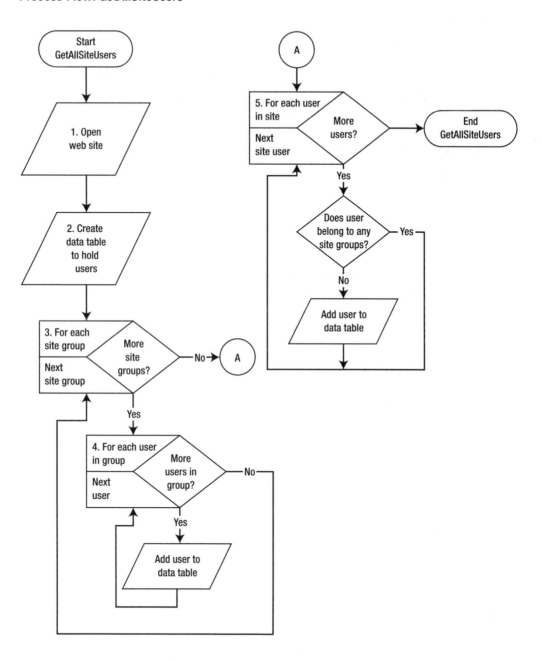

1. Open the web site to process.

2. Create a temporary data table to hold results.

3. Iterate through site groups in the target web site.

4. Iterate through the list of users in each site group, adding group users to the data table.

5. After obtaining all users who are members of one or more groups, add users who don't belong to any site groups but have been given site permissions directly.

Recipe—VB (See Project ObtainUsersInSite-VB, Class Default.aspx.vb)

```vb
Imports System
Imports System.Data
Imports System.Configuration
Imports System.Web
Imports System.Web.Security
Imports System.Web.UI
Imports System.Web.UI.WebControls
Imports System.Web.UI.WebControls.WebParts
Imports System.Web.UI.HtmlControls
Imports Microsoft.SharePoint
Imports System.Collections
Partial Public Class _Default
    Inherits System.Web.UI.Page
    Protected Sub Page_Load(ByVal sender As Object, _
            ByVal e As EventArgs) Handles Me.Load
        Dim siteUrl As String
        Dim webName As String = ""
        Dim fontSize As Integer = 14
        ' Validate site url
        Try
            siteUrl = Request.QueryString("siteUrl").ToString()
        Catch
            Response.Write("<div style='font-size: " & fontSize & _
                "pt; font-weight: bold; font-color: red'>")
            Response.Write("Please provide a value for 'siteUrl' " & _
                "in the querystring")
            Response.Write("</div>")
            Return
        End Try
        ' Validate web name
        Try
            webName = Request.QueryString("webName").ToString()
```

```vb
Catch
    Response.Write("<div style='font-size: " & fontSize & _
        "pt; font-weight: bold; font-color: red'>")
    Response.Write("Please provide a value for 'webName' " & _
        "in the querystring")
    Response.Write("</div>")
    Return
End Try
' Display banner and return link
Response.Write("<H1>List of users for web site '" & siteUrl & _
    "/" + webName + "</H1>")
Dim site As New SPSite(siteUrl)
Dim ADGroups As New ArrayList()
Dim userList As New DataTable()
userList = GetAllSiteUsers(siteUrl, webName)
Dim heading As String = "The following report displays all " & _
    "members of the '" & site.AllWebs(webName).Title & _
    "' as of " & DateTime.Now.ToLocalTime() & _
    "<br/><br/>"
Response.Write("<div style='font-size: " & fontSize & _
    "; font-weight: bold'>")
Response.Write(heading)
Response.Write("<hr/>")
Response.Write("</div>")
' Display users in all groups, and who are not members of any group.
Dim prevGroup As String = "..."
Dim table As New Table()
For Each userRow As DataRow In userList.Rows
    ' If a new GROUP, display heading info
    If prevGroup <> DirectCast(userRow("GroupName"), String) Then
        Response.Write("<br/>")
        If DirectCast(userRow("GroupName").ToString(), String) _
            <> "" Then
            Response.Write("<strong>Group: " & userRow("GroupName")& _
                " [" + userRow("GroupRoles") & _
                "]</strong><br/><br/>")
        Else
            Response.Write("<strong>The following users have " & _
                "been given explicit permissions" & _
                " </strong><br/><br/>")
        End If
        prevGroup = DirectCast(userRow("GroupName"), String)
    End If
    If userRow("UserName").ToString() <> "" Then
        Response.Write(userRow("UserName"))
```

```
            Else
                Response.Write(" (" + userRow("UserAlias") + ") ")
            End If
            If DirectCast(userRow("UserRoles"), String) <> "" Then
                Response.Write(" [" + userRow("UserRoles") + "] ")
            End If
            If DirectCast(userRow("IsADGroup"), String) <> "False" Then
                Response.Write("<font color='red'> " & _
                    "** Active Directory Security Group</font>")
            End If
            Response.Write("<br/>")
        Next
        Response.Write("</div>")
        site.Dispose()
    End Sub
    Private Function GetAllSiteUsers(ByVal siteUrl As String, _
        ByVal webName As String) As DataTable
        ' Step1: Open the web site to process
        Dim site As New SPSite(siteUrl)
        Dim web As SPWeb = site.AllWebs(webName)
        ' Step 2: Create a data table to hold list
        ' of site users
        Dim userList As New DataTable("UserList")
        Dim userRow As DataRow
        userList.Columns.Add("GroupName")
        userList.Columns.Add("GroupRoles")
        userList.Columns.Add("UserAlias")
        userList.Columns.Add("UserName")
        userList.Columns.Add("UserRoles")
        userList.Columns.Add("UserCompany")
        userList.Columns.Add("IsADGroup")
        ' Step 3: Iterate through site groups
        For Each group As SPGroup In web.SiteGroups
            ' Step 4: Get list of all users in this group
            ' and add to data table
            For Each user As SPUser In group.Users
                userRow = userList.NewRow()
                userRow("GroupName") = group.Name
                userRow("GroupRoles") = GetRoles(group)
                userRow("UserName") = user.Name
                userRow("UserAlias") = user.LoginName.ToString()
                userRow("UserRoles") = GetRoles(user)
                userRow("IsADGroup") = user.IsDomainGroup.ToString()
                userList.Rows.Add(userRow)
            Next
        Next
```

```vb
        ' Step 5: Get users who have been assigned
        ' explicit permissions
        For Each user As SPUser In web.Users
            If user.Groups.Count = 0 OrElse GetRoles(user) <> "" Then
                userRow = userList.NewRow()
                userRow("GroupName") = ""
                userRow("GroupRoles") = ""
                userRow("UserName") = user.Name
                userRow("UserAlias") = user.LoginName
                userRow("UserRoles") = GetRoles(user)
                userRow("IsADGroup") = user.IsDomainGroup.ToString()
                userList.Rows.Add(userRow)
            End If
        Next
        web.Dispose()
        site.Dispose()
        Return userList
    End Function
    ' Note: the SPUser.Roles collection has been
    ' deprecated in WSS 3.0, but it's still the
    ' simplest way to access roles assigned to a
    ' user.
    Private Function GetRoles(ByVal gu As SPPrincipal) As String
        Dim roleInfo As String = ""
        For Each role As SPRole In gu.Roles
            If roleInfo <> "" Then
                roleInfo = roleInfo + ","
            End If
            roleInfo = roleInfo + role.Name.ToString()
        Next
        Return roleInfo
    End Function
End Class
```

Recipe—C# (See Project ObtainUsersInSite-CS, Class Default.aspx.cs)

```csharp
using System;
using System.Data;
using System.Configuration;
using System.Web;
using System.Web.Security;
using System.Web.UI;
using System.Web.UI.WebControls;
using System.Web.UI.WebControls.WebParts;
using System.Web.UI.HtmlControls;
using Microsoft.SharePoint;
using System.Collections;
```

```csharp
public partial class _Default : System.Web.UI.Page
{
    protected void Page_Load(object sender, EventArgs e)
    {
        string siteUrl;
        string webName = "";
        int fontSize = 14;
        // Validate site url
        try
        {
            siteUrl = Request.QueryString["siteUrl"].ToString();
        }
        catch
        {
            Response.Write("<div style='font-size: " + fontSize
                + "pt; font-weight: bold; font-color: red'>");
            Response.Write("Please provide a value for 'siteUrl' "
                + "in the querystring");
            Response.Write("</div>");
            return;
        }
        // Validate web name
        try
        {
            webName = Request.QueryString["webName"].ToString();
        }
        catch
        {
            Response.Write("<div style='font-size: " + fontSize
                + "pt; font-weight: bold; font-color: red'>");
            Response.Write("Please provide a value for 'webName' in "
                + "the querystring");
            Response.Write("</div>");
            return;
        }
        //}
        // Display banner and return link
        Response.Write("<H1>List of users for web site \'"
            + siteUrl + "/" + webName + "</H1>");
        SPSite site = new SPSite(siteUrl);
        ArrayList ADGroups = new ArrayList();
        DataTable userList = new DataTable();
        userList = GetAllSiteUsers(siteUrl, webName);
        string heading = "The following report displays all members of the '"
            + site.AllWebs[webName].Title + "' as of "
            + DateTime.Now.ToLocalTime()
            + "<br/><br/>";
```

```
Response.Write("<div style='font-size: " + fontSize
    + "; font-weight: bold'>");
Response.Write(heading);
Response.Write("<hr/>");
Response.Write("</div>");
// Display users in all groups, and who are not members of
// any group.
string prevGroup = "...";
Table table = new Table();
foreach (DataRow userRow in userList.Rows)
{
    // If a new GROUP, display heading info
    if (prevGroup != (string)userRow["GroupName"])
    {
        Response.Write("<br/>");
        if ((string)userRow["GroupName"].ToString() != "")
        {
            Response.Write("<strong>Group: "
                + userRow["GroupName"] + "  ["
                + userRow["GroupRoles"] + "]</strong><br/><br/>");
        }
        else
        {
            Response.Write("<strong>The following users " +
                "have been given explicit permissions " +
                " </strong><br/><br/>");
        }
        prevGroup = (string)userRow["GroupName"];
    }
    if (userRow["UserName"].ToString() != "")
    {
        Response.Write(userRow["UserName"]);
    }
    else
    {
        Response.Write(" (" + userRow["UserAlias"] + ") ");
    }
    if ((string)userRow["UserRoles"] != "")
    {
        Response.Write("  [" + userRow["UserRoles"] + "] ");
    }
    if ((string)userRow["IsADGroup"] != "False")
    {
        Response.Write("<font color='red'> " +
            "** Active Directory Security Group</font>");
    }
    Response.Write("<br/>");
```

```
        }
        Response.Write("</div>");
        site.Dispose();
    }
    private DataTable GetAllSiteUsers(string siteUrl, string webName)
    {
        // Step1: Open the web site to process
        SPSite site = new SPSite(siteUrl);
        SPWeb web = site.AllWebs[webName];
        // Step 2: Create a data table to hold list
        //  of site users
        DataTable userList = new DataTable("UserList");
        DataRow userRow;
        userList.Columns.Add("GroupName");
        userList.Columns.Add("GroupRoles");
        userList.Columns.Add("UserAlias");
        userList.Columns.Add("UserName");
        userList.Columns.Add("UserRoles");
        userList.Columns.Add("UserCompany");
        userList.Columns.Add("IsADGroup");
        // Step 3: Iterate through site groups
        foreach (SPGroup group in web.SiteGroups)
        {
            // Step 4: Get list of all users in this group
            //  and add to data table
            foreach (SPUser user in group.Users)
            {
                userRow = userList.NewRow();

                userRow["GroupName"] = group.Name;
                userRow["GroupRoles"] = GetRoles(group);
                userRow["UserName"] = user.Name;
                userRow["UserAlias"] = user.LoginName.ToString();
                userRow["UserRoles"] = GetRoles(user);
                userRow["IsADGroup"] = user.IsDomainGroup.ToString();
                userList.Rows.Add(userRow);
            }
        }
        // Step 5: Get users who have been assigned
        //  explicit permissions
        foreach (SPUser user in web.Users)
        {
```

```
            if (user.Groups.Count == 0 || GetRoles(user) != "")
            {
                userRow = userList.NewRow();
                userRow["GroupName"] = "";
                userRow["GroupRoles"] = "";
                userRow["UserName"] = user.Name;
                userRow["UserAlias"] = user.LoginName;
                userRow["UserRoles"] = GetRoles(user);
                userRow["IsADGroup"] = user.IsDomainGroup.ToString();
                userList.Rows.Add(userRow);
            }
        }
        web.Dispose();
        site.Dispose();
        return userList;
    }
    // Note: the SPUser.Roles collection has been
    //   deprecated in WSS 3.0, but it's still the
    //   simplest way to access roles assigned to a
    //   user.
    string GetRoles(SPPrincipal gu)
    {
        string roleInfo = "";
        foreach (SPRole role in gu.Roles)
        {
            if (roleInfo != "")
            {
                roleInfo = roleInfo + ",";
            }
            roleInfo = roleInfo + role.Name.ToString();
        }
        return roleInfo;
    }
}
```

To Run

Start the application from within Visual Studio, or open a browser window and navigate to the application URL. Be sure to provide the siteUrl and webName query string parameters as part of the URL. You should see a page similar to Figure 2-1.

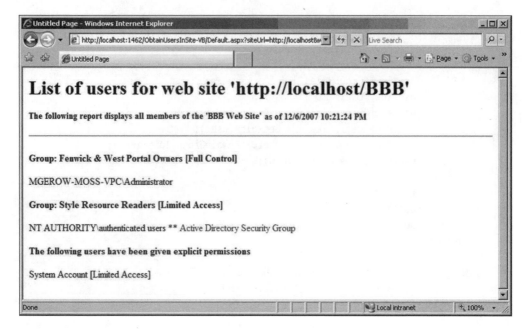

Figure 2-1. *Report of users for a given web site*

Variations

- Modify the application to allow the user to input the site URL and web name via a web form, and then to either navigate to the report page or display the results below the input fields.

- If you deploy the recipe to the 12/Template/Layouts directory, the recipe will be accessible from any site via http://server/site/_layouts/mypage.aspx, and you can use the context within SharePoint via the SPControl object (GetContextWeb()method) so that the page can determine which site you called it from.

Recipe 2-2. Adding Users to a Site by Using the Object Model

There are many times when manually adding users to a site is impractical. For example, if you are automating the provisioning of multiple sites, or you want to add a standard set of users to one or more sites quickly, you will want a way to programmatically add those users.

This recipe shows you how to add one or more users to an existing site group of a web site. Other recipes in this chapter will show you how to create new site groups and roles, and assign users to those programmatically as well.

Note Keep in mind that in SharePoint 2007, groups are defined, and their users managed, at the site collection level, not on individual web sites.

Recipe Type: .NET Console Application

Ingredients

Assembly References

- Windows SharePoint Services

Class Library References

- Microsoft.SharePoint

Special Considerations

- The user login should be provided in the form of [domain]\[login].

- This recipe provides essentially the same functionality as the STSADM ADDUSER command, with the addition that this application will prompt for parameters if they are not provided.

Preparation

1. Create a new .NET console application.

2. Add a reference to the Windows SharePoint Services .NET assembly.

3. Add an Imports or using statement at the top of the main program file referencing the Microsoft.SharePoint library.

Process Flow

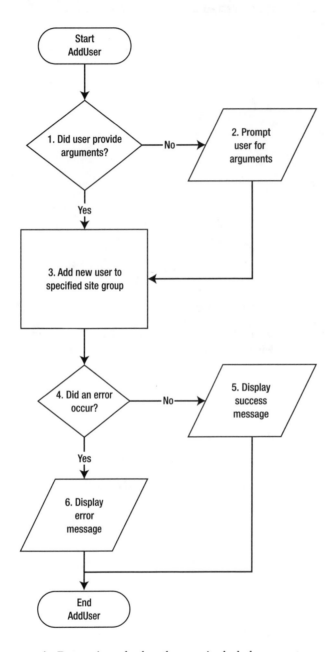

1. Determine whether the user included parameters on the command line.

2. If parameters were not included, prompt the user for them at the console.

3. Create SPSite and SPWeb objects representing the target site collection and web site and add the user.

4. Determine whether an error occurred while adding the new user.

5. If no error occurred, display a success message.

6. Otherwise, if an error did occur, return the error message to the console.

Recipe—VB (See Project AddUsersOM-VB, Module Module1.vb)

```vb
Imports Microsoft.SharePoint
Module Module1
    Sub Main(ByVal args() As String)
        'Step 1: If no arguments passed in, prompt for them now
        If (args.Length = 0) Then
            args = New String(7) {}
            args = GetParams(args)
        End If
        Try
            'Step 3a: Get handle to specified site collection and web site
            Dim site As New SPSite(args(0))
            Dim web As SPWeb = site.AllWebs(args(1))
            'Step 3b: Add the user to the specified site group
            web.SiteGroups(args(6)).AddUser(args(2),args(3),args(4),args(5))
            'Steps 4-5: Display success message
            Console.WriteLine("User '" & args(2) & _
               "' has been successfully added to site group '" & _
              args(6) & "'")
            web.Dispose()
            site.Dispose()
        Catch ex As Exception
            'Step 6: If error occurred, display error message
            Console.WriteLine(ex.Message)
        End Try
        Console.WriteLine()
        Console.WriteLine("Press any key to continue...")
        Console.Read()
    End Sub
    Private Function GetParams(ByRef args() As String) As String()
        Try
            ' Step 2: Get parameters from user
            Console.WriteLine()
            Console.Write("Site collection url: ")
            args(0) = Console.ReadLine
            Console.Write("Site (web): ")
            args(1) = Console.ReadLine
            Console.Write("User login: ")
            args(2) = Console.ReadLine
            Console.Write("Email address: ")
            args(3) = Console.ReadLine
```

```
                Console.Write("User name: ")
                args(4) = Console.ReadLine
                Console.Write("Notes: ")
                args(5) = Console.ReadLine
                Console.Write("Site Group to add user to: ")
                args(6) = Console.ReadLine
                Console.WriteLine()
                Console.WriteLine()
            Catch ex As Exception
                ' If an error occurred, display the error message
                Console.WriteLine()
                Console.WriteLine(ex.Message)
                Console.WriteLine()
            End Try
            Return args
        End Function
End Module
```

Recipe—C# (See Project AddUserOM-CS, File Program.cs)

```csharp
using System;
using System.Collections.Generic;
using System.Text;
using Microsoft.SharePoint;
class Module1
{
    static public void Main(string[] args)
    {
        //Step 1: If no arguments passed in, prompt for them now
        if ((args.Length == 0))
        {
            args = new string[8];
            args = GetParams(args);
        }
        try
        {
            //Step 3a: Get handle to specified site collection and web site
            SPSite site = new SPSite(args[0]);
            SPWeb web = site.AllWebs[args[1]];
            //Step 3b: Add the user to the specified site group
            web.SiteGroups[args[6]].AddUser(args[2], args[3],
              args[4], args[5]);
            //Steps 4-5: Display success message
            Console.WriteLine("User '" + args[2] +
               "' has been successfully added to site group '" +
              args[6] + "'");
```

```
                web.Dispose();
                siite.Dispose();
            }
        catch (Exception ex)
        {
            //Step 6: If error occurred, display error message
            Console.WriteLine(ex.Message);
        }
        Console.WriteLine();
        Console.WriteLine("Press any key to continue...");
        Console.Read();
    }
    static private string[] GetParams(string[] args)
    {
        try
        {
            // Step 2: Get parameters from user
            Console.WriteLine();
            Console.Write("Site collection url: ");
            args[0] = Console.ReadLine();
            Console.Write("Site (web): ");
            args[1] = Console.ReadLine();
            Console.Write("User login: ");
            args[2] = Console.ReadLine();
            Console.Write("Email address: ");
            args[3] = Console.ReadLine();
            Console.Write("User name: ");
            args[4] = Console.ReadLine();
            Console.Write("Notes: ");
            args[5] = Console.ReadLine();
            Console.Write("Site Group to add user to: ");
            args[6] = Console.ReadLine();
            Console.WriteLine();
            Console.WriteLine();
        }
        catch (Exception ex)
        {
            // If an error occurred, display the error message
            Console.WriteLine();
            Console.WriteLine(ex.Message);
            Console.WriteLine();
        }
        return args;
    }
}
```

To Run

Run the console application from a command window or from within Visual Studio. Unless you provide all data as command-line parameters, you will be prompted to provide them at runtime. Figure 2-2 shows this recipe running in a command window.

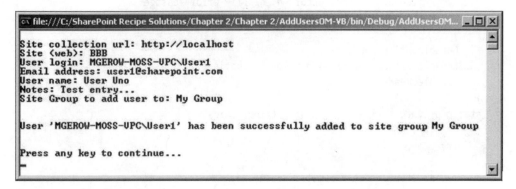

Figure 2-2. *Running the AddUserOM application in a console window*

Assuming no errors occur, the user will be added to the specified site group.

Variations

- Read user data from a database.

Recipe 2-3. Adding Users and Groups to a Site by Using the Web Services

Managing groups and users is one of several instances where the SharePoint web services are simpler to use than the object model. The signatures of the methods for managing users and groups are generally cleaner than their object model counterparts. And, of course, you have the advantage of being able to use them in programs running on any server that can make an HTTP call to one of the front-end servers in the SharePoint farm.

Recipe Type: .NET Console Application

Ingredients

Web Services References

- `http://[SharePoint server]/_vti_bin/UserGroup.asmx` web service

Special Considerations

- As with any web service call, be sure to set the instance object's credentials property to a network credential with permissions to access the SharePoint web server hosting the target site collection and web site.

Preparation

1. Create a .NET console application.

2. Add a web reference named `UserGroupService`, to `http://[SharePoint server]/_vti_bin/UserGroup.asmx`.

Process Flow

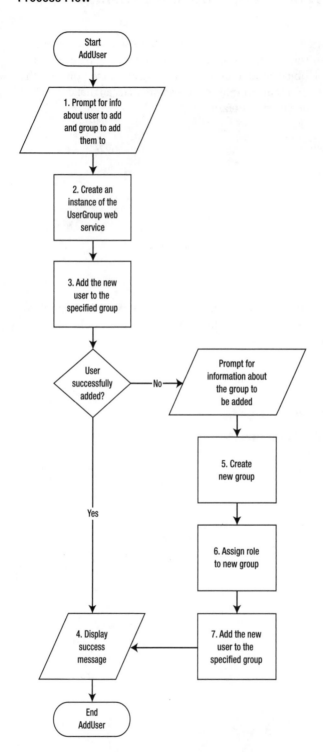

1. Get information about site collection, the web site, the user, and the target group.

2. Point the UserGroup web service to the target site collection and web site.

3. Try to add the new user to the specified group.

4. If an error occurs, assume it's because the target group doesn't exist, so get more information needed to create the group, including the group owner and role.

5. Create the new group.

6. Assign the specified role to the new group.

7. Add the new user. This time it should work!

Recipe—VB (See Project AddUserWS-VB, Module Module1.vb)

```
Module Module1
    'Define structure to hold user info
    Private Structure UserArgs
        Dim UserLogin As String
        Dim UserName As String
        Dim Email As String
        Dim UserDescription As String
        Dim GroupName As String
        Dim SiteUrl As String
        Dim WebName As String
    End Structure
    'Define structure to hold group info
    Private Structure GroupArgs
        Dim OwnerLogin As String
        Dim OwnerType As String
        Dim DefaultUserLogin As String
        Dim RoleName As String
        Dim Description As String
    End Structure
    Sub Main()
        'Step 1: Prompt for user info
        Dim userArgs As UserArgs = GetUserArgs()
        'Step 2: Create an instance of the UserGroup web service class
        '   and set its URL to the target site/web
        Dim objUserGroup As New UserGroupService.UserGroup
        objUserGroup.Url = userArgs.SiteUrl & "/" & _
            userArgs.WebName & "/_vti_bin/UserGroup.asmx"
        objUserGroup.Credentials = _
            System.Net.CredentialCache.DefaultCredentials
        'Attempt to add user to group; if error occurs, will need to get
        'some additional info about the group too
```

```vb
        Try
            'Step 3: Try adding user to the target group
            objUserGroup.AddUserToGroup( _
                userArgs.GroupName, _
                userArgs.UserName, _
                userArgs.UserLogin, _
                userArgs.Email, _
                userArgs.UserDescription)
        Catch exAddUser As Exception
            Try
                'Step 5: Initial user add attempt failed,
                '    so try to create the group
                Dim groupArgs As GroupArgs = GetGroupArgs()
                objUserGroup.AddGroup( _
                    userArgs.GroupName, _
                    groupArgs.OwnerLogin, _
                    groupArgs.OwnerType, _
                    groupArgs.DefaultUserLogin, _
                    groupArgs.Description)
                'Step 6: Assign the new group to desired role
                objUserGroup.AddGroupToRole( _
                    groupArgs.RoleName, _
                    userArgs.GroupName)
                'Step 7: Try adding user again now that group exists
                objUserGroup.AddUserToGroup( _
                    userArgs.GroupName, _
                    userArgs.UserName, _
                    userArgs.UserLogin, _
                    userArgs.Email, _
                    userArgs.UserDescription)
            Catch exAddGroup As Exception
                Console.WriteLine(exAddGroup.Message)
            End Try
        End Try
        'Step 4: Display success message
        Console.WriteLine("Successfully added user '" & _
            userArgs.UserLogin & _
            "' to group '" & _
            userArgs.GroupName & "'")
        Console.WriteLine()
        Console.WriteLine("Press any key to continue...")
        Console.Read()
    End Sub
    Private Function GetGroupArgs() As GroupArgs
        Dim groupArgs As New GroupArgs
```

```vbnet
        Try
            Console.WriteLine()
            Console.Write("Group owner login: ")
            groupArgs.OwnerLogin = Console.ReadLine()
            Console.Write("Group default user login: ")
            groupArgs.DefaultUserLogin = Console.ReadLine()
            Console.Write("Owner login type (User/Group): ")
            groupArgs.OwnerType = Console.ReadLine()
            Console.Write("Group role (Full Control/Contribute/Read): ")
            groupArgs.RoleName = Console.ReadLine()
            Console.Write("Group description: ")
            groupArgs.Description = Console.ReadLine()
            Console.WriteLine()
        Catch ex As Exception
            ' If an error occurred, display the error message
            Console.WriteLine()
            Console.WriteLine(ex.Message)
            Console.WriteLine()
        End Try
        Return groupArgs
    End Function
    Private Function GetUserArgs() As UserArgs
        Dim userArgs As New UserArgs
        Try
            Console.WriteLine()
            Console.Write("Site collection url: ")
            userArgs.SiteUrl = Console.ReadLine()
            Console.Write("Site (web): ")
            userArgs.WebName = Console.ReadLine()
            Console.Write("Site group to add user to: ")
            userArgs.GroupName = Console.ReadLine()
            Console.Write("User login: ")
            userArgs.UserLogin = Console.ReadLine()
            Console.Write("User name: ")
            userArgs.UserName = Console.ReadLine()
            Console.Write("User email: ")
            userArgs.Email = Console.ReadLine()
            Console.Write("Description: ")
            userArgs.UserDescription = Console.ReadLine()
            Console.WriteLine()
        Catch ex As Exception
            ' If an error occurred, display the error message
            Console.WriteLine()
            Console.WriteLine(ex.Message)
            Console.WriteLine()
        End Try
```

```
        Return userArgs
    End Function
End Module
```

Recipe—C# (See Project AddUserWS-CS, File Program.cs)

```csharp
using System;
using System.Collections.Generic;
using System.Text;
namespace AddUserWS_CS
{
    class program1
    {
        //Define structure to hold user info
        private struct UserArgs
        {
            public string UserLogin;
            public string UserName;
            public string Email;
            public string UserDescription;
            public string GroupName;
            public string SiteUrl;
            public string WebName;
        }
        //Define structure to hold group info
        private struct GroupArgs
        {
            public string OwnerLogin;
            public string OwnerType;
            public string DefaultUserLogin;
            public string RoleName;
            public string Description;
        }
        public static void Main()
        {
            //Step 1: Prompt for user info
            UserArgs userArgs = GetUserArgs();
            //Step 2: Create an instance of the UserGroup web service class
            // and set its URL to the target site/web
            UserGroupService.UserGroup objUserGroup =
                new UserGroupService.UserGroup();
            objUserGroup.Url = userArgs.SiteUrl + "/" +
                userArgs.WebName + "/_vti_bin/UserGroup.asmx";
            objUserGroup.Credentials =
                System.Net.CredentialCache.DefaultCredentials;
            //Attempt to add user to group; if error occurs, will need to get
            //some additional info about the group too
```

```
    try
    {
        //Step 3: Try adding user to the target group
        objUserGroup.AddUserToGroup(userArgs.GroupName,
            userArgs.UserName, userArgs.UserLogin, userArgs.Email,
            userArgs.UserDescription);
    }
    catch (Exception exAddUser)
    {
        try
        {
            //Step 5: Initial user add attempt failed,
            // so try to create the group
            GroupArgs groupArgs = GetGroupArgs();
            objUserGroup.AddGroup(userArgs.GroupName,
                groupArgs.OwnerLogin, groupArgs.OwnerType,
                groupArgs.DefaultUserLogin, groupArgs.Description);
            //Step 6: Assign the new group to desired role
            objUserGroup.AddGroupToRole(groupArgs.RoleName,
                userArgs.GroupName);
            //Step 7: Try adding user again now that group exists
            objUserGroup.AddUserToGroup(userArgs.GroupName,
                userArgs.UserName, userArgs.UserLogin,
                userArgs.Email, userArgs.UserDescription);
        }
        catch (Exception exAddGroup)
        {
            Console.WriteLine(exAddGroup.Message);
        }
    }
    //Step 4: Display success message
    Console.WriteLine("Successfully added user '" +
        userArgs.UserLogin + "' to group '" +
        userArgs.GroupName + "'");
    Console.WriteLine();
    Console.WriteLine("Press any key to continue...");
    Console.Read();
}
private static GroupArgs GetGroupArgs()
{
    GroupArgs groupArgs = new GroupArgs();
    try
    {
        Console.WriteLine();
        Console.Write("Group owner login: ");
        groupArgs.OwnerLogin = Console.ReadLine();
        Console.Write("Group default user login: ");
```

```
            groupArgs.DefaultUserLogin = Console.ReadLine();
            Console.Write("Owner login type (User/Group): ");
            groupArgs.OwnerType = Console.ReadLine();
            Console.Write("Group role (Full Control/Contribute/Read): ");
            groupArgs.RoleName = Console.ReadLine();
            Console.Write("Group description: ");
            groupArgs.Description = Console.ReadLine();
            Console.WriteLine();
        }
        catch (Exception ex)
        {
            // If an error occurred, display the error message
            Console.WriteLine();
            Console.WriteLine(ex.Message);
            Console.WriteLine();
        }
        return groupArgs;
    }
    private static UserArgs GetUserArgs()
    {
        UserArgs userArgs = new UserArgs();
        try
        {
            // Step 2: Get parameters from user
            Console.WriteLine();
            Console.Write("Site collection url: ");
            userArgs.SiteUrl = Console.ReadLine();
            Console.Write("Site (web): ");
            userArgs.WebName = Console.ReadLine();
            Console.Write("Site group to add user to: ");
            userArgs.GroupName = Console.ReadLine();
            Console.Write("User login: ");
            userArgs.UserLogin = Console.ReadLine();
            Console.Write("User name: ");
            userArgs.UserName = Console.ReadLine();
            Console.Write("User email: ");
            userArgs.Email = Console.ReadLine();
            Console.Write("Description: ");
            userArgs.UserDescription = Console.ReadLine();
            Console.WriteLine();
        }
        catch (Exception ex)
        {
            // If an error occurred, display the error message
            Console.WriteLine();
            Console.WriteLine(ex.Message);
            Console.WriteLine();
        }
```

```
            return userArgs;
        }
    }
}
```

To Run

Run the application from a command window or from within Visual Studio. You will be prompted for the target site collection and web site, the user login and name, and the group to add the user to. If the group doesn't already exist, you will be prompted for group information as well. Figure 2-3 shows the `AddUserWS` recipe in action.

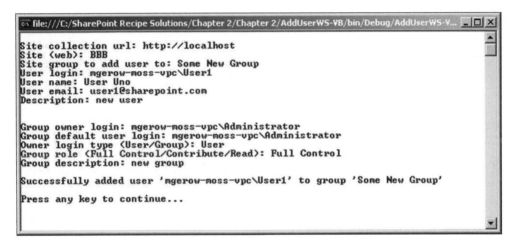

Figure 2-3. *Running the AddUserWS application in a console window*

You can verify that the program ran correctly by opening a browser and navigating to the `/_layouts/groups.aspx` page of the target site collection and web site.

■Note Through the SharePoint UI, you can access this page by using the Site Actions menu, clicking the Site Settings option, and then clicking the People and Groups link.

Variations

- Of course, a console application doesn't allow for much in the way of input validation, so you may want to modify this to use a web or Windows form instead.

Recipe 2-4. Adding Groups to a Site by Using the Object Model

As with users, groups can be added programmatically to a site. This recipe shows you how to add groups and assign them to a role (for example, Contribute or Full Control).

Recipe Type: .NET Console Application

Ingredients

Assembly References

- Windows SharePoint Services

Class Library References

- Microsoft.SharePoint

Classes Used

- SPWeb.SiteGroup collection

- SPWeb.Roles collection (See the following "Special Considerations" section for more on this collection.)

Special Considerations

- The SPWeb.Roles collection has been flagged as *obsolete* in SharePoint 2007. However, it is still functional and is the easiest way to manipulate roll assignments through the object model. Because simplicity is always my goal, I will continue to use it until Microsoft removes it from the object model. In the meantime, other than Visual Studio displaying warnings about it being obsolete, there is no negative impact from using this collection.

- The following example uses the SPWeb.SiteGroups and SPWeb.SiteUsers collections. These collections refer to the collection of cross-site groups and site users, respectively. To limit the scope to just site-specific groups and users, substitute the SPWeb.Groups and SPWeb.Users collections.

Preparation

1. Create a new .NET console application.

2. Add a reference to the Windows SharePoint Services .NET assembly.

3. Add an Imports or using statement at the top of the main program file referencing the Microsoft.SharePoint library.

Process Flow

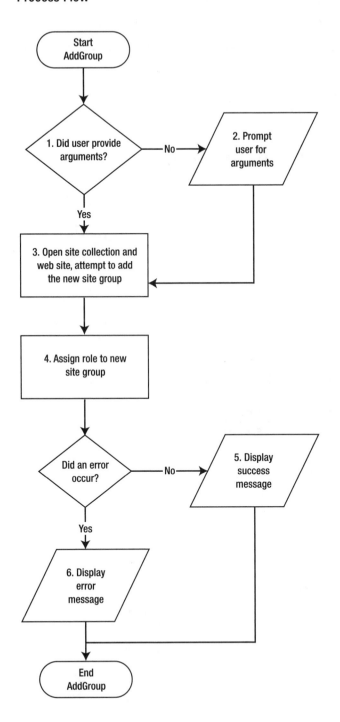

1. Determine whether the user provided necessary parameters on the command line.

2. If the user did not provide the parameters, prompt for them now.

3. Get a handle to the site collection and web site and add a new site group to the web site.

4. Assign an existing role to the new site group.

5. If no errors occurred, display a success message to the console.

6. Otherwise, display the error message to the console.

Recipe—VB (See Project AddGroupOM-VB, Module Module1.vb)

```vb
Imports System
Imports System.Collections.Generic
Imports System.Text
Imports Microsoft.SharePoint
Module Module1
    Public Shared Sub Main(ByVal args As String())
        'Steps 1-2: If no arguments passed in, prompt for them now
        If (args.Length = 0) Then
            args = New String(6) {}
            args = GetParams(args)
        End If
        Try
            'Step 3a: Get handle to specific site collection and web site
            Dim site As New SPSite(args(0))
            Dim web As SPWeb = site.AllWebs(args(1))
            'Step 3b: Add the specified site group
            web.SiteGroups.Add(args(2), web.SiteUsers(args(3)), _
                web.SiteUsers(args(4)), args(5))
            'Step 4: Assign specified role to the new group
            'Note: even though the SPWeb.Roles collection has been flagged as
            ' "obsolete" by Microsoft, it is still the easiest way to
            ' add roles to site groups in WSS/MOSS 2007
            web.Roles(args(6)).AddGroup(web.SiteGroups(args(2)))
            'Step 5: Display success message
            Console.WriteLine("Site group '" + args(2) + _
                "' has been successfully added")
            web.Dispose()
            site.Dispose()
        Catch ex As Exception
            'Step 6: If error occurred, display error message
            Console.WriteLine(ex.Message)
        End Try
        Console.WriteLine()
        Console.WriteLine("Press any key to continue...")
        Console.Read()
    End Sub
```

```vb
    Private Shared Function GetParams(ByVal args As String()) As String()
        Try
            ' Step 2: Get parameters from user
            Console.WriteLine()
            Console.Write("Site collection url: ")
            args(0) = Console.ReadLine()
            Console.Write("Site (web): ")
            args(1) = Console.ReadLine()
            Console.Write("Site group to add: ")
            args(2) = Console.ReadLine()
            Console.Write("Owner login: ")
            args(3) = Console.ReadLine()
            Console.Write("Default user: ")
            args(4) = Console.ReadLine()
            Console.Write("Site group description: ")
            args(5) = Console.ReadLine()
            Console.Write("Role (Full Control/Contribute/Read): ")
            args(6) = Console.ReadLine()
            Console.WriteLine()
            Console.WriteLine()
        Catch ex As Exception
            ' If an error occurred, display the error message
            Console.WriteLine()
            Console.WriteLine(ex.Message)
            Console.WriteLine()
        End Try
        Return args
    End Function
End Module
```

Recipe—C# (See Project AddGroupOM-CS, File Program.cs)

```csharp
using System;
using System.Collections.Generic;
using System.Text;
using Microsoft.SharePoint;
class Program1
{
    static public void Main(string[] args)
    {
        //Steps 1-2: If no arguments passed in, prompt for them now
        if ((args.Length == 0))
        {
            args = new string[7];
            args = GetParams(args);
        }
```

```csharp
    try
    {
        //Step 3a: Get handle to specific site collection and web site
        SPSite site = new SPSite(args[0]);
        SPWeb web = site.AllWebs[args[1]];
        //Step 3b: Add the specified site group
        web.SiteGroups.Add(args[2], web.SiteUsers[args[3]],
            web.SiteUsers[args[4]], args[5]);
        //Step 4: Assign specified role to the new group
        //Note: even though the SPWeb.Roles collection has
        //  been flagged as "obsolete" by Microsoft, it is
        //  still the easiest way to add roles to site
        //  groups in WSS/MOSS 2007
        web.Roles[args[6]].AddGroup(web.SiteGroups[args[2]]);
        //Step 5: Display success message
        Console.WriteLine("Site group '" + args[2] +
            "' has been successfully added");
        web.Dispose();
        site.Dispose();
    }
    catch (Exception ex)
    {
        //Step 6: If error occurred, display error message
        Console.WriteLine(ex.Message);
    }
    Console.WriteLine();
    Console.WriteLine("Press any key to continue...");
    Console.Read();
}
static private string[] GetParams(string[] args)
{
    try
    {
        // Step 2: Get parameters from user
        Console.WriteLine();
        Console.Write("Site collection url: ");
        args[0] = Console.ReadLine();
        Console.Write("Site (web): ");
        args[1] = Console.ReadLine();
        Console.Write("Site group to add: ");
        args[2] = Console.ReadLine();
        Console.Write("Owner login: ");
        args[3] = Console.ReadLine();
        Console.Write("Default user: ");
        args[4] = Console.ReadLine();
```

```
            Console.Write("Site group description: ");
            args[5] = Console.ReadLine();
            Console.Write("Role (Full Control/Contribute/Read): ");
            args[6] = Console.ReadLine();
            Console.WriteLine();
            Console.WriteLine();
        }
        catch (Exception ex)
        {
            // If an error occurred, display the error message
            Console.WriteLine();
            Console.WriteLine(ex.Message);
            Console.WriteLine();
        }
        return args;
    }
}
```

To Run

Run the application from a command window or directly from Visual Studio. Unless you have provided the necessary parameters on the command line, the program will prompt you to enter them from the console. See Figure 2-4 for an example of this recipe executing in a command window.

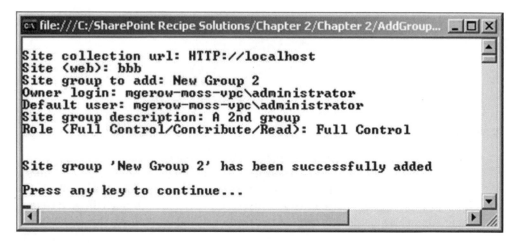

Figure 2-4. *Running the AddGroupOM application in a console window*

Variations

- As noted earlier, you can substitute the SPWeb.Groups and SPWeb.Users collections to limit the scope to groups and users in the current web site.

Recipe 2-5. Adding Roles to a Web Site by Using the Object Model

Roles (or *role definitions*) in SharePoint are essentially named permission sets. You're probably already familiar with the standard ones: Full Control, Contribute, and Read. But you can create custom role definitions to suit your particular needs.

In principle, you can assign one or more roles to an individual user, site group, or AD group to meet your security requirements. In practice, your best approach is to avoid assigning roles to individual users. Instead, you should assign roles to site groups, and add individual users or AD groups to those site groups.

Recipe Type: .NET Console Application

Ingredients

Assembly References

- Windows SharePoint Services .NET

Class Library References

- Microsoft.SharePoint

Classes Used

- SPSite class

- SPWeb class

- SPRoleDefinitionCollection collection

- SPRoleDefinition class

Special Considerations

- You can create new role definitions only in web sites that do not inherit permissions from their parent. Because the root site in a site collection by definition has no parent, you can always create new roles in the root. By default, however, child sites will inherit from the root, so you will need to break that inheritance either through the web UI or programmatically before you can use this method to add new roles to those web sites.

- SharePoint has 32 distinct base permissions, such as Manage Personal Views or Approve Items. The base permission sets, such as Full Control or Read are composed of different combinations of these 32 base permissions. Because of the large number of possible combinations, for the purposes of this recipe I have chosen to "clone" one of the standard permission sets rather than ask the user to choose from all or some of the base permissions. However, you shouldn't assume that you're restricted to any out-of-the-box set of permissions; you can mix and match from the 32 base permissions as needed.

Preparation

1. Create a new .NET console application.

2. Add a reference to the Windows SharePoint Services .NET assembly.

3. Add a using or Imports statement for the Microsoft.SharePoint library.

Process Flow

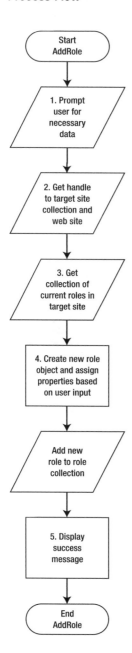

1. The user must provide the target site collection URL, web site name (blank for root), new role name, and base permission set to inherit from.

2. Create instances of the SPSite and SPWeb classes pointing to the target site collection and web site.

3. Create an instance of the SPRoleDefinitionCollection class pointing to the collection of existing roles in the target web site.

4. Create a new instance of the SPRoleDefinition class to represent the role to be added, assign all required properties, and add the target web site's role definition collection.

5. If no exceptions occurred along the way, let the user know it worked. Otherwise, display an error message.

Recipe—VB (See Project AddRoleOM-VB, Module Module1.vb)

```vb
Imports System
Imports System.Collections.Generic
Imports System.Text
Imports Microsoft.SharePoint
Namespace AddRoleOM_VB
    Module Module1
        Private Structure roleData
            Public SiteUr As String
            Public WebName As String
            Public RoleName As String
            Public RoleDescription As String
            Public PermissionMask As SPBasePermissions
        End Structure
        Public Shared Sub Main()
            'Step 1: Prompt data needed to define
            ' the new role
            Dim r As roleData = GetParams()
            Try
                'Step 2: Get handle to specific site collection and web site
                Dim site As New SPSite(r.SiteUr)
                Dim web As SPWeb = site.AllWebs(r.WebName)
                web.AllowUnsafeUpdates = True
                'Step 3: Get collection of current role definitions for site
                Dim roles As SPRoleDefinitionCollection = web.RoleDefinitions
                'Step 4: Create a new role using information passed in
                Dim role As New SPRoleDefinition()
                role.Name = r.RoleName
                role.Description = r.RoleDescription
                role.BasePermissions = r.PermissionMask
                roles.Add(role)
```

```vbnet
            'Step 5: Display success message
            Console.WriteLine("Role '" + r.RoleName + _
                "' has been successfully added")
            web.Dispose()
            site.Dispose()
        Catch ex As Exception
            'Step 6: If error occurred, display error message
            Console.WriteLine(ex.Message)
        End Try
        Console.WriteLine()
        Console.WriteLine("Press any key to continue...")
        Console.Read()
    End Sub
    Private Shared Function GetParams() As roleData
        Dim r As New roleData()
        Try
            ' Get the basic data
            Console.WriteLine()
            Console.Write("Site collection url: ")
            r.SiteUr = Console.ReadLine()
            Console.Write("Site (web): ")
            r.WebName = Console.ReadLine()
            Console.Write("Role to add: ")
            r.RoleName = Console.ReadLine()
            Console.Write("Description of role: ")
            r.RoleDescription = Console.ReadLine()
            ' Now get a character that represents the
            ' set of permissions the new role should
            ' inherit
            Console.Write("Role (F=Full Control, C=Contribute, R=Read): ")
            Dim strBasePermission As String = Console.ReadLine()
            'Only allow user to enter valid permission character,
            'keep looping until valid response provided
            Dim site As New SPSite(r.SiteUr)
            Dim web As SPWeb = site.AllWebs(r.WebName)
            r.PermissionMask = SPBasePermissions.EmptyMask
            While True
                Select Case strBasePermission.ToUpper()
                    Case "F"
                        r.PermissionMask = _
                            web.RoleDefinitions("Full Control").BasePermissions
                        Exit Select
                    Case "C"
                        r.PermissionMask = _
                            web.RoleDefinitions("Contribute").BasePermissions
                        Exit Select
```

```
                              Case "R"
                                  r.PermissionMask = _
                                      web.RoleDefinitions("Read").BasePermissions
                                  Exit Select
                          End Select
                          If r.PermissionMask <> SPBasePermissions.EmptyMask Then
                              Exit While
                          Else
                              Console.Write("Your selection was not valid" & _
                                  " (F=Full Control, C=Contribute, R=Read): ")
                              strBasePermission = Console.ReadLine()
                          End If
                      End While
                      Console.WriteLine()
                      Console.WriteLine()
                      web.Dispose()
                      site.Dispose()
                  Catch ex As Exception
                      ' If an error occurred, display the error message
                      Console.WriteLine()
                      Console.WriteLine(ex.Message)
                      Console.WriteLine()
                  End Try
                  Return r
              End Function
          End Module
    End Namespace
```

Recipe—C# (See Project AddRoleOM-CS, File Program.cs)

```csharp
using System;
using System.Collections.Generic;
using System.Text;
using Microsoft.SharePoint;
namespace AddRoleOM_CS
{
    class Program
    {
        private struct roleData
        {
            public string SiteUr;
            public string WebName;
            public string RoleName;
            public string RoleDescription;
            public SPBasePermissions PermissionMask;
        }
```

```csharp
static public void Main()
{
    //Step 1: Prompt data needed to define
    //  the new role
    roleData r = GetParams();
    try
    {
        //Step 2: Get handle to specific site collection and web site
        SPSite site = new SPSite(r.SiteUr);
        SPWeb web = site.AllWebs[r.WebName];
        web.AllowUnsafeUpdates = true;
        //Step 3: Get collection of current role definitions for site
        SPRoleDefinitionCollection roles = web.RoleDefinitions;

        //Step 4: Create a new role using information passed in
        SPRoleDefinition role = new SPRoleDefinition();
        role.Name = r.RoleName;
        role.Description = r.RoleDescription;
        role.BasePermissions = r.PermissionMask;
        roles.Add(role);
        //Step 5: Display success message
        Console.WriteLine(
            "Role '" + r.RoleName + "' has been successfully added");
        web.Dispose();
        site.Dispose();
    }
    catch (Exception ex)
    {
        //Step 6: If error occurred, display error message
        Console.WriteLine(ex.Message);
    }
    Console.WriteLine();
    Console.WriteLine("Press any key to continue...");
    Console.Read();
}
static private roleData GetParams()
{
    roleData r = new roleData();

    try
    {
        // Get the basic data
        Console.WriteLine();
        Console.Write("Site collection url: ");
        r.SiteUr = Console.ReadLine();
        Console.Write("Site (web): ");
        r.WebName = Console.ReadLine();
```

```
Console.Write("Role to add: ");
r.RoleName = Console.ReadLine();
Console.Write("Description of role: ");
r.RoleDescription = Console.ReadLine();
// Now get a character that represents the
// set of permissions the new role should
// inherit
Console.Write(
    "Role (F=Full Control, C=Contribute, R=Read): ");
string strBasePermission = Console.ReadLine();

//Only allow user to enter valid permission character,
//keep looping until valid response provided
SPSite site = new SPSite(r.SiteUr);
SPWeb web = site.AllWebs[r.WebName];
r.PermissionMask = SPBasePermissions.EmptyMask;
while (true)
{
    switch (strBasePermission.ToUpper())
    {
        case "F":
            r.PermissionMask =
                web.RoleDefinitions["Full Control"].BasePermissions;
            break;
        case "C":
            r.PermissionMask =
                web.RoleDefinitions["Contribute"].BasePermissions;
            break;
        case "R":
            r.PermissionMask =
                web.RoleDefinitions["Read"].BasePermissions;
            break;
    }
    if (r.PermissionMask != SPBasePermissions.EmptyMask)
        break;
    else
    {
        Console.Write("Your selection was not valid" +
            " (F=Full Control, C=Contribute, R=Read): ");
        strBasePermission = Console.ReadLine();
    }
}
Console.WriteLine();
Console.WriteLine();
web.Dispose();
site.Dispose();
}
```

```
        catch (Exception ex)
        {
            // If an error occurred, display the error message
            Console.WriteLine();
            Console.WriteLine(ex.Message);
            Console.WriteLine();
        }
        return r;
    }
  }
}
```

To Run

Run the application from within Visual Studio or at the command prompt. The application will prompt you for the target site collection and web site, a name and description, and a choice of one of three base permission sets to model the new role after.

In the example shown in Figure 2-5, I purposely entered the invalid entry *bad entry* at the role prompt to demonstrate the simple validation employed to ensure that the value is one of *F, C,* or *R*.

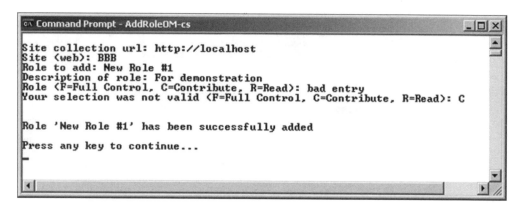

Figure 2-5. *Running the AddRoleOM application in a command window*

You can verify that the new role has been added by opening up the Site Settings/Permissions page of the target web site, as shown in Figure 2-6.

Clicking on the role name (titled Permission Level in the Role.aspx page shown) will display the detail page for that role, as shown in Figure 2-7.

In my example, I modeled the new role after the base Contribute role, and thus it inherited all the base permissions associated with that base role.

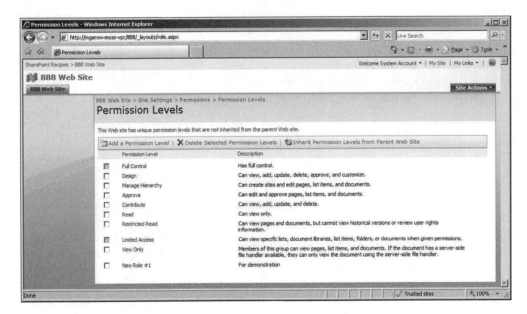

Figure 2-6. *Verifying the new permission level*

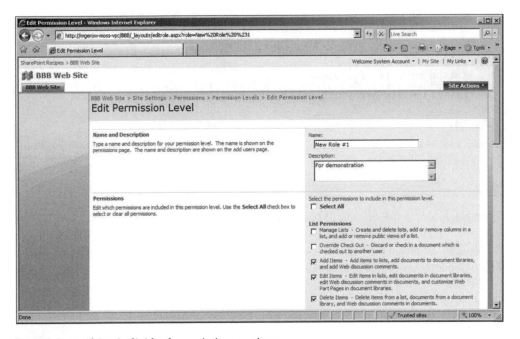

Figure 2-7. *Verifying individual permissions settings*

Variations

- In this recipe, I've used a .NET console application because it removes much of the complexity (and richness) of a web UI. However, you may want to create an ASP.NET web form that allows the user more flexibility in selecting the base permissions wanted in the new role, or to add the same new role to all site collections for a given web application.

- Perhaps the most likely scenario in which you'd want to programmatically provision roles for a web site might be when you are programmatically provisioning sites, and want to set up the security based on more- or less-complex business rules determined by data from another system (such as a customer relationship management database).

Recipe 2-6. Adding Roles to a Web Site by Using the Web Services

This recipe is similar to the previous one in that it shows you how to add a role to a web site. But in this case, we'll use a web service instead of the object model. As noted numerous times throughout this book, the web services have the advantage of allowing you to create distributed applications, rather than running your code on a SharePoint web server.

Adding a role by using the built-in `UserGroup.asmx` web service is actually very easy, with one exception—getting the permission flags necessary to assign a complex set of permissions to the new role. With that in mind, I will emphasize the `GetPermissionFlags()` method that is part of the recipe, showing how a combination of web service and OM calls can be used to clone permissions of an already existing role definition.

Recipe Type: ASP.NET Web Application

Ingredients

Assembly References

- Windows SharePoint Services

Class Library References

- `Microsoft.SharePoint` class library

Web Services References

- `http://[server name]/_vti_bin/usergroup.asmx`

Classes Used

- System.Xml class library

- SPBasePermissions enumeration

- UserGroup.GetRoleCollectionFromWeb() method

- UserGroup.AddRoleDef() method

Special Considerations

- In many instances, you would not expect to find a reference to the Windows SharePoint Services assembly in an application that uses SharePoint web services. This is because the web services are generally used when you want to build an application that doesn't need to run on a SharePoint web server, but the classes contained in the Windows SharePoint Services assembly assume that they are executed on a SharePoint server. The reason for including that assembly here is so we can get access to the SPBasePermissions enum type—and not to call any of the methods—so there is no conflict. We'll use the SPBasePermissions enum to help us construct the flags necessary to set permissions for the new role definition.

- As always with web services that require authentication (as all SharePoint web services do), you will want to attach a set of credentials that have authority to create new roles for the target web site.

- New roles may be added only to web sites that do not inherit their permissions from a parent site.

Preparation

1. Create a new ASP.NET web application.

2. Add a reference to the Windows SharePoint Services .NET assembly.

3. Add a web reference to the _vti_bin/UserGroup.asmx SharePoint web service.

4. Add a using or Imports statement for Microsoft.SharePoint.

5. Add a using or Imports statement for System.Xml, which will enable us to create the XmlNode object to hold the returned list of role definitions.

Process Flow: GetPermissionFlags()

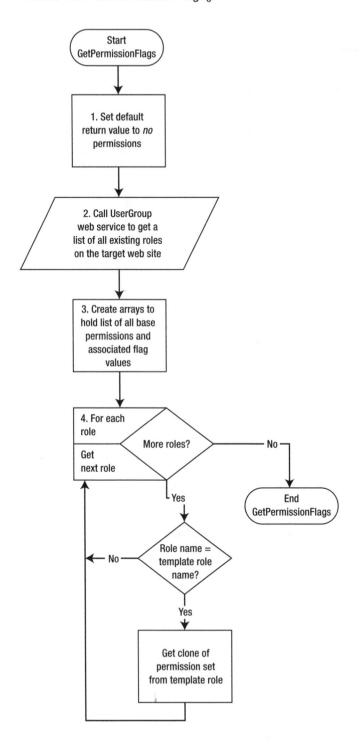

1. In case there is no existing role definition that matches the template name, default the permission flags to none.

2. Call the web service to get a list of existing roles in XML form. Associated with each entry will be a comma-delimited list of the base permissions associated with a given role definition.

3. Parse the `SPBasePermissions` enum to create arrays holding the list of all 32 base permissions and their associated flag values.

4. Loop through each role definition returned in step 2 to find the one whose name matches the desired template role. After you've found it, get the list of base permission names associated with that role, convert the list into an array, and then find the corresponding base permission value by using the arrays created in step 3. All the base permission values will be *OR*ed together to create the value that will be used to set the complete collection of base permissions associated with the new role.

Recipe—ASPX (See Project AddRoleWS-CS, File Default.aspx)

```
<%@ Page Language="C#" AutoEventWireup="true" Gerow_09614
        CodeFile="Default.aspx.cs" Inherits="_Default" %>
<!DOCTYPE html PUBLIC "-//W3C//DTD XHTML 1.0 Transitional//EN" ➥
        "http://www.w3.org/TR/xhtml1/DTD/xhtml1-transitional.dtd">
<html xmlns="http://www.w3.org/1999/xhtml" >
<head runat="server">
    <title>Untitled Page</title>
</head>
<body>
    <form id="form1" runat="server">
    <div>
        <table width="100%">
            <tr>
                <td>
                    Site collection Url:</td>
                <td style="width: 100px">
                    <asp:TextBox ID="txtSiteUrl" runat="server"></asp:TextBox></td>
                <td style="width: 100px">
                </td>
            </tr>
            <tr>
                <td>
                    Web site name:</td>
                <td style="width: 100px">
                    <asp:TextBox ID="txtWebName" runat="server"></asp:TextBox></td>
                <td style="width: 100px">
                </td>
            </tr>
```

```
<tr>
    <td>
        New role definition name:</td>
    <td style="width: 100px">
        <asp:TextBox ID="txtRoleName" runat="server"></asp:TextBox></td>
    <td style="width: 100px">
    </td>
</tr>
<tr>
    <td>
        New role definition</td>
    <td style="width: 100px">
        <asp:TextBox ID="txtRoleDefinition" runat="server" Rows="5"
            TextMode="MultiLine" Width="300px"></asp:TextBox></td>
    <td style="width: 100px">
    </td>
</tr>
<tr>
    <td>
        Copy permissions from which role:</td>
    <td style="width: 100px">
        <asp:RadioButtonList ID="rblTemplateRole" runat="server">
            <asp:ListItem>Full Control</asp:ListItem>
            <asp:ListItem>Contribute</asp:ListItem>
            <asp:ListItem Selected="True">Read</asp:ListItem>
        </asp:RadioButtonList></td>
    <td style="width: 100px">
    </td>
</tr>
<tr>
    <td style="width: 100px">
    </td>
    <td style="width: 100px">
        <asp:Button ID="cmdAddRole" runat="server"
            OnClick="cmdAddRole_Click" Text="Add Role" /></td>
    <td style="width: 100px">
    </td>
</tr>
<tr>
    <td style="width: 100px">
    </td>
    <td style="width: 100px">
         </td>
    <td style="width: 100px">
    </td>
</tr>
```

```
            <tr>
                <td style="width: 100px">
                </td>
                <td style="width: 100px">
                    <asp:Label ID="lblReturnMsg" runat="server"
                        ForeColor="Red"></asp:Label></td>
                <td style="width: 100px">
                </td>
            </tr>
        </table>

    </div>
    </form>
</body>
</html>
```

Recipe—VB (See Project AddRoleWS-VB, Class Default.aspx.vb)

```
Imports System
Imports System.Data
Imports System.Configuration
Imports System.Web
Imports System.Web.Security
Imports System.Web.UI
Imports System.Web.UI.WebControls
Imports System.Web.UI.WebControls.WebParts
Imports System.Web.UI.HtmlControls
Imports Microsoft.SharePoint
Imports System.Xml
Partial Public Class _Default
    Inherits System.Web.UI.Page
    Private objUserGroup As New UserGroupService.UserGroup()
    Private Function GetPermissionFlags(ByVal strRoleName As String) As ULong
        ' Step 1: Default to NO permissions
        Dim permissionFlags As ULong = CLng(SPBasePermissions.EmptyMask)
        ' Step 2: Get list of all current roles for this web site
        Dim xnRoles As XmlNode = objUserGroup.GetRoleCollectionFromWeb()
        ' Step 3: Even though we're using the web service to update
        ' the roles collection, we can use the built-in enum
        ' type to get the numeric values of the various base
        ' permissions.
        Dim enumBasePermissions As New SPBasePermissions()
        Dim arrBasePermissionNames As String() = _
            System.Enum.GetNames(enumBasePermissions.GetType())
        Dim arrBasePermissionValues As ULong() = _
            System.Enum.GetValues(enumBasePermissions.GetType())
```

```
' Step 4: Loop through all current roles in target site
' finding the role for which we want to duplicate permission
' flags.
For Each xnRole As XmlNode In xnRoles.FirstChild.ChildNodes
    If xnRole.Attributes("Name").Value.ToString().ToLower() = _
        strRoleName.ToLower() Then
        ' Turn the comma-delimited list of base permission names into
        ' an array so we can iterate through them
        Dim arrPermission As String() = _
            xnRole.Attributes("BasePermissions").Value.ToString().Split(",","c)
        ' Iterate through the complete list of base permissions to
        ' find the entry that matches the base permission from our
            ' template role
        For i As Integer = 0 To arrPermission.Length - 1
            For j As Integer = 0 To arrBasePermissionNames.Length - 1
                ' When we've found our base permission, "OR" its
                ' numeric value with that of any other base
                ' permissions to create the complete set of values
                If arrPermission(i).Trim() = _
                    arrBasePermissionNames(j) Then
                    permissionFlags = _
                        permissionFlags Or arrBasePermissionValues(j)
                End If
            Next
        Next
    End If
Next
Return permissionFlags
End Function
Protected Sub cmdAddRole_Click(ByVal sender As Object, _
    ByVal e As EventArgs) Handles cmdAddRole.Click
    Try
        ' Point the UserGroup web service to our target site collection
        ' and web site
        objUserGroup.Url = txtSiteUrl.Text + "/" + _
            txtWebName.Text + "/_vti_bin/usergroup.asmx"
        objUserGroup.Credentials = _
            System.Net.CredentialCache.DefaultCredentials
        ' Get the permission flags of the role to be cloned
        Dim permissionFlags As ULong = _
            GetPermissionFlags(rblTemplateRole.SelectedValue)
        ' Create the new role
        objUserGroup.AddRoleDef(txtRoleName.Text, _
            txtRoleDefinition.Text, permissionFlags)
        ' Display success message
        lblReturnMsg.Text = "Successfully added '" + _
            txtRoleName.Text + "' role."
```

```
            Catch ex As Exception
                lblReturnMsg.Text = "Error: " + ex.Message
            End Try
        End Sub
End Class
```

Recipe—C# (See Project AddRoleWS-CS, Class Default.aspx.cs)

```csharp
using System;
using System.Data;
using System.Configuration;
using System.Web;
using System.Web.Security;
using System.Web.UI;
using System.Web.UI.WebControls;
using System.Web.UI.WebControls.WebParts;
using System.Web.UI.HtmlControls;
using Microsoft.SharePoint;
using System.Xml;
public partial class _Default : System.Web.UI.Page
{
    private UserGroupService.UserGroup objUserGroup =
        new UserGroupService.UserGroup();
    protected void Page_Load(object sender, EventArgs e)
    {
    }
    private ulong GetPermissionFlags(string strRoleName)
    {
        // Step 1: Default to NO permissions
        ulong permissionFlags = (ulong)SPBasePermissions.EmptyMask;
        // Step 2: Get list of all current roles for this web site
        XmlNode xnRoles = objUserGroup.GetRoleCollectionFromWeb();
        // Step 3: Even though we're using the web service to update
        //   the roles collection, we can use the built-in enum
        //   type to get the numeric values of the various base
        //   permissions.
        SPBasePermissions enumBasePermissions =
            new SPBasePermissions();
        string[] arrBasePermissionNames =
            System.Enum.GetNames(enumBasePermissions.GetType());
        ulong[] arrBasePermissionValues =
            (ulong[])System.Enum.GetValues(enumBasePermissions.GetType());
        // Step 4: Loop through all current roles in target site
        //   finding the role for which we want to duplicate permission
        //   flags.
```

```csharp
        foreach (XmlNode xnRole in xnRoles.FirstChild.ChildNodes)
        {
            if (xnRole.Attributes["Name"].Value.ToString().ToLower()
              == strRoleName.ToLower())
            {
                // Turn the comma-delimited list of base permission
                // names into an array so we can iterate through them
                string[] arrPermission =
                    xnRole.Attributes["BasePermissions"].Value.ToString().Split(',');
                // Iterate through the complete list of base permissions to
                // find the entry that matches the base permission
                // from our template role
                for (int i = 0; i < arrPermission.Length; i++)
                    for (int j = 0; j < arrBasePermissionNames.Length; j++)
                        // When we've found our base permission, "OR" its
                        // numeric value with that of any other base
                        // permissions to create the complete set of values
                        if (arrPermission[i].Trim() ==
                          arrBasePermissionNames[j])
                            permissionFlags = permissionFlags |
                                arrBasePermissionValues[j];
            }
        }
        return permissionFlags;
    }
    protected void cmdAddRole_Click(object sender, EventArgs e)
    {
        try
        {
            // Point the UserGroup web service to our target site collection
            // and web site
            objUserGroup.Url = txtSiteUrl.Text + "/" +
                txtWebName.Text + "/_vti_bin/usergroup.asmx";
            objUserGroup.Credentials =
                System.Net.CredentialCache.DefaultCredentials;
            // Get the permission flags of the role to be cloned
            ulong permissionFlags =
              GetPermissionFlags(rblTemplateRole.SelectedValue);
            // Create the new role
            objUserGroup.AddRoleDef(txtRoleName.Text,
                txtRoleDefinition.Text, permissionFlags);
            // Display success message
            lblReturnMsg.Text = "Successfully added '" +
            txtRoleName.Text + "' role.";
        }
```

```
            catch (Exception ex)
            {
                lblReturnMsg.Text = "Error: " + ex.Message;
            }
        }
    }
}
```

To Run

Run the application from within Visual Studio, or by opening a web browser and navigating to the application page. Provide the target site collection URL, web name (if not creating the new role in the site collection's root web), role name, and optional definition. Select the template role you want to copy permissions from and click the Add Role button. See Figure 2-8 for an example of the page running in a browser.

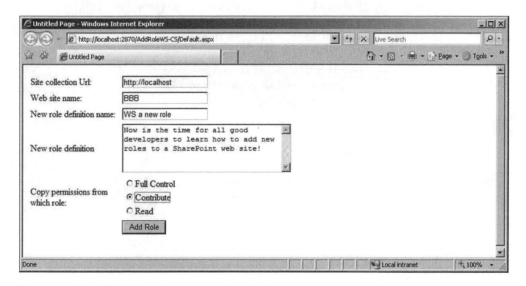

Figure 2-8. *The AddRole application running in a browser*

You can verify that the new role was created by opening the target web site's Site Settings/ Permissions page as shown in Figure 2-9. You should see the new role at the bottom of the list, along with any description you provided.

Clicking on the role name in the list (WS a New Role in this example) will display the detail page of the new role (shown in Figure 2-10). You can see the various base permissions that were copied from the selected template role definition.

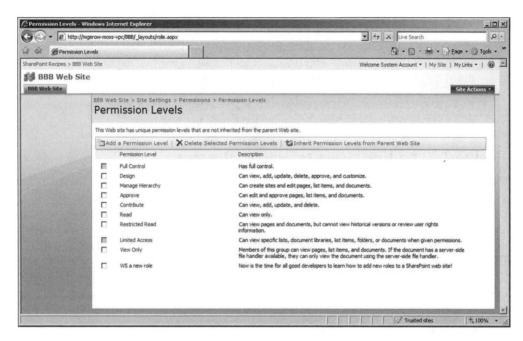

Figure 2-9. *Verifying the result of adding a new role*

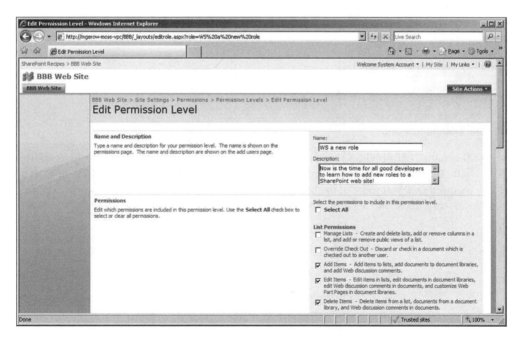

Figure 2-10. *Verifying the permission-level entries for the new role*

Variations

- Rather than hard-code the list of template sites (that is, Full Control, Contribute, Read), you can use the `UserGroup.GetRoleCollectionFromWeb()` method to populate a drop-down list of all existing roles for the user to select from.

- Add a test to make sure that the target web site is not set to inherit from a parent site, and allow the user to break inheritance if needed to add the new role.

Recipe 2-7. Adding Users to Active Directory

This recipe doesn't apply only to SharePoint, but is very handy in a SharePoint installation that uses Windows (rather than Forms-based) authentication. The reason is that SharePoint does not provide any means of creating new Windows user accounts, only for using accounts that already exist. There are times when you want to be able to programmatically create new accounts, and you may prefer not to require SharePoint administrators to use the standard Active Directory user utility.

The following application is built as a web service so that it can be used by a wide variety of calling programs, including ASP.NET, .NET console, and .NET Windows applications.

Recipe Type: ASP.NET Web Service

Ingredients

Assembly References

- `System.DirectoryServices`
- `System.Data`

Special Considerations

- Although .NET provides the `DirectoryServices` library and associated classes, working with Active Directory has a very different feel to working with native .NET classes. This recipe shows you some of the basics, but if you plan on doing a lot of work with AD, you will want to consult a general-purpose reference.

- One arcane aspect of Active Directory is the way connection strings are written. For example, if you are trying to connect to the Windows domain named test.domain, and open the folder NewUsers, you would create a connection string that looks like LDAP://CN=NewUsers,DC=test,DC=domain—not very intuitive!

■**Note** The account that the web service's application pool is running under will need permissions to connect to and manage AD, for the web services to run. An alternative is to connect to AD with specific credentials.

- As you'll notice in the following recipe, we set the password to never expire. This is because, unlike Windows, browsers provide no easy way to allow users to change their password. If you were to require users to change their password at first login (the AD standard), you would therefore effectively lock the user out of SharePoint.

Preparation

1. Create a new ASP.NET web service.

2. Add a reference to the System.DirectoryServices library.

3. Add a using or Imports statement for System.DirectoryServices.

4. Add a using or Imports statement for System.Data.

5. Ideally, make sure you can connect remotely or directly to a server that is acting as a domain controller for the Windows domain that you will be adding new users to. If not, you can still install the Active Directory Computers and Users utility on your development machine from www.microsoft.com/downloads/details.aspx?familyid=E487F885-F0C7-436A-A392-25793A25BAD7&displaylang=en. Running this setup will install various utilities under your Control Panel/Administrative Tools.

Process Flow

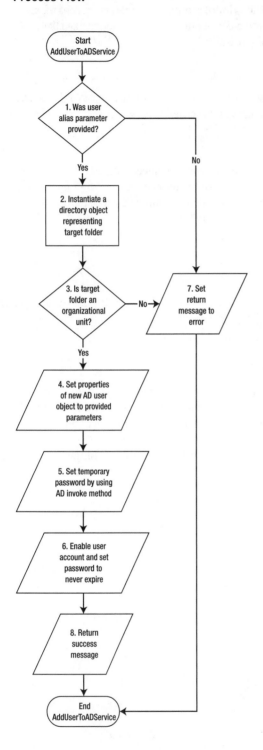

1. Because no processing is possible without a user alias, check that parameter first to make sure it's not empty. If it is empty, set an error message and return to the calling program.

2. Create a directory object pointing to the new user to be added, as well as the target AD directory.

3. If the specified target folder is not an AD *organizational unit*, return to the calling program with an error message.

4. Use the properties collection of the AD user object created in step 2 to write the values passed to this method to AD.

5. The password cannot be set by using the properties collection, so use the `invoke()` method to set that.

■**Note** The call to the `invoke()` method must be made before the password and account flags can be set.

---

6. Finally, set the password to Never Expire and enable the new account. Note that this must be done after the password has been set.

7. If an error occurs, return an error message to the calling program.

8. Otherwise, return all data from new user object, plus a success message to the calling program.

Recipe—VB (See Project AddUserToADService-VB, Class Service.vb)

```vb
Imports System.Web
Imports System.Web.Services
Imports System.Web.Services.Protocols
Imports System.DirectoryServices
Imports System.Data
<WebService(Namespace:="http://tempuri.org/")> _
<WebServiceBinding(ConformsTo:=WsiProfiles.BasicProfile1_1)> _
<Global.Microsoft.VisualBasic.CompilerServices.DesignerGenerated()> _
Public Class AddUserToADService
    Inherits System.Web.Services.WebService
    'The LDAP connection string needs to match the domain you'll
    'be adding users to.  For example, the connection string below
    'applies to a domain called 'test.domain', and will save new
    'user accounts in the 'NewUsers' organizational unit folder.
    Const LDAP_CONNECTION_STRING = "LDAP://OU=NewUsers,DC=test,DC=domain"
    'AD sets account flags by "AND'ing" together various numeric
    'values stored in HEX.  The following are the base-10
    'integer representations of the HEX values for the flags we
    'want to set.
```

```
Const AD_ENABLED = 512
Const AD_DISABLED = 514
Const AD_NEVER_EXPIRE = 65536
<WebMethod()> _
Public Function AddUserToAD(ByVal strAlias As String, _
        ByVal strName As String, _
        ByVal strCompany As String, _
        ByVal strEmail As String, _
        ByVal strPhone As String, _
        ByVal strNotes As String) As DataTable
    Dim strMsg As String = ""
    'Step 1: Verify that alias was provided
    If strAlias = "" Then
        strMsg = strMsg & "Valid user alias required"
    Else
        'Step 2: Instantiate a Directory Entry Object
        'to represent the folder to contain the new user
        Dim adUserFolder As New DirectoryEntry(LDAP_CONNECTION_STRING)
        Dim newADUser As New DirectoryEntry
        Dim existingADUser As New DirectoryEntry
        'Step 3: Check to make sure the folder is an
        '"organizational unit" object
        Try
            If adUserFolder.SchemaEntry.Name = "organizationalUnit" Then
                'Create a directory entry to represent the new user
                newADUser = adUserFolder.Children.Add( _
                    "CN=" & strAlias, "User")
                'If already a user with this alias,
                'set the fields to data for
                'this user and return message
                If DirectoryEntry.Exists(newADUser.Path) Then
                    existingADUser = adUserFolder.Children.Find( _
                        "CN=" & strAlias, "User")
                    strName = existingADUser.Properties( _
                        "displayName").Value
                    strCompany = existingADUser.Properties( _
                        "company").Value
                    strEmail = existingADUser.Properties("mail").Value
                    strPhone = existingADUser.Properties( _
                        "telephoneNumber").Value
                    strEmail = existingADUser.Properties("comment").Value
                    strMsg = "User '" & strAlias & _
                        "' already exists in Active Directory"
```

```vb
            Else
                'Step 4: Save caller-supplied properties
                newADUser.Properties("sAMAccountName").Add( _
                    strAlias & "")
                newADUser.Properties("displayName").Add(strName & "")
                newADUser.Properties("company").Add(strCompany & "")
                newADUser.Properties("mail").Add(strEmail & "")
                newADUser.Properties("telephoneNumber").Add( _
                    strPhone & "")
                newADUser.Properties("comment").Add(strNotes & "")
                newADUser.Properties("info").Value = _
                    "New SharePoint User"
                newADUser.CommitChanges()
                'Step 5: Set the password using the "Invoke" method.
                newADUser.Invoke("setPassword", "P@ssW0rd")
                'Step 6: Enable the user, set account to never expire
                newADUser.Properties("userAccountControl").Value = _
                    AD_NEVER_EXPIRE + AD_ENABLED
                newADUser.CommitChanges()
                strMsg = "User '" & strAlias & _
                    "' successfully added to Active Directory"
            End If
        End If
    Catch ex As Exception
        'Step 7: Return error message
        strMsg = "User '" & strName & _
            "' could not be added to Active Directory " & _
            "due to the following error: " & ex.Message
    End Try
End If
'Step 8: Construct a dataset to return values
Dim dtReturn As New Data.DataTable("result")
dtReturn.Columns.Add("Alias")
dtReturn.Columns.Add("Name")
dtReturn.Columns.Add("Company")
dtReturn.Columns.Add("Phone")
dtReturn.Columns.Add("Email")
dtReturn.Columns.Add("Notes")
dtReturn.Columns.Add("Message")
'Add a single row to the data table to contain
'information describing the results of the method call
Dim drReturn As Data.DataRow = dtReturn.NewRow
drReturn("Alias") = strAlias
drReturn("Name") = strName
```

```
            drReturn("Company") = strCompany
            drReturn("Phone") = strPhone
            drReturn("Email") = strEmail
            drReturn("Notes") = strNotes
            drReturn("Message") = strMsg
            dtReturn.Rows.Add(drReturn)
            dtReturn.AcceptChanges()
            Return dtReturn.Copy
        End Function
End Class
```

Recipe—C# (See Project AddUserToADService-CS, Class Service.cs)

```csharp
using System;
using System.Web;
using System.Web.Services;
using System.Web.Services.Protocols;
using System.DirectoryServices;
using System.Data;
[WebService(Namespace = "http://tempuri.org/")]
[WebServiceBinding(ConformsTo = WsiProfiles.BasicProfile1_1)]
public class AddUserToADService : System.Web.Services.WebService
{

    //The LDAP connection string needs to match the domain you'll
    //be adding users to. For example, the connection string  below
    //applies to a domain called 'test.domain', and will save new
    //user accounts in the 'NewUsers' organizational unit folder.
    const string LDAP_CONNECTION_STRING =
        "LDAP://OU=NewUsers,DC=test,DC=domain";

    //AD sets account flags by "AND'ing" together various numeric
    //values stored in HEX. The following are the base-10
    //integer representations of the HEX values for the flags we
    //want to set.
    const int AD_ENABLED = 512;
    const int AD_DISABLED = 514;
    const int AD_NEVER_EXPIRE = 65536;

    [WebMethod()]
    public DataTable AddUserToAD(string strAlias,
        string strName, string strCompany,
        string strEmail, string strPhone, string strNotes)
    {

        string strMsg = "";
```

```
//Step 1: Verify that alias was provided
if (strAlias == "") {

    strMsg = strMsg + "Valid user alias required";
}

else {

    //Step 2: Instantiate a Directory Entry Object to
    // represent the folder to contain the new user
    DirectoryEntry adUserFolder =
        new DirectoryEntry(LDAP_CONNECTION_STRING);
    DirectoryEntry newADUser = new DirectoryEntry();
    DirectoryEntry existingADUser = new DirectoryEntry();

    //Step 3: Check to make sure the folder is an
    //"organizational unit" object
    try {
        if (adUserFolder.SchemaEntry.Name == "organizationalUnit") {

            //Create a directory entry to represent the new user
            newADUser = adUserFolder.Children.Add("CN=" +
                strAlias, "User");

            //If already a user with this alias, set the
            //fields to data for
            //this user and return message
            if (DirectoryEntry.Exists(newADUser.Path)) {

                existingADUser = adUserFolder.Children.Find("CN=" +
                    strAlias, "User");

                strName =
                    (string)existingADUser.Properties["displayName"].Value;
                strCompany =
                    (string)existingADUser.Properties["company"].Value;
                strEmail =
                    (string)existingADUser.Properties["mail"].Value;
                strPhone =
(string)existingADUser.Properties["telephoneNumber"].Value;
                strNotes =
                    (string)existingADUser.Properties["comment"].Value;

                strMsg = "User '" + strAlias +
                    "' already exists in Active Directory";
            }
```

```
            else {

                //Step 4: Save caller-supplied properties
                newADUser.Properties["sAMAccountName"].Add(
                    strAlias + "");
                newADUser.Properties["displayName"].Add(
                    strName + "");
                newADUser.Properties["company"].Add(strCompany + "");
                newADUser.Properties["mail"].Add(strEmail + "");
                newADUser.Properties["telephoneNumber"].Add(
                    strPhone + "");
                newADUser.Properties["comment"].Add(strNotes + "");
                newADUser.Properties["info"].Value =
                    "New SharePoint User";
                newADUser.CommitChanges();

                //Step 5: Set the password using the "Invoke" method.
                newADUser.Invoke("setPassword", "P@ssW0rd");

                //Step 6: Enable the user, set account to
                //never expire
                newADUser.Properties["userAccountControl"].Value =
                    AD_NEVER_EXPIRE + AD_ENABLED;
                newADUser.CommitChanges();

                strMsg = "User '" + strAlias +
                    "' successfully added to Active Directory";

            }

        }
    }

    catch (Exception ex) {

        //Step 7: Return error message
        strMsg = "User '" + strName +
          "' could not be added to Active Directory " +
          "due to the following error: " + ex.Message;

    }

}
```

```
            //Step 8: Construct a dataset to return values
            DataTable dtReturn = new DataTable("result");
            dtReturn.Columns.Add("Alias");
            dtReturn.Columns.Add("Name");
            dtReturn.Columns.Add("Company");
            dtReturn.Columns.Add("Phone");
            dtReturn.Columns.Add("Email");
            dtReturn.Columns.Add("Notes");
            dtReturn.Columns.Add("Message");

            //Add a single row to the data table to contain
            //information describing the results of the method call
            DataRow drReturn = dtReturn.NewRow();
            drReturn["Alias"] = strAlias;
            drReturn["Name"] = strName;
            drReturn["Company"] = strCompany;
            drReturn["Phone"] = strPhone;
            drReturn["Email"] = strEmail;
            drReturn["Notes"] = strNotes;
            drReturn["Message"] = strMsg;
            dtReturn.Rows.Add(drReturn);
            dtReturn.AcceptChanges();

            return dtReturn.Copy();

    }
}
```

To Run

You can test the web service from within Visual Studio or by creating a test harness application that includes a reference to the web service. Because testing from within Visual Studio is the easiest, I'll show that process here.

When the web service project has been created, and the source code added as shown in the previous sections, press F5 to run the web service. Visual Studio automatically creates the necessary plumbing to enable you to execute the methods exposed by the service, in this case the AddUserToAD() method. Figure 2-11 shows the Visual Studio–generated web page for that method.

Fill in the strAlias field and any other fields desired, and then click the Invoke button, which will call the web service, passing the provided data as parameters.

Assuming no errors occurred, the web service method will return a .NET data table in XML form, similar to that in Figure 2-12, showing all data used in the creation of the new account, along with a message indicating success.

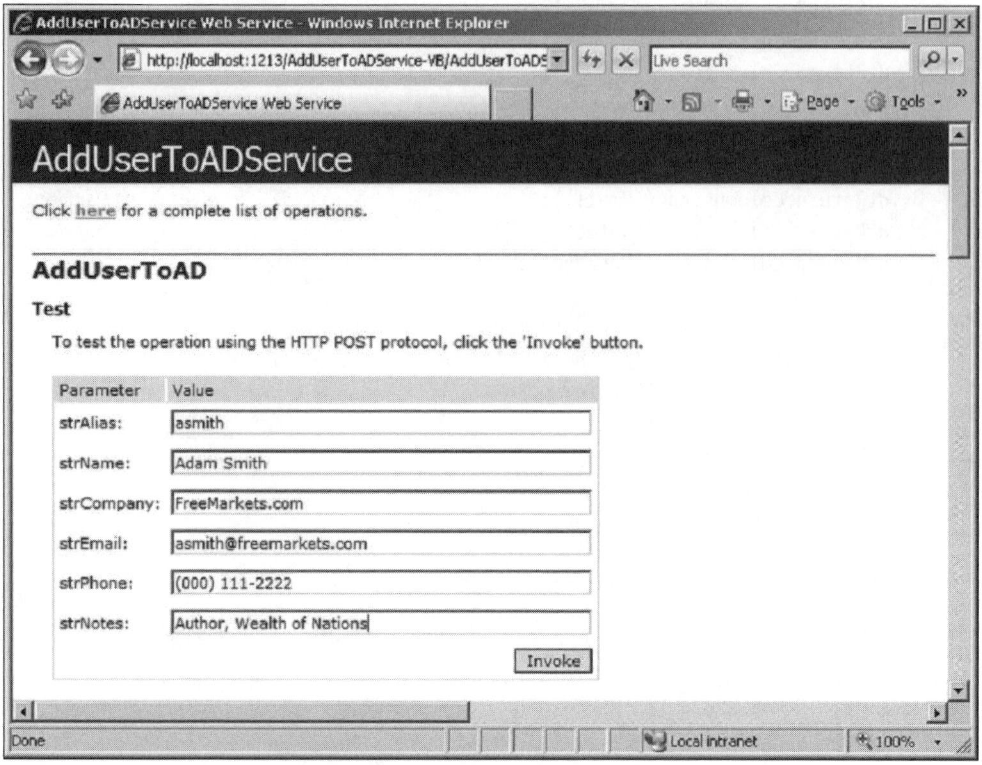

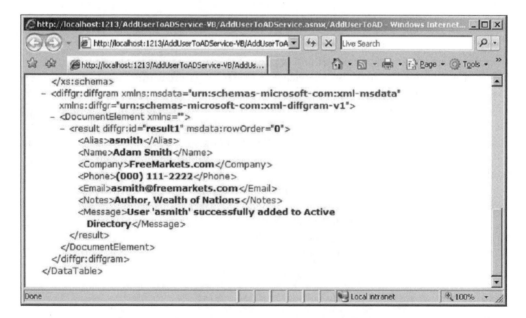

Figure 2-11. *Running the AddUserToADService from within Visual Studio*

Figure 2-12. *XML message returned by AddUserToADService web service*

You can verify that the new user was successfully added to Active Directory by opening the Active Directory Users and Computers utility (Dsa.msc). Open the NewUsers folder, and double-click on the account name just added. Figure 2-13 shows the General tab of the Active Directory properties dialog box for the user added in my example.

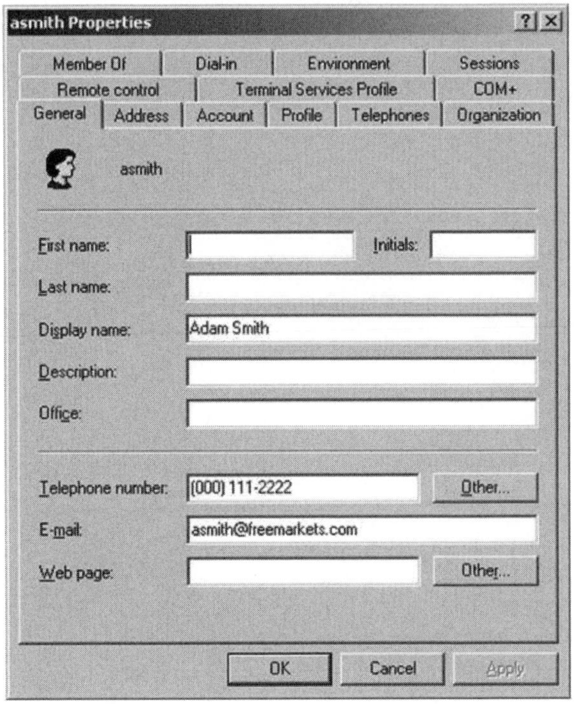

Figure 2-13. *Viewing the new AD account by using the Active Directory utility*

Variations

- The preceding recipe provides the basics required to add a new user account to Active Directory. However, you will probably want to add a routine to generate a random password for new users.

- Another useful method would allow users or administrators to change or reset passwords. This can be built around the Invoke("SetPassword") method used here to create the initial password.

- You could also provide the ability to disable an account by using the UserAccountControl property used here to set the password to never expire.

CHAPTER 3

■■■

Working with Lists

Ultimately, most content that your users will be interested in will be stored in lists—whether documents, events, tasks, contacts, or custom content you create.

The recipes in this chapter all relate to lists, and with the exception of document-specific programming tasks any of these recipes can be applied to lists of any type.

Recipes include those for creating a new list programmatically, both with the object model and web services. You'll also find recipes for uploading and removing documents from a document library—which of course apply to only that type of list. Finally, there's a recipe for modifying properties of a document library.

■**Note** One of the really exciting enhancements relating to lists in SharePoint 2007 centers around event handlers. You'll find recipes for those in Chapter 5.

Recipe 3-1. Creating a List by Using the Object Model

Lists are at the heart of what SharePoint is all about. List types include document libraries, task lists, event lists, custom lists, and many more. The ability to create lists programmatically gives you great flexibility in how you can provision and extend web sites. For example, you might want to provide your end users with a custom page that enables them to build lists based on complex business rules that would be difficult to encapsulate in a list template. Or you might decide that the built-in list definition pages provide too much information and would confuse some of your users.

In this recipe, you'll create a simple web page that enables the user to create a new list for a given web site, add a few custom fields if desired, and make sure any new fields appear on the default view.

Recipe Type: ASP.NET Web Application

Ingredients

Assembly References

- Windows SharePoint Services

Class Library References

- Microsoft.SharePoint

Classes Used

- SPSite class

- SPWeb class

- SPListCollection class

- SPList class

- SPView class

- SPField class

- SPListTemplate class

Special Considerations

- The network security credentials under which this web page runs will determine the permissions that the application has. You should therefore make sure that whatever security context it runs under has permissions to create new lists on the target web site, or that if a security violation does occur, you handle it appropriately.

Preparation

1. Create a new ASP.NET web application project.

2. Add a reference to the Windows SharePoint Services .NET assembly.

3. In the code-behind for the default web page (or whatever web page you decide to use for this application), add using or Imports statements for the Microsoft.SharePoint and System.Collections class libraries (the latter is to make ArrayLists available).

4. Add controls as shown in the following "To Run" section. The control names are as follows:

txtSiteUrl	txtUDFName1	ddlUDFType1
txtWebName	txtUDFName2	ddlUDFType2
txtListName	txtUDFName3	ddlUDFType3
ddlListType		

Process Flow

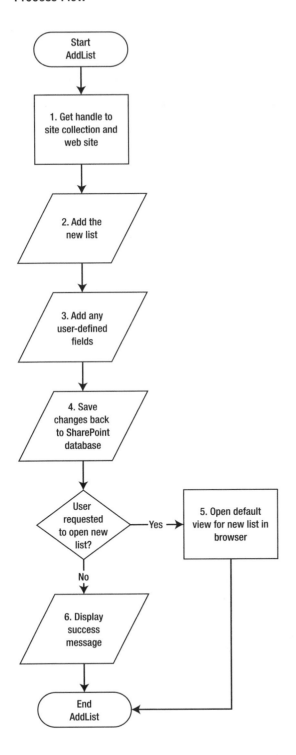

1. Create instances of the SPSite and SPWeb classes pointing at the site collection and web site that will contain the new list.

2. Add the new list. If an error occurs, display an error message and return to the web page.

3. If any custom column fields are not blank, add those fields to the list and to the list's default view. If an error occurs, display an error message and return to the web page.

4. Call the Update() methods on the list and web objects to update the SharePoint database.

5. If the user selected the checkbox to automatically open the new list, redirect the user to the default view page for that new list.

6. Otherwise, display an alert indicating success and return to the web page.

Recipe—VB (See Project CreateListOM-VB, Form Default.aspx.vb)

```vb
Imports System
Imports System.Data
Imports System.Configuration
Imports System.Web
Imports System.Web.Security
Imports System.Web.UI
Imports System.Web.UI.WebControls
Imports System.Web.UI.WebControls.WebParts
Imports System.Web.UI.HtmlControls
Imports Microsoft.SharePoint
Imports System.Collections
Partial Public Class _Default
    Inherits System.Web.UI.Page
    Protected Sub Page_Load(ByVal sender As Object, _
        ByVal e As EventArgs) Handles Me.Load
        If Not IsPostBack Then
            ' Get column types
            InitializeTypeDDL(ddlUDFType1)
            InitializeTypeDDL(ddlUDFType2)
            InitializeTypeDDL(ddlUDFType3)
        End If
    End Sub
    Protected Sub cmdCreateList_Click(ByVal sender As Object, _
        ByVal e As EventArgs) Handles cmdCreateList.Click
        Try
            lblErrorMsg.Visible = False
            ' Step 1: Get a handle to the site collection and web site
            Dim site As New SPSite(txtSiteUrl.Text)
            Dim web As SPWeb = site.AllWebs(txtWebName.Text)
            Dim listCollection As SPListCollection = web.Lists
            web.AllowUnsafeUpdates = True
```

```vbnet
        ' Step 2: Create the new list
        listCollection.Add(txtListName.Text, "", _
           web.ListTemplates(ddlListType.SelectedItem.Text))
        Dim newList As SPList = listCollection(txtListName.Text)
        ' Step 3: Add any user-defined fields
        If txtUDFName1.Text <> "" Then
            AddField(newList, txtUDFName1, ddlUDFType1)
        End If
        If txtUDFName2.Text <> "" Then
            AddField(newList, txtUDFName2, ddlUDFType2)
        End If
        If txtUDFName3.Text <> "" Then
            AddField(newList, txtUDFName3, ddlUDFType3)
        End If
        ' Step 4: Save the changes
        newList.Update()
        web.Update()
        ' Step 5: If requested, open new list
        If cbOpenList.Checked Then
            ' The following assumes the list title matches the
            ' list name; if this is not the case, use
            ' web.Url + newList.DefaultViewUrl() to
            ' obtain a path to the list's default view
            Response.Redirect(web.Url.ToString() + _
               "/lists/" + newList.Title.ToString())
        Else
            ' Step 6: Display success message
            Me.RegisterClientScriptBlock("Success", _
               "<script>alert ('List successfully added');</script>")
        End If
        web.Dispose()
        site.Dispose()
    Catch ex As Exception
        lblErrorMsg.Text = ex.Message
        lblErrorMsg.Visible = True
    End Try
End Sub
' Add the UDF to list and default view
Private Sub AddField(ByVal newList As SPList, ByVal tb As TextBox, _
   ByVal ddl As DropDownList)
    Dim defaultView As SPView = newList.DefaultView
    newList.Fields.Add(tb.Text, GetFieldType(ddl), False)
    Dim newField As SPField = newList.Fields(tb.Text)
    defaultView.ViewFields.Add(newField)
    defaultView.Update()
End Sub
```

```vb
' Return SP field type from ddl value for UDF type
Private Function GetFieldType(ByVal ddlUDFType As DropDownList) _
    As SPFieldType
    Select Case ddlUDFType.SelectedItem.Value
        Case ("Number")
            Return SPFieldType.Number
        Case ("Text")
            Return SPFieldType.Text
        Case ("Date")
            Return SPFieldType.DateTime
        Case Else
            Return SPFieldType.Text
    End Select
End Function
' Get a sorted list of all templates available
Protected Sub cmdLookupListTemplates_Click(ByVal sender As Object, _
    ByVal e As EventArgs) Handles cmdLookupListTemplates.Click
    Try
        lblErrorMsg.Visible = False
        Dim site As New SPSite(txtSiteUrl.Text)
        Dim web As SPWeb = site.AllWebs(txtWebName.Text)
        ' Get sorted list of available list templates
        Dim arrListItems As New ArrayList()
        For Each listTemplate As SPListTemplate In web.ListTemplates
            If Not listTemplate.Hidden Then
                arrListItems.Add(listTemplate.Name)
            End If
        Next
        arrListItems.Sort()
        ' Add them to the drop-down list
        ddlListType.Items.Clear()
        For Each templateName As String In arrListItems
            ddlListType.Items.Add(templateName)
        Next
        ddlListType.SelectedIndex = 0
        ' Show the rest of the form          Panel1.Visible = True
        web.Dispose()
        site.Dispose()
    Catch ex As Exception
        lblErrorMsg.Text = ex.Message
        lblErrorMsg.Visible = True
    End Try
End Sub
' Set standard type values for UDF type ddl's
```

```vbnet
    Private Sub InitializeTypeDDL(ByRef ddl As DropDownList)
        ddl.Items.Clear()
        ddl.Items.Add("Date")
        ddl.Items.Add("Number")
        ddl.Items.Add("Text")
        ddl.SelectedIndex = 2
    End Sub
End Class
```

Recipe—C# (See Project CreateListOM-CS, Form Default.aspx.cs)

```csharp
using System;
using System.Data;
using System.Configuration;
using System.Web;
using System.Web.Security;
using System.Web.UI;
using System.Web.UI.WebControls;
using System.Web.UI.WebControls.WebParts;
using System.Web.UI.HtmlControls;
using Microsoft.SharePoint;
using System.Collections;
public partial class _Default : System.Web.UI.Page
{
    protected void Page_Load(object sender, EventArgs e)
    {
        if (!IsPostBack)
        {
            // Get column types
            InitializeTypeDDL(ref ddlUDFType1);
            InitializeTypeDDL(ref ddlUDFType2);
            InitializeTypeDDL(ref ddlUDFType3);
        }
    }
    protected void cmdCreateList_Click(object sender, EventArgs e)
    {
        try
        {
            lblErrorMsg.Visible = false;
            // Step 1: Get a handle to the site collection and web site
            SPSite site = new SPSite(txtSiteUrl.Text);
            SPWeb web = site.AllWebs[txtWebName.Text];
            SPListCollection listCollection = web.Lists;
            web.AllowUnsafeUpdates = true;
```

```
            // Step 2: Create the new list
            listCollection.Add(txtListName.Text, "",
                web.ListTemplates[ddlListType.SelectedItem.Text]);
            SPList newList = listCollection[txtListName.Text];
            // Step 3: Add any user-defined fields
            if (txtUDFName1.Text != "")
                AddField(newList, txtUDFName1, ddlUDFType1);
            if (txtUDFName2.Text != "")
                AddField(newList, txtUDFName2, ddlUDFType2);
            if (txtUDFName3.Text != "")
                AddField(newList, txtUDFName3, ddlUDFType3);
            // Step 4: Save the changes
            newList.Update();
            web.Update();
            // Step 5: If requested, open new list
            if (cbOpenList.Checked)
            {
                // The following assumes the list title matches the
                // list name; if this is not the case, use
                // web.Url + newList.DefaultViewUrl() to
                // obtain a path to the list's default view
                Response.Redirect(web.Url.ToString() +
                    "/lists/" + newList.Title.ToString());
            }
            else
            {
                // Step 6: Display success message
                this.RegisterClientScriptBlock("Success",
                    "<script>alert ('List successfully added');</script>");
            }
            web.Dispose();
            site.Dispose();
        }
        catch (Exception ex)
        {
            lblErrorMsg.Text = ex.Message;
            lblErrorMsg.Visible = true;
        }
    }
    // Add the UDF to list and default view
```

```
private void AddField(SPList newList, TextBox tb, DropDownList ddl)
{
    SPView defaultView = newList.DefaultView;
    newList.Fields.Add(tb.Text, GetFieldType(ddl), false);
    SPField newField = newList.Fields[tb.Text];
    defaultView.ViewFields.Add(newField);
    defaultView.Update();
}
// Return SP field type from ddl value for UDF type
private SPFieldType GetFieldType(DropDownList ddlUDFType)
{
    switch (ddlUDFType.SelectedItem.Value)
    {
        case ("Number"):
            return SPFieldType.Number;
        case ("Text"):
            return SPFieldType.Text;
        case ("Date"):
            return SPFieldType.DateTime;
        default:
            return SPFieldType.Text;
    }
}
// Get a sorted list of all templates available
protected void cmdLookupListTemplates_Click(object sender, EventArgs e)
{
    try
    {
        lblErrorMsg.Visible = false;
        SPSite site = new SPSite(txtSiteUrl.Text);
        SPWeb web = site.AllWebs[txtWebName.Text];
        // Get sorted list of available list templates
        ArrayList arrListItems = new ArrayList();
        foreach (SPListTemplate listTemplate in web.ListTemplates)
        {
            if (!listTemplate.Hidden)
            {
                arrListItems.Add(listTemplate.Name);
            }
        }
```

```
            arrListItems.Sort();
            // Add them to the drop-down list
            ddlListType.Items.Clear();
            ListItem li;
            foreach (string templateName in arrListItems)
            {
                ddlListType.Items.Add(templateName);
            }
            ddlListType.SelectedIndex = 0;
            // Show the rest of the form
            Panel1.Visible = true;
            web.Dispose();
            site.Dispose();
        }
        catch (Exception ex)
        {
            lblErrorMsg.Text = ex.Message;
            lblErrorMsg.Visible = true;
        }
    }
    // Set standard type values for UDF type ddl's
    private void InitializeTypeDDL(ref DropDownList ddl)
    {
        ddl.Items.Clear();
        ddl.Items.Add("Date");
        ddl.Items.Add("Number");
        ddl.Items.Add("Text");
        ddl.SelectedIndex = 2;
    }
}
```

To Run

When the page is first displayed, only the first section (section I) will be displayed. This is because the list types must be read from the target web site before the list can be added. After you have filled in a site collection URL and web site name, click the Lookup List Templates button to populate the drop-down list of list templates and display the rest of the form, as shown in Figure 3-1.

Provide a new, unique list name, as well as up to three custom columns to add in addition to those that are part of the base list template when creating the new list.

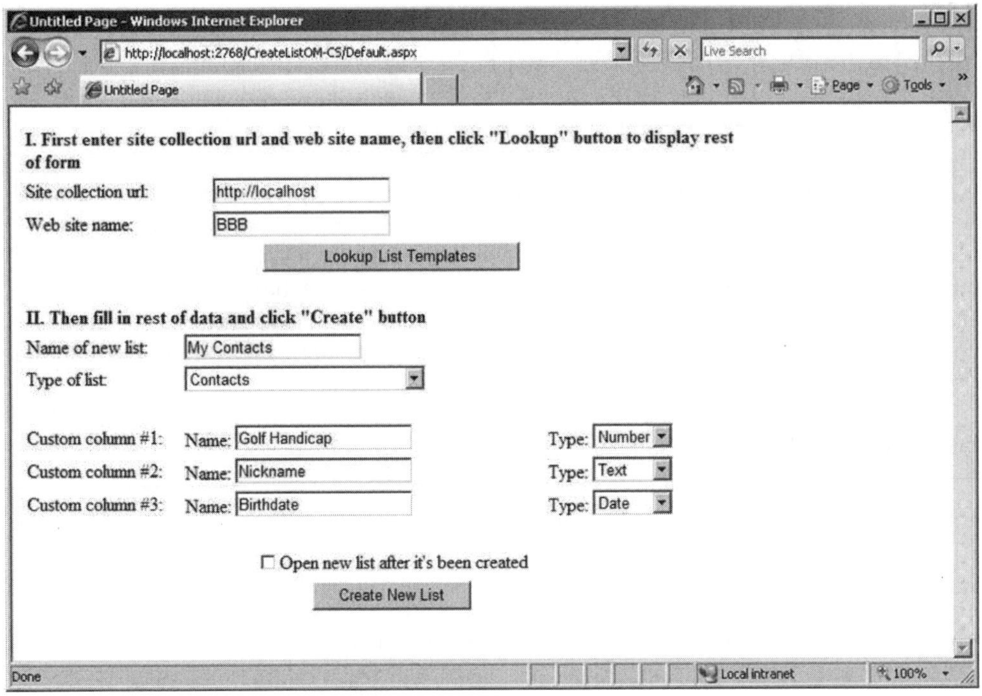

Figure 3-1. *Create list web form*

Clicking the Create New List button will use all the provided information to create the new list. If you selected the Open New List After It's Been Created checkbox, the browser will be redirected to the default view page of the new list. Otherwise, a success alert will be displayed and the page refreshed.

Variations

- This recipe provides a simple example of a whole class of applications that could be used to address one of two requirements: either 1) you want to limit end users' options when creating new lists or 2) end users need guidance when creating new lists to ensure that those lists are appropriate to the specific business purpose.

Related Recipes

- Recipe 3-2

Recipe 3-2. Creating a List by Using Web Services

This recipe shows how you can create a new list by using the built-in SharePoint web services. Using this approach, you can create a truly distributed application by placing the front-end web site, console, or Windows application anywhere in the world that can access one of the SharePoint front-end web servers.

Although many operations using the web services are as simple as or simpler than using the object model, this recipe shows one aspect of the web services that is more complex—namely the use of Collaborative Application Markup Language (CAML) to pass complex parameters to the web service methods. CAML has the advantage that complex information, such as a list of fields to add to a list, can be packaged as XML documents and sent to the service.

As you'll see next, to accomplish all we need to get done, we'll call on three separate web services: `Lists`, `Views`, and `Webs`.

Recipe Type: ASP.NET Web Application

Ingredients

Web Service References

- `http://[server name]/_vti_bin/Lists.asmx` web service

- `http://[server name]/_vti_bin/Views.asmx` web service

- `http://[server name]/_vti_bin/Webs.asmx` web service

Class Library References

- `System.Collections` library—to support the use of `ArrayLists`

- `System.Xml` library—to provide XML structures needed to call web service methods

Special Considerations

- Each instance of the `Lists`, `Views`, or `Webs` web service must be assigned a network credential with permissions to access and update the target site collection and web site.

Preparation

1. Create a new ASP.NET web application.

2. Add a reference to the `http://[server name]/_vti_bin/Lists.asmx` web service (you may use `localhost` instead of `[server name]` if you wish).

3. Add a reference to the `http://[server name]/_vti_bin/Views.asmx` web service (you may use `localhost` instead of `[server name]` if you wish).

4. Add a reference to the `http://[server name]/_vti_bin/Webs.asmx` web service (you may use `localhost` instead of `[server name]` if you wish).

5. Add a `using` or `Includes` statement at the top of the `Default.aspx` code-behind file to reference `System.Collections` and `System.Xml`.

Process Flow

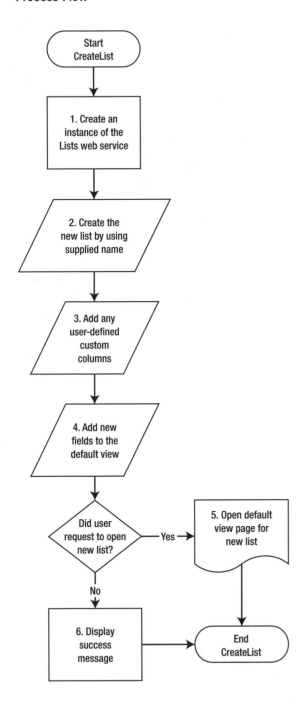

1. Create an instance of the `Lists.asmx` web service and assign its URL property to the target site collection and web site. Also set the `Credentials` property to either the default credentials or another credential that has permissions to create a new list in the target site.

2. Create the new list by using the selected template ID.

3. If the user has entered one or more custom columns, add those to the list by using the `UpdateList()` method.

4. Get the default view for the list by using the `Views` web service; add any new fields to the `ViewFields` property of the default view.

5. If the user selected the checkbox indicating that the new list should be displayed, redirect the user's browser to the default view page for the new list.

6. Otherwise, display a success message and refresh the page.

Recipe—VB (See Project CreateListService-VB, Form Default.aspx.vb)

```vb
Imports System
Imports System.Data
Imports System.Configuration
Imports System.Web
Imports System.Web.Security
Imports System.Web.UI
Imports System.Web.UI.WebControls
Imports System.Web.UI.WebControls.WebParts
Imports System.Web.UI.HtmlControls
Imports System.Xml
Imports System.Collections
Partial Public Class _Default
    Inherits System.Web.UI.Page
    Protected Sub Page_Load(ByVal sender As Object, _
        ByVal e As EventArgs) Handles Me.Load
        If Not IsPostBack Then
            ' Get column types
            InitializeTypeDDL(ddlUDFType1)
            InitializeTypeDDL(ddlUDFType2)
            InitializeTypeDDL(ddlUDFType3)
        End If
    End Sub
    ' Get a sorted list of available list templates
    Protected Sub cmdLookupListTemplates_Click(ByVal sender As Object, _
ByVal e As EventArgs) Handles cmdLookupListTemplates.Click
        Dim objWebs As New WebsService.Webs()
        objWebs.Url = txtSiteUrl.Text + "/" + txtWebName.Text + _
            "/_vti_bin/Webs.asmx"
        objWebs.Credentials = System.Net.CredentialCache.DefaultCredentials
```

```vb
    Dim xnListTemplates As XmlNode
    xnListTemplates = objWebs.GetListTemplates()
    ' Get sorted list of available list templates
    Dim arrListItems As New ArrayList()
    For Each xnListTemplate As XmlNode In xnListTemplates.ChildNodes
        Try
            If xnListTemplate.Attributes("Hidden").Value.ToString() _
                <> "TRUE" Then
                arrListItems.Add(xnListTemplate.Attributes("DisplayName").Value
                    + ":" + xnListTemplate.Attributes("Type").Value)
            End If
        Catch
            arrListItems.Add(xnListTemplate.Attributes("DisplayName").Value + _
              ":" + xnListTemplate.Attributes("Type").Value)
        End Try
    Next
    arrListItems.Sort()
    ' Add them to the drop-down list
    ddlListType.Items.Clear()
    Dim li As ListItem
    For Each templateData As String In arrListItems
        li = New ListItem(templateData.Split(":"c)(0), _
            templateData.Split(":"c)(1))
        ddlListType.Items.Add(li)
    Next
    ddlListType.SelectedIndex = 0
    ' Show the rest of the form
    Panel1.Visible = True
End Sub
' Add the new list
Protected Sub cmdCreateList_Click(ByVal sender As Object, _
    ByVal e As EventArgs) Handles cmdCreateList.Click
    Try
        lblErrorMsg.Visible = False
        ' Step 1: Create an instance of a list service
        Dim objLists As New ListsService.Lists()
        objLists.Url = txtSiteUrl.Text + "/" + txtWebName.Text + _
            "/_vti_bin/Lists.asmx"
        objLists.Credentials = _
          System.Net.CredentialCache.DefaultCredentials
        ' Step 2: Create the new list
        Dim listTemplateType As Integer = _
            Integer.Parse(ddlListType.SelectedValue)
        objLists.AddList(txtListName.Text, "", listTemplateType)
        ' Step 3: Add any user-defined fields - this requires
        ' a bit of CAML
        Dim xmlDoc As New XmlDocument()
```

```vb
Dim xnNewFields As XmlNode = _
    xmlDoc.CreateNode(XmlNodeType.Element, "Fields", "")
If txtUDFName1.Text <> "" Then
    xnNewFields.InnerXml += _
        "<Method ID='1'>" + _
        "<Field Type='" + ddlUDFType1.SelectedValue + _
        "' DisplayName='" + txtUDFName1.Text + "'/>" + _
        "</Method>"
End If
If txtUDFName2.Text <> "" Then
    xnNewFields.InnerXml += _
        "<Method ID='2'>" + _
        "<Field Type='" + ddlUDFType2.SelectedValue + _
        "' DisplayName='" + txtUDFName2.Text + "'/>" + _
        "</Method>"
End If
If txtUDFName3.Text <> "" Then
    xnNewFields.InnerXml += _
        "<Method ID='3'>" + _
        "<Field Type='" + ddlUDFType3.SelectedValue + _
        "' DisplayName='" + txtUDFName3.Text + "'/>" + _
        "</Method>"
End If
' We can pass "null" values for any parameters we don't
' need to change, so we're passing data for only the new fields
' we want to add
objLists.UpdateList(txtListName.Text, Nothing, xnNewFields, _
    Nothing, Nothing, Nothing)
' Step 4: Add any new fields to the default view
Dim objViews As New ViewsService.Views()
objViews.Url = txtSiteUrl.Text + "/" + txtWebName.Text + _
    "/_vti_bin/Views.asmx"
objViews.Credentials = _
    System.Net.CredentialCache.DefaultCredentials
' Get a handle to the view
Dim xnDefaultView As XmlNode = _
    objViews.GetView(txtListName.Text, "")
' Get the GUID of the view, which we'll need when we call the
' UpdateView() method below
Dim viewName As String = xnDefaultView.Attributes("Name").Value
' Get any existing fields in the view, so we can add the new
' fields to that list. To do this, we need to find the
' "ViewFields" node (if one exists), and grab its XML to use as
' a starting point.
Dim xnViewFields As XmlNode = _
    xmlDoc.CreateNode(XmlNodeType.Element, "ViewFields", "")
For Each childNode As XmlNode In xnDefaultView.ChildNodes
```

```vb
                If childNode.Name = "ViewFields" Then
                    xnViewFields.InnerXml += childNode.InnerXml
                End If
            Next
            ' Now add the new fields to end of the list of preexisting
            ' view fields.
            If txtUDFName1.Text <> "" Then
                xnViewFields.InnerXml += "<FieldRef Name='" + _
                    txtUDFName1.Text + "'/>"
            End If
            If txtUDFName2.Text <> "" Then
                xnViewFields.InnerXml += "<FieldRef Name='" + _
                    txtUDFName2.Text + "'/>"
            End If
            If txtUDFName3.Text <> "" Then
                xnViewFields.InnerXml += "<FieldRef Name='" + _
                    txtUDFName3.Text + "'/>"
            End If
            ' Update the view. As with the ListUpdate() method, we need to
            ' pass parameters only for data we want to change. We can pass
            ' "null" values for all the rest.
            objViews.UpdateView(txtListName.Text, viewName, Nothing, _
                Nothing, xnViewFields, Nothing, _
                Nothing, Nothing)
            ' Step 5: If requested, open new list
            If cbOpenList.Checked Then
                Response.Redirect(txtSiteUrl.Text.ToString() + "/" + _
                    txtWebName.Text.ToString() + "/lists/" + _
                    txtListName.Text.ToString())
            Else
                ' Step 6: Display success message
                Me.RegisterClientScriptBlock("Success", _
                    "<script>alert ('List successfully added');</script>")
            End If
        Catch ex As Exception
            lblErrorMsg.Text = ex.Message
            lblErrorMsg.Visible = True
        End Try
    End Sub
    ' Set standard type values for UDF type ddl's
    Private Sub InitializeTypeDDL(ByRef ddl As DropDownList)
        ddl.Items.Clear()
        ddl.Items.Add("DateTime")
        ddl.Items.Add("Number")
        ddl.Items.Add("Text")
        ddl.SelectedIndex = 2
    End Sub
End Class
```

Recipe—C# (See Project CreateListOM-CS, Form Default.aspx.cs)

```csharp
using System;
using System.Data;
using System.Configuration;
using System.Web;
using System.Web.Security;
using System.Web.UI;
using System.Web.UI.WebControls;
using System.Web.UI.WebControls.WebParts;
using System.Web.UI.HtmlControls;
using System.Xml;
using System.Collections;
public partial class _Default : System.Web.UI.Page
{
    protected void Page_Load(object sender, EventArgs e)
    {
        if (!IsPostBack)
        {
            // Get column types
            InitializeTypeDDL(ref ddlUDFType1);
            InitializeTypeDDL(ref ddlUDFType2);
            InitializeTypeDDL(ref ddlUDFType3);
        }
    }
    // Get a sorted list of available list templates
    protected void cmdLookupListTemplates_Click(object sender, EventArgs e)
    {
        WebsService.Webs objWebs = new WebsService.Webs();
        objWebs.Url = txtSiteUrl.Text + "/" + txtWebName.Text +
            "/_vti_bin/Webs.asmx";
        objWebs.Credentials = System.Net.CredentialCache.DefaultCredentials;
        XmlNode xnListTemplates;
        xnListTemplates = objWebs.GetListTemplates();
        // Get sorted list of available list templates
        ArrayList arrListItems = new ArrayList();
        foreach (XmlNode xnListTemplate in xnListTemplates.ChildNodes)
        {
            try
            {
                if (xnListTemplate.Attributes["Hidden"].Value.ToString()
                    != "TRUE")
                {
                    arrListItems.Add(xnListTemplate.Attributes["DisplayName"].Value
                        + ":" + xnListTemplate.Attributes["Type"].Value);
                }
            }
```

```
        catch
        {
            arrListItems.Add(xnListTemplate.Attributes["DisplayName"].Value +
                ":" + xnListTemplate.Attributes["Type"].Value);
        }
    }
    arrListItems.Sort();
    // Add them to the drop-down list
    ddlListType.Items.Clear();
    ListItem li;
    foreach (string templateData in arrListItems)
    {
        li = new ListItem(templateData.Split(':')[0],
            templateData.Split(':')[1]);
        ddlListType.Items.Add(li);
    }
    ddlListType.SelectedIndex = 0;
    // Show the rest of the form
    Panel1.Visible = true;
}
// Add the new list
protected void cmdCreateList_Click(object sender, EventArgs e)
{
    try
    {
        lblErrorMsg.Visible = false;
        // Step 1: Create an instance of a list service
        ListsService.Lists objLists = new ListsService.Lists();
        objLists.Url = txtSiteUrl.Text + "/" +
            txtWebName.Text + "/_vti_bin/Lists.asmx";
        objLists.Credentials =
            System.Net.CredentialCache.DefaultCredentials;
        // Step 2: Create the new list
        int listTemplateType = int.Parse(ddlListType.SelectedValue);
        objLists.AddList(txtListName.Text, "", listTemplateType);
        // Step 3: Add any user-defined fields - this requires
        //   a bit of CAML
        XmlDocument xmlDoc = new XmlDocument();
        XmlNode xnNewFields =
            xmlDoc.CreateNode(XmlNodeType.Element,"Fields","");
        if (txtUDFName1.Text != "")
        {
            xnNewFields.InnerXml +=
                "<Method ID='1'>" +
                "<Field Type='" + ddlUDFType1.SelectedValue +
                "' DisplayName='" + txtUDFName1.Text + "'/>" +
                "</Method>";
        }
```

```csharp
    if (txtUDFName2.Text != "")
    {
        xnNewFields.InnerXml +=
            "<Method ID='2'>" +
            "<Field Type='" + ddlUDFType2.SelectedValue +
            "' DisplayName='" + txtUDFName2.Text + "'/>" +
            "</Method>";
    }
    if (txtUDFName3.Text != "")
    {
        xnNewFields.InnerXml +=
            "<Method ID='3'>" +
            "<Field Type='" + ddlUDFType3.SelectedValue +
            "' DisplayName='" + txtUDFName3.Text + "'/>" +
            "</Method>";
    }
    // We can pass "null" values for any parameters we don't need to
    // change,so we're passing data for only the new fields we want
    // to add
    objLists.UpdateList(txtListName.Text,null,xnNewFields,
        null,null,null);
    // Step 4: Add any new fields to the default view
    ViewsService.Views objViews = new ViewsService.Views();
    objViews.Url = txtSiteUrl.Text + "/" +
        txtWebName.Text + "/_vti_bin/Views.asmx";
    objViews.Credentials =
        System.Net.CredentialCache.DefaultCredentials;
    // Get a handle to the view
    XmlNode xnDefaultView = objViews.GetView(txtListName.Text, "");
    // Get the GUID of the view, which we'll need when we call the
    // UpdateView() method below
    string viewName = xnDefaultView.Attributes["Name"].Value;
    // Get any existing fields in the view, so we can add the new
    // fields to that list.  To do this, we need to find the
    // "ViewFields"node (if one exists), and grab its XML to use as
    // a starting point.
    XmlNode xnViewFields =
        xmlDoc.CreateNode(XmlNodeType.Element, "ViewFields", "");
    foreach (XmlNode childNode in xnDefaultView.ChildNodes)
    {
        if (childNode.Name == "ViewFields")
        {
            xnViewFields.InnerXml += childNode.InnerXml;
        }
    }
```

```
            // Now add the new fields to end of the list of preexisting
            // view fields.
            if (txtUDFName1.Text != "")
               xnViewFields.InnerXml += "<FieldRef Name='" +
                  txtUDFName1.Text + "'/>";
            if (txtUDFName2.Text != "")
               xnViewFields.InnerXml += "<FieldRef Name='" +
                  txtUDFName2.Text + "'/>";
            if (txtUDFName3.Text != "")
               xnViewFields.InnerXml += "<FieldRef Name='" +
                  txtUDFName3.Text + "'/>";
            // Update the view.  As with the ListUpdate() method, we need
            // to pass parameters only for data we want to change.  We can
            // pass "null" values for all the rest.
            objViews.UpdateView(txtListName.Text, viewName,
               null, null, xnViewFields, null, null, null);
            // Step 5: If requested, open new list
            if (cbOpenList.Checked)
            {
                Response.Redirect(txtSiteUrl.Text.ToString() + "/" +
                   txtWebName.Text.ToString() + "/lists/" +
                   txtListName.Text.ToString());
            }
            else
            {
                // Step 6: Display success message
                this.RegisterClientScriptBlock(
                   "Success",
                   "<script>alert ('List successfully added');</script>");
            }
        }
        catch (Exception ex)
        {
            lblErrorMsg.Text = ex.Message;
            lblErrorMsg.Visible = true;
        }
    }
    // Set standard type values for UDF type ddl's
    private void InitializeTypeDDL(ref DropDownList ddl)
    {
        ddl.Items.Clear();
        ddl.Items.Add("DateTime");
        ddl.Items.Add("Number");
        ddl.Items.Add("Text");
        ddl.SelectedIndex = 2;
    }
}
```

To Run

Open a new web browser and navigate to the application page, or simply run the application from within Visual Studio. When the page is first displayed, only the Site Collection URL and Web Site Name fields will be displayed. Fill in at least the site collection URL (leaving the web name blank will indicate that you want the root web site of the site collection) and click the Lookup List Templates button. Clicking this button will cause the application to query Share-Point for a list of list templates available for the target web site, and will display the remainder of the web form.

Enter a new, unique list name and select the type of list you want to create. You may optionally add one to three custom columns. If you want the browser redirected to the new list after it's created, select the Open New List After It's Been Created checkbox. To create the list as specified, click the Create New List button (shown in Figure 3-2).

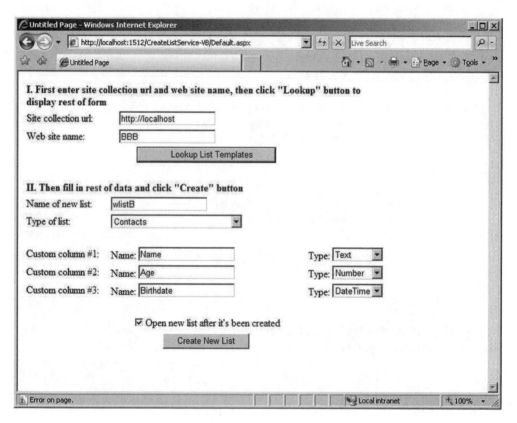

Figure 3-2. *Create list web form*

Assuming there were no errors, the list will be created. You can verify that the list was created correctly by navigating to the default view page of the new list.

Variations

- One of the great advantages of using web services instead of the object model classes is that you can call them from any application that can communicate via HTTP with one of the front-end SharePoint farm servers. This means that, for instance, you could create a Windows Forms application that could reside on the end user's desktop and use these same web services to create a view. Or, you could create a .NET console application that is scheduled to run on an entirely different server, which reads a database to obtain the needed information to create a new list.

Related Recipes

- Recipe 3-3

Recipe 3-3. Updating a List by Using the Object Model

This recipe shows how you can add, edit, or delete SharePoint list items by using the object model (OM). In effect, you are using a SharePoint list as a table to hold data to be manipulated by a custom ASP.NET web application running on the SharePoint front-end server.

Recipe Type: ASP.NET Web Application

Ingredients

Assembly References

- Windows SharePoint Services .NET assembly

Library References

- `Microsoft.SharePoint` library

Classes Used

- `SPSite` class
- `SPWeb` class
- `SPList` class
- `SPListItem` class

Special Considerations

- The code in this recipe is a bit more involved than that in most other recipes in this chapter. This is because I've included more of the form event-handling code than I typically do. However, this recipe provides a lot of useful techniques and essentially gives you a complete (although simplistic) model for handling additions, edits, and deletions to any SharePoint list.

- As with any application that makes changes to a SharePoint web site by using OM calls, you will need to set the `SPWeb.AllowUnsafeUpdates` property to `true` prior to attempting those changes. Failure to do so will result in a runtime error.

Preparation

1. Create a new ASP.NET web application project.

2. Add a reference to the Windows SharePoint Services .NET assembly.

3. Add a `using` or `Imports` statement for the `Microsoft.SharePoint` library at the top of the code-behind file for the default page.

4. Add all form fields as shown in the following "To Run" section. Fields include the following:

`txtEmpName`	`ddlCommand`
`txtJobTitle`	`ddlID`
`txtHireDate`	`lblReturnMsg`
`Button1`	

Process Flow

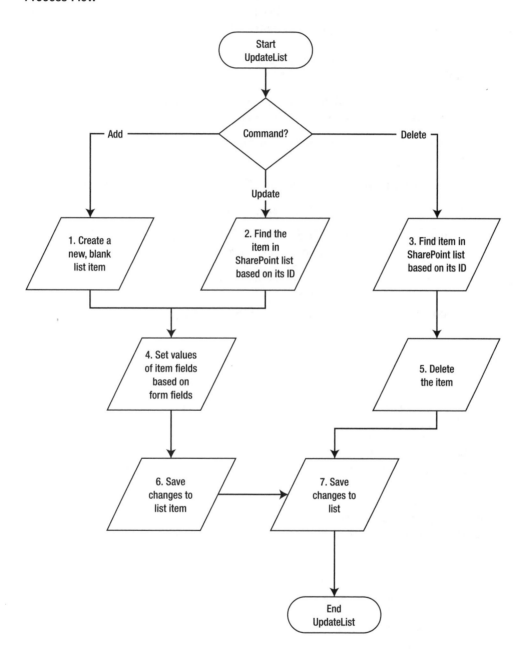

Several process flows are embodied in the program code because of the interactivity of the web form and the associated event handlers. I've therefore decided to focus on the process of updating the list when the command button is pressed.

1. If the user has selected New, use the `SPListItemCollection.Add()` method to create a new list item.

2. If the user has selected Update, use the `SPList.GetItemById()` method to find that item and return an `SPListItem` object pointing to it.

3. If the user has selected Delete, first get the `EmpName` property value by using the same technique as in step 2.

4. For New or Update, assign values from form fields to the associated `SPListItem` properties.

5. For Delete, call the `SPList.DeleteItemById()` method to remove the item from the list.

6. If changes were made via adding or updating, call the `SPListItem.Update()` method to save changes to item properties back to SharePoint.

7. In any case, call the `SPList.Update()` method to save all changes.

Recipe—VB (See Project UpdateListOM-VB Form Default.aspx.vb)

```vb
Imports System
Imports System.Data
Imports System.Configuration
Imports System.Web
Imports System.Web.Security
Imports System.Web.UI
Imports System.Web.UI.WebControls
Imports System.Web.UI.WebControls.WebParts
Imports System.Web.UI.HtmlControls
Imports Microsoft.SharePoint
Partial Public Class _Default
    Inherits System.Web.UI.Page
    Protected Sub Page_Load(ByVal sender As Object, ByVal e As EventArgs) _
        Handles Me.Load
        If Not IsPostBack Then
            ' Populate the "Command" drop-down list
            ddlCommand.Items.Add("Delete")
            ddlCommand.Items.Add("New")
            ddlCommand.Items.Add("Update")
            ddlCommand.SelectedIndex = 2
            ' Get list of current IDs
            GetIDs()
            ' Populate form fields
            setFields()
            ' Get Current entries in list
            RefreshEmployeeList()
        End If
```

```vb
End Sub
' Return list of employees currently in
' the SharePoint list
Private Function GetAllEmployees() As DataTable
    Dim site As New SPSite("http://localhost")
    Dim web As SPWeb = site.AllWebs("")
    Dim employees As SPList = web.Lists("Employee")
    Dim dtEmployees As DataTable = employees.Items.GetDataTable()
    Dim dtEmployeesNew As New DataTable("Employees")
    dtEmployeesNew.Columns.Add("ID")
    dtEmployeesNew.Columns.Add("EmpName")
    dtEmployeesNew.Columns.Add("JobTitle")
    dtEmployeesNew.Columns.Add("HireDate")
    For Each drEmployee As DataRow In dtEmployees.Rows
        Try
            Dim drEmployeeNew As DataRow = dtEmployeesNew.NewRow()
            drEmployeeNew("ID") = drEmployee("ID").ToString()
            drEmployeeNew("EmpName") = drEmployee("EmpName").ToString()
            drEmployeeNew("JobTitle") = drEmployee("JobTitle").ToString()
            drEmployeeNew("HireDate") = drEmployee("HireDate").ToString()
            dtEmployeesNew.Rows.Add(drEmployeeNew)
            dtEmployeesNew.AcceptChanges()
        Catch
        End Try
    Next
     web.Dispose()
     site.Dispose()
    Return dtEmployeesNew
End Function
' Return a drop-down list object containing
' all current IDs, unless the "New" command
' selected, in which case no ID is needed
Private Function GetIDs() As DropDownList
    ddlID.Items.Clear()
    If ddlCommand.SelectedValue = "New" Then
        ddlID.Enabled = False
        ddlID.Items.Add(New ListItem("N/A"))
    Else
        ddlID.Enabled = True
        Dim dtEmployees As New DataTable()
        dtEmployees = GetAllEmployees()
        For Each drEmployee As DataRow In dtEmployees.Rows
            Dim li As New ListItem(drEmployee("ID").ToString(), _
                drEmployee("ID").ToString())
            ddlID.Items.Add(li)
        Next
    End If
```

```
            ddlID.SelectedIndex = 0
            Return ddlID
    End Function
    ' Redraw grid-view listing all employees
    Private Sub RefreshEmployeeList()
        Dim dtEmployeeListData As New DataTable()
        dtEmployeeListData = GetAllEmployees()
        Me.GridView1.DataSource = dtEmployeeListData
        Me.GridView1.DataBind()
    End Sub
    ' Update form fields to reflect
    ' selected command and, if appropriate
    ' selected ID
    Private Sub setFields()
        ' Clear out data entry fields
        txtEmpName.Text = ""
        txtHireDate.Text = ""
        txtJobTitle.Text = ""
        ' By default, let user select an existing ID
        ddlID.Enabled = True
        ' Enable or disable fields as appropriate
        If ddlCommand.SelectedValue = "Delete" Then
            txtEmpName.Enabled = False
            txtHireDate.Enabled = False
            txtJobTitle.Enabled = False
        Else
            ' If "New", doesn't make sense for
            ' user to select an ID
            If ddlCommand.SelectedValue = "New" Then
                ddlID.Enabled = False
            Else
                ddlID.Enabled = True
                ' Retrieve existing data for selected employee
                Dim site As New SPSite("http://localhost")
                Dim web As SPWeb = site.AllWebs("")
                Dim list As SPList = web.Lists("Employee")
                Dim ID As Integer = Integer.Parse(ddlID.SelectedValue)
                Dim item As SPListItem = list.GetItemById(ID)
                ' Assign form field values from SharePoint list
                txtEmpName.Text = item("EmpName").ToString()
                txtHireDate.Text = item("HireDate").ToString()
                txtJobTitle.Text = item("JobTitle").ToString()
                web.Dispose()
                site.Dispose()
            End If
```

```
            txtEmpName.Enabled = True
            txtHireDate.Enabled = True
            txtJobTitle.Enabled = True
        End If
    End Sub
    Protected Sub ddlCommand_SelectedIndexChanged(ByVal sender As Object, _
        ByVal e As EventArgs) Handles ddlCommand.SelectedIndexChanged
        GetIDs()
        setFields()
    End Sub
    Protected Sub ddlID_SelectedIndexChanged(ByVal sender As Object, _
        ByVal e As EventArgs) Handles ddlID.SelectedIndexChanged
        setFields()
    End Sub
    Protected Sub Button1_Click(ByVal sender As Object, ByVal e As EventArgs) _
Handles Button1.Click
        Try
            Dim site As New SPSite("http://localhost")
            Dim web As SPWeb = site.AllWebs("")
            Dim list As SPList = web.Lists("Employee")
            Dim item As SPListItem
            Dim ID As Integer
            lblReturnMsg.Text = ""
            lblReturnMsg.Visible = True
            web.AllowUnsafeUpdates = True
            Select Case ddlCommand.SelectedValue
                Case "New"
                    item = list.Items.Add()
                    item("EmpName") = txtEmpName.Text
                    item("JobTitle") = txtJobTitle.Text
                    item("HireDate") = txtHireDate.Text
                    item.Update()
                    lblReturnMsg.Text = "'" & txtEmpName.Text & _
                        "' has been successfully added"
                    Exit Select
                Case "Update"
                    ID = Integer.Parse(ddlID.SelectedValue)
                    item = list.GetItemById(ID)
                    item("EmpName") = txtEmpName.Text
                    item("JobTitle") = txtJobTitle.Text
                    item("HireDate") = txtHireDate.Text
                    item.Update()
                    lblReturnMsg.Text = "'" & txtEmpName.Text & _
                        "' has been successfully updated"
                    Exit Select
```

```
                    Case "Delete"
                        ID = Integer.Parse(ddlID.SelectedValue)
                        item = list.GetItemById(ID)
                        Dim empName As String = item("EmpName").ToString()
                        list.Items.DeleteItemById(ID)
                        lblReturnMsg.Text = "'" & empName & _
                            "' has been successfully deleted"
                        Exit Select
                End Select
                list.Update()
                GetIDs()
                setFields()
                RefreshEmployeeList()
                web.Dispose()
                site.Dispose()
            Catch ex As Exception
                lblReturnMsg.Text = ex.Message
            End Try
        End Sub
    End Class
```

Recipe—C# (See Project UpdateListOM-CS Form Default.aspx.cs)

```csharp
using System;
using System.Data;
using System.Configuration;
using System.Web;
using System.Web.Security;
using System.Web.UI;
using System.Web.UI.WebControls;
using System.Web.UI.WebControls.WebParts;
using System.Web.UI.HtmlControls;
using Microsoft.SharePoint;
public partial class _Default : System.Web.UI.Page
{
    protected void Page_Load(object sender, EventArgs e)
    {
        if (!IsPostBack)
        {
            // Populate the "Command" drop-down list
            ddlCommand.Items.Add("Delete");
            ddlCommand.Items.Add("New");
            ddlCommand.Items.Add("Update");
            ddlCommand.SelectedIndex = 2;
            // Get list of current IDs
```

```
            GetIDs();
            // Populate form fields
            setFields();
            // Get Current entries in list
            RefreshEmployeeList();
        }
    }
    // Return list of employees currently in
    // the SharePoint list
    DataTable GetAllEmployees()
    {
        SPSite site = new SPSite("http://localhost");
        SPWeb web = site.AllWebs[""];
        SPList employees = web.Lists["Employee"];
        DataTable dtEmployees = employees.Items.GetDataTable();
        DataTable dtEmployeesNew = new DataTable("Employees");
        dtEmployeesNew.Columns.Add("ID");
        dtEmployeesNew.Columns.Add("EmpName");
        dtEmployeesNew.Columns.Add("JobTitle");
        dtEmployeesNew.Columns.Add("HireDate");
        foreach (DataRow drEmployee in dtEmployees.Rows)
        {
            try
            {
                DataRow drEmployeeNew = dtEmployeesNew.NewRow();
                drEmployeeNew["ID"] = drEmployee["ID"].ToString();
                drEmployeeNew["EmpName"] = drEmployee["EmpName"].ToString();
                drEmployeeNew["JobTitle"] =
                    drEmployee["JobTitle"].ToString();
                drEmployeeNew["HireDate"] =
                    drEmployee["HireDate"].ToString();
                dtEmployeesNew.Rows.Add(drEmployeeNew);
                dtEmployeesNew.AcceptChanges();
            }
            catch { }
        }
        web.Dispose();
        site.Dispose();
        return dtEmployeesNew;
    }
    // Return a drop-down list object containing
    // all current IDs, unless the "New" command
    // selected, in which case no ID is needed
```

```csharp
DropDownList GetIDs()
{
    ddlID.Items.Clear();
    if (ddlCommand.SelectedValue == "New")
    {
        ddlID.Enabled = false;
        ddlID.Items.Add(new ListItem("N/A"));
    }
    else
    {
        ddlID.Enabled = true;
        DataTable dtEmployees = new DataTable();
        dtEmployees = GetAllEmployees();
        foreach (DataRow drEmployee in dtEmployees.Rows)
        {
            ListItem li = new ListItem(drEmployee["ID"].ToString(),
                drEmployee["ID"].ToString());
            ddlID.Items.Add(li);
        }
    }
    ddlID.SelectedIndex = 0;
    return ddlID;
}
// Redraw grid-view listing all employees
void RefreshEmployeeList()
{
    DataTable dtEmployeeListData = new DataTable();
    dtEmployeeListData = GetAllEmployees();
    this.GridView1.DataSource = dtEmployeeListData;
    this.GridView1.DataBind();
}
// Update form fields to reflect
// selected command and, if appropriate
// selected ID
private void setFields()
{
    // Clear out data entry fields
    txtEmpName.Text = "";
    txtHireDate.Text = "";
    txtJobTitle.Text = "";
    lblReturnMsg.Text = "";
    // By default, let user select an existing ID
    ddlID.Enabled = true;
    // Enable or disable fields as appropriate
```

```csharp
        if (ddlCommand.SelectedValue == "Delete")
        {
            txtEmpName.Enabled = false;
            txtHireDate.Enabled = false;
            txtJobTitle.Enabled = false;
        }
        else
        {
            // If "New", doesn't make sense for
            // user to select an ID
            if (ddlCommand.SelectedValue == "New")
                ddlID.Enabled = false;
            else
            {
                ddlID.Enabled = true;
                // Retrieve existing data for selected employee
                SPSite site = new SPSite("http://localhost");
                SPWeb web = site.AllWebs[""];
                SPList list = web.Lists["Employee"];
                int ID = int.Parse(ddlID.SelectedValue);
                SPListItem item = list.GetItemById(ID);
                // Assign form field values from SharePoint list
                txtEmpName.Text = item["EmpName"].ToString();
                txtHireDate.Text = item["HireDate"].ToString();
                txtJobTitle.Text = item["JobTitle"].ToString();
            }
            txtEmpName.Enabled = true;
            txtHireDate.Enabled = true;
            txtJobTitle.Enabled = true;
            web.Dispose();
            site.Dispose();
        }
}
protected void ddlCommand_SelectedIndexChanged(object sender, EventArgs e)
{
    GetIDs();
    setFields();
}
protected void ddlID_SelectedIndexChanged(object sender, EventArgs e)
{
    setFields();
}
protected void Button1_Click(object sender, EventArgs e)
{
```

```csharp
try
{
    SPSite site = new SPSite("http://localhost");
    SPWeb web = site.AllWebs[""];
    SPList list = web.Lists["Employee"];
    SPListItem item;
    int ID;
    lblReturnMsg.Text = "";
    web.AllowUnsafeUpdates = true;
    switch (ddlCommand.SelectedValue)
    {
        case "New":
            item = list.Items.Add();
            item["EmpName"] = txtEmpName.Text;
            item["JobTitle"] = txtJobTitle.Text;
            item["HireDate"] = txtHireDate.Text;
            item.Update();
            lblReturnMsg.Text = "'" +
                txtEmpName.Text + "' has been successfully added";
            break;
        case "Update":
            ID = int.Parse(ddlID.SelectedValue);
            item = list.GetItemById(ID);
            item["EmpName"] = txtEmpName.Text;
            item["JobTitle"] = txtJobTitle.Text;
            item["HireDate"] = txtHireDate.Text;
            item.Update();
            lblReturnMsg.Text = "'" +
                txtEmpName.Text + "' has been successfully updated";
            break;
        case "Delete":
            ID = int.Parse(ddlID.SelectedValue);
            item = list.GetItemById(ID);
            string empName = item["EmpName"].ToString();
            list.Items.DeleteItemById(ID);
            lblReturnMsg.Text = "'" + empName +
                "' has been successfully deleted";
            break;
    }
    list.Update();
    GetIDs();
    setFields();
    RefreshEmployeeList();
    web.Dispose();
    site.Dispose();
}
```

```
        catch (Exception ex)
        {
            lblReturnMsg.Text = ex.Message;
        }
    }
}
```

To Run

Run the application from within Visual Studio, or open a web browser and navigate to the web page URL. When the page first loads, a list of existing items from the `http://localhost/` root web Employee list is displayed. Select Update, New, or Delete from the Command drop-down list. If you select New, the ID drop-down will also be set to New; otherwise, you may select one of the existing ID values.

For a New or Update command, enter text into any or all of the Employee Name, Job Title, or Hire Date fields (remember format requirements for the Hire Date value).

Click the Go button to process the command as shown in Figure 3-3.

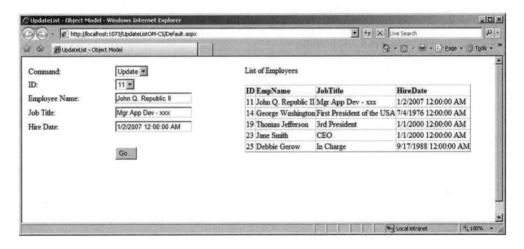

Figure 3-3. *List update web form*

After the update has been processed, a confirmation message will be displayed and the list of employees will be updated to reflect any changes.

Variations

- See Recipe 3-4.

Related Recipes

- Recipe 3-4

Recipe 3-4. Updating a List by Using Web Services

Lists in SharePoint are roughly analogous to SQL tables, with the exception that SharePoint does not support relational operations such as joins and intersections on lists. One very common task you might want to perform programmatically is to add, edit, or delete entries in a SharePoint list.

This recipe shows you how to create a simple web page to do just that. The page will display a list of current entries in an Employee list, and enable you to delete or update existing rows, and add new rows. Through this recipe, you'll work with two important SharePoint web services methods: `Lists.GetListItems()` and `Lists.UpdateListItems()`.

Recall that an important advantage of working with SharePoint through its web services is the ability to create applications (whether ASP.NET, .NET Windows, or .NET console applications) that can run on any computer that can connect to one of your SharePoint farm's front-end web servers. A particularly useful feature of the `Lists.UpdateListItems()` method is that you can pass a *batch* of commands to process in a single pass. For example, if you want to add 100 list items, you don't need to call the method 100 times. Rather, you create a chunk of XML describing all 100 rows to add, and `UpdateListItems()` does the rest.

And batches aren't limited to just one type of command. You can mix add, update, and delete operations in a single batch. This makes the `UpdateListItems()` method particularly useful for processing remote updates.

Recipe Type: ASP.NET Web Application

Ingredients

Web Service References

- `http://[Server]/_vti_bin/Lists.asmx`

Classes Used

- `System.Text`
- `System.XML`

Special Considerations

- As with any SharePoint web service, authentication is required, so you'll need to pass a network credential to the `Lists.asmx` service before calling any of its methods. Failure to do so will result in an exception being thrown, indicating that the calling program is not authorized.

- One of the fields updated in this recipe is of the date/time type. When passing data to SharePoint via the `<Batch><Method>` XML, you need to use the YYYY-MM-DD format. For example, the date 10/1/2007 needs to be encoded as 2007-10-1.

Preparation

1. Create a new ASP.NET web application.

2. Add a web reference to `http://localhost/_vti_bin/Lists.asmx`.

Process Flow: UpdateListWS

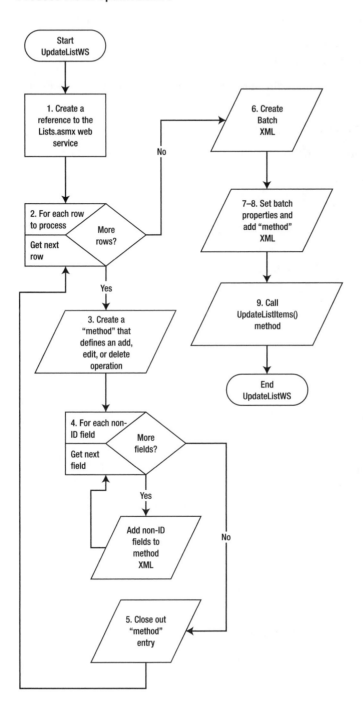

1. Create an instance of the Lists.asmx web service and assign valid credentials.

2. Loop through rows in the table of commands (only one row is passed in this recipe).

3. Create an XML fragment to contain a <Method> (for example, command) to add, edit, or delete a list item in the SharePoint list.

4. Loop through row columns, skipping the first column, because it contains the command, adding <Field> elements to the method.

5. After all columns have been processed, close out the </Method>.

6. Create a new <Batch> to contain the <Method> elements created in steps 3–5.

7. Set the <Batch> properties.

8. Add the <Method> elements.

9. Call the Lists.UpdateListItems() method, passing the <Batch>.

Recipe—VB (See Project UpdateListWS-VB, Form Default.aspx.vb)

```vb
Imports System
Imports System.Data
Imports System.Configuration
Imports System.Web
Imports System.Web.Security
Imports System.Web.UI
Imports System.Web.UI.WebControls
Imports System.Web.UI.WebControls.WebParts
Imports System.Web.UI.HtmlControls
Imports System.Text
Imports System.Xml
Partial Public Class _Default
    Inherits System.Web.UI.Page
    Protected Sub Page_Load(ByVal sender As Object, ByVal e As EventArgs) _
        Handles Me.Load
        If Not IsPostBack Then
            ' Populate the "Command" drop-down list
            ddlCommand.Items.Add("Delete")
            ddlCommand.Items.Add("New")
            ddlCommand.Items.Add("Update")
            ddlCommand.SelectedIndex = 2
            ' Populate the "ID" drop-down list
            ddlID = GetIDs()
            ' Get Current entries in list
            RefreshEmployeeList()
        End If
    End Sub
```

```vb
    Protected Sub ddlCommand_SelectedIndexChanged(ByVal sender As Object, _
        ByVal e As EventArgs) Handles ddlCommand.SelectedIndexChanged
            ddlID = GetIDs()
    End Sub
    Private Function GetAllEmployees() As DataTable
        Dim objListService As New ListsService.Lists()
        objListService.Url = "http://localhost/_vti_bin/lists.asmx"
        objListService.Credentials = _
            System.Net.CredentialCache.DefaultCredentials
        Dim dtEmployees As New DataTable("Employees")
        dtEmployees.Columns.Add("ID")
        dtEmployees.Columns.Add("EmpName")
        dtEmployees.Columns.Add("JobTitle")
        dtEmployees.Columns.Add("HireDate")
        Dim drEmployee As DataRow
        Dim xnEmployees As XmlNode = objListService.GetListItems( _
            "Employee", Nothing, Nothing, Nothing, Nothing, Nothing, _
            Nothing)
        For Each xnEmployee As XmlNode _
  In xnEmployees.ChildNodes(1).ChildNodes
            Try
                drEmployee = dtEmployees.NewRow()
                drEmployee("ID") = xnEmployee.Attributes("ows_ID").Value
                drEmployee("EmpName") = _
                    xnEmployee.Attributes("ows_EmpName").Value
                drEmployee("JobTitle") = _
                    xnEmployee.Attributes("ows_JobTitle").Value
                drEmployee("HireDate") = _
                    xnEmployee.Attributes("ows_HireDate").Value
                dtEmployees.Rows.Add(drEmployee)
            Catch
            End Try
        Next
        Return dtEmployees
    End Function
    ' Return a drop-down list object containing
    ' all current IDs, unless the "New" command
    ' selected, in which case the only valid
    ' value for ID is also "New"
    Private Function GetIDs() As DropDownList
        ddlID.Items.Clear()
        If ddlCommand.SelectedValue = "New" Then
            Dim li As New ListItem("New", "New")
            ddlID.Items.Add(li)
```

```vb
        Else
            Dim dtEmployees As New DataTable()
            dtEmployees = GetAllEmployees()
            For Each drEmployee As DataRow In dtEmployees.Rows
                Dim li As New ListItem(drEmployee("ID").ToString(), _
                    drEmployee("ID").ToString())
                ddlID.Items.Add(li)
            Next
        End If
        Return ddlID
End Function
' Redraw grid-view listing all employees
Private Sub RefreshEmployeeList()
    Dim dtEmployeeListData As New DataTable()
    dtEmployeeListData = GetAllEmployees()
    Me.GridView1.DataSource = dtEmployeeListData
    Me.GridView1.DataBind()
End Sub
' Build necessary batch XML and call the web service method
Private Sub UpdateListWS(ByVal listName As String, _
    ByVal dtListData As DataTable)
    ' Step 1: Create a reference to the "Lists" web service
    Dim objListService As New ListsService.Lists()
    objListService.Url = "http://localhost/_vti_bin/lists.asmx"
    objListService.Credentials = _
        System.Net.CredentialCache.DefaultCredentials
    ' Step 2: Loop through rows in data table,
    ' adding one add, edit, or delete command for each row
    Dim drListItem As DataRow
    Dim strBatch As String = ""
    For i As Integer = 0 To dtListData.Rows.Count - 1
        drListItem = dtListData.Rows(i)
        ' Step 3: Create a "Method" element to add to batch
        ' Assume that first column of data table was the 'Cmd'
        strBatch += "<Method ID='" + i.ToString() _
            + "' Cmd='" + drListItem("Cmd") + "'>"
        For j As Integer = 1 To drListItem.Table.Columns.Count - 1
            ' Step 4: Loop through fields 2-n, building
            ' one "method" in batch
            ' Include only columns with data
            If drListItem(j).ToString() <> "" Then
                strBatch += "<Field Name='" _
                    + drListItem.Table.Columns(j).ColumnName + "'>"
                strBatch += Server.HtmlEncode(drListItem(j).ToString())
                strBatch += "</Field>"
            End If
        Next
```

```
                   ' Step 5: Close out this method entry
                      strBatch += "</Method>"
            Next
            ' Step 6: Create the parent "batch" element
            Dim xmlDoc As XmlDocument = New System.Xml.XmlDocument()
            Dim xmlBatch As System.Xml.XmlElement = xmlDoc.CreateElement("Batch")
            ' Step 7: Tell SharePoint to keep processing if a single
            ' "Method" causes an error.
            xmlBatch.SetAttribute("OnError", "Continue")
            xmlBatch.SetAttribute("ListVersion", "1")
            xmlBatch.SetAttribute("ViewName", "")
            ' Step 8: Add method (i.e. add/update/delete command) to batch
            xmlBatch.InnerXml = strBatch
            ' Step 9: Process the batch
            Dim xmlReturn As XmlNode = objListService.UpdateListItems( _
                listName, xmlBatch)
            ' Display batch that was just run on web page
            lblBatchXML.Text = "<strong>Batch just processed</strong><br/><br/>" _
                + Server.HtmlEncode(xmlBatch.OuterXml)
            'Display the returned results
            lblReturnXML.Text = "<strong>Results</strong><br/><br/>" _
                + Server.HtmlEncode(xmlReturn.InnerXml)
    End Sub
    Protected Sub Button1_Click(ByVal sender As Object, ByVal e As EventArgs) _
Handles Button1.Click
            ' Define table to hold data to process
            Dim dtEmployees As New DataTable("Employee")
            ' New, Update, or Delete
            dtEmployees.Columns.Add("Cmd")
            ' New if adding, or ID of item
            dtEmployees.Columns.Add("ID")
            ' Builtin Title column
            dtEmployees.Columns.Add("Title")
            ' Employee name
            dtEmployees.Columns.Add("EmpName")
            ' Employee hire date
            dtEmployees.Columns.Add("HireDate")
            ' Employee title
            dtEmployees.Columns.Add("JobTitle")
            ' Call routine to update list
            Dim drEmployee As DataRow = dtEmployees.NewRow()
            drEmployee("Cmd") = ddlCommand.SelectedValue
            drEmployee("ID") = ddlID.SelectedValue
            drEmployee("EmpName") = txtEmpName.Text
            drEmployee("JobTitle") = txtJobTitle.Text
            drEmployee("HireDate") = txtHireDate.Text
            dtEmployees.Rows.Add(drEmployee)
```

```vbnet
        ' Update SharePoint
        UpdateListWS("Employee", dtEmployees)
        RefreshEmployeeList()
    End Sub
End Class
```

Recipe—C# (See Project UpdateListWS-CS, Form Default.aspx.cs)

```csharp
using System;
using System.Data;
using System.Configuration;
using System.Web;
using System.Web.Security;
using System.Web.UI;
using System.Web.UI.WebControls;
using System.Web.UI.WebControls.WebParts;
using System.Web.UI.HtmlControls;
using System.Text;
using System.Xml;
public partial class _Default : System.Web.UI.Page
{
    protected void Page_Load(object sender, EventArgs e)
    {
        if (!IsPostBack)
        {
            // Populate the "Command" drop-down list
            ddlCommand.Items.Add("Delete");
            ddlCommand.Items.Add("New");
            ddlCommand.Items.Add("Update");
            ddlCommand.SelectedIndex = 2;
            // Populate the "ID" drop-down list
            ddlID = GetIDs();
            // Get Current entries in list
            RefreshEmployeeList();
        }
    }
    protected void ddlCommand_SelectedIndexChanged(object sender,
        EventArgs e)
    {
        ddlID = GetIDs();
    }
    DataTable GetAllEmployees()
    {
        ListsService.Lists objListService = new ListsService.Lists();
        objListService.Url = "http://localhost/_vti_bin/lists.asmx";
```

```csharp
            objListService.Credentials =
                System.Net.CredentialCache.DefaultCredentials;
            DataTable dtEmployees = new DataTable("Employees");
            dtEmployees.Columns.Add("ID");
            dtEmployees.Columns.Add("EmpName");
            dtEmployees.Columns.Add("JobTitle");
            dtEmployees.Columns.Add("HireDate");
            DataRow drEmployee;
            XmlNode xnEmployees = objListService.GetListItems(
                "Employee", null, null, null, null, null, null);
            foreach (XmlNode xnEmployee in xnEmployees.ChildNodes[1].ChildNodes)
            {
                try
                {
                    drEmployee = dtEmployees.NewRow();
                    drEmployee["ID"] = xnEmployee.Attributes["ows_ID"].Value;
                    drEmployee["EmpName"] =
                        xnEmployee.Attributes["ows_EmpName"].Value;
                    drEmployee["JobTitle"] =
                        xnEmployee.Attributes["ows_JobTitle"].Value;
                    drEmployee["HireDate"] =
                        xnEmployee.Attributes["ows_HireDate"].Value;
                    dtEmployees.Rows.Add(drEmployee);
                }
                catch { }
            }
            return dtEmployees;
        }
        // Return a drop-down list object containing
        // all current IDs, unless the "New" command
        // selected, in which case the only valid
        // value for ID is also "New"
        DropDownList GetIDs()
        {
            ddlID.Items.Clear();
            if (ddlCommand.SelectedValue == "New")
            {
                ListItem li = new ListItem("New", "New");
                ddlID.Items.Add(li);
            }
            else
            {
                DataTable dtEmployees = new DataTable();
                dtEmployees = GetAllEmployees();
```

```
        foreach (DataRow drEmployee in dtEmployees.Rows)
        {
            ListItem li =
              new ListItem(drEmployee["ID"].ToString(),
             drEmployee["ID"].ToString());
            ddlID.Items.Add(li);
        }
    }
    return ddlID;
}
// Redraw grid-view listing all employees
void RefreshEmployeeList()
{
    DataTable dtEmployeeListData = new DataTable();
    dtEmployeeListData = GetAllEmployees();
    this.GridView1.DataSource = dtEmployeeListData;
    this.GridView1.DataBind();
}
// Build necessary batch XML and call the web service method
void UpdateListWS(string listName, DataTable dtListData)
{
    ListsService.Lists objListService = new ListsService.Lists();
    objListService.Url = "http://localhost/_vti_bin/lists.asmx";
    objListService.Credentials =
       System.Net.CredentialCache.DefaultCredentials;
    // Create XML containing "batch" of updates to process
    DataRow drListItem;
    string strBatch = "";
    for (int i = 0; i < dtListData.Rows.Count; i++)
    {
        drListItem = dtListData.Rows[i];
        // Create a "Method" element to add to batch
        strBatch += "<Method ID='" + i.ToString() + "' Cmd='"
          + drListItem["Cmd"] + "'>";
        // Asume that first column of data table was the 'Cmd'
        for (int j = 1; j < drListItem.Table.Columns.Count; j++)
        {
            // Include only columns with data
            if (drListItem[j].ToString() != "")
            {
                strBatch += "<Field Name='"
                    + drListItem.Table.Columns[j].ColumnName + "'>";
                strBatch += Server.HtmlEncode(drListItem[j].ToString());
                strBatch += "</Field>";
            }
        }
```

```csharp
            // Close out this entry
            strBatch += "</Method>";
        }
        // Create the parent "batch" element
        XmlDocument xmlDoc = new System.Xml.XmlDocument();
        System.Xml.XmlElement xmlBatch = xmlDoc.CreateElement("Batch");
        // Tell SharePoint to keep processing if a single
        // "Method" causes an error.
        xmlBatch.SetAttribute("OnError", "Continue");
        xmlBatch.SetAttribute("ListVersion", "1");
        xmlBatch.SetAttribute("ViewName", "");
        xmlBatch.InnerXml = strBatch;
        // Display batch that was just run on web page
        lblBatchXML.Text = "<strong>Batch just processed</strong><br/><br/>"
            + Server.HtmlEncode(xmlBatch.OuterXml);
        XmlNode xmlReturn = objListService.UpdateListItems(
            listName, xmlBatch);
        //Display the returned results
        lblReturnXML.Text = "<strong>Results</strong><br/><br/>"
            + Server.HtmlEncode(xmlReturn.InnerXml);
    }
    protected void Button1_Click(object sender, EventArgs e)
    {
        // Define table to hold data to process
        DataTable dtEmployees = new DataTable("Employee");
        dtEmployees.Columns.Add("Cmd");        // New, Update, or Delete
        dtEmployees.Columns.Add("ID");         // New if adding, or item ID
        dtEmployees.Columns.Add("Title");      // Builtin Title column
        dtEmployees.Columns.Add("EmpName");    // Employee name
        dtEmployees.Columns.Add("HireDate");   // Employee hire date
        dtEmployees.Columns.Add("JobTitle");   // Employee title
        // Call routine to update list
        DataRow drEmployee = dtEmployees.NewRow();
        drEmployee["Cmd"] = ddlCommand.SelectedValue;
        drEmployee["ID"] = ddlID.SelectedValue;
        drEmployee["EmpName"] = txtEmpName.Text;
        drEmployee["JobTitle"] = txtJobTitle.Text;
        drEmployee["HireDate"] = txtHireDate.Text;
        dtEmployees.Rows.Add(drEmployee);
        // Update SharePoint
        UpdateListWS("Employee", dtEmployees);
        RefreshEmployeeList();
    }
}
```

To Run

Run the application from within Visual Studio, or open a web browser and navigate to the web page URL. When the page first loads, a list of existing items from the `http://localhost/` root web Employee list is displayed. Select Update, New, or Delete from the Command drop-down list. If you select New, the ID drop-down will also be set to New; otherwise, you may select one of the existing ID values.

For a New or Update command, enter text into any or all of the Employee Name, Job Title, or Hire Date fields (remember format requirements for the Hire Date value). Click the Go (see Figure 3-4) button to process the command.

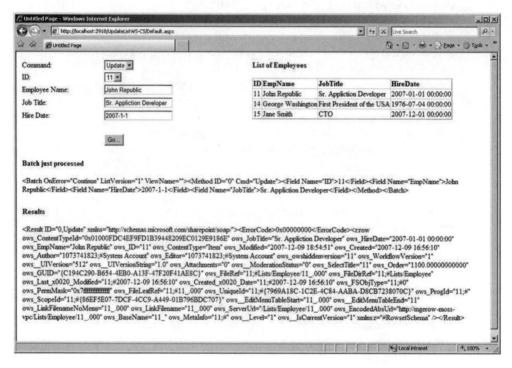

Figure 3-4. *List update form (web service)*

After the batch has been processed, the Batch Just Processed section will display the XML that was sent to the `Lists.UpdateListItems()` method, and the Results section will display the XML returned by the method, including a status code for each command in the batch, as well as full data for each item processed.

Variations

- This recipe processes only a single command, but the custom `UpdateListWS()` method is designed to receive a data table containing multiple commands. You can modify this recipe to enable the user to enter as many commands as you wish, and then process them together.

Related Recipes

- Recipe 3-3

Recipe 3-5. Adding a Document to a Document Library by Using the Object Model

Here's a useful little recipe to upload a document via an ASP.NET page. The user is asked to provide the site collection URL, the web site, and the name of a document library on the site. The user must also select a file for upload.

Recipe Type: ASP.NET Web Application

Ingredients

Assembly References

- Windows SharePoint Services assembly

Class Library References

- `Microsoft.SharePoint` library

Classes Used

- System.IO (to support the stream to read the file)

Special Considerations

- As always, the network credential under which the page runs needs to have permission to access and upload a document to the target document library.

- By default, ASP.NET web pages are limited to 4MB data transfers, which means that without making changes to the Web.config file, you will be able to upload only a 4MB file. Unless you expect all your files to be under 4MB, you will need to increase the maxRequestLength value in the web application's Web.config file. The element to add is <httpRuntime maxRequestLength="512000"/> (to increase the maximum upload size to 500MB) and should be added just after the <system.web> element. Failure to make this change will result in an error indicating that the file to be uploaded exceeds the maximum limit.

Preparation

1. Create a new ASP.NET web application.

2. Add a reference to the Windows SharePoint Services .NET assembly.

3. Add using or Imports statements for the following:

   - Microsoft.SharePoint

   - System.IO

4. Add web controls for all specified form fields:

   - txtSiteUrl (text box)

   - txtWebName (text box)

   - txtDocLibName (text box)

   - FileUpload1 (file upload)

   - cmdUploadFile (button)

   - lblErrorMsg (label)

Process Flow

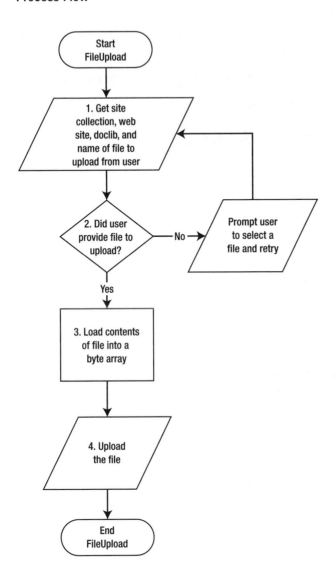

1. Prompt the user for the target site collection, web site, and document library name. The user also selects a file from disk to upload via the file upload control.

2. Verify that the name of the file to upload has been provided. If not, prompt the user to provide it now and return to the web form.

3. Assuming that the user has provided a valid file, read its contents into a byte array.

4. Upload the file to the target document library.

Recipe—VB (See Project FileUploadOM-VB, Form Default.aspx.vb)

```vb
Imports System
Imports System.Data
Imports System.Configuration
Imports System.Web
Imports System.Web.Security
Imports System.Web.UI
Imports System.Web.UI.WebControls
Imports System.Web.UI.WebControls.WebParts
Imports System.Web.UI.HtmlControls
Imports Microsoft.SharePoint
Imports System.IO
Partial Public Class _Default
    Inherits System.Web.UI.Page
    Protected Sub cmdUploadFile_Click(ByVal sender As Object, _
      ByVal e As EventArgs) Handles cmdUploadFile.Click
        Try
            lblErrorMsg.Visible = False
            ' Step 1: Get handle to site collection, web site, list
            Dim site As New SPSite(txtSiteUrl.Text)
            Dim web As SPWeb = site.AllWebs(txtWebName.Text)
            Dim dl As SPList = web.Lists(txtDocLibName.Text)
            Dim file As SPFile
            web.AllowUnsafeUpdates = True
            web.Lists.IncludeRootFolder = True
            ' Step 2: Make sure user has selected a file
            If FileUpload1.PostedFile.FileName <> "" Then
                ' Step 3: Load the content of the file into a byte array
                Dim fStream As Stream
                Dim contents As Byte() = _
                    New Byte(FileUpload1.PostedFile.InputStream.Length - 1) {}
                fStream = FileUpload1.PostedFile.InputStream
                fStream.Read(contents, 0, CInt(fStream.Length))
```

```
                        fStream.Close()
                        ' Step 4: Upload the file to SharePoint doclib
                        file = web.Files.Add(web.Url.ToString() + "/" + _
                            dl.Title.ToString() + "/" + _
                            FileUpload1.FileName, contents)
                    Else
                        lblErrorMsg.Text = "Please select a file to upload"
                        lblErrorMsg.Visible = True
                    End If
                    web.Dispose
                    site.Dispose()
                Catch ex As Exception
                    lblErrorMsg.Text = ex.Message
                    lblErrorMsg.Visible = True
                End Try
            End Sub
        End Class
```

Recipe—C# (See Project FileUploadOM-CS, Form Default.aspx.cs)

```csharp
using System;
using System.Data;
using System.Configuration;
using System.Web;
using System.Web.Security;
using System.Web.UI;
using System.Web.UI.WebControls;
using System.Web.UI.WebControls.WebParts;
using System.Web.UI.HtmlControls;
using Microsoft.SharePoint;
using System.IO;
public partial class _Default : System.Web.UI.Page
{
    protected void cmdUploadFile_Click(object sender, EventArgs e)
    {
        try
        {
            lblErrorMsg.Visible = false;
            // Step 1: Get handle to site collection, web site, list
            SPSite site = new SPSite(txtSiteUrl.Text);
            SPWeb web = site.AllWebs[txtWebName.Text];
            SPList dl = web.Lists[txtDocLibName.Text];
```

```
        SPFile file;
        web.AllowUnsafeUpdates = true;
        web.Lists.IncludeRootFolder = true;
        // Step 2: Make sure user has selected a file
        if (FileUpload1.PostedFile.FileName != "")
        {
            // Step 3: Load the content of the file into a byte array
            Stream fStream;
            Byte[] contents =
                new Byte[FileUpload1.PostedFile.InputStream.Length];
            fStream = FileUpload1.PostedFile.InputStream;
            fStream.Read(contents, 0, (int)fStream.Length);
            fStream.Close();
            // Step 4: Upload the file to SharePoint doclib
            file = web.Files.Add(web.Url.ToString() + "/" +
                dl.Title.ToString() + "/" +
                FileUpload1.FileName, contents);
            file.Update();
        }
        else
        {
            lblErrorMsg.Text = "Please select a file to upload";
            lblErrorMsg.Visible = true;
        }
        web.Dispose();
        site.Dispose();
    }
    catch (Exception ex)
    {
        lblErrorMsg.Text = ex.Message;
        lblErrorMsg.Visible = true;
    }
}
}
```

To Run

Run the application from within Visual Studio, or open a browser and navigate to the application's web page. Fill in all required information and select a file to upload from your computer or a network share. Click the Upload File button as in Figure 3-5.

Assuming no errors occurred, the page will return without messages after the file has been uploaded to the target document library. You can verify this by navigating to the library.

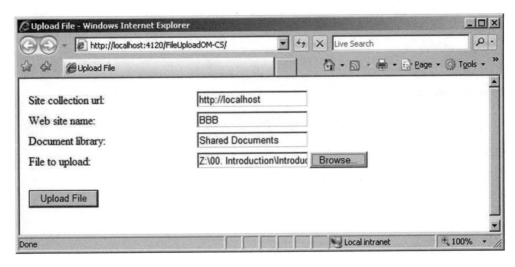

Figure 3-5. *Upload File form*

Variations

- One variation is to upload multiple files from a file share to a given destination. This can be done by reading the contents of a file system folder into an array and uploading each file in turn.

- In addition to uploading the file, set various custom columns of the document library with metadata about the document provided by the end user.

Related Recipes

- Recipe 3-6

Recipe 3-6. Adding a Document to a Document Library by Using Web Services

One of the odd omissions in SharePoint is a built-in web service method to upload a document to a document library. In this recipe, you'll create such a web service, which you'll find will come in handy in many instances.

The FileUpload web service is quite simple, taking advantage of .NET web services' ability to transfer byte arrays—which we use to hold the bytes composing any document. One "gotcha" that we need to handle is the problem of uploading large files. To handle this, we'll need to address two potential pitfalls: 1) file size restrictions and 2) transfer time restrictions. These are covered in the "Special Considerations" section that follows.

Recipe Type: ASP.NET Web Service and Console Application

Ingredients

Assembly References

- Windows SharePoint Services assembly

Class Library References

- Microsoft.SharePoint library

Classes Used

- SPSite class

- SPWeb class

Special Considerations

- As with any web service that requires authentication, you will need to attach network credentials with permissions to access both the service and SharePoint.

- Unless you expect all your files to be quite under 4MB, you will need to increase the maxRequestLength value in the web service's Web.config file. The element to add is <httpRuntime maxRequestLength="512000"/> and should be added just after the <system.web> element. Failure to make this change will result in an error indicating that the file to be uploaded exceeds the maximum limit. (In the preceding example, the maximum upload size has been increased to 500MB.)

- You may also want to increase the maximum file size that SharePoint allows. You can do this through the SharePoint Central Administration Website (SCAW) on the Web Application General Settings page. Change the value in the Maximum Upload Size field to reflect the setting made to the web service Web.config (for example, change the value to 500 for the preceding example).

- Finally, depending on the typical connection speed, you may need to increase the connection time-out value in IIS to enable connections to remain open longer for slow connections or large file uploads. You can set the connection time-out value on the Web Site tab of the web site property sheet in IIS.

Preparation

1. Create a new ASP.NET web service project in Visual Studio.

2. Add a reference to the Windows SharePoint Services assembly.

Process Flow

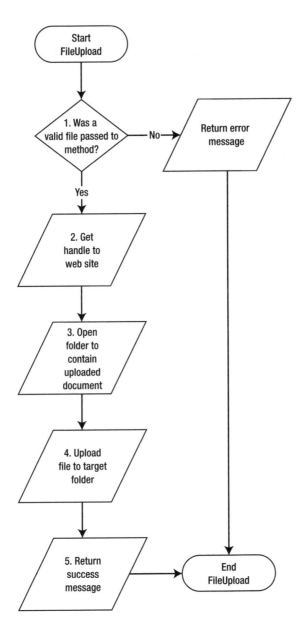

1. Verify that a non-null byte array was passed to the upload method. If the array is null, abort processing and return an error message.

2. If a valid byte array was passed, get a handle to the target web site.

3. Open the target folder. If the full target path doesn't exist, create any necessary folders or subfolders.

4. Upload the file.

5. Return a success message to the calling routine.

Recipe—VB: FileUploadService (See Project FileUploadService-VB, Class Service.vb)

```vb
Imports System
Imports System.Web
Imports System.Web.Services
Imports System.Web.Services.Protocols
Imports Microsoft.SharePoint
Imports Microsoft.SharePoint.WebControls
<WebService([Namespace]:="http://tempuri.org/")> _
<WebServiceBinding(ConformsTo:=WsiProfiles.BasicProfile1_1)> _
Public Class Service
    Inherits System.Web.Services.WebService
    'Uncomment the following line if using designed components
    'InitializeComponent();
    Public Sub New()
    End Sub
    <WebMethod()> _
    Public Function UploadFile2SharePoint( _
       ByVal fileName As String, _
       ByVal fileContents As Byte(), _
       ByVal siteUrl As String, _
       ByVal webName As String, _
       ByVal pathFolder As String) _
       As String
         ' Step 1: Make sure a valid file has been
         ' passed to the service method
        If fileContents Is Nothing Then
            Return "Missing File"
        End If
        Try
             ' Step 2: Open the target site and web
            Dim site As New SPSite(siteUrl)
            Dim web As SPWeb = site.AllWebs(webName)
             ' Step 3: Open the folder to hold the document
            Dim folder As SPFolder = _
               web.GetFolder(EnsureParentFolder(web, _
               pathFolder + "/" + fileName))
            Dim boolOverwrite As Boolean = True
             ' Step 4: Add the file
            Dim file As SPFile = _
               folder.Files.Add(fileName, fileContents, boolOverwrite)
            web.Dispose()
            site.Dispose()
```

```vb
                ' Step 5: Declare victory!
                Return "'" + file.Name + "' successfully written to '" + _
                    file.Item.Url + "'"
            Catch ex As System.Exception
                Return ex.Message
            End Try
        End Function
        ' This is a stock function from the WSS SDK to make
        ' sure that a folder path exists before we try to upload the
        ' file.
        Public Function EnsureParentFolder( _
            ByVal parentSite As SPWeb, ByVal destinUrl As String) As String
            destinUrl = parentSite.GetFile(destinUrl).Url
            Dim index As Integer = destinUrl.LastIndexOf("/")
            Dim parentFolderUrl As String = String.Empty
            If index > -1 Then
                parentFolderUrl = destinUrl.Substring(0, index)
                Dim parentFolder As SPFolder = parentSite.GetFolder(parentFolderUrl)
                If Not parentFolder.Exists Then
                    Dim currentFolder As SPFolder = parentSite.RootFolder
                    For Each folder As String In parentFolderUrl.Split("/"c)
                        currentFolder = currentFolder.SubFolders.Add(folder)
                    Next
                End If
            End If
            Return parentFolderUrl
        End Function
    End Class
```

Recipe—C#: FileUploadService (See Project FileUploadService, Class Service.cs)

```csharp
using System;
using System.Web;
using System.Web.Services;
using System.Web.Services.Protocols;
using Microsoft.SharePoint;
using Microsoft.SharePoint.WebControls;
[WebService(Namespace = "http://tempuri.org/")]
[WebServiceBinding(ConformsTo = WsiProfiles.BasicProfile1_1)]
public class Service : System.Web.Services.WebService
{
    public Service () {
        //Uncomment the following line if using designed components
        //InitializeComponent();
    }
    [WebMethod]
```

```
public string UploadFile2SharePoint(
    string fileName, byte[] fileContents, string siteUrl,
    string webName, string pathFolder)
{
    // Step 1: Make sure a valid file has been passed
    // to the service method
    if (fileContents == null)
    {
        return "Missing File";
    }
    try
    {
        // Step 2: Open the target site and web
        SPSite site = new SPSite(siteUrl);
        SPWeb web = site.AllWebs[webName];
        // Step 3: Open the folder to hold the document
        SPFolder folder =
            web.GetFolder(
            EnsureParentFolder(web,pathFolder+"/"+fileName));
        bool boolOverwrite = true;
        // Step 4: Add the file
        SPFile file = folder.Files.Add(
            fileName, fileContents, boolOverwrite);
        web.Dispose();
        site.Dispose();
        // Step 5: Declare victory!
        return "'" + file.Name + "' successfully written to '" +
            file.Item.Url + "'";
    }
    catch (System.Exception ex)
    {
        return ex.Message;
    }
}
// This is a stock function from the WSS SDK to make
// sure that a folder path exists before we try to upload the
// file.
public string EnsureParentFolder(SPWeb parentSite, string destinUrl)
{
    destinUrl = parentSite.GetFile(destinUrl).Url;
    int index = destinUrl.LastIndexOf("/");
    string parentFolderUrl = string.Empty;
    if (index > -1)
    {
        parentFolderUrl = destinUrl.Substring(0, index);
        SPFolder parentFolder
            = parentSite.GetFolder(parentFolderUrl);
```

```
            if (!parentFolder.Exists)
            {
                SPFolder currentFolder = parentSite.RootFolder;
                foreach (string folder in parentFolderUrl.Split('/'))
                {
                    currentFolder
                        = currentFolder.SubFolders.Add(folder);
                }
            }
        }
    }
    return parentFolderUrl;
}
}
```

Recipe—C#: TestFileUploadService

Note The following code assumes that a default namespace of TestFileUploadService has been specified in the project properties.

```csharp
using System;
using System.Collections.Generic;
using System.Text;
namespace TestFileUploadService
{
    class Program
    {
        static void Main(string[] args)
        {
            // If 3 arguments have not been passed
            // on command line, prompt user for inputs
            // via console
            if (args.Length < 4)
            {
                args = new string[4];
                Console.Write("Full path of source file: ");
                args[0] = Console.ReadLine();
                Console.Write("Target site url: ");
                args[1] = Console.ReadLine();
                Console.Write("Target web name: ");
                args[2] = Console.ReadLine();
                Console.Write("Target folder path: ");
                args[3] = Console.ReadLine();
            }
```

```
// Create an instance of the file upload service
// and assign credentials of an authorized user
FileUploadService.Service objFileUploadService =
    new FileUploadService.Service();
objFileUploadService.Credentials =
    System.Net.CredentialCache.DefaultCredentials;
// Read in source file
System.IO.FileStream fs =
    new System.IO.FileStream(args[0],System.IO.FileMode.Open);
byte[] fileContents = new byte[fs.Length];
fs.Read(fileContents,0,(int)fs.Length);
fs.Close();
// Get just the filename
string fileName =
    args[0].Split('\\')[args[0].Split('\\').Length-1];

// Upload the specified file
Console.WriteLine();
Console.WriteLine(
    objFileUploadService.UploadFile2SharePoint(
        fileName,
        fileContents,
        args[1],
        args[2],
        args[3])
        );
Console.WriteLine();
Console.WriteLine("Press any key to continue");
Console.Read();
        }
    }
}
```

To Run

Run the TestFileUploadService.exe application from within Visual Studio or from the Windows console. Enter a valid filename, site, web, and path that you wish to upload the file to, as shown in Figure 3-6.

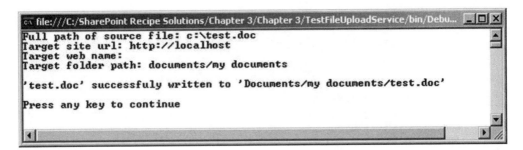

Figure 3-6. *Adding a document by using a web service*

Assuming that no errors occur, you will see a confirmation message indicating that the file has been successfully uploaded. You can verify this by opening a browser and navigating to the target folder.

Variations

- This example creates a SharePoint-specific file-upload routine. However, it's quite simple to create a variation that uploads the file to the file system instead of a SharePoint library by using a System.IO.FileStream object.

Related Recipes

- Recipe 3-5

CHAPTER 4

■ ■ ■

Working with Web Parts

SharePoint is a fascinating platform because it comprises so many technologies and subsystems, from site-definition templates to the object model, XML and XSLT, .NET and HTML, and everything in between.

Of all these, developing for the web-part framework is my favorite. The idea that you can create discrete bits of applications and reassemble them as needed is extremely powerful—and in fact is what object-oriented programming is all about. Web parts are the embodiment of that powerful idea in a web UI. You can build components (web parts) to meet a very specific requirement, confident that you'll be able to reuse them and even share data between them at a later time to meet future requirements as well.

With the release of SharePoint 2007—Windows SharePoint Services 3.0 (WSS 3.0) and Microsoft Office SharePoint Server (MOSS)—your web parts will be based on the ASP.NET 2.0 web-part framework rather than the SharePoint-specific framework in SharePoint 2003. This means that you can create and test web parts by using pure ASP.NET if you want. And if your web parts won't need access to the SharePoint object model, you can develop them on a computer that is not a SharePoint server, adding more flexibility to your development environment.

For those rare cases when you need some web-part feature that Microsoft has deprecated in the new framework, you can still instantiate a SharePoint web-part class. In SharePoint 2007, this class is simply a wrapper that maps the old 2003 web-part properties and methods onto the new ASP.NET 2.0 web-part class. But, for the most part, you'll want to stick with ASP.NET 2.0 web parts for flexibility and forward compatibility.

I need to say a few words about deploying the web parts you'll create by using the following recipes. There are several ways to deploy web parts, and here I use what I find the simplest for development purposes, which is to manually copy the web part's signed assembly (`.dll`) to the Global Assembly Cache (GAC), manually add the corresponding `<SafeControl>` element to SharePoint's `Web.config` file, and then use a site collection's web-part gallery pages to add the web part. However, when you're ready to move your web parts into production, you'll want to create a solution package to deploy it to your SharePoint farm. Creating a solution is, unfortunately, more work than it ought to be. But Microsoft has created an add-in called Windows SharePoint Services 3.0 Tools: Visual Studio 2005 Extensions, Version 1.1, which as of this writing can be found at `www.microsoft.com/downloads/details.aspx?FamilyID=3E1DCCCD-1CCA-433A-BB4D-97B96BF7AB63&displaylang=en`. Among the many features this add-on includes is a template for creating web parts that will make debugging and deploying your work much easier.

A few other things about web-part development to keep in mind before we begin:

- How you configure security and permissions in SharePoint, along with user permissions, will affect what operations can be performed by a web part at runtime, because web parts will run under the permissions of the current user unless you explicitly override those credentials.

- Use Try/Catch statements freely, because if your web part throws an unhandled error during runtime in production, SharePoint will provide virtually no information about the error, and the site administrator's only option may be to remove the web part from the page.

- Web parts must always be signed if they'll be placed in the GAC, and should always be signed anyway. There are arguments for and against GAC deployment. The argument against is that assemblies in the GAC are fully trusted, so if you place a web part there, it can do more harm than one deployed to SharePoint's \bin folder. The argument for GAC deployment is that it will make your life easier. If you are the source of all web parts in your production environment, go ahead and place them in the GAC. If you receive web parts from other sources (either commercial or separate development groups), you may want to use a \bin deployment.

- All web-part recipes developed here assume that SharePoint's security trust level is set to Full. If you are in charge of the SharePoint server and trust the quality and dependability of all code, setting trust to Full is not unreasonable. However, if you receive many web parts from other sources, you may want to use SharePoint's support for Code Access Security (CAS). You can find more on CAS in the SharePoint SDK.

Ultimately, the best way to learn any programming task is to roll up your sleeves and dig in. I'm confident that you'll find the following recipes both useful and instructive. Let's get to work!

Recipe 4-1. Creating a Simple RSS Feed Web Part

If you're new to creating SharePoint web parts, this is a great place to start. This web part will enable you to display an RSS source to any page, converting the underlying XML of the RSS feed into legible Hypertext Markup Language (HTML).

■**Note** A simple RSS Feed web part exists out of the box in MOSS, but this recipe will enable you to have an RSS Feed web part for WSS 3.0 environments and enable you to expand on the functionality to suit your needs.

Recipe Type: Web Part

Ingredients

Assembly References

- Windows SharePoint Services assembly
- `System.Web` .NET assembly

Class Library References

- `System.Web`
- `System.Web.UI`
- `System.Web.UI.WebControls`
- `System.Web.UI.WebControls.WebParts`
- `System.Web.UI.HtmlControls`

Special Considerations

- SharePoint 2007 web parts are simply ASP.NET 2.0 web parts designed for use in Share-Point. This was not the case with SharePoint 2003, which had web-part classes that were tightly tied to the SharePoint object model. The SharePoint 2007 object model still provides its own web-part classes for backward compatibility, but for most purposes you're better off using the generic ASP.NET web-part classes.

- The deployment instructions given in the "To Run" section will activate the web part for only a single site collection. The preferred method for deploying a web part for an entire SharePoint web application or web farm is through a SharePoint solution.

- One of the more interesting techniques shown in this recipe is that of reading a web page programmatically. We use this technique to get the RSS page Extensible Markup Language (XML), but can just as easily read any `http:` source in the same way. In this example, I'm calling an RSS feed that does not require authentication, and so I simply attach my default credentials. If I were reading a secure RSS feed that required authentication, I could attach a specific credential by using the `System.Net.NetworkCredential()` method.

Preparation

1. Create a new C# or Visual Basic .NET (VB.NET) class library.

2. Add references to the `System.Web` and `Windows.SharePoint.Services` .NET assemblies.

3. On the project properties Signing tab, select the Sign the Assembly checkbox and specify a new strong-name key file.

Process Flow

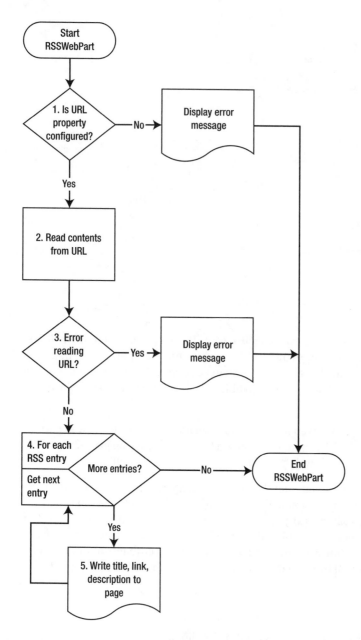

1. **Ensure** that the Url custom property of our RSS web part has been filled in. If not, display a message informing the user that it's required.

2. Read the RSS XML into an ADO DataSet object.

3. If an error occurred while reading the RSS source, display the resulting error to the web-part page.

4. Loop through each article returned in the RSS XML.

5. Write the title, description, and link to the page.

Recipe—VB (See Project RSSWebPartVB, Class RSSWebPartVB.vb)

```vb
Imports System
Imports System.Web
Imports System.Web.Security
Imports System.Web.UI
Imports System.Web.UI.WebControls
Imports System.Web.UI.WebControls.WebParts
Imports System.Web.UI.HtmlControls
Imports System.Xml
Imports System.Data
Namespace RSSWebPartVB
    Public Class RSSWebPart
        Inherits WebPart
        ' Local variables to hold web-part
        ' property values
        Private _url As String
        Private _newPage As Boolean = True
        Private _showDescription As Boolean = True
        Private _showUrl As Boolean = True
        ' Property to determine whether article should
        ' be opened in same or new page
        <Personalizable()> _
        <WebBrowsable()> _
        Public Property NewPage() As Boolean
            Get
                Return _newPage
            End Get
            Set(ByVal value As Boolean)
                _newPage = value
            End Set
        End Property
        ' Should Description be displayed?
        <Personalizable()> _
        <WebBrowsable()> _
        Public Property ShowDescription() As Boolean
            Get
                Return _showDescription
            End Get
            Set(ByVal value As Boolean)
                _showDescription = value
            End Set
        End Property
```

```vb
' Should URL be displayed?
<Personalizable()> _
<WebBrowsable()> _
Public Property ShowUrl() As Boolean
    Get
        Return _showUrl
    End Get
    Set(ByVal value As Boolean)
        _showUrl = value
    End Set
End Property
' Property to set URL of RSS feed
<Personalizable()> _
<WebBrowsable()> _
Public Property Url() As String
    Get
        Return _url
    End Get
    Set(ByVal value As String)
        _url = value
    End Set
End Property
' This is where the HTML gets rendered to the
' web-part page.
Protected Overloads Overrides Sub RenderContents( _
   ByVal writer As HtmlTextWriter)
   MyBase.RenderContents(writer)
    ' Step 1: Ensure Url property has been provided
    If Url <> "" Then
        ' Display heading with RSS location URL
        If ShowUrl Then
            writer.WriteLine("<hr/>")
            writer.WriteLine("<span style='font-size: larger;'>")
            writer.WriteLine("Results for: ")
            writer.WriteLine("<strong>")
            writer.WriteLine(Url)
            writer.WriteLine("</strong>")
            writer.WriteLine("</span>")
            writer.WriteLine("<hr/>")
        End If
        displayRSSFeed(writer)
    Else
        ' Tell user they need to fill in the Url property
        writer.WriteLine( _
            "<font color='red'>RSS Url cannot be blank</font>")
    End If
End Sub
```

```vb
        Private Sub displayRSSFeed(ByVal writer As HtmlTextWriter)
            Try
                ' Step 2: Read the RSS feed into memory
                Dim wReq As System.Net.WebRequest
                wReq = System.Net.WebRequest.Create(Url)
                wReq.Credentials = _
                    System.Net.CredentialCache.DefaultCredentials
                ' Return the response.
                Dim wResp As System.Net.WebResponse = wReq.GetResponse()
                Dim respStream As System.IO.Stream = _
                    wResp.GetResponseStream()
                ' Load RSS stream into a DataSet for easier processing
                Dim dsXML As New DataSet()
                dsXML.ReadXml(respStream)
                ' Step 4: Loop through all items returned, displaying results
                Dim target As String = ""
                If NewPage Then
                    target = "target='_new'"
                End If
                For Each item As DataRow In dsXML.Tables("item").Rows
                    ' Step 5: Write the title, link, and description to page
                    writer.WriteLine( _
                        "<a href='" + item("link") + "' " + target + _
                        ">" + item("title") + "</a>" + "<br/>" + _
                        "<span style='color:silver'>" + _
                        item("pubDate") + "</span>" + "<br/>" _
                        )
                    If ShowDescription Then
                        writer.WriteLine("<br/>" + item("description"))
                    End If
                    writer.WriteLine("<hr/>")
                Next
            Catch ex As Exception
                ' Step 3: If error occurs, notify end user
                writer.WriteLine("<font color='red'><strong>" + _
                    "An error occurred while attempting to process " + _
                    "the selected RSS feed. " + _
                    "Please verify that the url provided references " + _
                    "a valid RSS page." _
                    )
            End Try
        End Sub
    End Class
End Namespace
```

Recipe—C# (See Project RSSWebPartCS, Class RSSWebPart.cs)

```csharp
using System;
using System.Web;
using System.Web.Security;
using System.Web.UI;
using System.Web.UI.WebControls;
using System.Web.UI.WebControls.WebParts;
using System.Web.UI.HtmlControls;
using System.Xml;
using System.Data;
namespace RSSWebPartCS
{
    public class RSSWebPart : WebPart
    {
        // Local variables to hold web-part
        // property values
        string _url;
        bool _newPage = true;
        bool _showDescription = true;
        bool _showUrl = true;
        // Property to determine whether article should
        // be opened in same or new page
        [Personalizable]
        [WebBrowsable]
        public bool NewPage
        {
            get
            {
                return _newPage;
            }
            set
            {
                _newPage = value;
            }
        }
        // Should description be displayed?
        [Personalizable]
        [WebBrowsable]
        public bool ShowDescription
        {
            get
            {
                return _showDescription;
            }
```

```
        set
        {
            _showDescription = value;
        }
    }
    // Should URL be displayed?
    [Personalizable]
    [WebBrowsable]
    public bool ShowUrl
    {
        get
        {
            return _showUrl;
        }
        set
        {
            _showUrl = value;
        }
    }
    // Property to set URL of RSS feed
    [Personalizable]
    [WebBrowsable]
    public string Url
    {
        get
        {
            return _url;
        }
        set
        {
            _url = value;
        }
    }
    // This is where the HTML gets rendered to the
    // web-part page.
    protected override void RenderContents(HtmlTextWriter writer)
    {
        base.RenderContents(writer);
        // Step 1: Ensure Url property has been provided
        if (Url != "")
        {
            // Display heading with RSS location URL
            if (ShowUrl)
            {
                writer.WriteLine("<hr/>");
                writer.WriteLine("<span style='font-size: larger;'>");
                writer.WriteLine("Results for: ");
```

```
                    writer.WriteLine("<strong>");
                    writer.WriteLine(Url);
                    writer.WriteLine("</strong>");
                    writer.WriteLine("</span>");
                    writer.WriteLine("<hr/>");
                }
                displayRSSFeed(writer);
            }
            else
            {
                // Tell user they need to fill in the Url property
                writer.WriteLine(
                    "<font color='red'>RSS Url cannot be blank</font>");
            }
        }


        private void displayRSSFeed(HtmlTextWriter writer)
        {
            try
            {
                // Step 2: Read the RSS feed into memory
                System.Net.WebRequest wReq;
                wReq = System.Net.WebRequest.Create(Url);
                wReq.Credentials =
                    System.Net.CredentialCache.DefaultCredentials;
                // Return the response.
                System.Net.WebResponse wResp = wReq.GetResponse();
                System.IO.Stream respStream = wResp.GetResponseStream();
                // Load RSS stream into a DataSet for easier processing
                DataSet dsXML = new DataSet();
                dsXML.ReadXml(respStream);
                // Step 4: Loop through all items returned,
                // displaying results
                string target = "";
                if (NewPage)
                    target = "target='_new'";
                foreach (DataRow item in dsXML.Tables["item"].Rows)
                {
                    // Step 5: Write the title, link, and description to page
                    writer.WriteLine(
                        "<a href='" + item["link"] +
                        "' " + target + ">" + item["title"] + "</a>" +
                        "<br/>" +
                        "<span style='color:silver'>" +
                        item["pubDate"] + "</span>" +
                        "<br/>");
```

```
            if (ShowDescription)
                writer.WriteLine("<br/>" + item["description"]);
            writer.WriteLine("<hr/>");
        }
    }
    catch (Exception ex)
    {
        // Step 3: If error occurs, notify end user
        writer.WriteLine(
            "<font color='red'><strong>" +
            "An error occurred while attempting " +
            "to process the selected RSS feed. " +
            "Please verify that the url provided " +
            "references a valid RSS page." +
            "<BR/><BR/>" +
            ex.Message;
        );
    }
}
    }
  }
}
```

To Run

First, you'll need to install the web part so SharePoint recognizes it. To do so, compile the web part with a strong name. Next, copy the web part .dll to the GAC, which is usually located at C:\Windows\assembly. Last, create a <SafeControl> entry in the Web.config file of the target SharePoint web application that looks something like the following:

```
<SafeControl Assembly="RSSWebPartCS,
    Version=1.0.0.0,
    Culture=neutral,
    PublicKeyToken=5669ee1e85397acc"
    Namespace="RSSWebPartCS"
    TypeName="*"
    Safe="True" />
```

Of course, the Assembly, Version, PublicKeyToken, and Namespace attribute values will be those you assign rather than those shown in the preceding code.

■**Note** There are several ways to obtain the information needed to fill out the <SafeControl> element shown in the preceding code, including using the SN.exe (*strong name*) command or a third-party tool such as Reflector (www.aisto.com/roeder/dotnet/). The simplest in my opinion is to simply copy the signed assembly to the GAC, typically found at C:\Windows\assembly. Once there, you can right-click on the assembly name and open the properties dialog box to view the assembly name and public key.

Finally, navigate to the web-part gallery page for the site collection on which you want to place this web part (typically at `http://<yourserver>/<sitecol>_catalogs/wp/Forms/AllItems.aspx`, where `<sitecol>` is the root site of the collection). Click the New button and find your web part in the list of web-part type names. Select the checkbox to the left of the web-part type name, and click the Populate Gallery button.

Your web part should now be available to add to any web-part page in the current site collection. Select a web-part page and click the Site Actions ➤ Edit Page option. Then add your RSS web part to one of the available zones by clicking the Add a Web Part banner at the top of that zone. A list of available web parts will be displayed, including your custom RSS web part. Edit the web-part properties to provide an RSS site URL (in the following example, the target URL is `http://news.search.yahoo.com/news/rss?p=SharePoint+Search`). Figure 4-1 shows the property pane for the custom RSS web part.

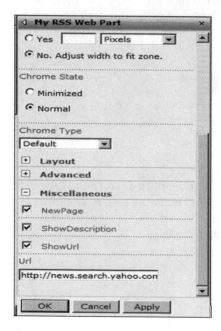

Figure 4-1. *The custom RSS web-part property pane*

Figure 4-2 shows the RSS web part in action.

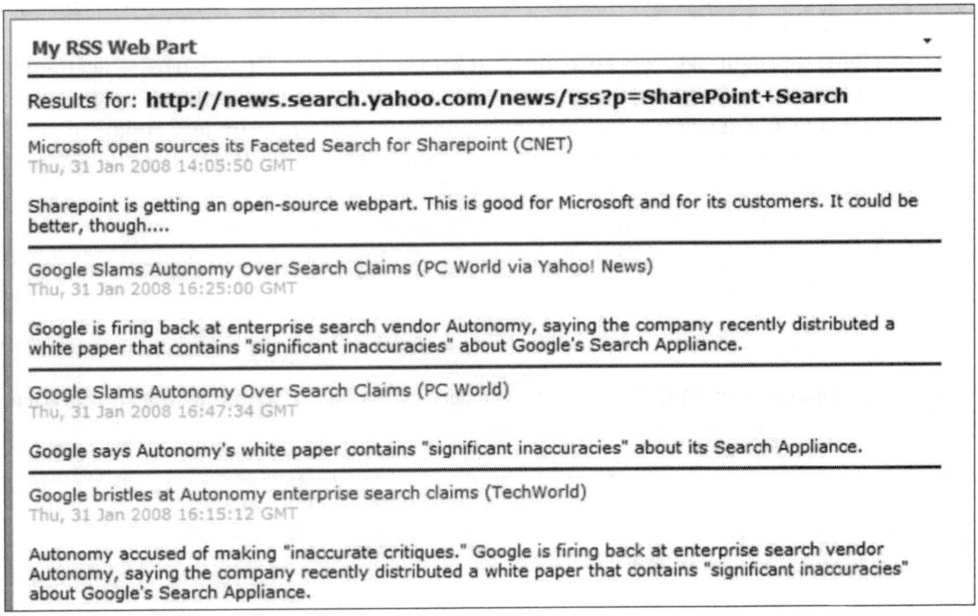

My RSS Web Part

Results for: **http://news.search.yahoo.com/news/rss?p=SharePoint+Search**

Microsoft open sources its Faceted Search for Sharepoint (CNET)
Thu, 31 Jan 2008 14:05:50 GMT

Sharepoint is getting an open-source webpart. This is good for Microsoft and for its customers. It could be better, though....

Google Slams Autonomy Over Search Claims (PC World via Yahoo! News)
Thu, 31 Jan 2008 16:25:00 GMT

Google is firing back at enterprise search vendor Autonomy, saying the company recently distributed a white paper that contains "significant inaccuracies" about Google's Search Appliance.

Google Slams Autonomy Over Search Claims (PC World)
Thu, 31 Jan 2008 16:47:34 GMT

Google says Autonomy's white paper contains "significant inaccuracies" about its Search Appliance.

Google bristles at Autonomy enterprise search claims (TechWorld)
Thu, 31 Jan 2008 16:15:12 GMT

Autonomy accused of making "inaccurate critiques." Google is firing back at enterprise search vendor Autonomy, saying the company recently distributed a white paper that contains "significant inaccuracies" about Google's Search Appliance.

Figure 4-2. *The custom RSS web part in action*

Variations

- MOSS does come with an RSS Feed web part, but this recipe adds that functionality to WSS 3.0. To mimic the MOSS web-part functionality, you could allow for the user to define XSLT that determines how the results are rendered.

Recipe 4-2. Creating an XML Web Part

As you saw in the RSS Feed recipe, XML documents can be easily loaded into an ADO.NET DataSet object. And after the XML is in a DataSet, it's a simple matter to format it by using a DataGrid web control, manipulate it programmatically, or transform it by using an XML web control (which, in my opinion would have been better named an *XSLT* control).

In this recipe, you'll create a generic web part that has several user-configurable properties indicating an XML source URL, whether the XML should be displayed by using a simple `DataGrid` or transformed by using an XSLT, and optional user credentials to use when accessing secure XML sources.

You might reasonably ask why go to the trouble of creating an XML web part, when there's one that ships with SharePoint or when you could use a `DataView` web part in SharePoint Designer. The answer is that as a developer, I want understanding and control—understanding of the underlying processes so I can anticipate and avoid problems, and control so I can deliver the specific solution that my end users need. In particular, this recipe addresses how to access secure XML sources by impersonating the currently logged-on user, or any other user, as required. It also enables you to insert any code you need to manipulate the source XML document prior to displaying it to the page.

Note This recipe builds on many of the concepts introduced in Recipe 4-1, so you may want to review that prior to whipping up an XML web part.

Recipe Type: Web Part

Ingredients

Assembly References

- `System.Web` .NET assembly

- `Windows.SharePoint.Services` .NET assembly

Special Considerations

- Because this web part uses the generic ASP.NET 2.0 web-part framework and doesn't need to communicate directly with SharePoint, we won't add a reference to the `Windows.SharePoint.Services` library. However, if you want to use the legacy SharePoint web-part framework, you will need to add that reference to the project.

Preparation

1. Create a new C# or VB.NET class library project.

2. Add a reference to the `System.Web` .NET assembly.

3. At the top of the class module, add `using` or `Includes` statements for the `System.Web.UI.WebControls` and `System.Web.UI.WebControls.WebParts` class libraries.

4. Open the project properties page, go to the Signing tab, select the Sign the Assembly checkbox, and add a new strong-name key file named something like `XMLWebPart.snk`.

Process Flow

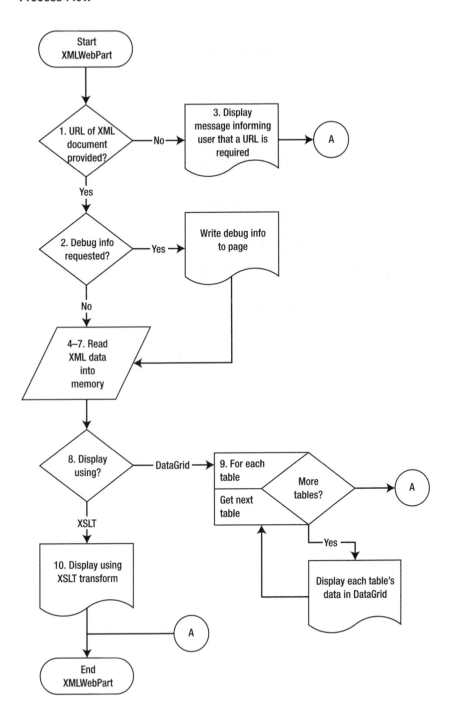

1. Make sure that the user has supplied the URL of an XML document to load. If the user has, go to step 2. If not, go to step 3.

2. If the URL has been provided, check to see whether the user has requested debug information to be displayed, and if so, display that information prior to displaying formatted XML data to the page. Go to step 4.

3. If the user *did not* supply a URL to load, display a message indicating that it's required and exit.

4. Create a new `WebRequest` object.

5. If the user has selected the `Impersonate` web-part property, set the request credentials to be those of the current user.

6. Otherwise, set the credentials based on the explicitly provided domain, user, and password.

7. Read the XML document into a `DataSet` object.

8. If the user has specified that the data should be displayed by using a `DataGrid`, go to step 9. Otherwise, go to step 10.

9. Loop through the collection of tables in the `DataSet` created in step 7, displaying the table name and a `DataGrid` containing all data in that table.

10. Create a new XML web control and set its contents to the XML in memory, read from the `DataSet` object. Set the XML web control's `TransformSource` to the path provided in the XSLT property of the web part.

Recipe—VB (See Project XMLWebPartVB, Class XMLWebPart.vb)

```vb
Imports System
Imports System.Web
Imports System.Web.Security
Imports System.Web.UI
Imports System.Web.UI.WebControls
Imports System.Web.UI.WebControls.WebParts
Imports System.Web.UI.HtmlControls
Imports System.Xml
Imports System.Data
Public Class XMLWebPart
    Inherits WebPart
    ' Local variable to hold property values
    Private _url As String = ""
    Private _impersonate As Boolean = True
    Private _domain As String = ""
    Private _user As String = ""
    Private _password As String = ""
    Private _debug As Boolean = False
    Private _formatUsing As enumFormatUsing = enumFormatUsing.DataGrid
```

```vb
Private _xsltPath As String = ""
'ENUM types will result in drop-down lists in
'the web-part property sheet
Public Enum enumFormatUsing
    DataGrid = 1
    XSLT = 2
End Enum
' Property to set URL of source XML document
<Personalizable()> _
<WebBrowsable()> _
<WebDisplayName("Url of XML document")> _
Public Property Url() As String
    Get
        Return _url
    End Get
    Set(ByVal value As String)
        _url = value
    End Set
End Property
'Create property to determine whether DataGrid or
'XSLT should be used to format output
<Personalizable(PersonalizationScope.[Shared]), _
    WebBrowsable(), _
    WebDisplayName("Format Using:"), _
    WebDescription("What method do you want " + _
    "to use to format the results.")> _
Public Property FormatUsing() As enumFormatUsing
    Get
        Return _formatUsing
    End Get
    Set(ByVal value As enumFormatUsing)
        _formatUsing = value
    End Set
End Property
'If XSLT will be used, this property specifies
'its server-relative path
<Personalizable(PersonalizationScope.[Shared]), _
    WebBrowsable(), _
    WebDisplayName("XSLT Path:"), _
    WebDescription("If formatting with XSLT, " + _
    "provide full path to XSLT document.")> _
Public Property XSLTPath() As String
    Get
        Return _xsltPath
    End Get
```

```vb
            Set(ByVal value As String)
                _xsltPath = value
            End Set
        End Property
        ' If explicit credentials have been requested,
        ' the following three properties, Domain, User, and
        ' Password, will be used to construct the credentials
        ' to pass to the page
        <Personalizable()> _
        <WebBrowsable()> _
        Public Property Domain() As String
            Get
                Return _domain
            End Get
            Set(ByVal value As String)
                _domain = value
            End Set
        End Property
        <Personalizable()> _
        <WebBrowsable()> _
        Public Property User() As String
            Get
                Return _user
            End Get
            Set(ByVal value As String)
                _user = value
            End Set
        End Property
        <Personalizable()> _
        <WebBrowsable()> _
        Public Property Password() As String
            Get
                Return _password
            End Get
            Set(ByVal value As String)
                _password = value
            End Set
        End Property
        ' If this option is checked, the web part will use
        ' the default credentials of the user viewing
        ' the web-part page.
        <Personalizable()> _
        <WebBrowsable()> _
        Public Property Impersonate() As Boolean
            Get
                Return _impersonate
            End Get
```

```vbnet
        Set(ByVal value As Boolean)
            _impersonate = value
        End Set
    End Property
    ' Display debug info?
    <Personalizable()> _
    <WebBrowsable()> _
    Public Property Debug() As Boolean
        Get
            Return _debug
        End Get
        Set(ByVal value As Boolean)
            _debug = value
        End Set
    End Property
    ' This is where the HTML gets rendered to the
    ' web-part page.
    Protected Overloads Overrides Sub RenderContents( _
       ByVal writer As HtmlTextWriter)
        MyBase.RenderContents(writer)
         ' Step 1: Ensure Url property has been provided
        If Url <> "" Then
            ' Step 2: If debug info requested, display it
            If Debug Then
                writer.WriteLine("Url: " + Url + "<br/>")
                writer.WriteLine("Impersonate: " + _
                    Impersonate.ToString() + "<br/>")
                writer.WriteLine("Domain: " + Domain + "<br/>")
                writer.WriteLine("User: " + User + "<br/>")
                writer.WriteLine("Password: " + Password + "<br/>")
                writer.WriteLine("Format using: " + _
                    FormatUsing.ToString() + "<br/>")
                writer.WriteLine("<hr/>")
            End If
            ' Call helper function to render data as HTML to page
            displayXML(writer)
        Else
            ' Step 3: Tell user they need to fill in the Url property
            writer.WriteLine( _
                "<font color='red'>Source XML url cannot be blank</font>")
        End If
    End Sub
    Private Sub displayXML(ByVal writer As HtmlTextWriter)
        Try
            ' Step 4: Read the XML document into memory
            Dim wReq As System.Net.WebRequest
            wReq = System.Net.WebRequest.Create(Url)
```

```vbnet
                    ' Step 5: Set the security as appropriate
                    If Impersonate Then
                        wReq.Credentials = _
                            System.Net.CredentialCache.DefaultCredentials
                    Else
                        wReq.Credentials = _
                            New System.Net.NetworkCredential(User, Password, Domain)
                    End If
                    wReq.Credentials = System.Net.CredentialCache.DefaultCredentials
                    ' Step 6: Return the response.
                    Dim wResp As System.Net.WebResponse = wReq.GetResponse()
                    Dim respStream As System.IO.Stream = wResp.GetResponseStream()
                    ' Step 7: Load XML stream into a DataSet for easier processing
                    Dim dsXML As New DataSet()
                    dsXML.ReadXml(respStream)
                    ' Step 8: Determine display mechanism to use
                    If FormatUsing = enumFormatUsing.DataGrid Then
                        ' Step 9: Loop through each table in the DataSet,
                        ' displaying each in a DataGrid
                        Dim dgXML As DataGrid
                        Dim lbl As Label
                        For Each dtXML As DataTable In dsXML.Tables
                            ' Display table name
                            lbl = New Label()
                            lbl.Text = "<br/><strong>" + _
                                dtXML.TableName.ToUpper() + "</strong><br/><br/>"
                            lbl.RenderControl(writer)
                            ' Now display the data
                            dgXML = New DataGrid()
                            dgXML.DataSource = dtXML
                            dgXML.DataBind()
                            dgXML.RenderControl(writer)
                        Next
                    Else
                        ' Step 10: Format using provided XSLT
                        Dim xml As New System.Web.UI.WebControls.Xml()
                        xml.DocumentContent = dsXML.GetXml()
                        xml.TransformSource = XSLTPath
                        xml.RenderControl(writer)
                    End If
                Catch ex As Exception
                    ' If error occurs, notify end user
                    writer.WriteLine("<font color='red'><strong>" + _
                        ex.Message + "</font>")
                End Try
            End Sub
        End Class
```

Recipe—C# (See Project XMLWebPartCS, Class XMLWebPart.cs)

```csharp
using System;
using System.Web;
using System.Web.Security;
using System.Web.UI;
using System.Web.UI.WebControls;
using System.Web.UI.WebControls.WebParts;
using System.Web.UI.HtmlControls;
using System.Xml;
using System.Data;
namespace XMLWebPartCS
{
    public class XMLWebPart : WebPart
    {
        // Local variable to hold property values
        string _url = "";
        bool _impersonate = true;
        string _domain = "";
        string _user = "";
        string _password = "";
        bool _debug = false;
        enumFormatUsing _formatUsing = enumFormatUsing.DataGrid;
        string _xsltPath = "";
        //ENUM types will result in drop-down lists in
        //the web-part property sheet
        public enum enumFormatUsing
        {
            DataGrid = 1,
            XSLT = 2
        }
        // Property to set URL of source XML document
        [Personalizable]
        [WebBrowsable]
        [WebDisplayName("Url of XML document")]
        public string Url
        {
            get
            {
                return _url;
            }
            set
            {
                _url = value;
            }
        }
```

```
//Create property to determine whether DataGrid or
//XSLT should be used to format output
[Personalizable(PersonalizationScope.Shared), WebBrowsable(),
    WebDisplayName("Format Using:"),
    WebDescription("What method do you want " +
        "to use to format the results.")]
public enumFormatUsing FormatUsing
{
    get { return _formatUsing; }
    set { _formatUsing = value; }
}
//If XSLT will be used, this property specifies
//its server-relative path
[Personalizable(PersonalizationScope.Shared),
    WebBrowsable(), WebDisplayName("XSLT Path:"),
    WebDescription("If formatting with XSLT, " +
        "provide full path to XSLT document.")]
public string XSLTPath
{
    get { return _xsltPath; }
    set { _xsltPath = value; }
}
// If explicit credentials have been requested,
// the following three properties, Domain, User, and
// Password, will be used to construct the credentials
// to pass to the page
[Personalizable]
[WebBrowsable]
public string Domain
{
    get
    {
        return _domain;
    }
    set
    {
        _domain = value;
    }
}
[Personalizable]
[WebBrowsable]
public string User
{
    get
    {
        return _user;
    }
```

```csharp
        set
        {
            _user = value;
        }
    }
    [Personalizable]
    [WebBrowsable]
    public string Password
    {
        get
        {
            return _password;
        }
        set
        {
            _password = value;
        }
    }
    // If this option is checked, the web part will use
    // the default credentials of the user viewing
    // the web-part page.
    [Personalizable]
    [WebBrowsable]
    public bool Impersonate
    {
        get
        {
            return _impersonate;
        }
        set
        {
            _impersonate = value;
        }
    }
    // Display debug info?
    [Personalizable]
    [WebBrowsable]
    public bool Debug
    {
        get
        {
            return _debug;
        }
        set
        {
            _debug = value;
        }
    }
```

```csharp
// This is where the HTML gets rendered to the
// web-part page.
protected override void RenderContents(HtmlTextWriter writer)
{
    base.RenderContents(writer);
    // Step 1: Ensure Url property has been provided
    if (Url != "")
    {
        // Step 2: If debug info requested, display it
        if (Debug)
        {
            writer.WriteLine("Url: " + Url + "<br/>");
            writer.WriteLine("Impersonate: " +
                Impersonate.ToString() + "<br/>");
            writer.WriteLine("Domain: " + Domain + "<br/>");
            writer.WriteLine("User: " + User + "<br/>");
            writer.WriteLine("Password: " + Password + "<br/>");
            writer.WriteLine("Format using: " + FormatUsing +
                "<br/>");
            writer.WriteLine("<hr/>");
        }
        // Call helper function to render data as HTML to page
        displayXML(writer);
    }
    else
    {
        // Step 3: Tell user they need to fill in the Url property
        writer.WriteLine(
            "<font color='red'>Source XML url cannot be blank</font>");
    }
}
private void displayXML(HtmlTextWriter writer)
{
    try
    {
        // Step 4: Read the XML data into memory
        System.Net.WebRequest wReq;
        wReq = System.Net.WebRequest.Create(Url);
        // Step 5: Set the security as appropriate
        if (Impersonate)
        {
            wReq.Credentials =
                System.Net.CredentialCache.DefaultCredentials;
        }
```

```
else
{
    wReq.Credentials = new System.Net.NetworkCredential(
        User, Password, Domain);
}
wReq.Credentials =
    System.Net.CredentialCache.DefaultCredentials;
// Step 6: Return the response.
System.Net.WebResponse wResp = wReq.GetResponse();
System.IO.Stream respStream = wResp.GetResponseStream();
// Step 7: Load XML stream into a DataSet for easier
// processing
DataSet dsXML = new DataSet();
dsXML.ReadXml(respStream);
// Step 8: Determine display mechanism to use
if (FormatUsing == enumFormatUsing.DataGrid)
{
    // Step 9: Loop through each table in the DataSet,
    // displaying each in a DataGrid
    DataGrid dgXML;
    Label lbl;
    foreach (DataTable dtXML in dsXML.Tables)
    {
        // Display table name
        lbl = new Label();
        lbl.Text = "<br/><strong>" +
            dtXML.TableName.ToUpper() +
            "</strong><br/><br/>";
        lbl.RenderControl(writer);
        // Now display the data
        dgXML = new DataGrid();
        dgXML.DataSource = dtXML;
        dgXML.DataBind();
        dgXML.RenderControl(writer);
    }
}
else
{
    // Step 10: Format using provided XSLT
    System.Web.UI.WebControls.Xml xml =
        new System.Web.UI.WebControls.Xml();
    xml.DocumentContent = dsXML.GetXml();
    xml.TransformSource = XSLTPath;
    xml.RenderControl(writer);
}
}
```

```
            catch (Exception ex)
            {
                // If error occurs, notify end user
                writer.WriteLine("<font color='red'><strong>" +
                    ex.Message + "</font>");
            }
        }
    }
}
```

Recipe—XML Document (See Project XMLWebPartCS, File SampleXMLSource.xml)

The following listing provides the sample XML document that was used in conjunction with the XSLT that appears in the next section. The XML web part is designed, however, to work with any valid XML document.

```xml
<?xml version="1.0" encoding="utf-8"?>
<CustomerData>
    <Customer>
        <Name>ABC Corp.</Name>
        <Address>100 Main Street</Address>
        <Phone>(415) 999-1234</Phone>
        <Order>
            <OrderNo>1000</OrderNo>
            <Product>Widgets</Product>
            <Qty>10</Qty>
            <UnitPrice>100</UnitPrice>
            <ExtPrice>1000</ExtPrice>
        </Order>
        <Order>
            <OrderNo>1001</OrderNo>
            <Product>Gadget</Product>
            <Qty>50</Qty>
            <UnitPrice>50</UnitPrice>
            <ExtPrice>2500</ExtPrice>
        </Order>
        <Order>
            <OrderNo>0113</OrderNo>
            <Product>WhatsIt</Product>
            <Qty>100</Qty>
            <UnitPrice>70</UnitPrice>
            <ExtPrice>7000</ExtPrice>
        </Order>
    </Customer>
```

```
    <Customer>
        <Name>XYZ Inc.</Name>
        <Address>123 Center Avenue</Address>
        <Phone>(650) 789-1234</Phone>
        <Order>
            <OrderNo>2000</OrderNo>
            <Product>Laptop</Product>
            <Qty>10</Qty>
            <UnitPrice>1000</UnitPrice>
            <ExtPrice>10000</ExtPrice>
        </Order>
        <Order>
            <OrderNo>2001</OrderNo>
            <Product>Memory</Product>
            <Qty>50</Qty>
            <UnitPrice>100</UnitPrice>
            <ExtPrice>5000</ExtPrice>
        </Order>
        <Order>
            <OrderNo>2003</OrderNo>
            <Product>LCD</Product>
            <Qty>100</Qty>
            <UnitPrice>300</UnitPrice>
            <ExtPrice>30000</ExtPrice>
        </Order>
    </Customer>
</CustomerData>
```

Recipe—XSLT

You could, of course, create any number of XSLT transforms to format the sample data. That's exactly the point of XSLT: to allow you to separate the source data from the means to display it. The following XSLT was used to provide the sample output in the "To Run" section:

```
<?xml version="1.0" encoding="utf-8"?>
<xsl:stylesheet version="1.0" xmlns:xsl="http://www.w3.org/1999/XSL/Transform">
   <xsl:output method="html"/>
   <xsl:template match="/">
      <xsl:for-each select="CustomerData/Customer">
         <h1>Orders for <xsl:value-of select="Name"/></h1>
         Address: <xsl:value-of select="Address"/><br/>
         Phone: <xsl:value-of select="Phone"/><br/><br/>
         <table cellpadding="3" cellspacing="3" width="80%">
            <tr valign="bottom">
               <td>
                  <strong>
                     <u>Order #</u>
                  </strong>
               </td>
```

```
    <td>
        <strong>
            <u>Product</u>
        </strong>
    </td>
    <td align="center">
        <strong>
            <u>Quanty</u>
        </strong>
    </td>
    <td align="right">
        <strong>
            Unit<br/><u>Price</u>
        </strong>
    </td>
    <td align="right">
        <strong>
            Extended<br/><u>Price</u>
        </strong>
    </td>
</tr>
<xsl:for-each select="Order">
    <tr>
        <td>
            <xsl:value-of select="OrderNo"/>
        </td>
        <td>
            <xsl:value-of select="Product"/>
        </td>
        <td align="center">
            <xsl:value-of select="Qty"/>
        </td>
        <td align="right">
        <xsl:value-of select="format-number(UnitPrice,'$ #,###')"/>
        </td>
        <td align="right">
        <xsl:value-of select="format-number(ExtPrice,'$ #,###')"/>
        </td>
    </tr>
</xsl:for-each>
```

```
        <tr>
          <td colspan="4"/>
          <td align="right">
            ==========
          </td>
        </tr>
        <tr>
          <td colspan="4"/>
          <td align="right">
      <xsl:value-of select="format-number(sum(Order/ExtPrice),'$ #,###')"/>
          </td>
        </tr>
      </table>
    </xsl:for-each>
  </xsl:template>
</xsl:stylesheet>
```

To Run

> **Note** Please see the "To Run" section of Recipe 4-1 for instructions on how to deploy a web part to a single site collection. After the web part has been successfully deployed, proceed with the following steps.

After the web part has been successfully deployed, you can add your custom XML web part to any page in the site collection, open the web-part property sheet, and provide a URL to an XML document.

> **Note** The SampleSourceXML used for the following example should be saved to a folder that is served by IIS or some other web server, and that can be read from your SharePoint server.

After you have set the URL property of the web part and selected the Debug checkbox, save your changes to display a result similar to that shown in Figure 4-3.

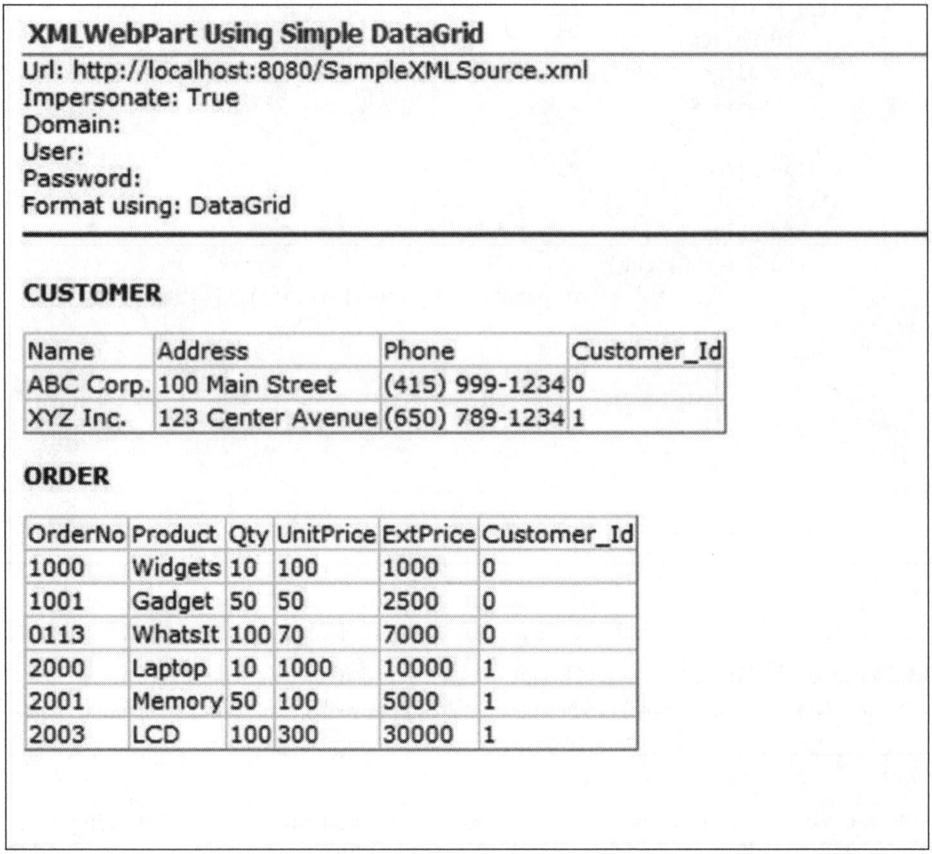

XMLWebPart Using Simple DataGrid

Url: http://localhost:8080/SampleXMLSource.xml
Impersonate: True
Domain:
User:
Password:
Format using: DataGrid

CUSTOMER

Name	Address	Phone	Customer_Id
ABC Corp.	100 Main Street	(415) 999-1234	0
XYZ Inc.	123 Center Avenue	(650) 789-1234	1

ORDER

OrderNo	Product	Qty	UnitPrice	ExtPrice	Customer_Id
1000	Widgets	10	100	1000	0
1001	Gadget	50	50	2500	0
0113	WhatsIt	100	70	7000	0
2000	Laptop	10	1000	10000	1
2001	Memory	50	100	5000	1
2003	LCD	100	300	30000	1

Figure 4-3. *The XML web part in debug mode*

Note that ADO.NET has inserted a Customer_Id column that did not appear in the source XML. .NET does this to maintain the parent-child relationship that is implicit in the XML.

Now let's spruce things up a bit. Open the web-part property pane and select XSLT from the Format drop-down list. Next enter a *server-relative* path to an XSLT document.

■Note The XSLT can simply be copied to a shared location on your SharePoint server. Then enter the Universal Naming Convention (UNC) of that location.

The resulting web-part output will look something like that shown in Figure 4-4.

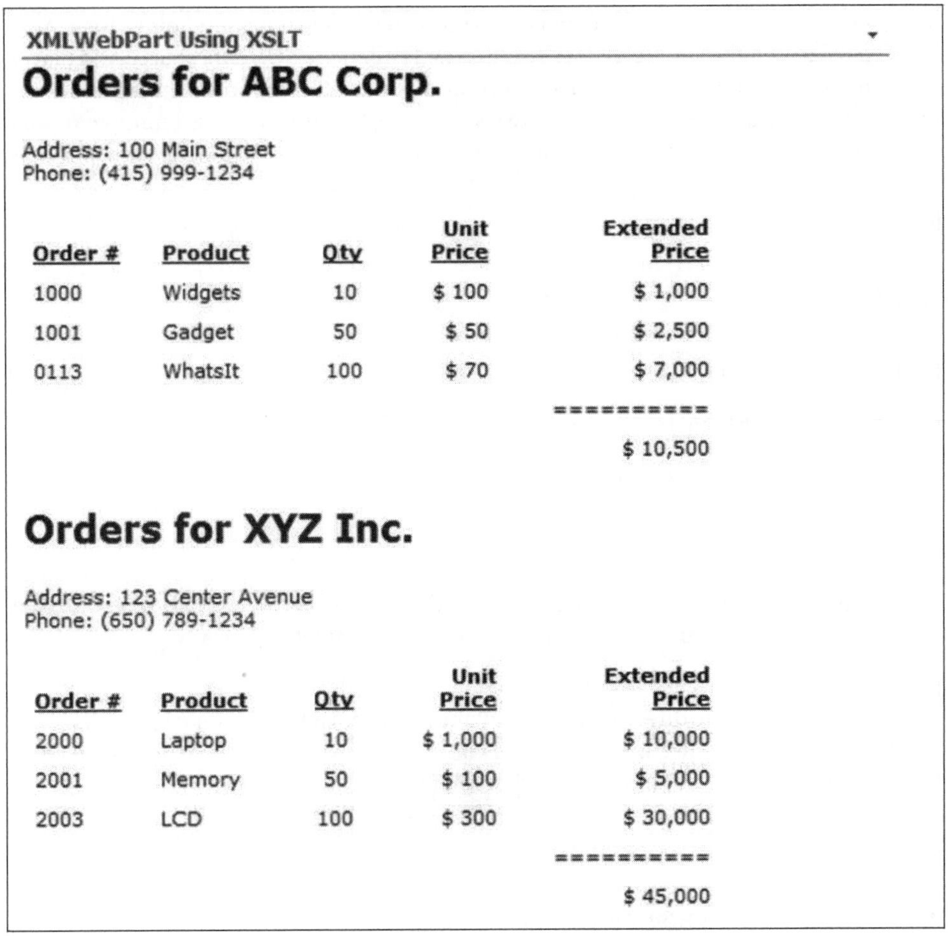

XMLWebPart Using XSLT   ▾

Orders for ABC Corp.

Address: 100 Main Street
Phone: (415) 999-1234

Order #	Product	Qty	Unit Price	Extended Price
1000	Widgets	10	$ 100	$ 1,000
1001	Gadget	50	$ 50	$ 2,500
0113	WhatsIt	100	$ 70	$ 7,000
				==========
				$ 10,500

Orders for XYZ Inc.

Address: 123 Center Avenue
Phone: (650) 789-1234

Order #	Product	Qty	Unit Price	Extended Price
2000	Laptop	10	$ 1,000	$ 10,000
2001	Memory	50	$ 100	$ 5,000
2003	LCD	100	$ 300	$ 30,000
				==========
				$ 45,000

Figure 4-4. *Fully formatted output using the XML web part*

Variations

- Modify the recipe to allow the XSLT to be retrieved from a document library in Share-Point rather than from the physical server, to allow for collaboration and development directly within the site.

Recipe 4-3. Creating a SQL Web Part

This recipe shows you how to create one of the most useful web parts, one that can be used to query and format any SQL data source that can be accessed from your SharePoint server. At its core, this web part is quite simple. It does two things: 1) queries a SQL data source and places the results of the query into a `DataSet` in memory, and 2) uses XSLT to format the result set and display it on the page using HTML. In those two simple steps, you'll find a vast number of solutions to the problem of formatting external SQL data sources.

Recipe Type: Web Part

Ingredients

Class Library References

- `System.Web.UI.WebControls.WebParts` class library

- `System.Web.UI.WebControls` class library

Special Considerations

- Remember that the queries are being executed from the SharePoint web server, so that server must have the ability to communicate with the target SQL server.

- Because this web part uses the generic ASP.NET 2.0 web-part framework and doesn't need to communicate directly with SharePoint, we won't add a reference to the `Windows.SharePoint.Services` library. However, if you want to use the legacy SharePoint web-part framework, you will need to add that reference to the project.

Preparation

1. Create a new C# or VB.NET class library project.

2. Add a reference to the `System.Web` .NET assembly.

3. At the top of the class module, add `using` or `Includes` statements for the `System.Web.UI.WebControls` and `System.Web.UI.WebControls.WebParts` class libraries.

4. Open the project properties page, go to the Signing tab, select the Sign the Assembly checkbox, and add a new strong-name key file named something like `SQLWebPart.snk`.

Process Flow

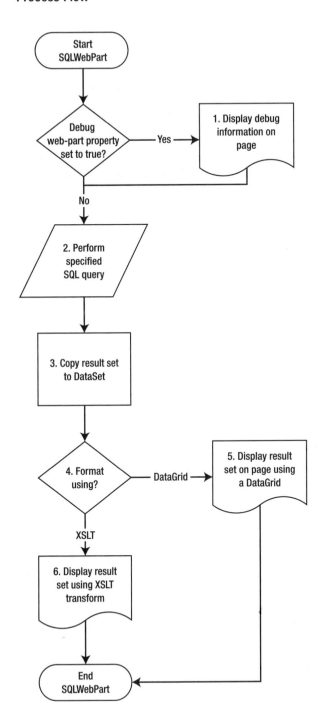

1. If the web part's debug property has been selected, display the property settings prior to displaying the formatted output.

2. Query the database to return one or more tables in a result set.

3. Load the result set into a DataSet object.

4. Determine whether the format property has been set to DataGrid or XSLT.

5. If it has been set to DataGrid, assign the DataSet as the source for a DataGrid web control and display that.

6. Otherwise, assign the specified XSLT document to the TransformSource property of the XML web control, assign the DataSet as the document, and then add the control to the page.

Recipe—VB (See Project SQLWebPartVB, Class SQLWebPart.vb)

```
Imports System.Web.UI.WebControls
Imports System.Web.UI.WebControls.WebParts
Imports System.Data
Imports System.Xml
Public Class SQLWebPart
    Inherits WebPart
    'Define local variables to contain property values
    Private _connectionString As String = ""
    Private _connectionKey As String = ""
    Private _query As String = ""
    Private _formatUsing As enumFormatUsing = enumFormatUsing.DataGrid
    Private _xsltPath As String = ""
    Private _includeDebugInfo As Boolean = False
    'ENUM types will result in drop-down lists in
    'the web-part property sheet
    Public Enum enumFormatUsing
        DataGrid = 1
        XSLT = 2
    End Enum
    'Create property to hold SQL connection string
    <Personalizable( _
        PersonalizationScope.Shared), _
        WebBrowsable(), _
        WebDisplayName("Connection String:"), _
        WebDescription("Connection string to use" & _
            " when connecting to SQL source.")> _
    Property ConnectionString() As String
        Get
            Return _connectionString
        End Get
```

```vb
            Set(ByVal Value As String)
                _connectionString = Value
            End Set
        End Property
        'Create property to hold SQL query
        <Personalizable( _
            PersonalizationScope.Shared), _
            WebBrowsable(), _
            WebDisplayName("SQL Query:"), _
            WebDescription("A valid SQL query to execute.")> _
        Property Query() As String
            Get
                Return _query
            End Get
            Set(ByVal Value As String)
                _query = Value
            End Set
        End Property
        'Create property to determine whether DataGrid or
        'XSLT should be used to format output
        <Personalizable( _
            PersonalizationScope.Shared), _
            WebBrowsable(), WebDisplayName("Format Using:"), _
            WebDescription("What method do you want " & _
                "to use to format the results.")> _
        Property FormatUsing() As enumFormatUsing
            Get
                Return _formatUsing
            End Get
            Set(ByVal Value As enumFormatUsing)
                _formatUsing = Value
            End Set
        End Property
        'If XSLT will be used, this property specifies
        'its path
        <Personalizable( _
            PersonalizationScope.Shared), _
            WebBrowsable(), _
            WebDisplayName("XSLT Path:"), _
            WebDescription("If formatting with XSLT, " & _
                "provide full path to XSLT document.")> _
        Property XSLTPath() As String
            Get
                Return _xsltPath
            End Get
```

```vbnet
            Set(ByVal Value As String)
                _xsltPath = Value
            End Set
        End Property
        'Even though our web parts never have bugs…
        <Personalizable( _
            PersonalizationScope.Shared), _
            WebBrowsable(), _
            WebDisplayName("Include Debug Info?:"), _
            WebDescription("If selected, will " & _
                "display values of web part properties.")> _
        Property IncludeDebugInfo() As Boolean
            Get
                Return _includeDebugInfo
            End Get
            Set(ByVal Value As Boolean)
                _includeDebugInfo = Value
            End Set
        End Property
        'This is where the real work happens!
        Protected Overrides Sub RenderContents( _
                ByVal writer As System.Web.UI.HtmlTextWriter)
            'Process any output from the base class first
            MyBase.RenderContents(writer)
            ' Step 1: Display debug info if requested
            If IncludeDebugInfo Then
                writer.Write("Connection String: " & ConnectionString)
                writer.WriteBreak()
                writer.Write("SQL Query: " & Query)
                writer.WriteBreak()
                writer.Write("Format Using: " & FormatUsing.ToString)
                writer.WriteBreak()
                writer.Write("XSLT Path: " & XSLTPath)
                writer.Write("<hr>")
            End If
            ' Step 2: Query SQL database and return the result set
            Dim con As New SqlClient.SqlConnection(ConnectionString)
            Try
                con.Open()
            Catch ex As Exception
                writer.Write("<font color='red'>" & ex.Message & "</font>")
                Exit Sub
            End Try
            Dim da As New SqlClient.SqlDataAdapter(Query, con)
            Dim ds As New DataSet
            ' Step 3: Copy result set to DataSet
```

```
        Try
            da.Fill(ds)
        Catch ex As Exception
            writer.Write("<font color='red'>" & ex.Message & "</font>")
            Exit Sub
        End Try
        ' Step 4: Format the output using an XSLT or DataGrid
        If FormatUsing = enumFormatUsing.DataGrid Then
            ' Step 5: Format using simple DataGrid
            Dim dg As New DataGrid
            dg.DataSource = ds
            dg.DataBind()
            dg.RenderControl(writer)
        Else
            ' Step 6: Format using provided XSLT
            Dim xml As New System.Web.UI.WebControls.Xml
            xml.DocumentContent = ds.GetXml
            xml.TransformSource = XSLTPath
            xml.RenderControl(writer)
        End If
    End Sub
End Class
```

Recipe—C# (See Project SQLWebPartCS, Class SQLWebPartCS.cs)

```csharp
using System;
using System.Collections.Generic;
using System.Text;
using System.Web.UI.WebControls;
using System.Web.UI.WebControls.WebParts;
using System.Data;
using System.Xml;
namespace SQLWebPartCS
{
    public class SQLWebPartCS : WebPart
    {
        //Define local variables to contain property values
        string _connectionString = "";
        string _query = "";
        enumFormatUsing _formatUsing = enumFormatUsing.DataGrid;
        string _xsltPath = "";
        bool _includeDebugInfo = false;
        //ENUM types will result in drop-down lists in
        //the web-part property sheet
```

```csharp
public enum enumFormatUsing
{
    DataGrid = 1,
    XSLT = 2
}
//Create property to hold SQL connection string
[Personalizable(PersonalizationScope.Shared),
    WebBrowsable(), WebDisplayName("Connection String:"),
    WebDescription("Connection string to use" +
    " when connecting to SQL source.")]
public string ConnectionString
{
    get { return _connectionString; }
    set { _connectionString = value; }
}
//Create property to hold SQL query
[Personalizable(PersonalizationScope.Shared),
    WebBrowsable(), WebDisplayName("SQL Query:"),
  WebDescription("A valid SQL query to execute.")]
public string Query
{
    get { return _query; }
    set { _query = value; }
}
//Create property to determine whether DataGrid or
//XSLT should be used to format output
[Personalizable(PersonalizationScope.Shared),
    WebBrowsable(), WebDisplayName("Format Using:"),
    WebDescription("What method do you want " +
    "to use to format the results.")]
public enumFormatUsing FormatUsing
{
    get { return _formatUsing; }
    set { _formatUsing = value; }
}
//If XSLT will be used, this property specifies
//its path
[Personalizable(PersonalizationScope.Shared),
    WebBrowsable(), WebDisplayName("XSLT Path:"),
    WebDescription("If formatting with XSLT, " +
    "provide full path to XSLT document.")]
public string XSLTPath
{
    get { return _xsltPath; }
    set { _xsltPath = value; }
}
```

```csharp
//Even though our web parts never have bugs…
[Personalizable(PersonalizationScope.Shared),
   WebBrowsable(), WebDisplayName("Include Debug Info?:"),
   WebDescription("If selected, will " +
   "display values of web part properties.")]
public bool IncludeDebugInfo
{
    get { return _includeDebugInfo; }
    set { _includeDebugInfo = value; }
}
//This is where the real work happens!
protected override void RenderContents(
   System.Web.UI.HtmlTextWriter writer)
{
    //Process any output from the base class first
    base.RenderContents(writer);
    // Step 1: Display debug info if requested
    if (IncludeDebugInfo)
    {
        writer.Write("Connection String: " + ConnectionString);
        writer.WriteBreak();
        writer.Write("SQL Query: " + Query);
        writer.WriteBreak();
        writer.Write("Format Using: " + FormatUsing.ToString());
        writer.WriteBreak();
        writer.Write("XSLT Path: " + XSLTPath);
        writer.Write("<hr>");
    }
    // Step 2: Query SQL database and return the result set
    System.Data.SqlClient.SqlConnection con =
       new System.Data.SqlClient.SqlConnection(ConnectionString);
    try
    {
        con.Open();
    }
    catch (Exception ex)
    {
        writer.Write("<font color='red'>" + ex.Message + "</font>");
        return;
    }
    System.Data.SqlClient.SqlDataAdapter da =
       new System.Data.SqlClient.SqlDataAdapter(Query, con);
    DataSet ds = new DataSet();
```

```
            // Step 3: Copy result set to DataSet
            try
            {
                da.Fill(ds);
            }
            catch (Exception ex)
            {
                writer.Write("<font color='red'>" + ex.Message + "</font>");
                return;
            }
            // Step 4: Format the output using an XSLT or DataGrid
            if (FormatUsing == enumFormatUsing.DataGrid)
            {
                // Step 5: Format using simple DataGrid
                DataGrid dg = new DataGrid();
                dg.DataSource = ds;
                dg.DataBind();
                dg.RenderControl(writer);
            }
            else
            {
                // Step 6: Format using provided XSLT
                System.Web.UI.WebControls.Xml xml =
                    new System.Web.UI.WebControls.Xml();
                xml.DocumentContent = ds.GetXml();
                xml.TransformSource = XSLTPath;
                xml.RenderControl(writer);
            }
        }
    }
}
```

Recipe—XSLT (See Project SQLWebPartVB, File Presidents.xslt)

As I've noted before, XML Transformations (XSLT) is an incredibly powerful technology for manipulating any XML source, including of course the contents of any .NET DataSet or DataTable object. XSLT can be used to render XML as HTML for display, or to write XML to a new XML document with a different structure. In this case, we want to use XSLT to render our sample data as HTML for display on a web-part page. The following XSLT will be used in our example:

```
<?xml version="1.0" encoding="UTF-8" ?>
<xsl:stylesheet version="1.0"
xmlns:xsl="http://www.w3.org/1999/XSL/Transform">
  <xsl:template match="/">
    <table cellpadding="3" cellspacing="0">
        <tr>
            <td>
                <u><strong>President</strong></u>
            </td>
```

```
                    <td align="center">
                        <u>
                            <strong>Years In Office</strong>
                        </u>
                    </td>
                    <td style="width: 10px"/>
                    <td style="background-color: silver; width: 1px"/>
                    <td style="width: 10px"/>
                    <td>
                        <u><strong>President</strong></u>
                    </td>
                    <td>
                        <u><strong>Years In Office</strong></u>
                    </td>
                </tr>
                <xsl:for-each select="NewDataSet/Table">
                    <xsl:if test="position() mod 2 = 1">
                        <xsl:text disable-output-escaping="yes">
                            &lt;tr&gt;
                        </xsl:text>
                    </xsl:if>
                    <td>
                        <xsl:value-of select="Name"/>
                    </td>
                    <td align="center">
                        <xsl:value-of select="YearsInOffice"/>
                    </td>
                    <xsl:if test="position() mod 2 = 1">
                        <td style="width: 10px"/>
                        <td style="background-color: silver; width: 1px"/>
                        <td style="width: 10px"/>
                    </xsl:if>
                    <xsl:if test="position() mod 2 = 0">
                        <xsl:text disable-output-escaping="yes">
                            &lt;/tr&gt;
                        </xsl:text>
                    </xsl:if>
                </xsl:for-each>
            </table>
        </xsl:template>
    </xsl:stylesheet>
```

■**Note** Although Visual Studio .NET has very basic XML and XSLT editing capabilities, you may want to investigate third-party editors such as Stylus Studio from Progress Software, or XMLSpy from Altova.

To Run

After you have added the SQL web part to a web-part page, you're ready to try it out.

■**Note** Please see the "To Run" section of Recipe 4-1 for instructions on how to deploy a web part to a single site collection. After the web part has been successfully deployed, proceed with the following steps.

The following example assumes the SQL data source provided in Table 4-1.

Table 4-1. *Presidents SQL Table Definition*

Database name	MyDatabase
Table name	Presidents
User login	MyDatabaseUser, password password
Connection string	Data Source=MGEROW-MOSS-VPC; Initial Catalog=MyDatabase; UID=MyDatabaseUser; PWD=password
SQL query	select * from Presidents
Table definition	CREATE TABLE [dbo].[Presidents]([Name] [varchar](50) NULL [YearsInOffice] [varchar](50) NULL, [Id] [int] IDENTITY(1,1) NOT NULL)

Of course, you will likely use a different server, and there is no requirement that you even use the same query—although if you choose to change the query, you will also need to change the XSLT accordingly.

Figure 4-5 shows the SQL web part in action. Figure 4-6 shows the associated custom properties on the web-part property sheet.

SQLWebPartCS - Presidents of the United States		edit ▾	×

Connection String: Data Source=MGEROW-MOSS-VPC; Initial Catalog=MyDatabase;
UID=MyDatabaseUser; PWD=password
SQL Query: select * from Presidents
Format Using: XSLT
XSLT Path: C:\SharePoint Recipe Solutions\Chapter 4\SQLWebPartVB\Presidents.xslt

President	Years In Office	President	Years In Office
George Washington	1789-1797	John Adams	1797-1801
Thomas Jefferson	1801-1809	James Madison	1809-1817
James Monroe	1817-1825	John Quincy Adams	1825-1829
Andrew Jackson	1829-1837	Martin Van Buren	1837-1841
William Henry Harrison	1841	John Tyler	1841-1845
James Knox Polk	1845-1849	Zachary Taylor	1849-1850
Millard Fillmore	1850-1853	Franklin Pierce	1853-1857
James Buchanan	1857-1861	Abraham Lincoln	1861-1865
Andrew Johnson	1865-1869	Ulysses Simpson Grant	1869-1877
Rutherford Birchard Hayes	1877-1881	James Abram Garfield	1881
Chester Alan Arthur	1881-1885	Grover Cleveland	1885-1889
Benjamin Harrison	1889-1893	Grover Cleveland	1893-1897
William McKinley	1897-1901	Theodore Roosevelt	1901-1909
William Howard Taft	1909-1913	Woodrow Wilson	1913-1921
Warren Gamaliel Harding	1921-1923	Calvin Coolidge	1923-1929
Herbert Clark Hoover	1929-1933	Franklin Delano Roosevelt	1933-1945
Harry S. Truman	1945-1953	Dwight David Eisenhower	1953-1961
John Fitzgerald Kennedy	1961-1963	Lyndon Baines Johnson	1963-1969
Richard Milhous Nixon	1969-1974	Gerald Rudolph Ford	1974-1977
James Earl Carter, Jr.	1977-1981	Ronald Wilson Reagan	1981-1989
George Herbert Walker Bush	1989-1993	William Jefferson Clinton	1993-2001

Figure 4-5. *The Presidents table displayed by using the SQL web part*

⊟ **Miscellaneous**

Connection String:

Data Source=MGEROW-MOSS

SQL Query:

select * from Presidents

Format Using:

XSLT ▼

XSLT Path:

C:\SharePoint Recipe Solutior

☑ Include Debug Info?:

Figure 4-6. *The SQL web part's property pane*

Variations

- One of the more interesting variations on the preceding example is to process more than one SQL result set at a time. This can be accomplished by specifying a Microsoft SQL stored procedure that returns multiple tables, rather than a simple SQL query, in the SQL Query parameter. The XSLT is then written to process multiple tables rather than just one. The final formatting can be quite involved, presenting exciting possibilities for rapid solutions when presenting complex business data.

Recipe 4-4. Creating a Page Viewer Web Part

As with the XML web part, you might be wondering, "Why create a Page Viewer web part when one ships with SharePoint?" The answer is, to gain more flexibility and control. For example, what do you do if the page you want to access requires authentication? The built-in Page Viewer web part doesn't provide any way to pass credentials to the page to be displayed.

Further, what if you want to perform some transformation on the page you're acquiring before displaying it? For example, suppose you want only a fragment of the page (what used to be referred to as *screen scraping*)? With our custom page viewer, we could add code to parse the HTML returned by the web page, extract the desired content, and display only that.

Recipe Type: Web Part

Ingredients

Class Library References

- `System.Web.UI.WebControls.WebParts` class library

- `System.Web.UI.WebControls` class library

Special Considerations

- Because this web part uses the generic ASP.NET 2.0 web-part framework and doesn't need to communicate directly with SharePoint, we won't add a reference to the `Windows.SharePoint.Services` library. However, if you want to use the legacy SharePoint web-part framework, you will need to add that reference to the project.

- This web part supports one of two authentication modes: 1) *impersonation*, where the web part will pass the currently logged-in user's credentials to the target page, or 2) *explicit*, where a user domain, name, and password are entered directly into the web-part's property sheet.

- Because this recipe loads the source HTML into the current SharePoint page, relative links on the source page to resources such as images, Cascading Style Sheets (CSS) sheets, JavaScript files, or hyperlinks will not work. So you will either need to find all `<A>` tags and fix the relative links, or use the alternative approach of creating an `<IFRAME>` (discussed at the end of this recipe).

■**Caution** Manipulating a web-part page's HTML by using JavaScript and the Document Object Model (DOM) may cause problems on the SharePoint page if there is embedded JavaScript in the target HTML that conflicts with, or overrides, the native SharePoint script. Because of these issues, you should use this technique only when you have a thorough understanding of or control over the target web page.

Preparation

1. Create a new C# or VB.NET class library project.

2. Add a reference to the `System.Web` .NET assembly.

3. At the top of the class module, add `using` or `Includes` statements for the `System.Web.UI.WebControls` and `System.Web.UI.WebControls.WebParts` class libraries.

4. Open the project properties page, go to the Signing tab, select the Sign the Assembly checkbox, and add a new strong-name key file named something like `SQLWebPart.snk`.

Process Flow

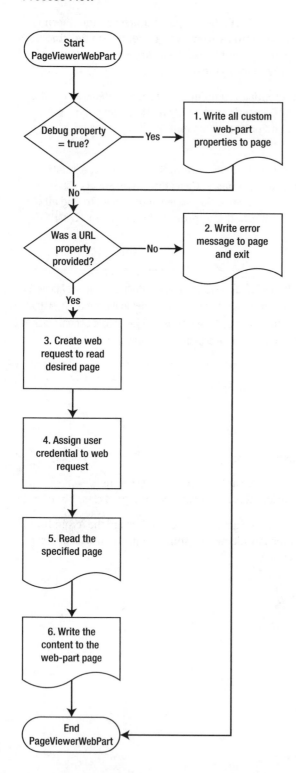

1. If the Debug property has been selected on the web-part properties page, write all properties to the web-part page.

2. If the URL property was *not* provided, there's nothing more to do. Warn the user that a URL is required and stop processing.

3. Create a .NET web request object to read the specified URL into memory.

4. Either assign the current user credentials (if Impersonate is selected), or the explicit domain/user/password provided to the web request before requesting the page.

5. Attempt to read the specified URL with the given credentials. If an error occurs, display it to the web-part page. If no error occurs, go to step 6.

6. Display the contents of the URL read.

Recipe—VB (See Project PageViewerWebPartVB, Class PageViewerWebPartVB.vb)

```vb
Imports System
Imports System.Web
Imports System.Web.Security
Imports System.Web.UI
Imports System.Web.UI.WebControls
Imports System.Web.UI.WebControls.WebParts
Imports System.Web.UI.HtmlControls
Imports System.Xml
Imports System.Data
Public Class PageViewerWebPartVB
    Inherits WebPart
    ' Local variable to hold property values
    Private _url As String = ""
    Private _impersonate As Boolean = True
    Private _domain As String = ""
    Private _user As String = ""
    Private _password As String = ""
    Private _debug As Boolean = False
    ' Property to set URL of page to display
    <Personalizable(), _
     WebBrowsable()> _
    Public Property Url() As String
        Get
            Return _url
        End Get
        Set(ByVal value As String)
            _url = value
        End Set
    End Property
```

```vb
' If explicit credentials have been requested,
' the following three properties will
' be used to construct the credentials
' to pass to the page
<Personalizable(), _
 WebBrowsable()> _
Public Property Domain() As String
    Get
        Return _domain
    End Get
    Set(ByVal value As String)
        _domain = value
    End Set
End Property
<Personalizable(), _
 WebBrowsable()> _
Public Property User() As String
    Get
        Return _user
    End Get
    Set(ByVal value As String)
        _user = value
    End Set
End Property
<Personalizable(), _
 WebBrowsable()> _
Public Property Password() As String
    Get
        Return _password
    End Get
    Set(ByVal value As String)
        _password = value
    End Set
End Property
' Should user be impersonated?
<Personalizable(), _
 WebBrowsable()> _
Public Property Impersonate() As Boolean
    Get
        Return _impersonate
    End Get
    Set(ByVal value As Boolean)
        _impersonate = value
    End Set
End Property
```

```vb
' Display debug info?
<Personalizable(), _
 WebBrowsable()> _
Public Property Debug() As Boolean
    Get
        Return _debug
    End Get
    Set(ByVal value As Boolean)
        _debug = value
    End Set
End Property
' This is where the HTML gets rendered to the
' web-part page.
Protected Overrides Sub RenderContents(ByVal writer As HtmlTextWriter)
    MyBase.RenderContents(writer)
    ' Step 1: If debug info requested, display it
    If Debug Then
        writer.WriteLine("Url: " + Url + "<br/>")
        writer.WriteLine("Impersonate: " + Impersonate.ToString _
            + "<br/>")
        writer.WriteLine("Domain: " + Domain + "<br/>")
        writer.WriteLine("User: " + User + "<br/>")
        writer.WriteLine("Password: " + Password + "<br/>")
        writer.WriteLine("<hr/>")
    End If
    ' Step 2: Make sure URL is provided
    If (Url = "") Then
        writer.WriteLine( _
            "<font color='red'>Please enter a valid Url</font>")
        Return
    End If
    ' Step 3: Create a web request to read desired page
    Dim wReq As System.Net.WebRequest
    wReq = System.Net.WebRequest.Create(Url)
    ' Step 4: Set the security as appropriate
    If Impersonate Then
        wReq.Credentials = System.Net.CredentialCache.DefaultCredentials
    Else
        wReq.Credentials = _
            New System.Net.NetworkCredential(User, Password, Domain)
    End If
    ' Step 5: Get the page contents as a string variable
```

```
        Try
            Dim wResp As System.Net.WebResponse = wReq.GetResponse
            Dim respStream As System.IO.Stream = wResp.GetResponseStream
            Dim respStreamReader As System.IO.StreamReader = _
                New System.IO.StreamReader(respStream, _
                System.Text.Encoding.ASCII)
            Dim strHTML As String = respStreamReader.ReadToEnd
            ' Step 6: Render the HTML to the web-part page
            writer.Write(strHTML)
        Catch e As Exception
            writer.Write(("<font color='red'>" + e.Message))
        End Try
    End Sub
End Class
```

Recipe—C# (See Project PageViewerWebPartCS, Class PageViewerWebPartCS.cs)

```csharp
using System;
using System.Web;
using System.Web.Security;
using System.Web.UI;
using System.Web.UI.WebControls;
using System.Web.UI.WebControls.WebParts;
using System.Web.UI.HtmlControls;
using System.Xml;
using System.Data;
namespace PageViewerWebPartCS
{
    public class PageViewerWebPartCS : WebPart
    {
        // Local variable to hold property values
        string _url = "";
        bool _impersonate = true;
        string _domain = "";
        string _user = "";
        string _password = "";
        bool _debug = false;
        // Property to set URL of page to display
        [Personalizable]
        [WebBrowsable]
        public string Url
        {
            get
            {
                return _url;
            }
        }
```

```csharp
        set
        {
            _url = value;
        }
    }
    // If explicit credentials have been requested,
    // the following three properties will
    // be used to construct the credentials
    // to pass to the page
    [Personalizable]
    [WebBrowsable]
    public string Domain
    {
        get
        {
            return _domain;
        }
        set
        {
            _domain = value;
        }
    }
    [Personalizable]
    [WebBrowsable]
    public string User
    {
        get
        {
            return _user;
        }
        set
        {
            _user = value;
        }
    }
    [Personalizable]
    [WebBrowsable]
    public string Password
    {
        get
        {
            return _password;
        }
        set
        {
            _password = value;
        }
    }
```

```csharp
// Should user be impersonated?
[Personalizable]
[WebBrowsable]
public bool Impersonate
{
    get
    {
        return _impersonate;
    }
    set
    {
        _impersonate = value;
    }
}
// Display debug info?
[Personalizable]
[WebBrowsable]
public bool Debug
{
    get
    {
        return _debug;
    }
    set
    {
        _debug = value;
    }
}
// This is where the HTML gets rendered to the
// web-part page.
protected override void RenderContents(HtmlTextWriter writer)
{
    base.RenderContents(writer);
    // Step 1: If debug info requested, display it
    if (Debug)
    {
        writer.WriteLine("Url: " + Url + "<br/>");
        writer.WriteLine("Impersonate: " + Impersonate.ToString() +
            "<br/>");
        writer.WriteLine("Domain: " + Domain + "<br/>");
        writer.WriteLine("User: " + User + "<br/>");
        writer.WriteLine("Password: " + Password + "<br/>");
        writer.WriteLine("<hr/>");
    }
    // Step 2: Make sure URL is provided
```

```
        if (Url == "")
        {
            writer.WriteLine(
                "<font color='red'>Please enter a valid Url</font>");
            return;
        }
        // Step 3: Create a web request to read desired page
        System.Net.WebRequest wReq;
        wReq = System.Net.WebRequest.Create(Url);
        // Step 4: Set the security as appropriate
        if (Impersonate)
        {
            wReq.Credentials =
                System.Net.CredentialCache.DefaultCredentials;
        }
        else
        {
            wReq.Credentials =
                new System.Net.NetworkCredential(User, Password, Domain);
        }
        // Step 5: Get the page contents as a string variable
        try
        {
            System.Net.WebResponse wResp = wReq.GetResponse();
            System.IO.Stream respStream = wResp.GetResponseStream();
            System.IO.StreamReader respStreamReader =
                new System.IO.StreamReader(respStream,
                System.Text.Encoding.ASCII);
            string strHTML = respStreamReader.ReadToEnd();
            // Step 6: Render the HTML to the web-part page
            writer.Write(strHTML);
        }
        catch (Exception e)
        {
            writer.Write("<font color='red'>" + e.Message);
        }
    }
  }
}
```

To Run

■**Note** Please see the "To Run" section of Recipe 4-1 for instructions on how to deploy a web part to a single site collection. After the web part has been successfully deployed, proceed with the following steps.

After you have deployed the web part to your site collection, place an instance of the web part on a web-part page. Initially an error message will be displayed stating that you must provide a URL to a web page. To do so, open the web-part property sheet, fill in the URL, and click the OK button. The result is shown in Figure 4-7.

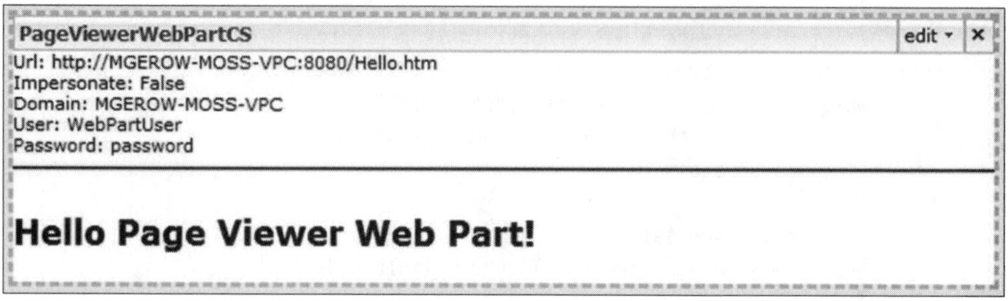

Figure 4-7. *A simple web page displayed by using the custom Page Viewer web part*

Assuming that the account under which you are currently logged in has permissions to that URL (or the site allows anonymous access), the page should be displayed. If your current account doesn't have the necessary permissions, you can deselect the Impersonate property and provide a specific domain, user, and password. Figure 4-8 shows the property settings to force the custom Page Viewer web part to connect as the user WebPartUser.

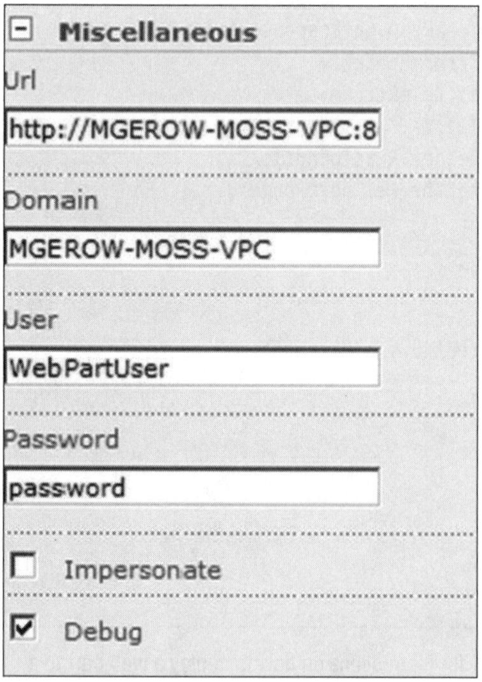

Figure 4-8. *The custom Page Viewer web part's property pane*

Variations

- As noted earlier, this web part provides significant flexibility not available in the out-of-the-box Page Viewer web part provided with SharePoint. One variation is to create a custom version of this web part to extract a known portion of another page. This might be appropriate if you have an internal web site that provides some useful data on a page, but all you want is a part of that page. Assuming you know the structure of the underlying HTML of that page, you could extract the desired HTML fragment by using string manipulation after the page has been read into a .NET string variable, writing just that fragment out to the web-part page.

- Rather than allow the end user to explicitly enter a domain, user name, and password, another variation is to store that information in an external source such as SQL Server or SharePoint's `Web.config` file. The credential information could be looked up based on the value of the URL.

- Make the URL property a drop-down list rather than a text box to allow end users to select from a controlled list of pages to display.

- As noted in the "Special Considerations" section at the beginning of this recipe, the preceding approach has the disadvantage that relative links on the source page will be broken. An alternative to reading the page into a string variable is to construct an `<IFRAME>` tag to hold the source. The disadvantage is that you cannot then handle authentication or perform any processing on the page before you display it. To use the `<IFRAME>` approach, replace the code in the `RenderContents()` method with a single statement that looks something like the following:

```
writer.Write("<IFRAME src=" + Url + " FRAMEBORDER='none'
ALIGN='TOP' VSPACE='0' scrolling='no' WIDTH='100%' HEIGHT='100%'> ➡
</IFRAME>");
```

Recipe 4-5. Creating a Connectable Page Viewer Web Part

One of the most exciting aspects of web-part technology is the ability to pass data between web parts. This capability enables web parts to interoperate in complex and flexible ways, and enables well-designed web parts to be used in ways that weren't originally anticipated at design time.

This recipe is for one such web part, which is a variation of the earlier custom Page Viewer web part that enables your users to select predefined target sites from a drop-down list. The drop-down list is populated from a list of sites that you can define via a delimited list.

Recipe Type: Web Part

Ingredients

Class Library References

- `System.Web.UI.WebControls.WebParts` class library

- `System.Web.UI.WebControls` class library

Special Considerations

- Because this web part uses the generic ASP.NET 2.0 web-part framework and doesn't need to communicate directly with SharePoint, we won't add a reference to the Windows.SharePoint.Services library. However, if you want to use the legacy SharePoint web-part framework, you will need to add that reference to the project.

- In this example, I have placed the custom interface and both web-part classes in the sample project class file. In most instances you will probably place the interface in its own file or even its own project so that it may be easily shared between any number of web parts that need to use that interface.

- This recipe shows an alternative approach to displaying a web page's contents to that shown in Recipe 4-4. In that case, we used the ASP.NET System.Net.WebRequest class to read the contents of the target page into memory and then write it out to our web-part page. In this recipe, we simply render an <IFRAME> tag to the web-part page with the SRC attribute set to the target URL. The first approach has the advantage that we can explicitly pass credentials, which may or may not be those of the currently logged-in user, to the target page. We can also manipulate the returned HTML prior to rendering if we wish because we have a copy of that HTML in memory. One disadvantage of the WebRequest approach is that relative references (such as relative HREF attributes in <A> tags, or SRC attributes referencing CSS or JavaScript includes) will not work when the contents are rendered to the web-part page. This is because those references will now be relative to the current page, and thus, most likely, be invalid. The <IFRAME> approach used in this recipe eliminates both the benefits and the drawbacks of the WebRequest approach. The credentials passed to the target page will always be those of the current user; there is no way to preprocess the page before it's displayed, but all relative links and references will remain intact.

Preparation

1. Create a new C# or VB.NET class library project.

2. Add a reference to the System.Web .NET assembly.

3. At the top of the class module, add using or Includes statements for the System.Web.UI.WebControls and System.Web.UI.WebControls.WebParts class libraries.

4. Open the project properties page, go to the Signing tab, select the Sign the Assembly checkbox, and add a new strong-name key file named something like ConnectablePageViewer.snk.

Process Flow

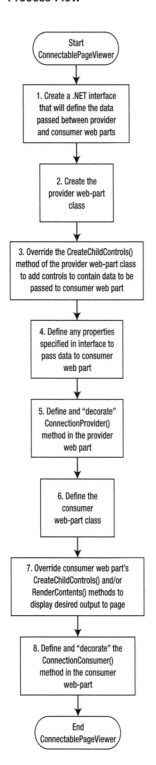

■**Note** The process highlighted here pertains to the generic steps required to create a connectable web part, rather than the steps required to create a Page Viewer web part per se.

---

1. A .NET interface is like a class, but it contains only property and method signatures without any code. The purpose of the interface in this case is to provide both the provider and consumer web parts with a common data structure to use when data is passed from the provider to the consumer.

2. Create a provider web-part class. Note that this class will also implement the interface created in step 1.

3. Override the web-part class's base `CreateChildControls()` method to add any web controls required to acquire data from the end user. In this case, we need one drop-down list that will contain the list of web sites that may be displayed.

4. Because the provider web part implements the interface defined in step 1, it must implement any properties in the interface. In our example, we need to implement the `Url` read-only property, returning the currently selected value of the drop-down list.

5. A provider web part must have a public method that returns an instance of the provider web part, as viewed through the properties defined in the interface created in step 1. This method is defined to the ASP.NET web-part framework by decorating the method with the `ConnectionProvider()` attribute.

6. Create a consumer web-part class.

7. In the consumer web-part class, override either the `CreateChildControls()` or `RenderContents()` base web-part methods, adding code to render the desired HTML to the web-part page.

8. A consumer web part must have a public method that can receive the data from the provider web part's `ConnectionProvider()` method—defined in step 5. This method must be decorated with the `ConnectionConsumer()` attribute to indicate to the ASP.NET web-part framework so that it can receive the data made available by the provider web part. In our example, the `ConnectionConsumer()` method receives an instance of the provider class, limited by the properties defined for the interface in step 1, which in this case is simply the `Url` property.

Recipe—VB (See Project ConnectablePageViewerVB, Class ConnectablePageViewerVB.vb)

```
Imports System
Imports System.Collections.Generic
Imports System.Text
Imports System.Web.UI.WebControls
Imports System.Web.UI.WebControls.WebParts
Namespace ConnectablePageViewerVB
```

```
' Step 1: Create the Interface
' ----------------------------
' The interface is the glue between the "provider" web part
' that sends data to the "consumer" web page. It provides
' a structure in which to pass the data. In this case
' we're just passing a single string value that represents
' the URL to display, but we could pass multiple data
' items by providing multiple properties
Public Interface IUrl
    ReadOnly Property Url() As String
End Interface
' Step 2: Create the provider web-part class
' ------------------------------------------
' The "provider" web part will display a drop-down list
' or site-name/URL pairs. When the user selects a value,
' the selected URL will be passed to the "consumer".
Public Class UrlProvider
    Inherits WebPart
    Implements IUrl
    Private ddlUrl As DropDownList = Nothing
    Private _urls As String = _
        "Microsoft;http://www.microsoft.com;Yahoo!;" & _
        "http://www.yahoo.com;Apress;http://www.apress.com"
    ' The "Urls" property will store a semicolon-delimited
    ' list of site-name/URL pairs to populate the drop-down list
    <Personalizable()> _
    <WebBrowsable()> _
    Public Property Urls() As String
        Get
            Return _urls
        End Get
        Set(ByVal value As String)
            _urls = value
        End Set
    End Property
    ' Step 3: Override the "CreateChildControls()" method
    ' ---------------------------------------------------
    ' The CreateChildControls() base method is called
    ' to populate the drop-down list of sites and
    ' add to the web-part output
    Protected Overloads Overrides Sub CreateChildControls()
        MyBase.CreateChildControls()
```

```vbnet
        Try
            ' Create the drop-down list of URLs from
            ' the parsed string in "Urls" property
            Dim arrUrls As String() = _urls.Split(";"c)
            Dim li As ListItem
            ddlUrl = New DropDownList()
            ddlUrl.Items.Add(New ListItem("[Please select a Url]", ""))
            Dim i As Integer = 0
            While i < arrUrls.Length
                li = New ListItem(arrUrls(i), arrUrls(i + 1))
                ddlUrl.Items.Add(li)
                i = i + 2
            End While
            ddlUrl.Items(0).Selected = True
            ddlUrl.AutoPostBack = True
            Me.Controls.Add(ddlUrl)
        Catch ex As Exception
            Dim lbl As New Label()
            lbl.Text = ex.Message
            Me.Controls.Add(lbl)
        End Try
    End Sub
    ' Step 4: Define any methods required by the interface
    ' ---------------------------------------------------
    ' This is the single method that was
    ' specified in the Interface, and must be provided
    ' to pass the selected URL to the "consumer" web
    ' part
    Public ReadOnly Property Url() As String Implements IUrl.Url
        Get
            Return ddlUrl.SelectedValue.ToString()
        End Get
    End Property
    ' Step 5: Define and "decorate" the ConnectionProvider() method
    ' ------------------------------------------------------------
    ' This method is required to wire up the
    ' "provider" with one or more "consumers."
    ' Note the "ConnectionProvider" decoration
    ' that tells .NET to make this the provider's
    ' connection point
    <ConnectionProvider("Url Provider")> _
    Public Function GetUrl() As IUrl
        Return Me
    End Function
End Class
```

```vbnet
' Step 6: Define the consumer web-part class
' ------------------------------------------
' This class defines the "consumer" web part that will
' obtain the URL from the "provider"
Public Class ConnectablePageViewer
    Inherits WebPart
    Private _url As String = ""
    ' Step 7: Override either or both the CreateChildControls() and/or
    ' RenderContents() base methods
    ' ------------------------------------------------------------------
    ' In the RenderContents() method we get the URL value
    ' which has been written to the _url local variable by
    ' the "UrlConsumer()" method that automatically fires
    ' when this web part is wired up with a "provider"
    Protected Overloads Overrides Sub RenderContents( _
        ByVal writer As System.Web.UI.HtmlTextWriter)
        MyBase.RenderContents(writer)
        Try
            If _url <> "" Then
                ' Create an <IFRAME> HTML tag and set the
                ' source to the selected url
                writer.Write("Opening page: " + _url)
                writer.Write("<hr/>")
                writer.Write("<div>")
                writer.Write("<iframe src='" + _url + _
                    "' width='100%' height='800px'></iframe>")
                writer.Write("</div>")
            Else
                writer.Write("Please select a Url from the provider.")
            End If
        Catch ex As Exception
            writer.Write(ex.Message)
        End Try
    End Sub
    ' Step 8: Define a ConnectionConsumer() method to receive
    ' data from the provider
    ' -------------------------------------------------------
    ' The UrlConsumer() method is wired up using the
    ' "ConnectionConsumer()" decoration, that tells
    ' .NET to automatically fire this method when
    ' the consumer is connected to a provider
    <ConnectionConsumer("Url Consumer")> _
    Public Sub UrlConsumer(ByVal url As IUrl)
        Try
            _url = url.Url
            ' No op
```

```vb
            Catch ex As Exception
            End Try
        End Sub
    End Class
End Namespace
```

Recipe—C# (See Project ConnectablePageViewerCS, Class ConnectablePageViewerCS.cs)

```csharp
using System;
using System.Collections.Generic;
using System.Text;
using System.Web.UI.WebControls;
using System.Web.UI.WebControls.WebParts;
namespace ConnectablePageViewerCS
{
    // Step 1: Create the Interface
    // ----------------------------
    // The interface is the glue between the "provider" web part
    // that sends data to the "consumer" web page.  It provides
    // a structure in which to pass the data.  In this case
    // we're just passing a single string value that represents
    // the URL to display, but we could pass multiple data
    // items by providing multiple properties.
    public interface IUrl
    {
        string Url { get; }
    }
    // Step 2: Create the provider web-part class
    // -------------------------------------------
    // The "provider" web part will display a drop-down list
    // or site-name/URL pairs.  When the user selects a value,
    // the selected URL will be passed to the "consumer."
    public class UrlProvider : WebPart, IUrl
    {
        DropDownList ddlUrl = null;
        string _urls =
          "Microsoft;http://www.microsoft.com; " +
          "Yahoo!;http://www.yahoo.com;Apress;http://www.apress.com";
        // The "Urls" property will store a semicolon-delimited
        // list of site-name/URL pairs to populate the drop-down list
        [Personalizable]
        [WebBrowsable]
        public string Urls
        {
            get { return _urls; }
```

```
            set { _urls = value;   }
        }
        // Step 3: Override the "CreateChildControls()" method
        // ----------------------------------------------------
        // The CreateChildControls() base method is called
        // to populate the drop-down list of sites and
        // add to the web-part output
        protected override void CreateChildControls()
        {
            base.CreateChildControls();
            try
            {
                // Create the drop-down list of URLs from
                // the parsed string in "Urls" property
                string[] arrUrls = _urls.Split(';');
                ListItem li;
                ddlUrl = new DropDownList();
                ddlUrl.Items.Add(new ListItem("[Please select a Url]", ""));
                for (int i = 0; i < arrUrls.Length; i = i + 2)
                {
                    li = new ListItem(arrUrls[i], arrUrls[i + 1]);
                    ddlUrl.Items.Add(li);
                }
                ddlUrl.Items[0].Selected = true;
                ddlUrl.AutoPostBack = true;
                this.Controls.Add(ddlUrl);
            }
            catch (Exception ex)
            {
                Label lbl = new Label();
                lbl.Text = ex.Message;
                this.Controls.Add(lbl);
            }
        }
        // Step 4: Define any methods required by the interface
        // ----------------------------------------------------
        // This is the single method that was
        // specified in the Interface, and must be provided
        // to pass the selected URL to the "consumer" web
        // part
        public string Url
        {
            get { return ddlUrl.SelectedValue; }
        }
```

```
        // Step 5: Define and "decorate" the ConnectionProvider method
    // ------------------------------------------------------------
    // This method is required to wire up the
        // "provider" with one or more "consumers."
        // Note the "ConnectionProvider" decoration
        // that tells .NET to make this the provider's
        // connection point
        [ConnectionProvider("Url Provider")]
        public IUrl GetUrl()
        {
            return this;
        }
    }
    // Step 6: Define the consumer web-part class
    // -----------------------------------------
    // This class defines the "consumer" web part that will
    // obtain the URL from the "provider"
    public class ConnectablePageViewer : WebPart
    {
        string _url = "";
        // Step 7: Override either or both the CreateChildControls() and/or
        //    RenderContents() base methods
        // ------------------------------------------------------------------
        // In the RenderContents() method, we get the URL value
        // that has been written to the _url local variable by
        // the "UrlConsumer()" method that automatically fires
        // when this web part is wired up with a "provider"
        protected override void RenderContents(
            System.Web.UI.HtmlTextWriter writer)
        {
            base.RenderContents(writer);
            try
            {
                if (_url != "")
                {
                    // Create an <IFRAME> HTML tag and set the
                    // source to the selected URLl
                    writer.Write("Opening page: " + _url);
                    writer.Write("<hr/>");
                    writer.Write("<div>");
                    writer.Write("<iframe src='" + _url +
                        "' width='100%' height=800px'></iframe>");
                    writer.Write("</div>");
                }
```

```
        else
        {
            writer.Write("Please select a Url from the provider.");
        }
    }
    catch (Exception ex)
    {
        writer.Write(ex.Message);
    }
}
// Step 8: Define a ConnectionConsumer() method to receive
// data from the provider
// --------------------------------------------------------
// The UrlConsumer() method is wired up using the
// "ConnectionConsumer()" decoration that tells
// .NET to automatically fire this method when
// the consumer is connected to a provider
[ConnectionConsumer("Url Consumer")]
public void UrlConsumer(IUrl url)
{
    try
    {
        _url = url.Url;
    }
    catch (Exception ex)
    {
        // No op
    }
}
    }
  }
}
```

To Run

■Note Please see the "To Run" section of Recipe 4-1 for instructions on how to deploy a web part to a single site collection. After the web part has been successfully deployed, proceed with the following steps.

Open a web-part page in the site collection where you have just deployed your two web parts, and then add both web parts to the page as shown in Figure 4-9.

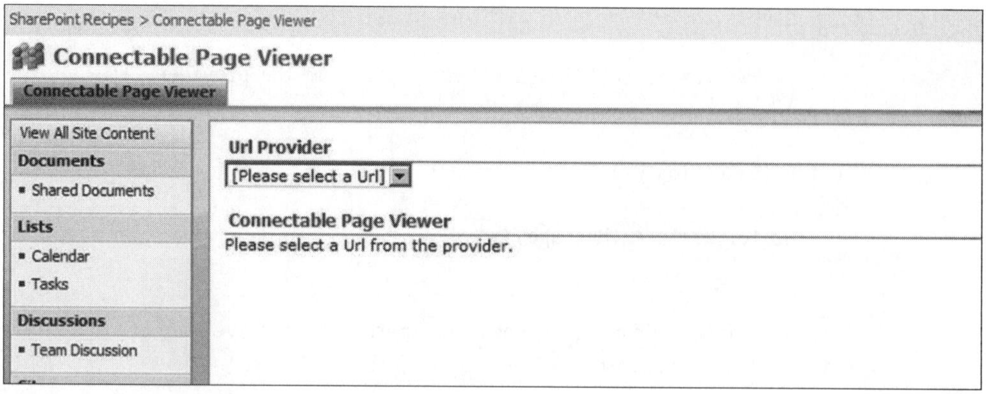

Figure 4-9. *The connectable Page Viewer waiting for the user to select a URL*

Note that because no URL has yet been selected, the Connectable Page Viewer web part displays the message "Please select a URL from the provider." Before the Page Viewer part will recognize that a URL has been selected, however, you must connect the web parts. To do so, choose the Site Actions ➤ Edit Page menu option, and then choose the Connections ➤ Send URL Provider To ➤ Connectable Page Viewer option from the Edit menu of the URL Provider web part, as shown in Figure 4-10. This will "wire up" the provider and Page Viewer web parts.

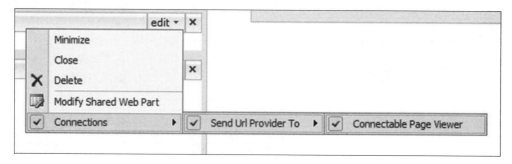

Figure 4-10. *Connecting the connectable Page Viewer to the URL source*

Finally, select a site name from the URL provider web part to display the corresponding site in the Connectable Page Viewer, as shown in Figure 4-11.

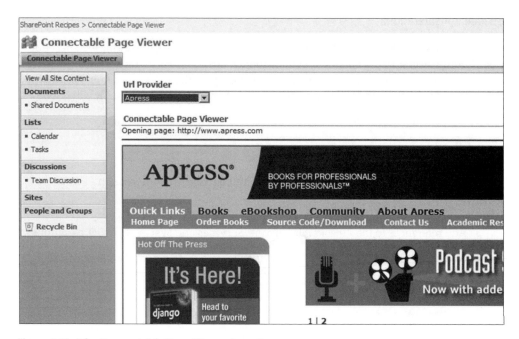

Figure 4-11. *The Connectable Page Viewer in action*

Related Recipes

- Recipe 4-4

Recipe 4-6. Reading Web-Part Parameters from the Querystring

There are many scenarios in which it would be useful for one or more web parts on a page to display differently depending on what, if any, parameters are included in the URL querystring. For example, you might wish to create a single web-part page to display client information, and pass the client ID as a parameter. That way, you can have a single web-part page that serves up information for thousands of clients.

In this recipe, you'll create a variation of the XML web part that will check the querystring for a client ID and use that to filter data from a SharePoint list, to format and display data for the specified client.

Recipe Type: Web Part

Ingredients

Assembly References

- Windows.SharePoint.Services .NET assembly

- System.Web .NET assembly

Special Considerations

- Note that, unlike most web-part recipes in this chapter, the Querystring web part does require access to the SharePoint object model. The reason is that we are using a Share-Point list as our data source. If you try one of the variations that use a non-SharePoint data source, the reference to the `Windows.SharePoint.Services` assembly will not be required.

Preparation

1. Create a custom list called `Clients` as described in the "To Run" section.

2. Create a new C# or VB.NET class library.

3. Add references to the `Windows.SharePoint.Services` and `System.Web` .NET assemblies.

4. Add `using` or `Includes` (depending on language used) statements for the following:

   - `Microsoft.SharePoint`

   - `Microsoft.SharePoint.WebControls`

   - `System.Web.UI.WebControls`

   - `System.Web.UI.WebControls.WebParts`

   - `System.Data`

5. Add the properties specified in the following source code.

6. Override the `RenderContents()` base web part method.

7. Add the custom `displayClientData()` method.

8. Create an XML transform (XSLT) to format the resulting data.

Process Flow

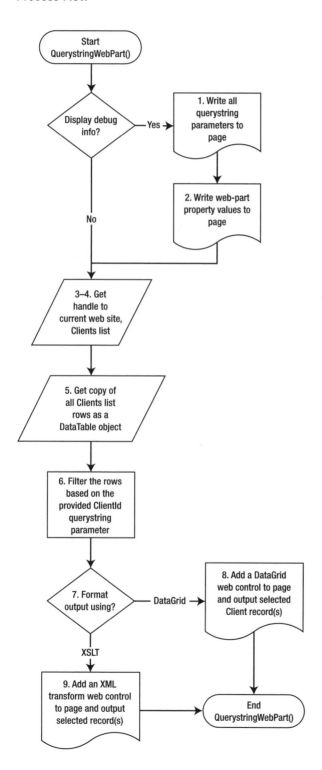

1. If the Debug checkbox is selected, loop through each querystring parameter and write to the web-part page.

2. Write values of web-part properties that determine output format and (if format is XSLT) the XSLT transform file to use.

3. Instantiate an SPWeb object representing the web site that the current web-part page is a member of.

4. Get a handle to the Clients list—assuming one exists.

5. Use the SPListItems.GetDataTable() method to write the entire contents of the list into an ADO.NET DataTable for easier processing.

6. Use an ADO.NET DataView object to filter the DataTable created in step 4 based on the client ID passed in the querystring.

7. Determine whether the web part has been set to format data by using a DataGrid or XSLT.

8. If the web part will use a DataGrid, create a new DataGrid object, assign the DataView object created in step 6 to its DataSource property, and then render the DataGrid to the page.

9. Otherwise, create a new XML transform web control, set its content to an XML representation of the DataView's data (by way of a DataSet and the DataView.ToTable() method). Set the transform path to that provided by the web part's XSLT path property, and render the XML to the page.

Recipe—VB (See Project QuerystringWebPartVB, Class QuerystringWebPart.vb)

```vb
Imports System
Imports System.Collections.Generic
Imports System.Text
Imports System.Web.UI.WebControls
Imports System.Web.UI.WebControls.WebParts
Imports Microsoft.SharePoint
Imports Microsoft.SharePoint.WebControls
Imports System.Data
Public Class QueryStringWebPartVB
    Inherits WebPart
    ' Define local variables
    Private _debug As Boolean = False
    Private _formatUsing As enumFormatUsing = enumFormatUsing.DataGrid
    Private _xsltPath As String = ""
    'ENUM types will result in drop-down lists in
    'the web-part property sheet
    Public Enum enumFormatUsing
        DataGrid = 1
        XSLT = 2
    End Enum
```

```vb
' Display debug info?
<Personalizable()> _
<WebBrowsable()> _
<WebDisplayName("Debug?")> _
<WebDescription("Check to cause debug information to be displayed")> _
Public Property Debug() As Boolean
    Get
        Return _debug
    End Get
    Set(ByVal value As Boolean)
        _debug = value
    End Set
End Property
'Create property to determine whether DataGrid or
'XSLT should be used to format output
<Personalizable(PersonalizationScope.[Shared]), _
    WebBrowsable(), WebDisplayName("Format Using:"), _
    WebDescription("What method do you want to use " & _
    "to format the results.")> _
Public Property FormatUsing() As enumFormatUsing
    Get
        Return _formatUsing
    End Get
    Set(ByVal value As enumFormatUsing)
        _formatUsing = value
    End Set
End Property
'If XSLT will be used, this property specifies
'its server-relative path
<Personalizable(PersonalizationScope.[Shared]), _
    WebBrowsable(), WebDisplayName("XSLT Path:"), _
    WebDescription("If formatting with XSLT, " & _
    "provide full path to XSLT document.")> _
Public Property XSLTPath() As String
    Get
        Return _xsltPath
    End Get
    Set(ByVal value As String)
        _xsltPath = value
    End Set
End Property
Protected Overloads Overrides Sub RenderContents(ByVal writer As _
    System.Web.UI.HtmlTextWriter)
    MyBase.RenderContents(writer)
```

```vbnet
        Try
            Dim qs As System.Collections.Specialized.NameValueCollection = _
                Page.Request.QueryString
            If _debug Then
                ' Step 1: Parse the querystring and display
                If qs.Count > 0 Then
                    writer.Write("<strong>Querystring parameters: </strong>")
                    writer.Write("<blockquote>")
                    For i As Integer = 0 To qs.Count - 1
                        writer.Write(qs.Keys(i) + " = " + qs(i) + "<br/>")
                    Next
                    writer.Write("</blockquote>")
                Else
                    writer.Write("No querystring parameters exist<br/>")
                End If
                ' Step 2: Display web-part property values
                writer.Write("<strong>Format output using:</strong> " + _
                    _formatUsing.ToString() + "<br/>")
                writer.Write("<strong>XSLT path:</strong> " + _
                    _xsltPath.ToString() + "<br/>")
                writer.Write("<hr/>")
            End If
            ' Step 3: Display items from Client list based on provided ID
            Dim clientId As String = qs("clientId")
            If clientId IsNot Nothing Then
                displayClientData(clientId, writer)
            Else
                writer.Write("Client ID was not provided in querystring")
            End If
        Catch e As Exception
            writer.Write("<font color='red'>" + e.Message + "</font>")
        End Try
    End Sub
    Private Sub displayClientData(ByVal clientId As String, _
        ByVal writer As System.Web.UI.HtmlTextWriter)
        Try
            ' Step 4: Get handle to current web site and client list
            Dim web As SPWeb = SPControl.GetContextWeb(Context)
            Dim clients As SPList = web.Lists("Clients")
            ' Step 5: Copy clients' data into a DataTable object
            ' for easier manipulation
            Dim dsClients As New DataSet("Clients")
            Dim dtClients As DataTable = clients.Items.GetDataTable()
            dtClients.TableName = "Clients"
```

```vb
            ' Step 6: Filter for the specified client ID
            Dim dvClients As New DataView()
            dvClients.Table = dtClients
            dvClients.RowFilter = "ClientId = '" + clientId + "'"
            ' Step 7: Determine display mechanism to use
            If FormatUsing = enumFormatUsing.DataGrid Then
                ' Step 8: Display as DataGrid
                Dim dgClients As New DataGrid()
                dgClients.DataSource = dvClients
                dgClients.DataBind()
                dgClients.RenderControl(writer)
            Else
                ' Step 9: Format using provided XSLT
                Dim xml As New System.Web.UI.WebControls.Xml()
                dsClients.Tables.Add(dvClients.ToTable("Clients"))
                xml.DocumentContent = dsClients.GetXml()
                xml.TransformSource = XSLTPath
                xml.RenderControl(writer)
            End If
        Catch ex As Exception
            ' If error occurs, notify end-user
            writer.WriteLine("<font color='red'><strong>" + _
                ex.Message + "</font>")
        End Try
    End Sub
End Class
```

Recipe—C# (See Project QuerystringWebPartCS, Class QuerystringWebPart.cs)

```csharp
using System;
using System.Collections.Generic;
using System.Text;
using System.Web.UI.WebControls;
using System.Web.UI.WebControls.WebParts;
using Microsoft.SharePoint;
using Microsoft.SharePoint.WebControls;
using System.Data;
namespace QuerystringWebPartCS
{
    public class QueryStringWebPartCS : WebPart
    {
        // Define local variables
        bool _debug = false;
        enumFormatUsing _formatUsing = enumFormatUsing.DataGrid;
        string _xsltPath = "";
        //ENUM types will result in drop-down lists in
        //the web-part property sheet
```

```csharp
public enum enumFormatUsing
{
    DataGrid = 1,
    XSLT = 2
}
// Display debug info?
[Personalizable]
[WebBrowsable]
[WebDisplayName("Debug?")]
[WebDescription("Check to cause debug information to be displayed")]
public bool Debug
{
    get { return _debug; }
    set { _debug = value; }
}
//Create property to determine whether DataGrid or
//XSLT should be used to format output
[Personalizable(PersonalizationScope.Shared), WebBrowsable(),
    WebDisplayName("Format Using:"),
    WebDescription("What method do you want " +
        "to use to format the results.")]
public enumFormatUsing FormatUsing
{
    get { return _formatUsing; }
    set { _formatUsing = value; }
}
//If XSLT will be used, this property specifies
//its server-relative path
[Personalizable(PersonalizationScope.Shared),
    WebBrowsable(), WebDisplayName("XSLT Path:"),
    WebDescription("If formatting with XSLT, " +
        "provide full path to XSLT document.")]
public string XSLTPath
{
    get { return _xsltPath; }
    set { _xsltPath = value; }
}
protected override void RenderContents(
    System.Web.UI.HtmlTextWriter writer)
{
    base.RenderContents(writer);
    try
    {
        System.Collections.Specialized.NameValueCollection qs =
            Page.Request.QueryString;
```

```
    if (_debug)
    {
        // Step 1: Parse the querystring and display
        if (qs.Count > 0)
        {
            writer.Write(
                "<strong>Querystring parameters: </strong>");
            writer.Write("<blockquote>");
            for (int i = 0; i < qs.Count; i++)
            {
                writer.Write(qs.Keys[i] + " = " + qs[i] +
                    "<br/>");
            }
            writer.Write("</blockquote>");
        }
        else
        {
            writer.Write("No querystring parameters exist<br/>");
        }
        // Step 2: Display web-part property values
        writer.Write("<strong>Format output using:</strong> " +
            _formatUsing + "<br/>");
        writer.Write("<strong>XSLT path:</strong> " +
            _xsltPath + "<br/>");
        writer.Write("<hr/>");
    }
    // Step 3: Display items from Client list
    // based on provided ID
    string clientId = qs["clientId"];
    if (clientId != null)
    {
        displayClientData(clientId, writer);
    }
    else
    {
        writer.Write(
            "Client ID was not provided in querystring");
    }
}
catch (Exception e)
{
    writer.Write("<font color='red'>" + e.Message + "</font>");
}
}
```

```
private void displayClientData(
    string clientId, System.Web.UI.HtmlTextWriter writer)
{
    try
    {
        // Step 4: Get handle to current web site and client list
        SPWeb web = SPControl.GetContextWeb(Context);
        SPList clients = web.Lists["Clients"];
        // Step 5: Copy clients' data into a DataTable object
        // for easier manipulation
        DataSet dsClients = new DataSet("Clients");
        DataTable dtClients = clients.Items.GetDataTable();
        dtClients.TableName = "Clients";
        // Step 6: Filter for the specified client ID
        DataView dvClients = new DataView();
        dvClients.Table = dtClients;
        dvClients.RowFilter = "ClientId = '" + clientId + "'";
        // Step 7: Determine display mechanism to use
        if (FormatUsing == enumFormatUsing.DataGrid)
        {
            // Step 8: Display as DataGrid
            DataGrid dgClients = new DataGrid();
            dgClients.DataSource = dvClients;
            dgClients.DataBind();
            dgClients.RenderControl(writer);
        }
        else
        {
            // Step 9: Format using provided XSLT
            System.Web.UI.WebControls.Xml xml =
                new System.Web.UI.WebControls.Xml();
            dsClients.Tables.Add(dvClients.ToTable("Clients"));
            xml.DocumentContent = dsClients.GetXml();
            xml.TransformSource = XSLTPath;
            xml.RenderControl(writer);
        }
    }
    catch (Exception ex)
    {
        // If error occurs, notify end user
        writer.WriteLine("<font color='red'><strong>" +
            ex.Message + "</font>");
    }
}
```

Recipe—Clients.xslt (See Project QuerystringWebPartCS, File Clients.xslt)

This is the XML transform used to format the XML representation of the selected client data as HTML on the page. This XSLT simply builds a well-formed HTML <TABLE> from the XML provided by the DataSet.

```
<?xml version="1.0" encoding="UTF-8" ?>
<xsl:stylesheet version="1.0" xmlns:xsl="http://www.w3.org/1999/XSL/Transform">
    <xsl:template match="/">
        <!-- Display each matching client -->
        <table cellpadding="10" border="1">
        <xsl:for-each select="Clients/Clients">
            <tr>
                <td>
                    Client Id:
                </td>
                <td>
                    <strong>
                        <xsl:value-of select="ClientId"/>
                    </strong>
                </td>
            </tr>
            <tr>
                <td>
                    Client Name:
                </td>
                <td>
                    <strong>
                        <xsl:value-of select="ClientName"/>
                    </strong>
                </td>
            </tr>
            <tr>
                <td>
                    Address:
                </td>
                <td>
                    <strong>
                        <xsl:value-of select="Address"/>
                    </strong>
                </td>
            </tr>
        </xsl:for-each>
        </table>
    </xsl:template>
</xsl:stylesheet>
```

To Run

■**Note** Please see the "To Run" section of Recipe 4-1 for instructions on how to deploy a web part to a single site collection. After the web part has been successfully deployed, proceed with the following steps.

The next step is to create a new list called Clients that includes three fields: ClientId, ClientName, and Address (actually, the only field the web part requires is ClientId, but the sample XSLT shown in the preceding section assumes all three fields will be in the XML output of the DataSet).

After you have created the Clients list, add some rows as shown in Figure 4-12.

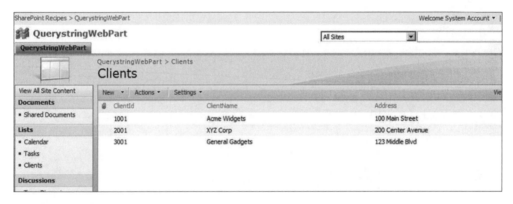

Figure 4-12. *Client data to use with the Querystring web part*

After the Clients list has been created and a few rows have been added, navigate to a web-part page in the same site and add the Querystring web part. Initially, you will receive an error message indicating that a client ID was not provided in the querystring. To remedy this, simply add some text such as ?clientid=1001 to the end of the URL in the browser's location field. Figure 4-13 shows the Querystring web part using custom XSLT to format the output.

■**Note** Any querystring is always preceded by the question mark (?) character, whereas parameters within a querystring are separated with an ampersand (&) character. So if clientid is the first (or only) parameter, it will be preceded by a ?. If it appears after one or more other parameters, it will be preceded by the & character.

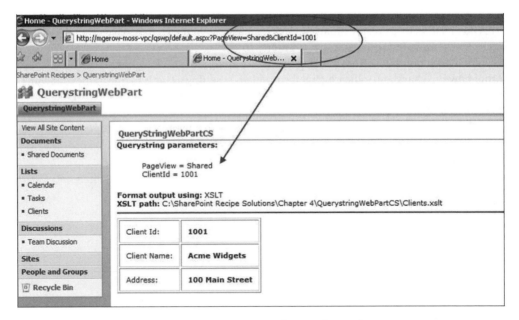

Figure 4-13. *The Querystring web part using XSLT to format the results*

Variations

- The preceding recipe always assumes that the parameter that will provide the filter data is called ClientId, that the list that holds the source data is named Clients, and that the field to compare to is named ClientId, just like the querystring parameter. Adding three additional web-part properties to contain the name of the querystring parameter, the list containing source records, and the field in that list to compare against the querystring parameter will allow this web part to address a virtually unlimited number of applications where you need to filter data in a list based on the querystring.

- Modify this recipe to obtain its data from an XML document source or a SQL query.

Related Recipes

- Recipe 4-1
- Recipe 4-2
- Recipe 4-3

Recipe 4-7. Using the SmartPart to Expose a .NET User Control

You're probably already aware of the wide range of freeware, shareware, and commercial web parts that are available. One that deserves special attention is the SmartPart by Jan Tielens. This part does something very elegant and, at least conceptually, simple. SmartPart makes it possible to use standard ASP.NET user controls as web parts. The reason this is useful is that while Visual Studio doesn't provide a What You See Is What You Get (WYSIWYG) design surface for web parts (which are really just a special type of server control), VS does for user controls. This means that, by using the SmartPart, you can lay out your web parts visually and assign complex event handling if necessary. It's pretty cool!

In this recipe, you'll create and deploy a web part that your colleagues can use to tell each other how busy they are, indicating their workload by setting a status to one of the following: green = need more work, yellow = pretty busy but will be available for more soon, or red = overloaded, don't bother me.

The status will be stored in a shared custom list, with an entry for each user.

Recipe Type: Web Part

Ingredients

Classes Used

- `SPSite` class

- `SPWeb` class

- `SPList` class

- `SPListItem` class

Other Ingredients

- Three `.ico` files that ship with Microsoft development environments: `Trffc10a.ico`, `Trffc10b.ico`, and `Trffc10c.ico`. These three files should be placed in SharePoint's image folder.

Special Considerations

- Any custom assemblies that your user control requires must be installed to either the `\bin` folder of the target web application or to the GAC.

Preparation

1. Download and install the SmartPart, which as of this writing is available at `www.codeplex.com/smartpart/Release/ProjectReleases.aspx?ReleaseId=10697`.

2. Create a `UserControls` folder under your target SharePoint web application folder. For example, if you are using the standard web application on port 80, create a new folder at `C:\Inetpub\wwwroot\wss\VirtualDirectories\80\UserControls`.

3. Create a new C# or VB.NET ASP.NET web application project.

4. Add a user control to the project and name it something like `SmartPartStatusWebPart.ascx`.

5. Add a reference to the `Windows.SharePoint.Services` .NET assembly.

6. Add using or Includes statements for the Microsoft.SharePoint and Microsoft.SharePoint.WebControls namespaces.

7. Copy the three icon files to the SharePoint images folder, which is typically at C:\Program Files\Common Files\Microsoft Shared\web server extensions\12\TEMPLATE\IMAGES.

8. Create a new SharePoint custom list named Status with two text fields: UserAlias and Status. Make sure that all users have Contribute rights to this list.

Process Flow: GetProfileStatus()

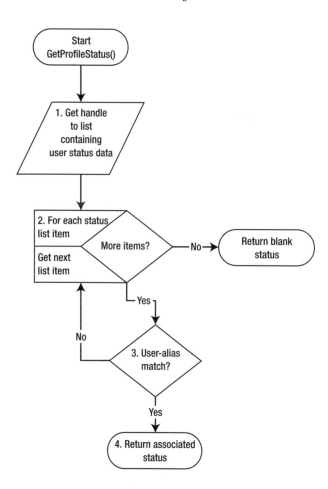

1. Instantiate SPSite, SPWeb, and SPList objects to obtain a handle to the list.

2. Step through the list of items to find the one that matches the current user alias. *For large lists, use an* SPQuery *object for better performance.*

3. If a match is found, return the associated value of the Status column and exit.

4. Otherwise, if no match is found, return an empty string.

Process Flow: UpdateStatus()

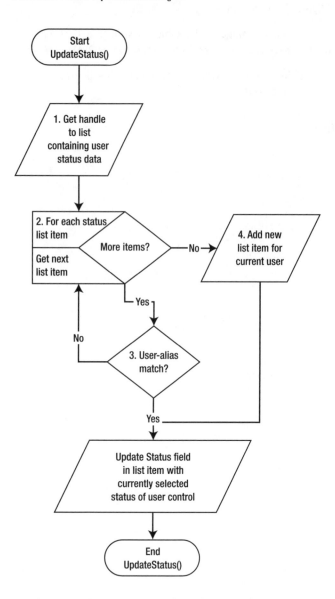

1. Instantiate SPSite, SPWeb, and SPList objects to obtain a handle to the list.

2. Step through the list of items to find the one that matches the current user alias. *For large lists, use an* SPQuery *object for better performance.*

3. If a match is found, update the Status field with the color value of the currently selected radio button.

4. If no match is found, this must be the first time the user has set their status, so insert a new item into the list and set the user alias and status accordingly.

Recipe—Page Layout (See Project SmartPartStatusWebPartCS, File SmartPartStatusWebPart.ascx)

Unlike standard web parts, where all UI elements are defined in the source code, an ASP.NET user control includes design surface elements as well as code. The following screen shot displays the elements of the layout. The radio buttons are named radRed, radYellow, and radGreen, respectively. The images are imgRed, imgYellow, and imgGreen. Figure 4-14 shows the user control displayed in Visual Studio's design surface.

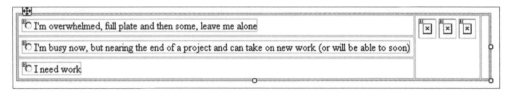

Figure 4-14. *The .ascx page shown in design view*

■**Note** All of the preceding radio buttons need to be given the same GroupName property, and their AutoPostBack property needs to be set to true.

Recipe—VB (See Project SmartPartStatusWebPartCS, Code-Behind SmartPartStatusWebPart.ascx.vb)

■**Note** Be sure that the variables _statusListSiteUrl, _statusListWeb, and _statusList reflect the actual location of the list that will contain user status information.

```vb
Imports Microsoft.SharePoint
Imports Microsoft.SharePoint.WebControls
Partial Class SmartPartStatusWebPart
    Inherits System.Web.UI.UserControl
    'Define local variables
    Private _showImage As Boolean = True
    Private _statusListSiteUrl As String = "http://localhost"
    Private _statusListWeb As String = "spwp"
    Private _statusList As String = "Status"
    Private Sub Page_PreRender(ByVal sender As Object, _
        ByVal e As System.EventArgs) Handles MyBase.PreRender
        'Only run this code if this is the first time the
        'user control has been displayed on the current
        'page since it was opened
```

```vb
            If Not IsPostBack Then
                HideAllImages()
                Select Case GetProfileStatus()
                    Case "Green"
                        Me.imgGreen.Visible = True
                        Me.radGreen.Checked = True
                    Case "Yellow"
                        Me.imgYellow.Visible = True
                        Me.radYellow.Checked = True
                    Case "Red"
                        Me.imgRed.Visible = True
                        Me.radRed.Checked = True
                    Case Else
                End Select
            End If
    End Sub
    Private Function GetProfileStatus() As String
        Try
            'Step 1: Define necessary objects
            Dim site As SPSite = New SPSite(_statusListSiteUrl)
            Dim web As SPWeb = site.AllWebs(_statusListWeb)
            Dim list As SPList = web.Lists(_statusList)
            'Step 2: Find the list item for the current user, and update its status
            'web.AllowUnsafeUpdates = True
            For Each ListItem As SPListItem In list.Items
                Try
                    'Step 3: If user is found, return their status
                    If ListItem("UserAlias").ToString.ToLower = _
                            Context.User.Identity.Name.ToLower Then
                        Return ListItem("Status")
                        Exit For
                    End If
                Catch ex As Exception
                    'No op
                End Try
            Next
            web.Dispose()
            site.Dispose()
        Catch ex As Exception
            'No op
        End Try
        'Step 4: If we got this far, no entry was found for the current user
        Return ""
    End Function
```

```vb
Private Sub UpdateStatus()
    Try
        'Step 1: Get a handle to the list that we're using to store
        'user status information
        Dim site As SPSite = New SPSite(_statusListSiteUrl)
        Dim web As SPWeb = site.AllWebs(_statusListWeb)
        Dim list As SPList = web.Lists(_statusList)
        Dim listItem As SPListItem
        Dim boolFound As Boolean = False
        'Step 2: Find the list item for the current user, and update its status
        For Each listItem In list.Items
            Try
                'Step 3: If found, update the user's status
                If listItem("UserAlias").ToString.ToLower = _
                    Context.User.Identity.Name.ToLower Then
                    listItem("Status") = GetUserControlStatus()
                    listItem.Update()
                    boolFound = True
                    Exit For
                End If
            Catch ex As Exception
            End Try
        Next
        'Step 4: If an entry for the current user wasn't found in the list,
        'add one now.
        If Not boolFound Then
            listItem = list.Items.Add()
            listItem("UserAlias") = Context.User.Identity.Name
            listItem("Status") = GetUserControlStatus()
            listItem.Update()
        End If
        web.Dispose()
        site.Dispose()
    Catch ex As Exception
        Dim lbl As New Label
        lbl.Text = "<font color='red'>" & ex.Message & "</font><br/>"
        Me.Controls.Add(lbl)
    End Try
End Sub
'Get the currently selected status from
'the user control UI
Private Function GetUserControlStatus() As String
    If radRed.Checked Then
        Return "Red"
    ElseIf radYellow.Checked Then
        Return "Yellow"
```

```vb
            Else
                Return "Green"
            End If
        End Function
        'Helper function to make sure all images are
        'hidden prior to displaying the selected one
        Public Sub HideAllImages()
            Me.imgGreen.Visible = False
            Me.imgYellow.Visible = False
            Me.imgRed.Visible = False
        End Sub
        'The following event handlers process button clicks to
        'display the image corresponding to the selected status
        Public Sub radGreen_CheckedChanged(ByVal sender As System.Object, _
            ByVal e As System.EventArgs) Handles radGreen.CheckedChanged
            HideAllImages()
            If radGreen.Checked Then
                If _showImage Then
                    imgGreen.Visible = True
                End If
            End If
            UpdateStatus()
        End Sub
        Public Sub radYellow_CheckedChanged(ByVal sender As System.Object, _
            ByVal e As System.EventArgs) Handles radYellow.CheckedChanged
            HideAllImages()
            If radYellow.Checked Then
                If _showImage Then
                    imgYellow.Visible = True
                End If
            End If
            UpdateStatus()
        End Sub
        Public Sub radRed_CheckedChanged(ByVal sender As System.Object, _
            ByVal e As System.EventArgs) Handles radRed.CheckedChanged
            HideAllImages()
            If radRed.Checked Then
                If _showImage Then
                    imgRed.Visible = True
                End If
            End If
            UpdateStatus()
        End Sub
    End Class
```

Recipe—C# (See Project SmartPartStatusWebPartCS, Code-Behind SmartPartStatusWebPartCS.ascx.cs)

■**Note** Be sure that the variable _statusListSiteUrl, _statusListWeb, and _statusList reflect the actual location of the list that will contain user status information.

```csharp
using System;
using System.Data;
using System.Configuration;
using System.Collections;
using System.Web;
using System.Web.Security;
using System.Web.UI;
using System.Web.UI.WebControls;
using System.Web.UI.WebControls.WebParts;
using System.Web.UI.HtmlControls;
using Microsoft.SharePoint;
using Microsoft.SharePoint.WebControls;
partial class SmartPartStatusWebPartCS : System.Web.UI.UserControl
{
    //Define local variables
    private bool _showImage = true;
    private string _statusListSiteUrl = "http://localhost";
    private string _statusListWeb = "spwp";
    private string _statusList = "Status";
    private void Page_PreRender(object sender, System.EventArgs e)
    {
        //Only run this code if this is the first time the
        //user control has been displayed on the current
        //page since it was opened
        if (!IsPostBack)
        {
            HideAllImages();
            switch (GetProfileStatus())
            {
                case "Green":
                    this.imgGreen.Visible = true;
                    this.radGreen.Checked = true;
                    break;
                case "Yellow":
                    this.imgYellow.Visible = true;
                    this.radYellow.Checked = true;
                    break;
```

```
                case "Red":
                    this.imgRed.Visible = true;
                    this.radRed.Checked = true;
                    break;
                default:
                    break;
            }
        }
    }
    private string GetProfileStatus()
    {
        try
        {
            //Step 1: Define necessary objects
            SPSite site = new SPSite(_statusListSiteUrl);
            SPWeb web = site.AllWebs[_statusListWeb];
            SPList list = web.Lists[_statusList];
            //Step 2: Find the list item for the current user, and update its status
            //web.AllowUnsafeUpdates = True
            foreach (SPListItem ListItem in list.Items)
            {
                try
                {
                    //Step 3: If found, return their status
                    if (ListItem["UserAlias"].ToString().ToLower() ==
                        Context.User.Identity.Name.ToLower())
                    {
                        return ListItem["Status"].ToString();
                    }
                }
                catch (Exception ex)
                {
                    //No op
                }
            }
            web.Dispose();
            site.Dispose();
        }
        catch (Exception ex)
        {
            //No op
        }
        //Step 4: If we got this far, no entry was found for the current user
        return "";
    }
```

```
private void UpdateStatus()
{
    try {
        //Step 1: Get a handle to the list that we're using to store
        //user status information
        SPSite site = new SPSite(_statusListSiteUrl);
        SPWeb web = site.AllWebs[_statusListWeb];
        SPList list = web.Lists[_statusList];
        SPListItem listItem;
        bool boolFound = false;
        //Step 2: Find the list item for the current user, and update its status
        foreach (SPListItem li in list.Items) {
            try {
                //Step 3: If found, set their status
                if (li["UserAlias"].ToString().ToLower() ==
                    Context.User.Identity.Name.ToLower()) {
                    li["Status"] = GetUserControlStatus();
                    li.Update();
                    boolFound = true;
                    break;
                }
            }
            catch (Exception ex) {
            }
        }
        //Step 4: If an entry for the current user wasn't found in the list,
        //add one now.
        if (!boolFound) {
            listItem = list.Items.Add();
            listItem["UserAlias"] = Context.User.Identity.Name;
            listItem["Status"] = GetUserControlStatus();
            listItem.Update();
        }
        web.Dispose();
        site.Dispose();
    }
    catch (Exception ex) {
        Label lbl = new Label();
        lbl.Text = "<font color='red'>" + ex.Message + "</font><br/>";
        this.Controls.Add(lbl);
    }
}
```

```csharp
//Get the currently selected status from
//the user control UI
private string GetUserControlStatus()
{
    if (radRed.Checked)
    {
        return "Red";
    }
    else if (radYellow.Checked)
    {
        return "Yellow";
    }
    else
    {
        return "Green";
    }
}
//Helper function to make sure all images are
//hidden prior to displaying the selected one
public void HideAllImages()
{
    this.imgGreen.Visible = false;
    this.imgYellow.Visible = false;
    this.imgRed.Visible = false;
}
//The following event handlers process button clicks to
//display the image corresponding to the selected status
public void radGreen_CheckedChanged(object sender, EventArgs e)
{
    HideAllImages();
    if (radGreen.Checked)
    {
        if (_showImage)
        {
            imgGreen.Visible = true;
        }
    }
    UpdateStatus();
}
public void radYellow_CheckedChanged(object sender, EventArgs e)
{
    HideAllImages();
    if (radYellow.Checked)
    {
        if (_showImage)
        {
            imgYellow.Visible = true;
```

```
        }
    }
    UpdateStatus();
}
public void radRed_CheckedChanged(object sender, EventArgs e)
{
    HideAllImages();
    if (radRed.Checked)
    {
        if (_showImage)
        {
            imgRed.Visible = true;
        }
    }
    UpdateStatus();
}
}
```

To Run

After you have successfully compiled your ASP.NET application containing the status user control, copy the user control .ascx and code-behind files (either .ascx.cs or .ascx.vb depending on the language you're using) to the UserControls folder you created earlier.

Next, navigate to a web-part page and place a SmartPart web part on the page. Open the SmartPart's property sheet and select the user control from the drop-down list of user controls in the UserControl folder. That's all there is to it!

When the status control is displayed for a given user for the first time, no image will be displayed. Clicking on one of the radio buttons will cause a new entry for the current user to be inserted into the status list. From that point forward, the Status web part will "remember" the user's status by looking up the user's entry in the status list. Figure 4-15 shows the Status web part as it will display on a web-part page.

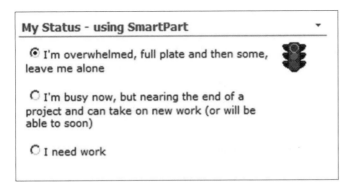

Figure 4-15. *The Status web part in action*

Recipe 4-8. Creating a ZoneTab Web Part

There must be some deep-seated, primal reason why end users love tabs! Not sure why, but they do. In this recipe, you'll learn how to create a web part that displays one to six tabs in a web-part page zone, and enables the user to configure which web parts to display when a particular tab is selected.

This recipe demonstrates several interesting techniques, including these:

- Programmatically hiding or unhiding web parts on a web-part page

- Creating event handlers that execute custom code when a control that belongs to a web part fires an event

- Dynamically modifying attributes of controls when an event occurs

Because there's so much happening in this recipe, it's a bit longer than most of those you'll find in this book, but I'm confident it will be worth the extra work!

Recipe Type: Web Part

Ingredients

Assembly References

- `System.Web` .NET assembly

- `System.Drawing` .NET assembly

Special Considerations

- Because this web part uses the generic ASP.NET 2.0 web-part framework and doesn't need to communicate directly with SharePoint, we won't add a reference to the `Windows.SharePoint.Services` library. However, if you want to use the legacy SharePoint web-part framework, you will need to add that reference to the project.

Preparation

1. Create a new C# or VB.NET class library.

2. Add references to the `System.Web` and `System.Drawing` .NET assemblies.

3. On the project properties Signing tab, select the Sign the Assembly checkbox and specify a new strong-name key file.

4. Add public properties as shown in the following source code.

5. Override the `CreateChildControls()` base web-part method.

6. Create an event handler for the tab `Click` events.

7. Create the `ShowHideWebParts()` custom method as shown in the following source code.

8. Override the `RenderContents()` method to call the `ShowHideWebParts()` method.

Process Flow: CreateChildControls()

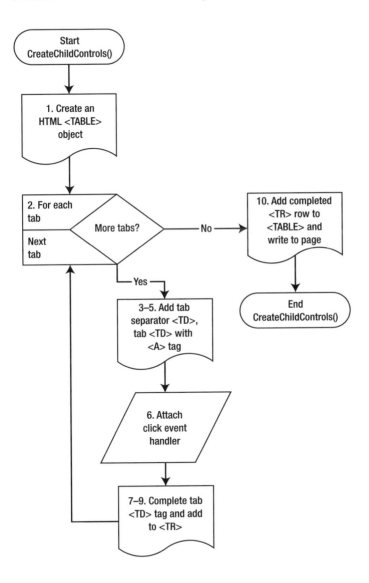

The first of the two most interesting processes in this recipe is the overridden `CreateChildControls()` method that is responsible for drawing the tab menu.

1. Create an in-memory representation of an HTML `<TABLE>` element, and a single `<TR>` element that will contain our tabs.

2. Loop through the list of tabs and their associated named web parts. Tabs are designated by a leading asterisk (*) in the `_tabData` variable.

3. Add a space between tabs.

4. Add a new `<TD>` (cell) object to hold the tab, and assign it a unique ID so we can reference it later in our code.

5. Add a new `<A>` (hyperlink) object that the user can click to display all named web parts associated with a tab. Give the hyperlink a unique ID as well so we can also reference it later in the code.

6. Attach an event handler to the hyperlink object (specifically, it's an ASP.NET `LinkButton` control) that will fire when the user clicks the hyperlink.

7. Finish setting properties that will affect how each tab displays.

8. Add the `<A>` hyperlink object to the `<TD>` table cell object.

9. Add the `<TD>` cell to the `<TR>` table row object.

10. When all tabs have been added to the `<TR>` object, add that to the `<TABLE>` object and render the entire `<TABLE>` to the page.

Process Flow: ShowHideWebParts()

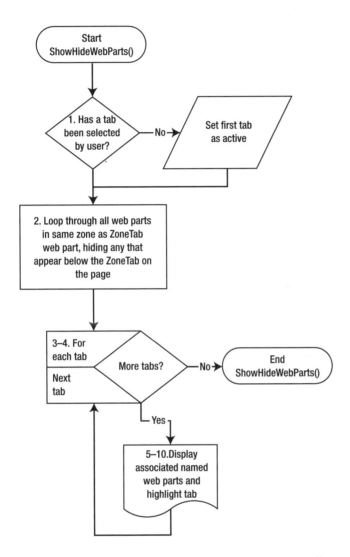

The second interesting method is ShowHideWebParts(). This is a custom method that loops through all web parts in the current zone that are below the ZoneTab web part, and hides those that are not associated with the currently selected tab.

1. If no tab has yet been selected, select the first (leftmost) tab.

2. Get a handle to the collection of all web parts in the same zone as the ZoneTab web part and hide any web parts below the ZoneTab.

3. Loop through the collection of tabs and associated named web parts.

4.–7. When the selected tab is found, unhide any associated web parts.

8. Bring the selected tab to the "front" by changing the border of the associated <TD> table cell element.

9. Highlight the <A> hyperlink element.

10. If it isn't the selected tab, move it to the "back" by changing the associated <TD> table cell element.

11. Unhighlight the tab.

Recipe—VB (See Project ZoneTabWebPartVB, Class ZoneTabWebPart.vb)

```vb
Imports System
Imports System.Collections.Generic
Imports System.Text
Imports System.Web.UI.WebControls
Imports System.Web.UI.WebControls.WebParts
Imports System.Drawing
Namespace ZoneTabWebPartVB
    Public Class ZoneTabWebPart
        Inherits WebPart
        ' Local variables
        Private _tabData As String = ""
        Private _debug As Boolean = False
        Private _selectedTab As String
        Private _tabWidth As Integer = 100
        Private _tabBackgroundColorSelected As String = "white"
        Private _tabBackgroundColorDeselected As String = "whitesmoke"
        <Personalizable()> _
        <WebBrowsable()> _
        <WebDisplayName( _
        "Flag indicating whether debug info should be displayed")> _
        Public Property Debug() As Boolean
            Get
                Return _debug
            End Get
            Set(ByVal value As Boolean)
                _debug = value
            End Set
        End Property
        ' String containing semicolon-delimited list
        ' of tab names. Tab names are preceded by "*".
        '
        ' Example: *Tab 1;webpart1;webpart2;*Tab 2;webpart3
        '
```

```vb
<Personalizable()> _
<WebBrowsable()> _
<WebDisplayName( _
"A delimited list of tab names and associated web parts")> _
Public Property TabData() As String
    Get
        Return _tabData
    End Get
    Set(ByVal value As String)
        _tabData = value
    End Set
End Property
<Personalizable()> _
<WebBrowsable()> _
<WebDescription("Color of selected tab")> _
Public Property SelectedColor() As String
    Get
        Return _tabBackgroundColorSelected
    End Get
    Set(ByVal value As String)
        _tabBackgroundColorSelected = value
    End Set
End Property
<Personalizable()> _
<WebBrowsable()> _
<WebDescription("Color of un-selected tab")> _
Public Property DeSelectedColor() As String
    Get
        Return _tabBackgroundColorDeselected
    End Get
    Set(ByVal value As String)
        _tabBackgroundColorDeselected = value
    End Set
End Property
<Personalizable()> _
<WebBrowsable()> _
<WebDisplayName("Width in pixels for each tab")> _
Public Property TabWidth() As Integer
    Get
        Return _tabWidth
    End Get
    Set(ByVal value As Integer)
        _tabWidth = value
    End Set
End Property
```

```vb
' Add tab-links to page
Protected Overloads Overrides Sub CreateChildControls()
    MyBase.CreateChildControls()
    Try
        Dim arrTabs As String() = _tabData.Split(";"c)
        ' Build list of tabs in the form
        ' of an HTML <TABLE> with <A> tags
        ' for each tab
        ' Step 1: Define <TABLE> and <TR> HTML elements
        Dim tbl As New Table()
        tbl.CellPadding = 0
        tbl.CellSpacing = 0
        Dim tr As New TableRow()
        tr.HorizontalAlign = HorizontalAlign.Left
        ' Step 2: Loop through list of tabs, adding
        ' <TD> and <A> HTML elements for each
        Dim tc As TableCell
        Dim tab As LinkButton
        Dim tabCount As Integer = 0
        For i As Integer = 0 To arrTabs.Length - 1
            If arrTabs(i).IndexOf("*") = 0 Then
                ' Step 3: Add a blank separator cell
                tc = New TableCell()
                tc.Text = " "
                tc.Width = _
                    System.Web.UI.WebControls.Unit.Percentage(1)
                tc.Style("border-bottom") = "black 1px solid"
                tr.Cells.Add(tc)
                ' Step 4: Create a <TD> HTML element to hold the tab
                tc = New TableCell()
                tc.ID = "tc_" + _
                    arrTabs(i).Substring(1).Replace(" ", "_")
                tc.Width = _
                    System.Web.UI.WebControls.Unit.Pixel(_tabWidth)
                ' Step 5: Create an <A> HTML element to represent
                ' the tab. Discard first character, which
                ' was a "*"
                tab = New LinkButton()
                tab.ID = "tab_" + _
                    arrTabs(i).Substring(1).Replace(" ", "_")
                tab.Text = arrTabs(i).Substring(1)
                ' Step 6: Attach event handler that will execute when
                ' user clicks on tab link
                AddHandler tab.Click, AddressOf tab_Click
                ' Step 7: Set any other properties as desired
                tab.Width = _
                    System.Web.UI.WebControls.Unit.Pixel(_tabWidth-2)
```

```vb
                        tab.Style("text-align") = "center"
                        tab.Style("font-size") = "larger"
                        ' Step 8: Insert tab <A> element into <TD> element
                        tc.Controls.Add(tab)
                        ' Step 9: Insert <TD> element into <TR> element
                        tr.Cells.Add(tc)
                        tabCount += 1
                    End If
                Next
                ' Add final blank cell to cause horizontal line to
                ' run across entire zone width
                tc = New TableCell()
                tc.Text = " "
                tc.Width = _
                    System.Web.UI.WebControls.Unit.Pixel(_tabWidth * 10)
                tc.Style("border-bottom") = "black 1px solid"
                tr.Cells.Add(tc)
                ' Step 10: Insert the <TR> element into <TABLE> and
                ' add the HTML table to the page
                tbl.Rows.Add(tr)
                Me.Controls.Add(tbl)
            Catch ex As Exception
                Dim lbl As New Label()
                lbl.Text = "Error: " + ex.Message
                Me.Controls.Add(lbl)
            End Try
        End Sub
        Protected Overloads Overrides Sub RenderContents( _
            ByVal writer As System.Web.UI.HtmlTextWriter)
            If _debug Then
                writer.Write("Tab Data: " + _tabData + "<hr/>")
            End If
            ShowHideWebParts(writer)
            MyBase.RenderContents(writer)
        End Sub
        ' Show web parts for currently selected tab,
        ' hide all others
        Private Sub ShowHideWebParts( _
            ByVal writer As System.Web.UI.HtmlTextWriter)
            Try
                Dim lbl As New Label()
                Dim arrTabs As String() = _tabData.Split(";"c)
                ' Step 1: If a tab has not been selected, assume
                ' the first one
                If _selectedTab Is Nothing Then
                    _selectedTab = arrTabs(0).Substring(1)
                End If
```

```
' Step 2: Hide all web parts in zone that are
' below the ZoneTab part
For Each wp As WebPart In Me.Zone.WebParts
    If wp.ZoneIndex > Me.ZoneIndex Then
        wp.Hidden = True
    End If
Next
For i As Integer = 0 To arrTabs.Length - 1
    ' Step 3: Get web-part names associated with this tab
    ' Step 4: Find the selected tab
    If arrTabs(i) = "*" + _selectedTab Then
        For j As Integer = i + 1 To arrTabs.Length - 1
            ' Step 5: Get associated web-part names
            ' Step 6: Loop until next tab name found,
            ' or end of list
            If arrTabs(j).IndexOf("*") <> 0 Then
                ' Step 7: Show named web parts
                For Each wp As WebPart In Me.Zone.WebParts
                    If wp.Title = arrTabs(j) Then
                        wp.Hidden = False
                    End If
                Next
            Else
                Exit For
            End If
        Next
        ' Step 8: Bring tab border to "front"
        Dim tc As TableCell = _
            DirectCast(Me.FindControl("tc_" + _
            arrTabs(i).Substring(1).Replace(" ", "_")), _
            TableCell)
        tc.Style("border-bottom") = "white 1px solid"
        tc.Style("border-top") = "black 1px solid"
        tc.Style("border-left") = "black 1px solid"
        tc.Style("border-right") = "black 1px solid"
        tc.Style("background-color") = _
            _tabBackgroundColorSelected
        ' Step 9: Highlight selected tab
        Dim tab As LinkButton = _
            DirectCast(Me.FindControl("tab_" + _
            arrTabs(i).Substring(1).Replace(" ", "_")), _
            LinkButton)
        tab.Style("background-color") = _
            _tabBackgroundColorSelected
```

```
                    Else
                        If arrTabs(i).IndexOf("*") = 0 Then
                            ' Step 10: Send tab border to "back"
                            Dim tc As TableCell = _
                                DirectCast(Me.FindControl("tc_" + _
                                arrTabs(i).Substring(1).Replace(" ", "_")), _
                                TableCell)
                            tc.Style("border-bottom") = "black 1px solid"
                            tc.Style("border-top") = "gray 1px solid"
                            tc.Style("border-left") = "gray 1px solid"
                            tc.Style("border-right") = "gray 1px solid"
                            tc.Style("background-color") = _
                                _tabBackgroundColorDeselected
                            ' Step 11: Lowlight selected tab
                            Dim tab As LinkButton = _
                                DirectCast(Me.FindControl("tab_" + _
                                arrTabs(i).Substring(1).Replace(" ", "_")), _
                                LinkButton)
                            tab.Style("background-color") = _
                                _tabBackgroundColorDeselected
                        End If
                    End If
                Next
            Catch ex As Exception
                writer.Write("Error: " + ex.Message)
            End Try
        End Sub
        ' This is the click event handler that was assigned
        ' to all tab LinkButton objects in CreateChildControls()
        ' method.
        Private Sub tab_Click(ByVal sender As Object, ByVal e As EventArgs)
            Try
                ' Set flag indicated current tab, for
                ' use in RenderContents() method
                Dim tab As LinkButton = DirectCast(sender, LinkButton)
                _selectedTab = tab.Text
            Catch ex As Exception
                Dim lbl As New Label()
                lbl.Text = ex.Message
                Me.Controls.Add(lbl)
            End Try
        End Sub
    End Class
End Namespace
```

Recipe—C# (See Project ZoneTabWebPartCS, Class ZoneTabWebPart.cs)

```csharp
using System;
using System.Collections.Generic;
using System.Text;
using System.Web.UI.WebControls;
using System.Web.UI.WebControls.WebParts;
using System.Drawing;
namespace ZoneTabWebPartCS
{
    public class ZoneTabWebPart : WebPart
    {
        // Local variables
        string _tabData = "";
        bool _debug = false;
        string _selectedTab;
        int _tabWidth = 100;
        string _tabBackgroundColorSelected = "white";
        string _tabBackgroundColorDeselected = "whitesmoke";
        [Personalizable]
        [WebBrowsable]
        [WebDisplayName(
           "Flag indicating whether debug info should be displayed")]
        public bool Debug
        {
            get { return _debug; }
            set { _debug = value; }
        }
        // String containing semicolon-delimited list
        // of tab names.  Tab names are preceded by "*".
        //
        // Example: *Tab 1;webpart1;webpart2;*Tab 2;webpart3
        //
        [Personalizable]
        [WebBrowsable]
        [WebDisplayName(
           "A delimited list of tab names and associated web parts")]
        public string TabData
        {
            get { return _tabData; }
            set { _tabData = value; }
        }
```

```csharp
[Personalizable]
[WebBrowsable]
[WebDescription("Color of selected tab")]
public string SelectedColor
{
    get { return _tabBackgroundColorSelected; }
    set { _tabBackgroundColorSelected = value; }
}
[Personalizable]
[WebBrowsable]
[WebDescription("Color of un-selected tab")]
public string DeSelectedColor
{
    get { return _tabBackgroundColorDeselected; }
    set { _tabBackgroundColorDeselected = value; }
}
[Personalizable]
[WebBrowsable]
[WebDisplayName("Width in pixels for each tab")]
public int TabWidth
{
    get { return _tabWidth; }
    set { _tabWidth = value; }
}
// Add tab links to page
protected override void CreateChildControls()
{
    base.CreateChildControls();
    try
    {
        string[] arrTabs = _tabData.Split(';');
        // Build list of tabs in the form
        // of an HTML <TABLE> with <A> tags
        // for each tab
        // Step 1: Define <TABLE> and <TR> HTML elements
        Table tbl = new Table();
        tbl.CellPadding = 0;
        tbl.CellSpacing = 0;
        TableRow tr = new TableRow();
        tr.HorizontalAlign = HorizontalAlign.Left;
        // Step 2: Loop through list of tabs, adding
        //   <TD> and <A> HTML elements for each
        TableCell tc;
        LinkButton tab;
        int tabCount = 0;
```

```
for (int i = 0; i < arrTabs.Length; i++)
{
    if (arrTabs[i].IndexOf("*") == 0)
    {
        // Step 3: Add a blank separator cell
        tc = new TableCell();
        tc.Text = " ";
        tc.Width =
            System.Web.UI.WebControls.Unit.Percentage(1);
        tc.Style["border-bottom"] = "black 1px solid";
        tr.Cells.Add(tc);
        // Step 4: Create a <TD> HTML element to hold the tab
        tc = new TableCell();
        tc.ID = "tc_" +
            arrTabs[i].Substring(1).Replace(" ", "_");
        tc.Width =
            System.Web.UI.WebControls.Unit.Pixel(_tabWidth);
        // Step 5: Create an <A> HTML element to represent
        // the tab.  Discard first character, which
        // was a "*"
        tab = new LinkButton();
        tab.ID = "tab_" +
            arrTabs[i].Substring(1).Replace(" ", "_");
        tab.Text = arrTabs[i].Substring(1);
        // Step 6: Attach event handler that will execute
        // when user clicks tab link
        tab.Click += new EventHandler(tab_Click);
        // Step 7: Set any other properties as desired
        tab.Width =
            System.Web.UI.WebControls.Unit.Pixel(_tabWidth-2);
        tab.Style["text-align"] = "center";
        tab.Style["font-size"] = "larger";
        // Step 8: Insert tab <A> element into <TD> element
        tc.Controls.Add(tab);
        // Step 9: Insert <TD> element into <TR> element
        tr.Cells.Add(tc);
        tabCount++;
    }
}
// Add final blank cell to cause horizontal line to
// run across entire zone width
tc = new TableCell();
tc.Text = " ";
tc.Width =
    System.Web.UI.WebControls.Unit.Pixel(_tabWidth * 10);
tc.Style["border-bottom"] = "black 1px solid";
tr.Cells.Add(tc);
```

```
            // Step 10: Insert the <TR> element into <TABLE> and
            // add the HTML table to the page
            tbl.Rows.Add(tr);
            this.Controls.Add(tbl);
        }
        catch (Exception ex)
        {
            Label lbl = new Label();
            lbl.Text = "Error: " + ex.Message;
            this.Controls.Add(lbl);
        }
    }
    protected override void RenderContents(
        System.Web.UI.HtmlTextWriter writer)
    {
        if (_debug)
        {
            writer.Write("Tab Data: " + _tabData + "<hr/>");
        }
        ShowHideWebParts(writer);
        base.RenderContents(writer);
    }
    // Show web parts for currently selected tab,
    // hide all others
    void ShowHideWebParts(System.Web.UI.HtmlTextWriter writer)
    {
        try
        {
            Label lbl = new Label();
            string[] arrTabs = _tabData.Split(';');
            // Step 1: If a tab has not been selected, assume
            // the first one
            if (_selectedTab == null)
                _selectedTab = arrTabs[0].Substring(1);
            // Step 2: Hide all web parts in zone that are
            // below the ZoneTab part
            foreach (WebPart wp in this.Zone.WebParts)
            {
                if (wp.ZoneIndex > this.ZoneIndex)
                {
                    wp.Hidden = true;
                }
            }
            // Step 3: Get web-part names associated with this tab
```

```csharp
for (int i = 0; i < arrTabs.Length; i++)
{
    // Step 4: Find the selected tab
    if (arrTabs[i] == "*" + _selectedTab)
    {
        // Step 5: Get associated web-part names
        for (int j = i + 1; j < arrTabs.Length; j++)
        {
            // Step 6: Loop until next tab name found,
            // or end of list
            if (arrTabs[j].IndexOf("*") != 0)
            {
                // Step 7: Show named web parts
                foreach (WebPart wp in this.Zone.WebParts)
                {
                    if (wp.Title == arrTabs[j])
                        wp.Hidden = false;
                }
            }
            else
            {
                break;
            }
        }
        // Step 8: Bring tab border to "front"
        TableCell tc =
            (TableCell)this.FindControl("tc_" +
            arrTabs[i].Substring(1).Replace(" ", "_"));
        tc.Style["border-bottom"] = "white 1px solid";
        tc.Style["border-top"] = "black 1px solid";
        tc.Style["border-left"] = "black 1px solid";
        tc.Style["border-right"] = "black 1px solid";
        tc.Style["background-color"] =
            _tabBackgroundColorSelected;
        // Step 9: Highlight selected tab
        LinkButton tab =
            (LinkButton)this.FindControl("tab_" +
            arrTabs[i].Substring(1).Replace(" ", "_"));
        tab.Style["background-color"] =
            _tabBackgroundColorSelected;
    }
    else
    {
        if (arrTabs[i].IndexOf("*") == 0)
        {
```

```
                          // Step 10: Send tab border to "back"
                          TableCell tc =
                              (TableCell)this.FindControl("tc_" +
                              arrTabs[i].Substring(1).Replace(" ", "_"));
                          tc.Style["border-bottom"] = "black 1px solid";
                          tc.Style["border-top"] = "gray 1px solid";
                          tc.Style["border-left"] = "gray 1px solid";
                          tc.Style["border-right"] = "gray 1px solid";
                          tc.Style["background-color"] =
                              _tabBackgroundColorDeselected;
                          // Step 11: Lowlight selected tab
                          LinkButton tab =
                              (LinkButton)this.FindControl("tab_" +
                              arrTabs[i].Substring(1).Replace(" ", "_"));
                          tab.Style["background-color"] =
                              _tabBackgroundColorDeselected;
                      }
                  }
              }
          }
          catch (Exception ex)
          {
              writer.Write("Error: " + ex.Message);
          }
      }
      // This is the click event handler that was assigned
      // to all tab LinkButton objects in CreateChildControls()
      // method.
      void tab_Click(object sender, EventArgs e)
      {
          try
          {
              // Set flag indicating current tab, for
              // use in RenderContents() method
              LinkButton tab = (LinkButton)sender;
              _selectedTab = tab.Text;
          }
          catch (Exception ex)
          {
              Label lbl = new Label();
              lbl.Text = ex.Message;
              this.Controls.Add(lbl);
          }
      }
  }
}
```

To Run

■**Note** Please see the "To Run" section of Recipe 4-1 for instructions on how to deploy a web part to a single site collection. After the web part has been successfully deployed, proceed with the following steps.

After you have deployed the ZoneTab web part, browse to a web-part page in the site collection to which the ZoneTab has been deployed. Add the ZoneTab to a page and set the properties as shown in Figures 4-16 and 4-17.

■**Note** Your actual values may vary depending on the web parts you want to show or hide on your page.

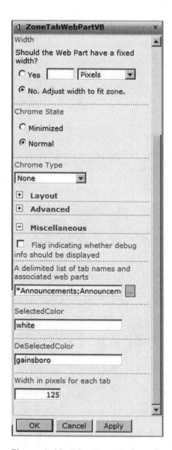

Figure 4-16. *The ZoneTab web part's property sheet*

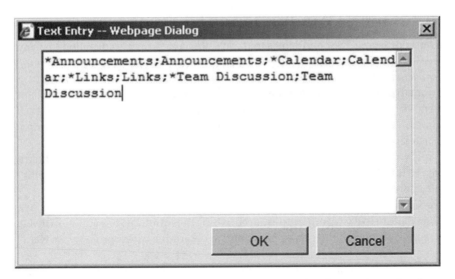

Figure 4-17. *Syntax for entering tab names and associated web parts for each tab*

In the preceding screen shots, you can see the ZoneTab web-part property sheet, along with an expanded view of the text that defines the tabs and associated named web parts, which will be displayed when a particular tab is selected. Figure 4-18 shows the ZoneTab web part as it will display on a web-part page.

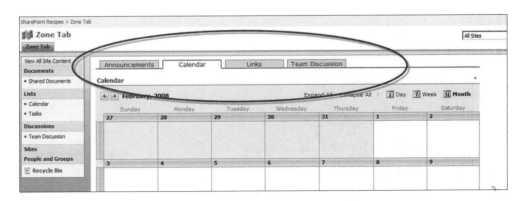

Figure 4-18. *The ZoneTab web part in action*

Variations

- This recipe uses simple outlining to give the impression of tabs. Alternatively, you can set a background image for the <TD> table cells that represent the tabs to give a more realistic impression of tabs.

- When a page refresh occurs, the first tab will always be reselected. You could save the selected tab to a cookie on the user's computer, and then reset the tab based on the cookie value, to cause the last selected tab to be reselected when the user returns to this page.

Recipe 4-9. Creating a Web Part to Edit SPWeb Properties

One of the better-kept secrets in SharePoint is that each site has a property collection that you can use to store site-specific data, *as long as you don't delete or edit the properties that Microsoft stores in that collection.* This collection can be a convenient place to store small amounts of data that you want to use to control a web site. For example, you could use it to store the client code of the client for which a particular site was created, and retrieve that property in other web parts or programs to control their behavior. Retrieving a property is simpler than storing the same data in a SharePoint list, so it means less code.

In this recipe, you'll create a little web part to add, edit, or delete site properties that have a specific prefix. Using a settable prefix, we can filter properties so we don't accidentally edit one of the built-in properties used internally by SharePoint.

This recipe takes the use of web-part events a step further than the ZoneTab recipe by attaching a Delete button to each property displayed, wiring those buttons to a common delete event handler, and using data in the sender parameter to determine which property we want to delete.

Because this web part manipulates site information, it must know whether a user is a site administrator to determine whether the list of properties should be read-only or editable. To accomplish that, we'll use the SPWeb.CurrentUser.IsSiteAdmin property.

■**Tip** If you want this recipe to work for users who have Full Control rights on the site but are not necessarily site collection administrators, use SPWeb.UserIsWebAdmin.

Recipe Type: Web Part

Ingredients

Assembly References

- System.Web .NET assembly

- Windows.SharePoint.Services .NET assembly

Special Considerations

- Unlike several earlier web-part recipes, we'll need the Microsoft.SharePoint namespaces because we're retrieving and manipulating data about a SharePoint web site.

- SharePoint creates a number of properties for every site that should not be changed or deleted, so this recipe uses a prefix for every property created. The prefix default is mg_ but you can change it to any value you want, as long as you don't use vti_ (which is the prefix used by Microsoft).

Preparation

1. Create a new C# or VB.NET class library.

2. Add references to the System.Web and Windows.SharePoint.Services .NET assemblies.

3. On the project properties Signing tab, select the Sign the Assembly checkbox and specify a new strong-name key file.

4. Add public properties as shown in the following source code.

5. Override the `CreateChildControls()` base web-part method as shown in the following code.

6. Add the `btnClick()` and `delbtnClick()` event handlers.

7. Override the `RenderContents()` method to call the `ShowHideWebParts()` method.

Process Flow: CreateChildControls()

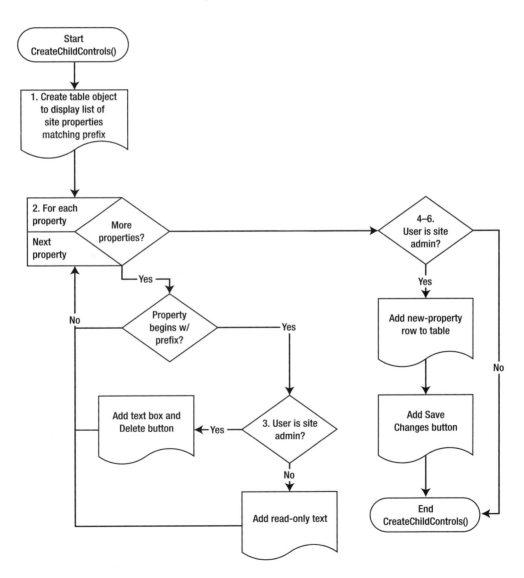

The `CreateChildControls()` method is fairly interesting in that in it we build a dynamic `<TABLE>` to contain the list of properties in the site matching our prefix, and for site administrators, Add, Delete, and Save buttons as well.

1. Create an in-memory `<TABLE>` object to hold the list of matching properties.

2. Loop through the properties for this web site, finding those whose key begins with the prefix specified in the web part `prefix` property.

3. If the user is a site administrator, place the property value in a text box, and include a Delete button to the right of the text box. Otherwise, just write the literal text of the property value to the page.

4. When finished writing all matching properties, determine whether the user is a site administrator.

5. If the user is the site administrator, add a blank row in which the user can add a new property.

6. Add a button to enable the user to save changes to existing or new properties.

Process Flow: btn_Click()

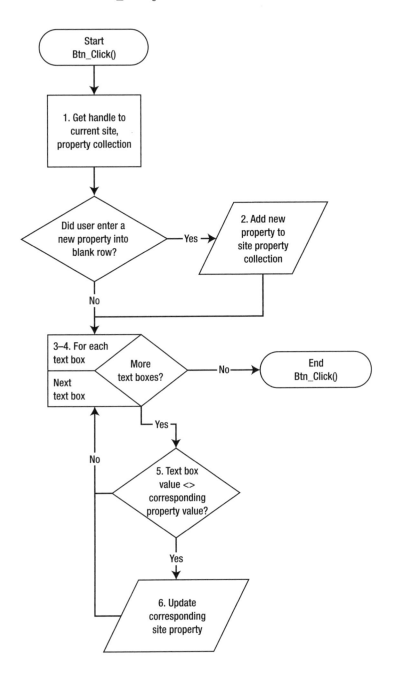

The btn_Click() event handler fires when the user clicks the Save Changes button, and is responsible for writing changed or new properties back to SharePoint.

1. Create an SPWeb object from the current context that points to the web site in which the current web-part page exists.

2. If the user entered a new property in the blank row at the bottom of the form, add a new property to the site with the same key name and value.

3. Loop through all text boxes in the web part that have an ID of key_<n>, where <n> is between 1 and 999.

4. Continue looping until no more text boxes with that ID pattern are found.

5. Determine whether the text box found has a text value that is different from the corresponding site property.

6. If the text box does have a different value, update the site property with the text box's value.

Process Flow: delbtn_Click()

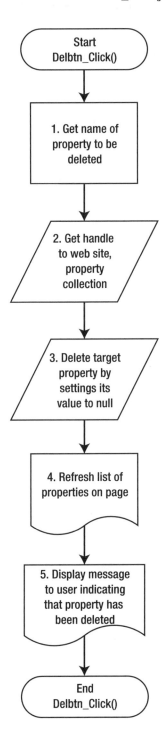

The `delbtn_Click()` event handler fires when the user clicks a Delete button to the right of an editable property, and is responsible for removing the corresponding site property from the property collection.

1. Find the name of the property to delete by inspecting the object (in this case, the specific Delete button) that fired the event.

2. Create an `SPWeb` object pointing to the current site.

3. Set the value of the property to be deleted to `null`, which will cause it to be removed from the collection. Note that there is a `Remove()` method on the `Properties` collection, but it failed to delete the property, so I chose this method instead.

4. Call the `CreateChildControls()` method again to redraw the `<TABLE>` of matching properties without the deleted property.

5. Display a message below the table informing the end user that the property has been deleted.

Recipe—VB (See Project WebPropertiesWebPartVB, Class WebPropertiesWebPart.vb)

```vb
Imports System
Imports System.Collections.Generic
Imports System.Text
Imports System.Web.UI.WebControls
Imports System.Web.UI.WebControls.WebParts
Imports Microsoft.SharePoint
Imports Microsoft.SharePoint.WebControls
Imports Microsoft.SharePoint.Utilities
Public Class WebPropertiesWebPart
    Inherits WebPart
    ' Define location variables
    Private _debug As Boolean = False
    Private _prefix As String = "mg_"
    <Personalizable()> _
    <WebBrowsable()> _
    <WebDescription("Check to display debug information")> _
    <WebDisplayName("Debug?")> _
    Public Property Debug() As Boolean
        Get
            Return _debug
        End Get
        Set(ByVal value As Boolean)
            _debug = value
        End Set
    End Property
```

```vbnet
<Personalizable()> _
<WebBrowsable()> _
<WebDescription("Prefix to use when storing & retrieving properties")> _
<WebDisplayName("Property prefix: ")> _
Public Property Prefix() As String
    Get
        Return _prefix
    End Get
    Set(ByVal value As String)
        _prefix = value
    End Set
End Property
Protected Overloads Overrides Sub CreateChildControls()
    MyBase.CreateChildControls()
    Try
        ' Step 1: Create table to hold existing, new properties
        Dim tbl As New Table()
        Dim tr As TableRow
        Dim tc As TableCell
        Dim delBtn As ImageButton
        Dim tb As TextBox
        Dim lbl As Label
        Dim i As Integer = 1
        ' Just a bit of formatting
        tbl.CellPadding = 3
        tbl.CellSpacing = 3
        tbl.BorderStyle = BorderStyle.Solid
        ' Add a heading
        tr = New TableRow()
        ' #
        tc = New TableCell()
        tr.Cells.Add(tc)
        ' Key
        tc = New TableCell()
        tc.Text = "Property Key"
        tc.Font.Bold = True
        tr.Cells.Add(tc)
        ' Value
        tc = New TableCell()
        tc.Text = "Value"
        tc.Font.Bold = True
        tr.Cells.Add(tc)
        tbl.Rows.Add(tr)
        ' Delete button
        tc = New TableCell()
        tr.Cells.Add(tc)
        tc.Font.Bold = True
```

```vb
tr.Cells.Add(tc)
tbl.Rows.Add(tr)
' Step 2: Loop through existing properties that match prefix
' and are not null, add to table
Dim web As SPWeb = SPControl.GetContextWeb(Context)
Dim properties As SPPropertyBag = web.Properties
Dim isAdmin As Boolean = web.CurrentUser.IsSiteAdmin
For Each key As Object In properties.Keys
    If key.ToString().IndexOf(_prefix) = 0 _
        AndAlso properties(key.ToString()) IsNot Nothing Then
        ' Create a new row for current property
        tr = New TableRow()
        ' #
        tc = New TableCell()
        tc.Text = i.ToString() + ". "
        tr.Cells.Add(tc)
        ' Key
        tc = New TableCell()
        tc.Text = key.ToString().Substring(_prefix.Length)
        tc.ID = "key_" + i.ToString()
        tr.Cells.Add(tc)
        ' Value
        tc = New TableCell()
        ' 3. For admin users, show value in
        ' an editable text box + delete button
        If isAdmin Then
            tb = New TextBox()
            tb.Text = properties(key.ToString())
            tb.ID = "value_" + i.ToString()
            tc.Controls.Add(tb)
            tr.Cells.Add(tc)
            tc = New TableCell()
            delBtn = New ImageButton()
            delBtn.ImageUrl = "/_layouts/images/delete.gif"
            AddHandler delBtn.Click, AddressOf delBtn_Click
            delBtn.ID = "delete_" + i.ToString()
            tc.Controls.Add(delBtn)
            tr.Cells.Add(tc)
        Else
            ' for non-admin users, just show read-only
            lbl = New Label()
            lbl.Text = properties(key.ToString())
            tc.Controls.Add(lbl)
            tr.Cells.Add(tc)
        End If
```

```vb
                        ' Add new row to table
                        tbl.Rows.Add(tr)
                        i += 1
                    End If
            Next
            ' Step 4: Add a final row to allow user
            ' to add new properties if current user is site admin
            If isAdmin Then
                tr = New TableRow()
                ' #
                tc = New TableCell()
                tc.Text = "*. "
                tr.Cells.Add(tc)
                ' Key
                tc = New TableCell()
                tb = New TextBox()
                tb.Text = ""
                tb.ID = "key_new"
                tc.Controls.Add(tb)
                tr.Cells.Add(tc)
                ' Value
                tc = New TableCell()
                tb = New TextBox()
                tb.Text = ""
                tb.ID = "value_new"
                tc.Controls.Add(tb)
                tr.Cells.Add(tc)
                tbl.Rows.Add(tr)
            End If
            ' Step 5: Add the completed table to the page
            Me.Controls.Add(tbl)
            ' Step 6: Now add a button to save changes,
            ' if current user is site admin
            If isAdmin Then
                lbl = New Label()
                lbl.Text = "<br/>"
                Me.Controls.Add(lbl)
                Dim btn As New Button()
                btn.Text = "Save changes"
                AddHandler btn.Click, AddressOf btn_Click
                Me.Controls.Add(btn)
            End If
        Catch ex As Exception
            Dim lbl As New Label()
            lbl.Text = "Error: " + ex.Message
            Me.Controls.Add(lbl)
        End Try
    End Sub
```

```vb
' Handles "Save Changes" button click event
Private Sub btn_Click(ByVal sender As Object, ByVal e As EventArgs)
    Try
        ' Step 1: Get handle to web site property
        ' collection
        Dim isChanged As Boolean = False
        Dim web As SPWeb = SPControl.GetContextWeb(Context)
        Dim properties As SPPropertyBag = web.Properties
        web.AllowUnsafeUpdates = True
        ' Step 2: Add new property
        Dim tbNewKey As TextBox = _
            DirectCast(Me.FindControl("key_new"), TextBox)
        Dim tbNewValue As TextBox = _
            DirectCast(Me.FindControl("value_new"), TextBox)
        If tbNewKey.Text <> "" Then
            properties(_prefix + tbNewKey.Text) = tbNewValue.Text
            web.Properties.Update()
            isChanged = True
        End If
        ' Step 3: Loop through text boxes in web part,
        ' updating corresponding site property if
        ' checkbox has been changed.
        Dim tc As TableCell
        Dim tb As TextBox
        For i As Integer = 1 To 998
            tc = DirectCast( _
                Me.FindControl("key_" + i.ToString()), TableCell)
            ' Step 4: If a control with the name "key_<n>" exists, get
            ' it, otherwise assume no more custom properties to edit
            If tc IsNot Nothing Then
                ' Step 5: Ok, we found the text box containing the
                ' property value, now let's see if the value in the
                ' text box has been changed to something other than that
                ' in the corresponding web property.
                tb = DirectCast( _
                    Me.FindControl("value_" + i.ToString()), TextBox)
                If properties(_prefix + tc.Text).Trim() _
                    <> tb.Text.Trim() Then
                    ' Step 6: The value was changed, update the web
                    ' property and set the flag indicating that web part
                    ' needs to be redrawn
                    properties(_prefix + tc.Text) = tb.Text
                    web.Properties.Update()
                    isChanged = True
                End If
            Else
                Exit For
            End If
```

```vb
            Next
            ' Step 7: If any changes made, redraw web part
            ' to reflect changed/added properties
            If isChanged Then
                Me.Controls.Clear()
                CreateChildControls()
            End If
        Catch ex As Exception
            Dim lbl As New Label()
            lbl.Text = "<br/><br/>Error: " + ex.Message
            Me.Controls.Add(lbl)
        End Try
End Sub
' Handles individual property delete button click
Private Sub delBtn_Click(ByVal sender As Object, _
    ByVal e As System.Web.UI.ImageClickEventArgs)
    Try
        ' Step 1. Get handle to name of property to be
        ' deleted
        Dim delBtn As ImageButton = DirectCast(sender, ImageButton)
        Dim _id As String = delBtn.ID.Replace("delete_", "")
        Dim tc As TableCell = _
            DirectCast(Me.FindControl("key_" + _id), TableCell)
        ' Step 2: Get handle to web site, property collection
        Dim web As SPWeb = SPControl.GetContextWeb(Context)
        Dim properties As SPPropertyBag = web.Properties
        web.AllowUnsafeUpdates = True
        ' Step 3: Delete the unwanted property by setting
        ' its value to null (note: for some reason using
        ' the Remove() method was not sufficient to cause
        ' SharePoint to delete the property).
        web.Properties(_prefix + tc.Text) = Nothing
        web.Properties.Update()
        web.Update()
        ' Step 4: Refresh list
        Me.Controls.Clear()
        CreateChildControls()
        ' Step 5: Display message to user informing them
        ' that property has been deleted
        Dim lbl As New Label()
        lbl.Text = "<br/><br/>You deleted property '" + tc.Text + "'"
        Me.Controls.Add(lbl)
    Catch ex As Exception
        Dim lbl As New Label()
        lbl.Text = "<br/><br/>Error: " + ex.Message
        Me.Controls.Add(lbl)
    End Try
```

```vbnet
    End Sub
    Protected Overloads Overrides Sub RenderContents( _
        ByVal writer As System.Web.UI.HtmlTextWriter)
        MyBase.RenderContents(writer)
        If _debug Then
            writer.Write("<hr/>")
            writer.Write("<strong>Prefix:</strong> " + _prefix)
            writer.Write("<hr/>")
        End If
    End Sub
End Class
```

Recipe—C# (See Project WebPartPropertiesCS, Class WebPartProperties.cs)

```csharp
using System;
using System.Collections.Generic;
using System.Text;
using System.Web.UI.WebControls;
using System.Web.UI.WebControls.WebParts;
using Microsoft.SharePoint;
using Microsoft.SharePoint.WebControls;
using Microsoft.SharePoint.Utilities;
namespace WebPropertiesWebPartCS
{
    public class WebPropertiesWebPart : WebPart
    {
        // Define location variables
        bool _debug = false;
        string _prefix = "mg_";
        [Personalizable]
        [WebBrowsable]
        [WebDescription("Check to display debug information")]
        [WebDisplayName("Debug?")]
        public bool Debug
        {
            get { return _debug; }
            set { _debug = value; }
        }
        [Personalizable]
        [WebBrowsable]
        [WebDescription(
            "Prefix to use when storing and retrieving properties")]
        [WebDisplayName("Property prefix: ")]
        public string Prefix
        {
            get { return _prefix; }
            set { _prefix = value; }
        }
```

```
protected override void CreateChildControls()
{
    base.CreateChildControls();
    try
    {
        // Step 1: Create table to hold existing, new properties
        Table tbl = new Table();
        TableRow tr;
        TableCell tc;
        ImageButton delBtn;
        TextBox tb;
        Label lbl;
        int i = 1;
        // Just a bit of formatting
        tbl.CellPadding = 3;
        tbl.CellSpacing = 3;
        tbl.BorderStyle = BorderStyle.Solid;
        // Add a heading
        tr = new TableRow();
        // #
        tc = new TableCell();
        tr.Cells.Add(tc);
        // Key
        tc = new TableCell();
        tc.Text = "Property Key";
        tc.Font.Bold = true;
        tr.Cells.Add(tc);
        // Value
        tc = new TableCell();
        tc.Text = "Value";
        tc.Font.Bold = true;
        tr.Cells.Add(tc);
        tbl.Rows.Add(tr);
        // Delete button
        tc = new TableCell();
        tr.Cells.Add(tc);
        tc.Font.Bold = true;
        tr.Cells.Add(tc);
        tbl.Rows.Add(tr);
        // Step 2: Loop through existing properties that match prefix
        // and are not null, add to table
        SPWeb web = SPControl.GetContextWeb(Context);
        SPPropertyBag properties = web.Properties;
        bool isAdmin = web.CurrentUser.IsSiteAdmin;
```

```
foreach (object key in properties.Keys)
{
    if (key.ToString().IndexOf(_prefix) == 0
        && properties[key.ToString()] != null)
    {
        // Create a new row for current property
        tr = new TableRow();
        // #
        tc = new TableCell();
        tc.Text = i.ToString() + ". ";
        tr.Cells.Add(tc);
        // Key
        tc = new TableCell();
        tc.Text = key.ToString().Substring(_prefix.Length);
        tc.ID = "key_" + i.ToString();
        tr.Cells.Add(tc);
        // Value
        tc = new TableCell();
        // 3. For admin users, show value in
        // an editable text box + delete button
        if (isAdmin)
        {
            tb = new TextBox();
            tb.Text = properties[key.ToString()];
            tb.ID = "value_" + i.ToString();
            tc.Controls.Add(tb);
            tr.Cells.Add(tc);
            tc = new TableCell();
            delBtn = new ImageButton();
            delBtn.ImageUrl = "/_layouts/images/delete.gif";
            delBtn.Click += new
                System.Web.UI.ImageClickEventHandler(delBtn_Click);
            delBtn.ID = "delete_" + i.ToString();
            tc.Controls.Add(delBtn);
            tr.Cells.Add(tc);
        }
        else // for non-admin users, just show read-only
        {
            lbl = new Label();
            lbl.Text = properties[key.ToString()];
            tc.Controls.Add(lbl);
            tr.Cells.Add(tc);
        }
        // Add new row to table
        tbl.Rows.Add(tr);
        i++;
    }
}
```

```csharp
                // Step 4: Add a final row to allow user
                // to add new properties if current user is site admin
                if (isAdmin)
                {
                    tr = new TableRow();
                    // #
                    tc = new TableCell();
                    tc.Text = "*. ";
                    tr.Cells.Add(tc);
                    // Key
                    tc = new TableCell();
                    tb = new TextBox();
                    tb.Text = "";
                    tb.ID = "key_new";
                    tc.Controls.Add(tb);
                    tr.Cells.Add(tc);
                    // Value
                    tc = new TableCell();
                    tb = new TextBox();
                    tb.Text = "";
                    tb.ID = "value_new";
                    tc.Controls.Add(tb);
                    tr.Cells.Add(tc);
                    tbl.Rows.Add(tr);
                }
                // Step 5: Add the completed table to the page
                this.Controls.Add(tbl);
                // Step 6: Now add a button to save changes,
                // if current user is site admin
                if (isAdmin)
                {
                    lbl = new Label();
                    lbl.Text = "<br/>";
                    this.Controls.Add(lbl);
                    Button btn = new Button();
                    btn.Text = "Save changes";
                    btn.Click += new EventHandler(btn_Click);
                    this.Controls.Add(btn);
                }
            }
            catch (Exception ex)
            {
                Label lbl = new Label();
                lbl.Text = "Error: " + ex.Message;
                this.Controls.Add(lbl);
            }
        }
```

```csharp
// Handles "Save Changes" button click event
void btn_Click(object sender, EventArgs e)
{
    try
    {
        // Step 1: Get handle to web site property
        // collection
        bool isChanged = false;
        SPWeb web = SPControl.GetContextWeb(Context);
        SPPropertyBag properties = web.Properties;
        web.AllowUnsafeUpdates = true;
        // Step 2: Add new property
        TextBox tbNewKey = (TextBox)this.FindControl("key_new");
        TextBox tbNewValue = (TextBox)this.FindControl("value_new");
        if (tbNewKey.Text != "")
        {
            properties[_prefix+tbNewKey.Text] = tbNewValue.Text;
            web.Properties.Update();
            isChanged = true;
        }
        // Step 3: Loop through text boxes in web part
        // updating corresponding site property if
        // checkbox has been changed.
        TableCell tc;
        TextBox tb;
        for (int i = 1; i < 999; i++)
        {
            tc = (TableCell)this.FindControl("key_"+i.ToString());
            // Step 4: If a control with the name "key_<n>"
            // exists, get it, otherwise assume no more custom
            // properties to edit
            if (tc != null)
            {
                // Step 5: Ok, we found the text box containing the
                // property value, now let's see if the value in the
                // text box has been changed to something other than
                // that in the corresponding web property.
                tb = (TextBox)this.FindControl("value_" +
                    i.ToString());
                if (properties[_prefix+tc.Text].Trim() !=
                    tb.Text.Trim())
                {
                    // Step 6: The value was changed, update the web
                    // property and set the flag indicating that web
                    // part needs to be redrawn
                    properties[_prefix+tc.Text] = tb.Text;
```

```
                    web.Properties.Update();
                    isChanged = true;
                }
            }
            else
            {
                break;
            }
        }
        // Step 7: If any changes made, redraw web part
        // to reflect changed/added properties
        if (isChanged)
        {
            this.Controls.Clear();
            CreateChildControls();
        }
    }
    catch (Exception ex)
    {
        Label lbl = new Label();
        lbl.Text = "<br/><br/>Error: " + ex.Message;
        this.Controls.Add(lbl);
    }
}
// Handles individual property delete button click
void delBtn_Click(object sender, System.Web.UI.ImageClickEventArgs e)
{
    try
    {
        // Step 1. Get handle to name of property to be
        // deleted
        ImageButton delBtn = (ImageButton)sender;
        string _id = delBtn.ID.Replace("delete_", "");
        TableCell tc = (TableCell)this.FindControl("key_" + _id);
        // Step 2: Get handle to web site, property collection
        SPWeb web = SPControl.GetContextWeb(Context);
        SPPropertyBag properties = web.Properties;
        web.AllowUnsafeUpdates = true;
        // Step 3: Delete the unwanted property by setting
        // its value to null (note: for some reason using
        // the Remove() method was not sufficient to cause
        // SharePoint to delete the property).
        web.Properties[_prefix + tc.Text] = null;
        web.Properties.Update();
        web.Update();
```

```
                // Step 4: Refresh list
                this.Controls.Clear();
                CreateChildControls();
                // Step 5: Display message to user informing them
                // that property has been deleted
                Label lbl = new Label();
                lbl.Text = "<br/><br/>You deleted property '" +
                    tc.Text + "'";
                this.Controls.Add(lbl);
            }
            catch (Exception ex)
            {
                Label lbl = new Label();
                lbl.Text = "<br/><br/>Error: " + ex.Message;
                this.Controls.Add(lbl);
            }
        }
        protected override void RenderContents(
            System.Web.UI.HtmlTextWriter writer)
        {
            base.RenderContents(writer);
            if (_debug)
            {
                writer.Write("<hr/>");
                writer.Write("<strong>Prefix:</strong> " + _prefix);
                writer.Write("<hr/>");
            }
        }
    }
}
```

To Run

■Note Please see the "To Run" section of Recipe 4-1 for instructions on how to deploy a web part to a single site collection. After the web part has been successfully deployed, proceed with the following steps.

Open a web-part page in the site collection to which you have deployed the Web Properties web part, edit the page, and add an instance of the web part. Edit the web part properties to set the prefix you wish to use for properties that will be added or edited through this web part.

Figure 4-19 shows a Web Properties web part as it will be displayed for a user who is a site collection administrator, on a site where five properties have already been added: client#, client name, status, matter name, and #. A new property with a key of new key and value of new value will be added to the property collection when the Save Changes button is clicked. Figure 4-19 shows the Web Properties web part with several custom web site properties already added.

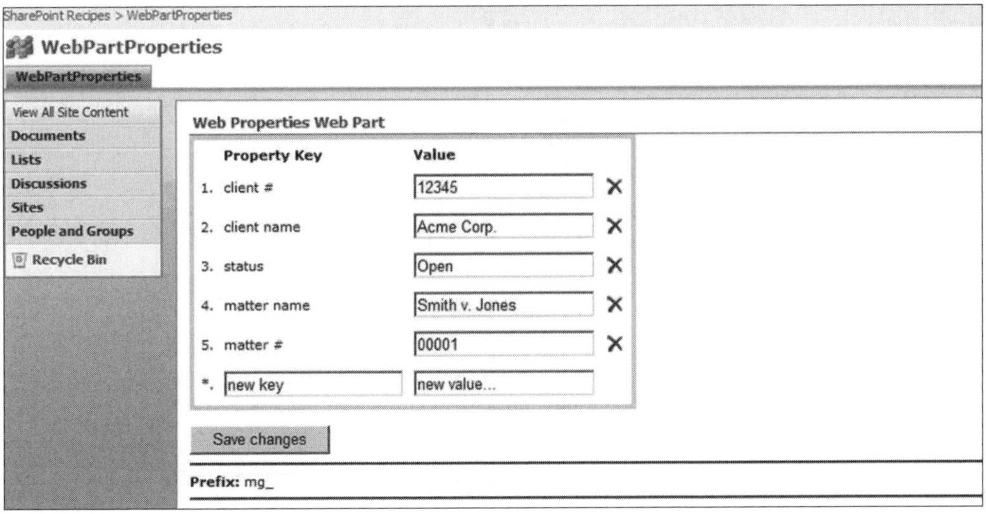

Figure 4-19. *The Web Properties web part shown with custom web properties*

Variations

- Although this recipe is designed to edit the current site's property collection, the general pattern can be adapted to any collection of key/value pairs. This could be items from a SharePoint list or even from an external database—with minor changes, the event handling will be the same.

- The recipe does not currently prompt the user to confirm a deletion. It would be fairly simple to add some client-side JavaScript to confirm that the user wants to delete a selected property and cancel the event if requested.

- Make a connectable web part that reads from the property bag (for instance, store the primary key of the web's associated entity) and then provides the value to multiple other web parts on the page that then use that value to read information from a database or filter their data.

CHAPTER 5

■ ■ ■

Working with Event Handlers

SharePoint 2007 has a significantly expanded event-handling capability that can be used to add custom pre- or postprocessing of list events. Such handlers dramatically expand what SharePoint can do with lists. And after you've mastered the basics, there's really no limit to the code that you can attach to an event handler. In this chapter, you'll find several recipes that will show you their flexibility and potential, including how to validate and update list item data, send a custom email upon task completion, and prevent users from deleting items based on custom business rules.

Note Everything shown in this chapter will work in either MOSS 2007 or WSS 3.0.

Why Create an Event Handler?

SharePoint's native list handling provides significant functionality out of the box, but there are times that you'll want more. Some example cases include the following:

- Performing complex data validation prior to allowing edits to be saved

- Filling fields with data from external systems

- Sending a thank-you email to a survey respondent

- Logging events to the file system or custom database

Caution Limited though event handling was in SharePoint 2003, it was often used to create simple workflow applications for document or form libraries (the only list types that supported event handling in that version of SharePoint). SharePoint now provides a rich framework (Workflow Foundation) for creating both sequential and state workflows. Therefore, you want to avoid creating highly complex event handlers. As a rule of thumb, if your event handler must perform more than one or two operations (for example, updating some fields, validating data, or sending an email), you should consider using a workflow rather than an event handler.

When to Use an Event Handler Rather Than a Workflow?

The key to answering that question is to understand that event handlers and workflows have fundamentally different design objectives, although they can be used to address similar problems. *Event handlers* respond in near real-time to user-initiated actions on a list (for example, adding a new document, updating properties, or deleting an item). *Workflows*, on the other hand, are most appropriate for long-running processes that may span minutes, hours, or days and involve multiple individuals (for example, a purchase order approval process). You could use event handlers to piece together workflows, and you could use a workflow to respond to list events in real time, but in either case you'd be doing more work than needed to get the job done. Having said that, there might be very simple workflows in which an event handler would be the easier approach. (When it comes to programming, sloth is a virtue in my book.)

■**Note** In general, you will want to create an event handler rather than a workflow when you need to attach small bits of code that will run immediately before or after a list event has occurred.

Event Handler Enhancements in SharePoint 2007

The two most significant improvements to SharePoint list handling are full support for all list types, and an increase in the number of events to which you can attach custom code.

Support for All List Types

In SharePoint 2003, only document and form libraries supported events. That left contacts, tasks, events (that is, calendar), and all other lists out in the cold! Now you can attach custom code to any list, significantly expanding how you can customize SharePoint.

More Events

The events that SharePoint 2003 could respond to were also quite limited. In SharePoint 2007, virtually anything a user (or an application) can do to a list will raise an event that you can attach to. In addition, SharePoint now exposes two types of events: *synchronous*, which fire before the event is processed by SharePoint, and *asynchronous*, which fire after. Synchronous events are new to SharePoint 2007 and provide the option of cancelling an event if desired. For example, you might use a synchronous event to perform complex validation on edits made to a list item and, if the validation fails, prevent the changes from being saved to the SharePoint content database by cancelling the update event. In the scenario I discuss in this section, I use the synchronous `ItemDeleting` event so I can access the soon-to-be deleted `ListItem` object before it's deleted.

■**Note** In this chapter, I focus on list event handlers, but SharePoint 2007 supports several other event handler classes, including `SPWebEventReceiver`, which allows you to handle web/site deletion and moves; `SPListEventReceiver`, which allows you to handle field (columns) additions/updates/deletions; and `SPItemEventReceiver`, which is the focus of this chapter and allows you to handle list item additions/updates/deletions/check-in/checkout/attachments.

Recipe 5-1. Updating List Fields When Adding a Document to a Document Library

As you are probably already aware, SharePoint allows defaults to be set on fields associated with items in any list. This feature is handy when most, if not all, items will have the same value. But what if the defaults should be set at the folder level, rather than for the document library as a whole?

In this recipe, I'll show you how to build and deploy an event handler that executes when a new document is added to a library, setting select field values to folder-level defaults. These defaults will be set regardless of how the end user adds the document: web form, explorer view, multidocument upload, or Windows Explorer.

To accomplish this, in addition to the event handler, we'll use a small hidden file in each folder to provide the defaults. Specifically, in this recipe, we'll set two fields: `client` and `matter`, which represent a client code and matter (or engagement) code.

Recipe Type: Event Handler

Ingredients

Assembly References

- `Windows SharePoint Services` .NET assembly

Class Library References

- `Microsoft.SharePoint` class library

Classes Used

- `SPItemEventReceiver` class
- `SPItemEventProperties` class

Special Considerations

- This recipe assumes that all users can read the document named [defaults] in each folder, or in the root if none is found in a given folder. To avoid confusing the end user, we'll set the default view to hide that document.

- Debugging event handlers is a lot like debugging web parts in that you can't run them directly. Rather, you must attach to the W3wp.exe process and step through the event handler when the event is raised by SharePoint.

Preparation

1. Create a new .NET class library project in Visual Studio to contain your event handler.

2. Add a .NET console application project to the same solution. This project will contain your installer.

3. In both projects, add a reference to the Windows SharePoint Services .NET assembly.

4. Assign a strong-name key file to the project in the Signing tab of the class library project.

5. Add the event handler code to the class library, as shown in the following code.

6. Add the installer code to the console application, as shown in the following code. You will need to obtain the strong-name key value for your compiled event handler assembly by one of the following methods:

   - Use the SN.exe command

   - Copy your assembly to the GAC and view its properties

   - Use a utility such as .NET Reflector

7. Create a document library on a SharePoint web site with the following fields:

   - client (single line of text)

   - matter (single line of text)

Process Flow

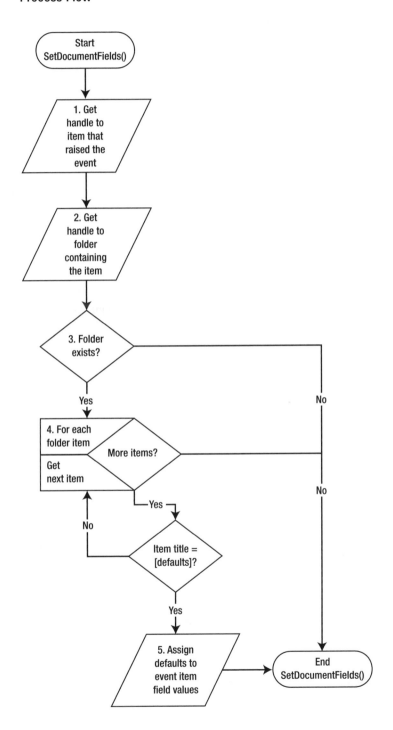

1. Create an `SPListItem` object to hold the list item that raised the `ItemAdded` event.

2. Find the folder that contains the list item. If there is none, assume the root folder.

3. If there was a problem accessing the folder (unlikely, but possible), exit the event handler. Otherwise, proceed to step 4.

4. Loop through each item in the folder containing the item that raised the event, searching for the [defaults] item.

■**Note** For large lists, a more efficient approach is to use `SPList.GetItems(SPQuery)`.

---

5. If the item is found, update the `client` and `matter` fields with those of the [defaults] item.

Recipe—VB (See Project SetDocumentFields-VB, Class Class1.vb)

■**Note** The root namespace, as specified in the project properties page, is `"SetDocumentFields_VB"`.

```vb
Imports System.
Imports System.Collections.Generic
Imports System.Text
Imports Microsoft.SharePoint
Public Class SetDocumentFields
    Inherits SPItemEventReceiver
    ' Name of hidden item that contains default properties
    Const DEFAULT_FILE_TITLE As String = "[defaults]"
    ' Local variable to contain data passed in from SharePoint
    Private _properties As SPItemEventProperties
    ' Method called AFTER a new item has been added
    Public Overloads Overrides Sub ItemAdded( _
      ByVal properties As SPItemEventProperties)
        MyBase.ItemAdded(properties)
        _properties = properties
        ' Run under system account
        SPSecurity.RunWithElevatedPrivileges(AddressOf setFields)
    End Sub
    Private Sub setFields()
        ' Step 1: Get a handle to the item that raised the event
        Dim item As SPListItem = _properties.ListItem
```

```vb
        ' Step 2: Get a handle to folder containing the
        ' document just uploaded
        Dim folder As SPFolder = Nothing
        Try
            If item.File.ParentFolder IsNot Nothing Then
                folder = item.File.ParentFolder
            Else
                folder = item.ParentList.RootFolder
            End If
            ' No op
        Catch ex As Exception
        End Try
        ' Step 3: Assuming a folder was found (which
        ' should be in all cases), find the associated
        ' [defaults] document.
        If folder IsNot Nothing Then
            Dim files As SPFileCollection = folder.Files
            Dim client As String = ""
            Dim matter As String = ""
            ' Step 4: Find the document containing defaults, and
            ' use its "Client" and "Matter" values for
            ' new document
            For Each file As SPFile In files
                Try
                    If file.Title.ToLower() = DEFAULT_FILE_TITLE Then
                        client = file.Item("Client").ToString()
                        matter = file.Item("Matter").ToString()
                        Exit For
                    End If
                Catch
                End Try
            Next
            item("Client") = client
            item("Matter") = matter
            ' Step 5: Save changes without updating the
            ' MODIFIED, MODIFIED BY fields
            item.SystemUpdate(False)
        End If
    End Sub
End Class
```

Recipe—VB: Installer (See Project InstallSetDocumentFields-VB, Module Module1.vb)

■Note The root namespace for this project, as specified in the project property page, is
"InstallSetDocumentFields_VB".

```vb
Imports System.
Imports System.Collections.Generic
Imports System.Text
Imports Microsoft.SharePoint
Module Module1
    Sub Main(ByVal args As String())
        ' Get handle to target site, web, and list
        Dim site As New SPSite("http://mgerow-moss-vpc")
        Dim web As SPWeb = site.AllWebs("EventHandlers")
        Dim list As SPList = web.Lists("MyDocs")
        For i As Integer = list.EventReceivers.Count - 1 To 0 Step -1
            ' Remove any preexisting event receivers
            list.EventReceivers(i).Delete()
        Next
        ' Add the new event receiver
        Dim asmName As String = "SetDocumentFields_VB, Version=1.0.0.0, " & _
            "Culture=neutral, PublicKeyToken=cf284223dc97522f"
        Dim className As String = "SetDocumentFields_VB.SetDocumentFields"
        list.EventReceivers.Add(SPEventReceiverType.ItemAdded, asmName, className)
        web.Dispose()
        site.Dispose()
    End Sub
End Module
```

Recipe—C#: Event Handler (See Project SetDocumentFields-CS, Class SetDocumentFields.cs)

■**Note** The default namespace for this project, as specified in the project properties page, is
"SetDocumentFields_CS".

```csharp
using System;
using System.Collections.Generic;
using System.Text;
using Microsoft.SharePoint;
namespace SetDocumentFields_CS
{
    public class SetDocumentFields : SPItemEventReceiver
    {
        // Name of hidden item that contains default properties
        const string DEFAULT_FILE_TITLE = "[defaults]";
        // Local variable to contain data passed in from SharePoint
        private SPItemEventProperties _properties;
        // Method called AFTER a new item has been added
        public override void ItemAdded(SPItemEventProperties properties)
        {
            base.ItemAdded(properties);
            _properties = properties;
```

```
        // Run under system account
        SPSecurity.RunWithElevatedPrivileges(setFields);
}
private void setFields()
{
    // Step 1: Get a handle to the item that raised the event
    SPListItem item = _properties.ListItem;
    // Step 2: Get a handle to folder containing the
    // document just uploaded
    SPFolder folder = null;
    try
    {
        if (item.File.ParentFolder != null)
        {
            folder = item.File.ParentFolder;
        }
        else
        {
            folder = item.ParentList.RootFolder;
        }
    }
    catch (Exception ex)
    {
        // No op
    }
    // Step 3: Assuming a folder was found (which
    // should be in all cases), find the associated
    // [defaults] document.
    if (folder != null)
    {
        SPFileCollection files = folder.Files;
        string client = "";
        string matter = "";
        // Step 4: Find the document containing defaults, and
        // use its "Client" and "Matter" values for
        // new document
        foreach (SPFile file in files)
        {
            try
            {
                if (file.Title.ToLower() == DEFAULT_FILE_TITLE)
                {
                    client = file.Item["Client"].ToString();
                    matter = file.Item["Matter"].ToString();
                    break;
                }
            }
        }
```

```
                    catch (Exception ex)
                    {
                        // no op
                    }
                }
                item["Client"] = client;
                item["Matter"] = matter;
                // Step 5: Save changes without updating the
                // MODIFIED, MODIFIED BY fields
                item.SystemUpdate(false);
            }
        }
    }
}
```

Recipe—C#: Installer (See Project InstallSetDocumentFields-CS, Class Program.cs)

■**Note** The default namespace for this project, as specified in the project properties page, is
"InstallSetDocumentFields_CS".

```
using System;
using System.Collections.Generic;
using System.Text;
using Microsoft.SharePoint;
namespace InstallSetDocumentFields_CS
{
    class Program
    {
        static void Main(string[] args)
        {
            // Get handle to target site, web, and list
            SPSite site = new SPSite("http://mgerow-moss-vpc");
            SPWeb web = site.AllWebs["EventHandlers"];
            SPList list = web.Lists["MyDocs"];
            // Remove any preexisting event receivers
            for (int i = list.EventReceivers.Count - 1; i > -1; i--)
            {
                list.EventReceivers[i].Delete();
            }
```

```
            // Add the new event receiver
            string asmName = "SetDocumentFields-CS, Version=1.0.0.0, "
                + " Culture=neutral, PublicKeyToken=453cdb407c59801a";
            string className = "SetDocumentFields_CS.SetDocumentFields";
            list.EventReceivers.Add(
                SPEventReceiverType.ItemAdded, asmName, className);
            web.Dispose();
            site.Dispose()
        }
    }
}
```

To Run

After you've compiled your event handler, place the resulting assembly in the GAC, run your installer, and you're ready to test your work.

■**Note** There are also some widely used, free third-party tools for managing event handlers, including Patrick Tisseghem's EventHandler Explorer (http://blog.u2u.info/DottextWeb/patrick/archive/ 2006/07/31/27876.aspx) and Brian Wilson's Manage Event Handlers site settings feature (http:// blogs.msdn.com/brianwilson/archive/2007/03/18/event-handlers-part-3-register- event-handlers-plus-free-site-settings-manage-event-handlers-add-on.aspx).

First, add a new document to the root folder of your MyDocs library, giving it a title of [defaults] and filling in the desired values for the Client and Matter fields, as shown in Figure 5-1.

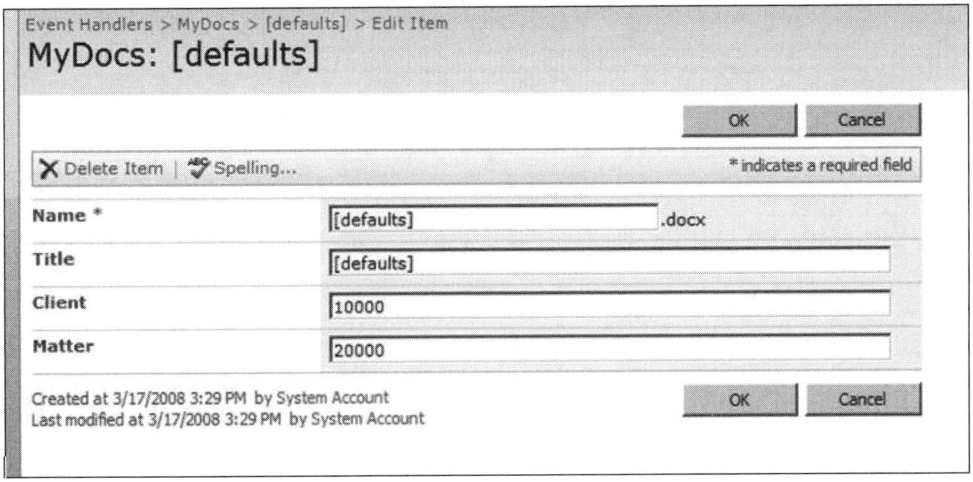

Figure 5-1. *Creating the [defaults] document*

Now upload or create a new document as you would normally. The Client and Matter fields will be automatically populated with the same values you entered for your [defaults] document, as shown in Figure 5-2.

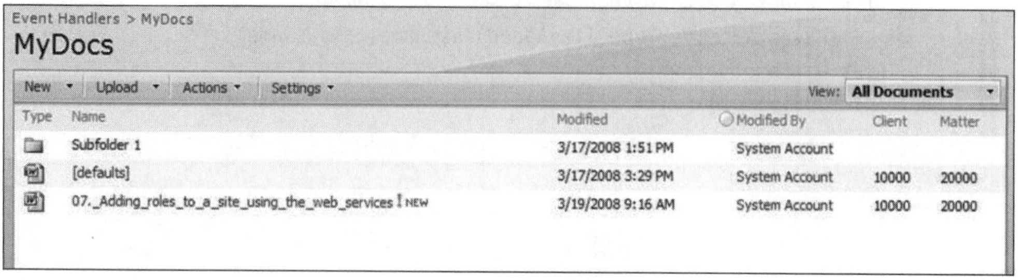

Figure 5-2. *New document with autogenerated field values*

Finally, to avoid confusion, hide the [defaults] document by setting a filter on the All Documents view, as shown in Figure 5-3.

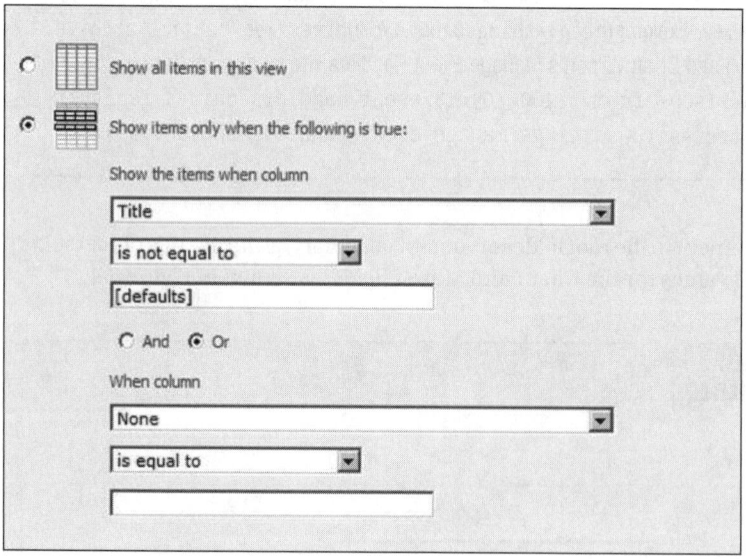

Figure 5-3. *Hiding the [defaults] document*

Variations

- In this recipe, we hard-coded the names of the fields to copy (`client` and `matter`). Instead, if you make the assumption of only one content type in your library, you could simply iterate through the fields collection, copying the value of each field in the [`defaults`] document to the corresponding field in the new item.

- Instead of using a [`default`] file to determine the defaults, you can extend the Folder content type to include the fields used by documents, and then set the values that should be used by default directly on the folder item within the library.

Recipe 5-2. Sending an Email When a Task Is Completed

SharePoint has the ability to send alerts to individuals who request them. But what if you want to send emails proactively and based on some specific business logic? For example, you may want to alert an individual or group when a task in a task list is flagged as complete.

In this recipe, you'll see how easy it is to write an event handler to do just that. The event handler you'll create here will respond to the `ItemUpdated` event that fires after updates to a task have been written back to the SharePoint database. It's a simple matter of checking the value of the task `Status` field to see if it's been flagged as `Completed`, and to send the email.

Recipe Type: Event Handler

Ingredients

Assembly References

- `Windows SharePoint Services` .NET assembly

Class Library References

- `Microsoft.SharePoint` class library

Classes Used

- `SPItemEventReceiver` class

- `SPItemEventProperties` class

- `System.Net.Mail.MailMessage` class

- `System.Net.Mail.smtpClient` class

Special Considerations

- This recipe assumes you have access to a Simple Mail Transfer Protocol (SMTP) mail server (such as Microsoft Exchange Server). If you don't have access to such a server, it is possible to set one up in a test environment. See the Microsoft article "SMTP Server Setup (IIS 6.0)" at www.microsoft.com/technet/prodtechnol/WindowsServer2003/Library/ IIS/e4cf06f5-9a36-474b-ba78-3f287a2b88f2.mspx?mfr=true.

Preparation

1. Create a new .NET class library project in Visual Studio to contain your event handler.

2. Add a .NET console application project to the same solution. This project will contain your installer.

3. In both projects, add a reference to the Windows SharePoint Services .NET assembly.

4. Assign a strong-name key file to the project in the Signing tab of the class library project.

5. If a task list doesn't already exist on your target web site, create one.

6. Add the event handler code to the class library, as shown in the following code . Be sure to replace the Recipient and Sender email addresses with ones that are appropriate for your development environment.

7. Add the installer code to the console application, as shown in the following code. Be sure that the list referenced by the SPList object is the one you created in the previous step. You will need to obtain the strong-name key value for your compiled event handler assembly by using one of the following methods:

   - Use the SN.exe command

   - Copy your assembly to the GAC and view its properties

   - Use a utility such as .NET Reflector

Process Flow

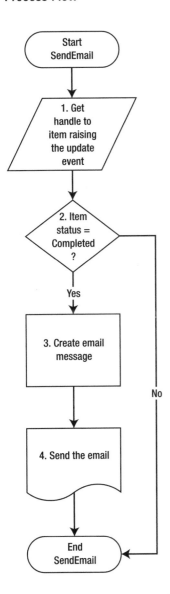

1. Create an SPListItem object to represent the list item that raised the ItemUpdated event.

2. If the list item's status is equal to Completed, move to step 3. Otherwise, exit the event handler.

3. Create a System.Net.Mail.MailMessage object and set its properties.

4. Send the mail message to the appropriate recipient.

Recipe—VB: Event Handler (See Project SendEmail-VB, Class SendEmail.vb)

■**Note** The root namespace specified for this project in the project properties page is `SendEmail_VB`.

```vb
Imports System.Web
Imports Microsoft.SharePoint
Public Class SendEmail
    Inherits SPItemEventReceiver
    Private _properties As SPItemEventProperties
    Public Overrides Sub ItemUpdated( _
        ByVal properties As Microsoft.SharePoint.SPItemEventProperties)
        MyBase.ItemUpdated(properties)
        _properties = properties
        SPSecurity.RunWithElevatedPrivileges(AddressOf emailIfComplete)
    End Sub
    Private Sub emailIfComplete()
        'Step 1: Get a handle to the task that
        '   raised the update event
        Dim item As SPListItem = _properties.ListItem
        'Step 2: Determine if email should be sent based
        '   on current status of task.  If so...
        If item("Status") = "Completed" Then
            SendEmail( _
                "user@somedomain.com", _
                "tasklist@somedomain.com", _
                "Task '" & item("Title").ToString() & "' is Complete", _
                "The task was marked complete by '" & _
                _properties.UserDisplayName.ToString() & "'.", _
                "MySMTPServer")
        End If
    End Sub
    Private Sub SendEmail( _
        ByVal Recipient As String, _
        ByVal Sender As String, _
        ByVal Subject As String, _
        ByVal Message As String, _
        ByVal Server As String _
        )
        'Step 3: Create message and SMTP client objects
        Dim msg As System.Net.Mail.MailMessage
        Dim smtpClient As System.Net.Mail.SmtpClient = _
            New System.Net.Mail.SmtpClient(Server)
```

```
            'Step 4: Construct and send the message
            msg = New System.Net.Mail.MailMessage(Sender, Recipient, Subject, Message)
            msg.IsBodyHtml = True
            smtpClient.Send(msg)
        End Sub
End Class
```

Recipe—VB: Installer (See Project InstallSendEmail-VB, Class Class1.vb)

■**Note** The root namespace specified for this project in the project properties page is
InstallSendEmail_VB.

```
Imports Microsoft.SharePoint
Module Module1
    Sub Main()
        Dim site As New SPSite("http://mgerow-moss-vpc")
        Dim web As SPWeb = site.AllWebs("EventHandlers")
        Dim tasks As SPList = web.Lists("Tasks")
        Dim i As Integer
        For i = tasks.EventReceivers.Count - 1 To 0 Step -1
            tasks.EventReceivers(i).Delete()
        Next
        'Add the SendEmail event handler
        Dim asmName As String = & _
            "SendEmail-VB, Version=1.0.0.0, Culture=neutral," &_
            "PublicKeyToken=4eb0175192d1b499"
        Dim className As String = "SendEmail_VB.SendEmail"
        tasks.EventReceivers.Add(SPEventReceiverType.ItemUpdated, _
            asmName, className)
        tasks.Update()
        web.Dispose()
        site.Dispose()
    End Sub
End Module
```

Recipe—C#: Event Handler (See Project SendEmail-CS, Class SendEmail.cs)

■**Note** The default namespace specified for this project in the project properties page is SendEmail_CS.

```csharp
using System.Web;
using Microsoft.SharePoint;
namespace SendEmail_CS
{
    public class SendEmail : SPItemEventReceiver
    {
        private SPItemEventProperties _properties;
        public override void
            ItemUpdated(Microsoft.SharePoint.SPItemEventProperties properties)
        {
            base.ItemUpdated(properties);
            _properties = properties;
            SPSecurity.RunWithElevatedPrivileges(emailIfComplete);
        }
        private void emailIfComplete()
        {
            //Step 1: Get a handle to the task that
            // raised the update event
            SPListItem item = _properties.ListItem;
            //Step 2: Determine if email should be sent based
            // on current status of task. If so...
            if (item["Status"].ToString() == "Completed")
            {
                _SendEmail(
                    "user@somedomain.com",
                    "tasklist@somedomain.com",
                    "Task '" + item["Title"].ToString() + "' is Complete",
                    "The task was marked complete by '"
                        + _properties.UserDisplayName.ToString()
                        + "'.",
                    " MySMTPServer ");
            }
        }
        private void _SendEmail(
            string Recipient,
            string Sender,
            string Subject,
            string Message,
            string Server)
        {
            //Step 3: Create message and SMTP client objects
            System.Net.Mail.MailMessage msg;
            System.Net.Mail.SmtpClient smtpClient =
                new System.Net.Mail.SmtpClient(Server);
```

```
            //Step 4: Construct and send the message
            msg = new System.Net.Mail.MailMessage(
                    Sender, Recipient, Subject, Message);
            msg.IsBodyHtml = true;
            smtpClient.Send(msg);
        }
    }
}
```

Recipe—C#: Installer (See Project InstallSendEmail-CS, Class Program.cs)

> ■**Note** The default namespace specified for this project in the project properties page is
> InstallSendEmail_CS.

```
using System;
using System.Collections.Generic;
using System.Text;
using Microsoft.SharePoint;
namespace InstallSetDocumentFields_CS
{
    class Program
    {
        static void Main(string[] args)
        {
            SPSite site = new SPSite("http://mgerow-moss-vpc");
            SPWeb web = site.AllWebs["EventHandlers"];
            SPList tasks = web.Lists["Tasks"];
            int i;
            for (i = tasks.EventReceivers.Count - 1; i >= 0; i += -1)
            {
                tasks.EventReceivers[i].Delete();
            }
            //Add the send email event handler
            string asmName = "SendEmail-CS, Version=1.0.0.0, Culture=neutral, " +
                "PublicKeyToken=6b31e633957e0e4d";
            string className = "SendEmail_CS.SendEmail";
            tasks.EventReceivers.Add(SPEventReceiverType.ItemUpdated, _
                asmName, className);
            tasks.Update();
            web.Dispose();
            site.Dispose();
        }
    }
}
```

To Run

After you have compiled and installed your event handler, create a new task in the list to which you've attached your event handler. Then set its Status to Completed. You should receive an email similar to that shown in Figure 5-4.

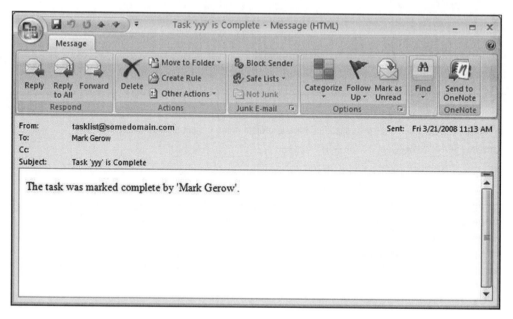

Figure 5-4. *Email generated by event handler*

Variations

- In this recipe, we hard-coded both the email sender and recipient. You could determine the appropriate recipient programmatically, for example by looking up the project manager in another SharePoint list or external SQL database, searching Active Directory for the user's manager, or using the SPUser.Email property.

- As with the recipient, the format of our email has been hard-coded. It would be more flexible to pass that into the event handler, so you could use the same event handler in multiple situations that require different email formatting. You can do this by using the Data property of the event receiver. For example, by adding the line tasks.EventReceivers[0].Data = "My subject line;My body text"; to the installer, just before you call the Update() method, you are telling your task list to pass this string into the event receiver whenever it's called. Inside your event receiver, you can access the Data property to retrieve the text to use in your emails. Because the string contained in the Data property can vary for each instance of your event receiver, different lists can use different values, and thus produce different emails.

- Users also may want to have their event handler handle the ItemAdded event so when a user adds a new Task item with a status of Completed, the email is sent out (in this recipe, only the update event is being handled, so new items are not checked).

Recipe 5-3. Preventing Deletion by Using an Event Handler

Through the use of permissions, you can prevent deletion of list items for some or all items based on user identity. But it's essentially an all-or-nothing proposition; either users can delete an item or they can't. There is no provision for conditional permissions based on data in the list item itself. For example, you may want to prevent users from deleting items that have a `Completed` status.

In this recipe, you'll add an event handler that prevents deletion of tasks in a task list after the status has been moved beyond `Not Started` or the `%Complete` is greater than zero unless the user is a site administrator. You can use a similar approach to prevent deletion (or other changes) to an item based on arbitrary business rules.

Recipe Type: Event Handler

Ingredients

Assembly References

- `Windows SharePoint Services` .NET assembly

Class Library References

- `Microsoft.SharePoint` class library

Classes Used

- `SPItemEventReceiver` class

- `SPItemEventProperties` class

- `SPListItem` class

- `SPUser` class

- `SPWeb` class

Special Considerations

- Debugging event handlers is a lot like debugging web parts in that you can't run them directly. Rather, you must attach to the `W3wp.exe` process and step through the event handler when the event is raised by SharePoint.

Preparation

1. Create a new .NET class library project in Visual Studio to contain your event handler.

2. Add a .NET console application project to the same solution. This project will contain your installer.

3. In both projects, add a reference to the `Windows SharePoint Services` .NET assembly.

4. Assign a strong-name key file to the project in the Signing tab of the class library project.

5. Add the event handler code to the class library, as shown in the following code listing.

6. Add the installer code to the console application, as shown in the following code. You will need to obtain the strong-name key value for your compiled event handler assembly by using one of the following methods:

   • Use the SN.exe command

   • Copy your assembly to the GAC and view its properties

   • Use a utility such as .NET Reflector

7. Create a task list (or use an existing one) on a SharePoint site (no special fields are required for this recipe).

Process Flow

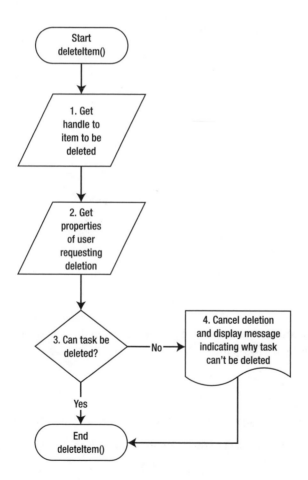

1. Instantiate an SPListItem object to contain information about the item to be deleted.

2. Instantiate SPWeb and SPUser objects to contain information about the user who is requesting that the list item be deleted.

3. Determine whether the task has not yet started, or whether the current user is a member of the site collection administrators collection, or is running under the System Account. If so, allow the deletion event to complete. Otherwise, proceed to step 4.

4. Cancel the deletion event and display a message to the user indicating that tasks that have begun may be cancelled only by site or system administrators.

Recipe—VB: Event Handler (See Project PreventDeletion-VB, Class PreventDeletion.vb)

■Note The root namespace specified for this project in the project properties page is PreventDeletion_VB.

```vb
Imports System
Imports System.Collections.Generic
Imports System.Text
Imports Microsoft.SharePoint
Public Class PreventDeletion
    Inherits SPItemEventReceiver
    Private _properties As SPItemEventProperties
    Public Overloads Overrides Sub ItemDeleting(_
        ByVal properties As SPItemEventProperties)
        MyBase.ItemDeleting(properties)
        _properties = properties
        SPSecurity.RunWithElevatedPrivileges(AddressOf deleteItem)
    End Sub
    Private Sub deleteItem()
        ' Step 1: Get handle to list item that raised
        ' the delete event
        Dim item As SPListItem = _properties.ListItem
        ' Step 2: Get object representing the user
        ' attempting to delete the task
        Dim web As SPWeb = _properties.ListItem.ParentList.ParentWeb
        Dim user As SPUser = web.SiteUsers(_properties.UserLoginName)
        ' Step 3: Determine whether task can
        ' be deleted
        If item("% Complete") Is Nothing Then
            item("% Complete") = 0
        End If
```

```vb
            Dim ok2Delete As Boolean = _
                (item("Status").ToString() = "Not Started" _
                    And Single.Parse(item("% Complete").ToString()) = 0) _
                Or user.IsSiteAdmin _
                Or _properties.UserDisplayName = "System Account"
            ' Step 4: If task is in progress and user
            ' requesting deletion isn't a site administrator
            ' or the "System Account", prevent the
            ' deletion.
            If Not ok2Delete Then
                _properties.Cancel = True
                _properties.ErrorMessage = "Unable to delete task '" _
                    + item("Title").ToString() + _
                    ". Only site administrators may delete " + _
                    "tasks on which work has already begun."
            End If
            web.Dispose()
        End Sub
End Class
```

Recipe—VB: Installer (See Project InstallPreventDeletion-VB, Module Module1.vb)

■Note The root namespace for this project specified in the project properties page is
InstallPreventDeletion_VB.

```vb
Imports System
Imports System.Collections.Generic
Imports System.Text
Imports Microsoft.SharePoint
Module Module1
    Sub Main(ByVal args As String())
        ' Get handle to target site, web, and list
        Dim site As New SPSite("http://mgerow-moss-vpc")
        Dim web As SPWeb = site.AllWebs("EventHandlers")
        Dim list As SPList = web.Lists("Tasks")
        For i As Integer = list.EventReceivers.Count - 1 To -1 + 1 Step -1
            ' Remove any pre-existing event receivers
            list.EventReceivers(i).Delete()
        Next
        ' Add the new event receiver
        Dim asmName As String = _
            "PreventDeletion-VB, Version=1.0.0.0, Culture=neutral, " & _
            "PublicKeyToken=551b0daa60f2e217"
        Dim className As String = "PreventDeletion_VB.PreventDeletion"
```

```
        list.EventReceivers.Add( _
            SPEventReceiverType.ItemDeleting, asmName, className)
        web.Dispose()
        site.Dispose()
    End Sub
End Module
```

Recipe—C#: Event Handler (See Project PreventDeletion-CS, Class PreventDeletion.cs)

■**Note** The default namespace specified for this project in the project properties page is
PreventDeletion_CS.

```csharp
using System;
using System.Collections.Generic;
using System.Text;
using Microsoft.SharePoint;
namespace PreventDeletion_CS
{
    public class PreventDeletion : SPItemEventReceiver
    {
        private SPItemEventProperties _properties;

        public override void ItemDeleting(SPItemEventProperties properties)
        {
            base.ItemDeleting(properties);
            _properties = properties;
            SPSecurity.RunWithElevatedPrivileges(deleteItem);
        }
        private void deleteItem()
        {
            // Step 1: Get handle to list item that raised
            //   the delete event
            SPListItem item = _properties.ListItem;
            // Step 2: Get object representing the user
            //   attempting to delete the task
            SPWeb web = _properties.ListItem.ParentList.ParentWeb;
            SPUser user = web.SiteUsers[_properties.UserLoginName];
            // Step 3: Determine whether task can
            //   be deleted
            bool ok2Delete =
                (item["Status"].ToString() == "Not Started"
                    && float.Parse(item["% Complete"].ToString()) == 0)
                || user.IsSiteAdmin
                || _properties.UserDisplayName == "System Account";
```

```
            // Step 4: If task is in progress and user
            //   requesting deletion isn't a site administrator
            //   or the "System Account", prevent the
            //   deletion.
            if (!ok2Delete)
            {
                _properties.Cancel = true;
                _properties.ErrorMessage = "Unable to delete task "
                    + item["Title"].ToString()
                    + ".  Only site administrators may delete tasks "
                    + "on which work has already begun.";
            }
            web.Dispose();
        }
    }
}
```

Recipe—C#: Installer (See Project InstallPreventDeletion-CS, Class Program.cs)

■**Note** The default namespace specified for this project in the project properties page is
`InstallPreventDeletion_CS`.

```
using System;
using System.Collections.Generic;
using System.Text;
using Microsoft.SharePoint;
namespace InstallSetDocumentFields_CS
{
    class Program
    {
        static void Main(string[] args)
        {
            // Get handle to target site, web, and list
            SPSite site = new SPSite("http://mgerow-moss-vpc");
            SPWeb web = site.AllWebs["EventHandlers"];
            SPList list = web.Lists["Tasks"];
            // Remove any preexisting event receivers
            for (int i = list.EventReceivers.Count - 1; i > -1; i--)
            {
                list.EventReceivers[i].Delete();
            }
```

```
                // Add the new event receiver
                string asmName = _
                    "PreventDeletion-CS, Version=1.0.0.0, Culture=neutral, " +
                    "PublicKeyToken=236c1d4aa4b4d71f";
                string className = "PreventDeletion_CS.PreventDeletion";
                list.EventReceivers.Add(_
                    SPEventReceiverType.ItemDeleting, asmName, className);
                web.Dispose();
                site.Dispose();
            }
        }
}
```

To Run

To test this recipe, do the following:

1. Sign in to SharePoint with a user account that is not a site administrator.

2. Add a new item to the task list to which you've just attached the event handler.

3. Change the Status field to In Progress.

4. Save your change.

5. From the new item's context menu, select the Delete Item option and click OK when prompted to confirm.

You should see an error message similar to that shown in Figure 5-5.

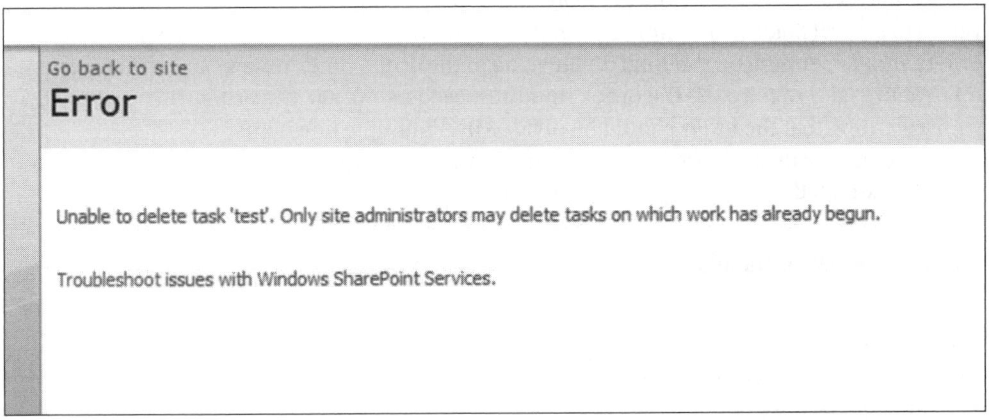

Figure 5-5. *Error message when attempting to delete an in-progress task*

Variations

- This recipe used simple and straightforward rules to determine whether to allow a list item to be deleted. You could easily imagine scenarios where you might check entries in related lists or even external databases, or determine whether the user was a member of one or more SharePoint security groups.

- Instead of preventing deletion, you could move the list item to another list, sending an alert to the project manager to review and authorize the deletion.

- A related scenario is to prevent users from editing certain columns. Because there is no column-level security, you can use event handlers to prevent column *X* from being changed while allowing editing of all other columns. This would use the `ItemUpdating` event but is related to the example in this recipe because you are preventing some action, cancelling the event, and returning a message.

Related Recipes

- Recipe 5-2

Recipe 5-4. Creating a Calculated Field by Using an Event Handler

You're probably aware that you can define calculated fields for any SharePoint list. Such calculations are fine for simple arithmetic, in which all inputs are constants or the values of other fields in the same list item. By creating an event handler, you can break through that limitation to derive field values based on any business logic you wish. For example, you could look up data from another SharePoint list, from Active Directory, or from a SQL database to determine the appropriate values to insert.

In this recipe, you'll see how to create and deploy a simple event handler that will assign values to several fields in a custom list. In this scenario, you'll use a list for tracking customer orders and, depending on the total dollar value of the order, determine what level of management approval is required. If the order amount exceeds $100,000, the order will be rejected, with a warning that the order should be divided into multiple line items.

Although the business logic in this recipe is artificially simple, you will see how easily it could be extended to accommodate more complex rules.

Recipe Type: Event Handler

Ingredients

Assembly References

- Windows SharePoint Services .NET assembly

Class Library References

- Microsoft.SharePoint class library

Special Considerations

- SharePoint event handlers are intended to allow you to attach small bits of logic to the intrinsic events of list items, but your custom event code can have a significant impact on the server's performance if not carefully designed. When writing event handlers, always consider the likely frequency of events and the time it will take your code to complete. For complex logic, you may be better off with a scheduled console application rather than close-to-real-time execution.

- As with web parts, be sure to include appropriate exception handling. Unlike web parts, event handlers may not display any visible signs of failure if an unhandled exception occurs because they don't run in the context of the user's session.

Preparation

1. Create a new .NET class library project in Visual Studio to contain your event handler.

2. Add a .NET console application project to the same solution. This project will contain your installer.

3. In both projects, add a reference to the `Windows SharePoint Services` .NET assembly.

4. Assign a strong-name key file to the project in the Signing tab of the class library project.

5. Add the event handler code to the class library, as shown in the following code.

6. Add the installer code to the console application, as shown in the following code. You will need to obtain the strong-name key value for your compiled event handler assembly by one of the following methods:

   - Use the `SN.exe` command

   - Copy your assembly to the GAC and view its properties

   - Use a utility such as .NET Reflector

7. Create a list on a SharePoint web site with the following fields:

   - Customer (text)

   - Product (text)

   - Price (currency)

   - Quantity (number)

   - Extended Price (currency)

   - Approval Required? (Yes/No)

   - Approver (text)

   - Notes (multiline plain text)

8. Test and modify to taste.

Process Flow

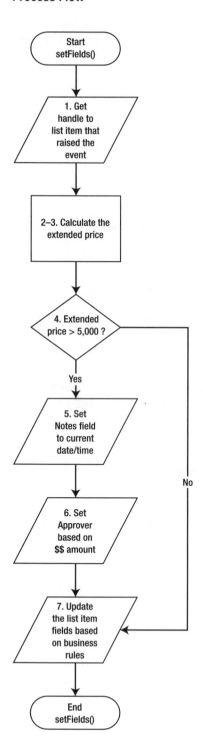

1. Obtain a handle to the list item that raised the event from the `properties` object that SharePoint passed in to the event handler.

2.–3. Calculate the extended price (as price x quantity) and determine whether approval will be required.

4.–6. If approval is required, determine the manager responsible for reviewing the order. If the order amount is greater than $5,000, determine what level of approval is required. If the order is greater than $100,000, set the quantity and extended price to 0 and place an error message in the Notes field.

7. Call the list item's `SystemUpdate()` method to update fields in the content database without modifying the date/time stamp of the list item.

Recipe—VB: Event Handler (See Project UpdateFieldsEventHandler-VB, Class UpdateFieldsEventHandler.vb)

■**Note** The root namespace specified in the project properties is `UpdateFieldsEventHandler_VB`.

```vb
Imports System
Imports System.Collections.Generic
Imports System.Text
Imports Microsoft.SharePoint
Imports Microsoft.SharePoint.WebControls
Public Class UpdateFieldsEventHandler
    Inherits SPItemEventReceiver
    ' Local variable used to pass event properties to
    ' setFields() method.
    Private _properties As SPItemEventProperties
    Const errMsg As String = "Rejected because order $Amt too large, " & _
        "please break into orders of less than $100,000."
    ' The ItemAdding method is called BEFORE the item is
    ' written to the SharePoint content database. If
    ' this event is cancelled, the item will be discarded.
    Public Overrides Sub ItemAdding(ByVal properties As SPItemEventProperties)
        MyBase.ItemAdding(properties)
        _properties = properties
        ' Run as system account to avoid any permission issues
        Microsoft.SharePoint.SPSecurity.RunWithElevatedPrivileges( _
            AddressOf validateAddUpdate)
    End Sub
    ' The ItemAdding method is called AFTER the item has been
    ' written to the content database. Place code or method
    ' calls here that will update fields or take action based
    ' on data saved.
```

```vb
Public Overrides Sub ItemAdded(ByVal properties As SPItemEventProperties)
    MyBase.ItemAdded(properties)
    _properties = properties
    ' Run as system account to avoid any permission issues
    Microsoft.SharePoint.SPSecurity.RunWithElevatedPrivileges( _
        AddressOf setFields)
End Sub
' The ItemUpdated method is called after changes are written
' to the SharePoint content database. Place code or method
' calls here to update fields or take action based on values
' written.
Public Overrides Sub ItemUpdated(ByVal properties As SPItemEventProperties)
    MyBase.ItemUpdated(properties)
    _properties = properties
    ' Run as system account to avoid any permission issues
    Microsoft.SharePoint.SPSecurity.RunWithElevatedPrivileges( _
        AddressOf setFields)
End Sub
' Validation has been passed, so apply business
' rules to update the approval fields.
Private Sub setFields()
    Try
        ' Step 1: Get a handle to the list item
        ' that raised this event
        Dim li As SPListItem = _properties.ListItem
        ' Step 2: Calculate the extended price
        Dim extPrice As Single = Single.Parse(li("Price").ToString()) * _
            Single.Parse(li("Quantity").ToString())
        ' Step 3: Determine if approval is required
        Dim approvalRequired As Boolean = (extPrice > 5000)
        li("Extended Price") = extPrice
        li("Approval Required?") = approvalRequired
        ' Step 4: If approval is required, assign to approver
        If approvalRequired Then
            ' Step 5: Assign default value to note field
            li("Notes") = "Approver assigned at " + DateTime.Now.ToString()
            ' Step 6: This is where the business logic gets applied.
            ' Of course your business logic will likely be more
            ' complex, but the process is the same
            If extPrice < 10000 Then
                li("Approver") = "Dept Mgr"
            Else
                If extPrice < 25000 Then
                    li("Approver") = "CFO"
                Else
                    If extPrice < 100000 Then
                        li("Approver") = "President/CEO"
```

```vb
                    Else
                        li("Notes") = errMsg
                        li("Approver") = ""
                        li("Approval Required?") = False
                        li("Quantity") = 0
                        li("Extended Price") = 0
                    End If
                End If
            End If
        End If
        ' Step 7: Update item, but don't reset
        ' the MODIFIED or MODIFIED BY fields.
        li.SystemUpdate()
        ' Handle error
    Catch ex As Exception
    End Try
End Sub
' This method checks to see if user has entered
' Price and/or Quantity that results in an
' Extended Amount in excess of $100,000
Private Sub validateAddUpdate()
    Dim extPrice As Single = _
        Single.Parse(_properties.AfterProperties("Price").ToString()) * _
        Single.Parse(_properties.AfterProperties("Quantity").ToString())
    ' Check to see if new item exceeds extended price limit of $100,000
    If extPrice > 99999 AndAlso _properties.EventType = _
        SPEventReceiverType.ItemAdding Then
        _properties.Cancel = True
        _properties.ErrorMessage = errMsg
    End If
End Sub
End Class
```

Recipe—VB: Installer (See Project InstallUpdateFieldsEventHandler-VB, Module Module1.vb)

Note The root namespace specified in the project properties is `InstallUpdateFieldsEventHandler_VB`.

```vb
Imports System
Imports System.Collections.Generic
Imports System.Text
Imports Microsoft.SharePoint
```

```
Module Module1
    Sub Main(ByVal args As String())
        ' Get handle to target site, web, and list
        Dim site As New SPSite("http://mgerow-moss-vpc")
        Dim web As SPWeb = site.AllWebs("EventHandlers")
        Dim list As SPList = web.Lists("UpdateFieldsList")
        For i As Integer = list.EventReceivers.Count - 1 To 0 Step -1
            ' Remove any preexisting event receivers
            list.EventReceivers(i).Delete()
        Next
        ' Add the new event receiver
        Dim asmName As String = "UpdateFieldsEventHandler-VB, Version=1.0.0.0, " & _
            "Culture=neutral, PublicKeyToken=809b67cef68bed7f"
        Dim className As String = _
            "UpdateFieldsEventHandler_VB.UpdateFieldsEventHandler"
        list.EventReceivers.Add(SPEventReceiverType.ItemAdded, asmName, className)
        list.EventReceivers.Add(SPEventReceiverType.ItemAdding, asmName, className)
        list.EventReceivers.Add(SPEventReceiverType.ItemUpdated, asmName, className)
        web.Dispose()
        site.Dispose()
    End Sub
End Module
```

Recipe—C#: Event Handler (See Project UpdateFieldsEventHandler-CS, Class UpdateFieldsEventHandler.cs)

■**Note** The default namespace specified for this project in the project properties page is UpdateFieldsEventHandler_CS.

```
using System;
using System.Collections.Generic;
using System.Text;
using Microsoft.SharePoint;
using Microsoft.SharePoint.WebControls;
namespace UpdateFieldsEventHandler_CS
{
    public class UpdateFieldsEventHandler : SPItemEventReceiver
    {
        // Local variable used to pass event properties to
        // setFields() method.
```

```
private SPItemEventProperties _properties;
const string errMsg =
    "Rejected because order $Amt too large, "
    + "please break into orders of less than $100,000.";
// The ItemAdding method is called BEFORE the item is
// written to the SharePoint content database.  If
// this event is cancelled, the item will be discarded.
public override void ItemAdding(SPItemEventProperties properties)
{
    base.ItemAdding(properties);
    _properties = properties;
    // Run as system account to avoid any permission issues
    Microsoft.SharePoint.SPSecurity.RunWithElevatedPrivileges(
        validateAddUpdate);
}
// The ItemAdding method is called AFTER the item has been
// written to the content database.  Place code or method
// calls here that will update fields or take action based
// on data saved.
public override void ItemAdded(SPItemEventProperties properties)
{
    base.ItemAdded(properties);
    _properties = properties;
    // Run as system account to avoid any permission issues
    Microsoft.SharePoint.SPSecurity.RunWithElevatedPrivileges(setFields);
}
// The ItemUpdated method is called after changes are written
// to the SharePoint content database.  Place code or method
// calls here to update fields or take action based on values
// written.
public override void ItemUpdated(SPItemEventProperties properties)
{
    base.ItemUpdated(properties);
    _properties = properties;
    // Run as system account to avoid any permission issues
    Microsoft.SharePoint.SPSecurity.RunWithElevatedPrivileges(setFields);
}
// Validation has been passed, so apply business
// rules to update the approval fields.
```

```csharp
private void setFields()
{
    try
    {
        // Step 1: Get a handle to the list item
        //   that raised this event
        SPListItem li = _properties.ListItem;
        // Step 2: Calculate the extended price
        float extPrice = float.Parse(li["Price"].ToString())
            * float.Parse(li["Quantity"].ToString());
        // Step 3: Determine if approval is required
        bool approvalRequired = (extPrice > 5000);
        li["Extended Price"] = extPrice;
        li["Approval Required?"] = approvalRequired;
        // Step 4: If approval is required, assign to approver
        if (approvalRequired)
        {
            // Step 5: Assign default value to note field
            li["Notes"] = "Approver assigned at " + DateTime.Now.ToString();
            // Step 6: This is where the business logic gets applied.
            // Of course your business logic will likely be more
            // complex, but the process is the same
            if (extPrice < 10000) {
                li["Approver"] = "Dept Mgr";
            }
            else {
                if (extPrice < 25000) {
                    li["Approver"] = "CFO";
                }
                else {
                    if (extPrice < 100000) {
                        li["Approver"] = "President/CEO";
                    }
                    else {
                        li["Notes"] = errMsg;
                        li["Approver"] = "";
                        li["Approval Required?"] = false;
                        li["Quantity"] = 0;
                        li["Extended Price"] = 0;
                    }
                }
            }
        }
    }
}
```

```
                // Step 7: Update item, but don't reset
                // the MODIFIED or MODIFIED BY fields.
                li.SystemUpdate();
            }
            catch (Exception ex)
            {
                // Handle error
            }
        }
        // This method checks to see if user has entered
        // Price and/or Quantity that results in an
        // Extended Amount in excess of $100,000
        private void validateAddUpdate()
        {
            float extPrice =
                float.Parse(_properties.AfterProperties["Price"].ToString())
                * float.Parse(_properties.AfterProperties["Quantity"].ToString());
            // Check to see if new item exceeds extended price limit of $100,000
            if (extPrice > 99999 &&
                _properties.EventType == SPEventReceiverType.ItemAdding)
            {
                _properties.Cancel = true;
                _properties.ErrorMessage = errMsg;
            }
        }
    }
}
```

Recipe—C#: Installer (See Project InstallUpdateFieldsEventHandler-CS, Class Program.cs)

■**Note** The default namespace specified for this project in the project properties page is
`InstallUpdateFieldsEventHandler_CS`.

```
using System;
using System.Collections.Generic;
using System.Text;
using Microsoft.SharePoint;
namespace InstallUpdateFieldsEventHandler_CS
{
```

```
class Program
{
    static void Main(string[] args)
    {
        // Get handle to target site, web, and list
        SPSite site = new SPSite("http://mgerow-moss-vpc");
        SPWeb web = site.AllWebs["EventHandlers"];
        SPList list = web.Lists["UpdateFieldsList"];
        // Remove any preexisting event receivers
        for (int i = list.EventReceivers.Count-1; i > -1 ; i--)
        {
            list.EventReceivers[i].Delete();
        }
        // Add the new event receiver
        string asmName =
            "UpdateFieldsEventHandler-CS, Version=1.0.0.0, Culture=neutral, "
          +"PublicKeyToken=4b4bd299aaa7406b";
        string className =
            "UpdateFieldsEventHandler_CS.UpdateFieldsEventHandler";
        list.EventReceivers.Add(
            SPEventReceiverType.ItemAdded, asmName, className);
        list.EventReceivers.Add(
            SPEventReceiverType.ItemAdding, asmName, className);
        list.EventReceivers.Add(
            SPEventReceiverType.ItemUpdated, asmName, className);
        web.Dispose();
        site.Dispose();
    }
}
}
```

To Run

After your event handler has been installed by running the installer application, you're ready to test it by adding a new item to your list. First, add an order that will result in an extended price of $10,000 as shown in Figure 5-6.

■**Note** You need to fill in only the Customer, Product, Price, and Quantity fields.

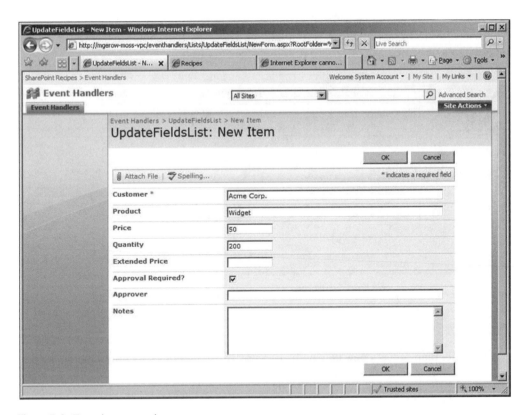

Figure 5-6. *Entering a new item*

After clicking the OK button, you should see an entry that looks similar to that in Figure 5-7.

Figure 5-7. *Item after event handler has run*

Now enter a new item for which the product of its price multiplied by its quantity exceeds $100,000. After you save your entry, you should see a page like that shown in Figure 5-8. This is SharePoint's standard error page with your message displayed.

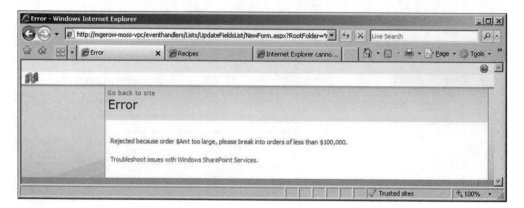

Figure 5-8. *Error message displayed when event handler cancels ItemAdding event*

Variations

- Rather than cancel a new item with an excessive extended price, simply change the values, as is done with the updates.

- Add email notifications for approving managers (see related recipes).

- Enable Content Approval on the list acnd automatically approve the item if it is under a certain amount; otherwise, proceed with emailing the approving manager.

Related Recipes

- Recipe 5-2

■ ■ ■

Working with Templates and Other XML Files

Although this book is focused primarily on how you can customize SharePoint through programming, you can do a great deal simply by modifying the XML files that control SharePoint's behavior and that control site provisioning. In this chapter, you'll look at several modifications that are of particular interest to developers:

- Associating new icon images with document library file types

- Adding custom menu items to the standard Site Settings and document context menus

- Creating a custom site definition to include specific web parts on various web-part pages when a new site is provisioned

- Adding a custom web form and code that SharePoint will run as part of the provisioning process

Not only can these recipes be used as is, but they are suggestive of a range of opportunities for customizing or automating SharePoint with XML alone or in conjunction with custom .NET programming.

Let's jump right in.

Recipe 6-1. Adding a PDF Image to Docicon.xml

Because Adobe Acrobat PDF files are so common, this is something that I've had to do for every SharePoint installation I've been involved with. I'm sure there's some good reason why Microsoft and Adobe haven't worked out a way to include the PDF icon in the out-of-the-box SharePoint installation; I just can't think what it would be! The process of adding an icon is quick and simple, and it provides a good introduction to the many XML files that underpin your SharePoint installation.

Recipe Type: CAML

Ingredients

- Adobe Acrobat PDF file icon

- Docicon.xml

Special Considerations

- Because SharePoint caches image files at startup, you'll need to execute the IISRESET command after you've added the icon file and updated the Docicon.xml file.

- According to the Adobe web site, you may use the PDF icon under the following conditions:

  - You may display the Adobe PDF file icon only on your web site, and not in any other manner.

  - The Adobe PDF file icon must appear by itself, with minimum spacing (the height of the icon) between each side of the icon and any other graphic or textual elements on your web page.

  - You may not alter the Adobe PDF file icon in any manner (including size, proportions, colors, elements, and so forth) or animate, morph, or otherwise distort its perspective or appearance.

  - Your use may not be obscene or pornographic, and may not be disparaging, defamatory, or libelous to Adobe, any of its products, or any other person or entity.

  - Your use may not directly or indirectly imply Adobe's sponsorship, affiliation, or endorsement of your product or service.

  - Your use may not infringe on any Adobe intellectual property or other rights, may not violate any state or federal laws, and must comply with international IP laws.

  - You may not create a frame or border environment around Adobe content.

  - You may not present false or misleading information about Adobe products or services.

  - Your reference to Adobe, its products, and its web site must comply with the general trademark guidelines.

  - These guidelines do not give you permission to use any other Adobe logos, icons, or trademarks. Adobe reserves the right in its sole discretion to terminate or modify your permission to display the Adobe PDF file icon at any time.

Preparation

- Download a copy of the Adobe PDF file icon from www.adobe.com/misc/linking.html#pdficon.

Process Flow

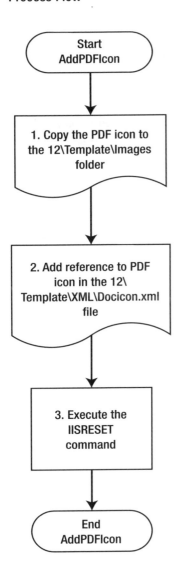

1. Obtain a copy of the `Pdficon_small.gif` file from the site www.adobe.com/misc/
   linking.html#pdficon and copy it to the `C:\Program Files\Common Files\Microsoft
   Shared\Web Server Extensions\12\Template\Images` folder.

■**Note** The preceding location is standard for language pack 1033 (English). If you are using another
language version of SharePoint, the target folder may be different.

---

2. Open the file `C:\Program Files\Common Files\Microsoft Shared\Web Server Extensions\ 12\Template\XML\Docicon.xml` and add an entry for PDF files within the `<ByExtension>` element.

3. Open a command window and execute the `IISRESET` command to force SharePoint to reload all document image icons.

■**Caution** When you execute the `IISRESET` command, SharePoint will become temporarily unavailable. If you are installing the PDF icon on a production server, you should perform this operation outside of normal business hours.

Recipe—PDF Entry in Docicon.xml

The following is a fragment of the `Docicon.xml` file showing a new entry for files with a `.pdf` extension, and the associated `Pdficon_small.gif` file.

```xml
<?xml version="1.0" encoding="utf-8"?>
<DocIcons>…
    <ByExtension>
            <Mapping Key="pdf" Value="pdficon_small.gif" />
            <Mapping Key="accdt" Value="icaccdb.gif"/>
            <Mapping Key="accdc" Value="icaccdb.gif"/>
            <Mapping Key="asax" Value="icasax.gif" OpenControl=""/>
…
    </ByExtension>
…
</DocIcons>
```

To Run

After you've run `IISRESET`, you can test that the new icon is correctly associated with PDF files by simply uploading a file with that extension to a document library anywhere on your site. Figure 6-1 shows the new icon associated with an uploaded PDF file.

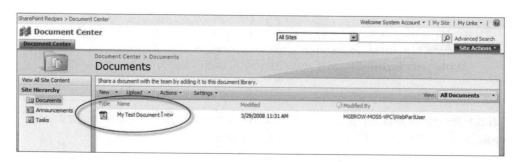

Figure 6-1. *PDF icon associated with uploaded Adobe Acrobat file*

Recipe 6-2. Adding Custom Menus by Using a Feature

One of the really cool new capabilities of SharePoint 2007 is that you can add your own options to virtually all of the menus, making it much easier to extend the native SharePoint interface to integrate your custom add-ons. SharePoint exposes this capability through the new Feature interface, which provides a standard (and supported) mechanism to add in all sorts of customizations, including menu items, event handlers, workflows, list definitions, and custom ASP.NET applications. If you ever made modifications to Onet.xml in SharePoint 2003, you know that after a new web site was provisioned in that version, changes to the Onet.xml file had no impact. The site-definition template was applied at provisioning time, and that was it!

SharePoint 2007 takes many of the template components that were static after provisioning in 2003, and allows you to "staple" them onto preexisting sites—providing significantly enhanced flexibility of design.

So, although this recipe is about adding custom menu items (or *custom actions*, as Microsoft calls them), the Feature framework allows you similar flexibility in managing many other components of your site design.

Recipe Type: Feature + ASP.NET Web Application

Ingredients

In this recipe, you'll add the ability for end users to provide comments on any document in any library on a site. The recipe will have several components:

- A custom action on the drop-down menu associated with document library list items, allowing users to add a comment about the document

- An ASP.NET web form for entering and saving those comments

- A custom list where the comments will be stored

- A custom action on the Site Actions menu that will show users all comments entered by document

- A Feature definition for the two custom actions

- A batch file containing STSADM commands to deploy our feature

Of course, we'll need the standard SharePoint components:

Assembly References

- Windows SharePoint Services .NET assembly

Class Library References

- Microsoft.SharePoint class library

Classes Used

- SPSite class

- SPWeb class

- SPList class

- SPListItem

Special Considerations

- Features can be deployed at the Web, Site, WebApplication, or Farm level. The level determines the scope of activation and deactivation. For example, a feature with a scope of Web must be activated or deactivated for each individual web site, whereas a feature with a scope of Farm will be activated or deactivated across all web sites, in all site collections, on all web applications at once. You should therefore select the scope based on how granular you need control to be.

- Site, web application, or farm administrators (depending on scope) will have the ability to deactivate or activate any features installed at their level of authority. In fact, most of the base functionality that you can access through the SharePoint Central Administration web site (SCAW) and Site Settings pages in SharePoint 2007 is defined through features.

Preparation

1. Create a new folder under C:\Program Files\Common Files\Microsoft Shared\ Web Server Extensions\12\Template\Features\ named DocumentComments. This folder will hold our feature definition XML.

2. Create a new ASP.NET web application called AddComment to provide a web form through which users will add their comments.

3. Add a reference to the Windows SharePoint Services library to the project.

4. Add a custom list named DocComments to hold user comments. This list should be accessible to all users who will be adding or viewing comments.

5. Add a using (C#) or Imports (VB.NET) statement to the to the top of the CodeBehind file of the Default.aspx page of the AddComment ASP.NET web application referencing the Microsoft.SharePoint class library.

Process Flow

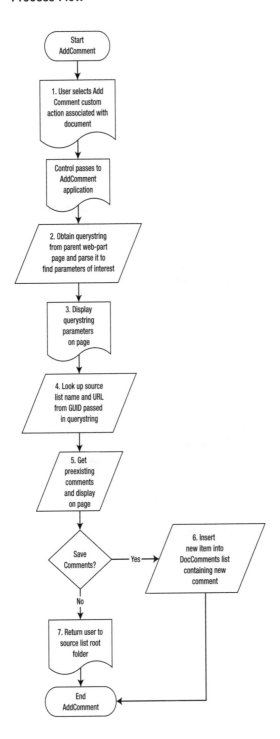

1. The user clicks the Add Comment custom action installed through the feature. This custom action redirects the browser to the web-part page with the Page Viewer web part referring to our `AddComment` application.

2. The page load event of the `AddComment` application retrieves the querystring of the web-part page, and parses out the parameters sent to it from the Add Comment custom action.

3. The extracted parameters are written to the web-part page.

4. One of the parameters passed in to the `AddComment` application was the GUID of the source list. We want to get a handle to the list based on that GUID to find its name and the URL to its root folder.

5. The last bit of information we want to display on the page is a list of already existing comments for the source document. We'll do that by getting a handle to the `DocComments` list, which contains all user comments, converting the list items collection to a `DataTable`, filtering the data by using a `DataView`, and then displaying that data by using a `GridView` web control.

6. If the user clicks the Save button, we'll write the text from the `Comment` control to a new item in the `DocComments` list (writing to lists was covered in Chapter 3).

7. All that's left is to return the user to the list page from which they came. Because the `AddComment` application is running in a Page Viewer web part, a `Response.Redirect()` would display the list page in that same page viewer, which is not what we want. To force the list page to display at the top level, we'll write a `window.open()` JavaScript command to the page.

Note An alternative way of deploying these types of add-ons is to deploy them to a subfolder of the `_layouts` directory (`C:\Program Files\Common Files\Microsoft Shared\Web Server Extensions\12\Template\Layouts`) and then redirect the browser to that page. This removes the need to create virtual directories in IIS. This also allows you to use the `application.master` page in the layouts directory so that the custom page maintains the SharePoint look and feel. However, I generally prefer to deploy custom applications outside of the `...\12\Template\Layouts` folder so as to avoid modifying the out-of-the-box SharePoint structure to the extent possible. For more information, see `http://msdn2.microsoft.com/en-us/library/cc297200.aspx`.

Recipe—Feature

Each feature in SharePoint is stored in its own folder under the `.../12/Template/Features` folder. In this case, we'll name our feature `DocumentComments`. Place the following XML in a file named `Feature.xml` in the `.../12/Template/Features/DocumentComments` folder.

```xml
<?xml version="1.0" encoding="utf-8" ?>
<Feature xmlns="http://schemas.microsoft.com/sharepoint/"
    Id="FD20EE04-D0C4-4bad-B909-D453D89CF7F5"
    Scope="Web"
    Title="DocumentComments"
    Version="1.0.0.0"
    Description="Add Document Comments feature.">
        <ElementManifests>
            <ElementManifest Location="DocumentComments.xml" />
        </ElementManifests>
</Feature>
```

Key components of each feature are as follows:

Id: A unique GUID identifying this feature to SharePoint. You can use the Visual Studio Tools ➤ Create GUID menu option to generate this.

■**Caution** The Create GUID utility will generate a GUID enclosed in {} brackets. You will need to remove these after you paste the GUID into your feature definition, or SharePoint will throw an error when you attempt to install your feature.

Scope: Can be one of Web, Site, WebApplication, or Farm. For our purposes, we'll set the Scope to Web.

Title: The title displayed in the Site Features page under Site Settings.

Description: The description displayed in the Site Features page under Site Settings.

ElementManifest: This points to the external file containing the custom action definitions.

Recipe—Feature Element

Each feature references one or more ElementManifests. In our example, we have just one, DocumentComments.xml.

■**Note** Be sure to change the URL references to http://<yourserver>/<yoursiteurl>/Pages/ Comments.aspx in the following <UrlAction> element to point to the server and site, and replace <yourdoclib> with the document library where you will be adding your Comments.aspx page.

```
<Elements xmlns="http://schemas.microsoft.com/sharepoint/">

    <!-- Action to add to drop-down menu associated with -->
    <!-- document library list items. -->
    <CustomAction
        Id="DC5D5B12-9ACA-4d95-AC54-0E42D4BB4051"
        RegistrationType="List"
        RegistrationId="101"
        Location="EditControlBlock"
        Sequence="999"
        ImageUrl="/_layouts/images/NMW16.GIF"
        Title="Add Comment...">
        <UrlAction Url="http://<yourserver>/<yoursiteurl>/<yourdoclib>/ ➥
            Comments.aspx?itemId={ItemId}&amp;itemUrl={ItemUrl} ➥
            &amp;siteUrl={SiteUrl}&amp;listId={ListId}"/>
    </CustomAction>

    <!-- Action to add to Site Actions menu -->
    <!-- The "UrlAction" element should point to the list where your -->
    <!-- AddComments application is storing the user comments -->
    <CustomAction
        Id="E1E69684-CDFC-4981-B7E0-57DE6EB3C3C8"
        GroupId="SiteActions"
        Location="Microsoft.SharePoint.StandardMenu"
        Sequence="999"
        ImageUrl="/_layouts/images/NMW16.GIF"
        Title="View Comments...">
        <UrlAction Url="http://<yourserver>/<yoursiteurl>/lists/DocComments"/>
    </CustomAction>

</Elements>
```

■Note The image file `Doclibrary.gif` ships with MOSS but is not installed in WSS-only installations. If you are running a WSS-only installation, you may substitute any other available image file found in the ...\12\Template\Images folder, such as `Editicon.gif`.

Key components of each element manifest are as follows:

Type: In our case, this element is of type `CustomAction`. Note that different feature element types will have differing sets of required and optional properties.

Id: As with the parent feature definition, this must be a unique GUID with the leading and trailing braces removed.

Location: This tells SharePoint which menu to attach this custom action to.

Sequence: The ordinal position of this menu item on the target menu.

ImageUrl: An optional icon image file to associate with this menu item.

Title: The text to display on the menu.

UrlAction: The page to redirect the user's browser to when this menu item is selected.

■Note The UrlAction for the EditControlBlock action refers to the web-part page on which we will place a Page Viewer web part to contain our AddComment application. Be sure to pass all the querystring parameters to the web-part page, so that the AddComment application can extract them at runtime.

Recipe—Installer Script

The following commands, entered into a Windows .cmd file, will save you time when installing and reinstalling your feature. They also provide good examples of the STSADM commands you'll use when working with features.

■Note To execute the STSADM command, you will need to open a command window and navigate to C:\Program Files\Common Files\Microsoft Shared\Web Server Extensions\12\bin, or add that path to your environment. Also, be sure to replace <yourserver> and <yoursite> in the following example with the appropriate values for your SharePoint environment.

```
stsadm -o deactivatefeature -filename DocumentComments\feature.xml ➥
-url http://<yourserver>/<yoursite>
```

This command deactivates the feature if it is activated. When you first run the script, you'll receive a warning that the feature had not already been activated. Note that the -url parameter references a web site URL because the feature Scope is Web.

```
stsadm -o uninstallfeature -filename DocumentComments\feature.xml –force
```

After a feature is deactivated, it can be uninstalled from the web site. As with the preceding command, the first time you run the script, you will receive a warning that the specified feature is not installed yet.

```
stsadm -o installfeature -filename DocumentComments\feature.xml –force
```

Here we're installing the feature. Note that SharePoint assumes that the path to the specified feature folder will be under ...\12\Template\Features.

```
stsadm -o activatefeature -filename DocumentComments\feature.xml ➥
-url http://<yourserver>/<yoursite>
```

Finally, the activatefeature STSADM command turns the feature on. This is equivalent to a site administrator navigating to the Site Settings ➤ Site Features page and then manually activating the feature.

Recipe—VB: Default.aspx (See Project AddComment-VB, Class Default.aspx.vb)

```vb
Imports System
Imports System.Data
Imports System.Configuration
Imports System.Web
Imports System.Web.Security
Imports System.Web.UI
Imports System.Web.UI.WebControls
Imports System.Web.UI.WebControls.WebParts
Imports System.Web.UI.HtmlControls
Imports Microsoft.SharePoint
Imports Microsoft.SharePoint.WebControls
Partial Public Class _Default
    Inherits System.Web.UI.Page
    Const COMMENTS_SITE_URL As String = "http://<yourserver>/<siteurl>"
    Const COMMENTS_WEB_NAME As String = "<webname>"
    Const COMMENTS_LIST As String = "DocComments"
    Protected Sub Page_Load(ByVal sender As Object, ByVal e As EventArgs)
        Try
            ' Step 2: Get parse querystring for parameters.
            ' We are assuming that this page is hosted in
            ' a page viewer web part on a web-part page.
            ' So get the parameters passed to the web-part
            ' page contining this page in a PageViewer
            Dim querystring As String() = _
          Server.UrlDecode( _
            Request.UrlReferrer.Query).ToLower().Replace("?", "").Split("&"c)
            For i As Integer = 0 To querystring.Length - 1
                ' Step 3: Display querystring parameters
                If querystring(i).IndexOf("itemid=") <> -1 Then
                    lblItemId.Text = querystring(i).Split("="c)(1)
                End If
                If querystring(i).IndexOf("itemurl=") <> -1 Then
                    hlItemUrl.NavigateUrl = querystring(i).Split("="c)(1)
                    hlItemUrl.Text = querystring(i).Split("="c)(1)
                End If
                If querystring(i).IndexOf("listid=") <> -1 Then
                    lblListId.Text = querystring(i).Split("="c)(1)
                End If
                If querystring(i).IndexOf("siteurl=") <> -1 Then
                    hlSiteUrl.NavigateUrl = querystring(i).Split("="c)(1)
                    hlSiteUrl.Text = querystring(i).Split("="c)(1)
                End If
            Next
```

```vbnet
            ' Step 4: Get the list name and URL from its GUID
            Dim site As New SPSite(hlSiteUrl.NavigateUrl)
            'Extract the web name
Dim webUrl As String
webUrl = hlSiteUrl.NavigateUrl.ToLower().Replace(site.Url, "")
If webUrl.IndexOf("/") = 0 Then
    webUrl = webUrl.Substring(1)
EndIf
Dim web As SPWeb = site.OpenWeb(webUrl);
        Dim guid As New Guid(lblListId.Text)
        Dim origList As SPList = web.Lists(guid)
        lblListName.Text = origList.Title
        hlListUrl.NavigateUrl = web.Url + "/" + origList.RootFolder.Url
        hlListUrl.Text = web.Url + "/" + origList.RootFolder.Url
        ' Step 5: Display existing comments for this document
        Dim siteComments As New SPSite(COMMENTS_SITE_URL)
        Dim webComments As SPWeb = _
           siteComments.OpenWeb(COMMENTS_WEB_NAME)
        Dim docComments As SPList = webComments.Lists(COMMENTS_LIST)
        Dim dtComments As DataTable = docComments.Items.GetDataTable()
        dtComments.TableName = "Comments"
        Dim dvComments As New DataView( _
            dtComments, "ItemUrl='" + hlItemUrl.NavigateUrl + "'", _
            "Created DESC", DataViewRowState.CurrentRows)
        GridView1.DataSource = dvComments
        GridView1.DataBind()
        webComments.Dispose()
        siteComments.Dispose()
    Catch ex As Exception
    End Try
End Sub
Protected Sub cmdSave_Click(ByVal sender As Object, ByVal e As EventArgs) _
    Handles cmdSave.Click
    ' Get handle to web
    Dim siteComments As New SPSite(COMMENTS_SITE_URL)
    Dim webComments As SPWeb = _
       siteComments.OpenWeb(COMMENTS_WEB_NAME)
    webComments.AllowUnsafeUpdates = True
    ' Step 6: Write new comment to DOCCOMMENTS list
    Dim docComments As SPList = webComments.Lists(COMMENTS_LIST)
    Dim item As SPListItem = docComments.Items.Add()
    item("ItemId") = lblItemId.Text
    item("ItemUrl") = hlItemUrl.NavigateUrl
    item("ListId") = lblListId.Text
    item("SiteUrl") = hlSiteUrl.NavigateUrl
    item("Comment") = txtComments.Text
    item.Update()
```

```
            webComments.Dispose()
            siteComments.Dispose()
            ' Step 7: Return user to list
            returnToList()
        End Sub
        Protected Sub cmdCancel_Click(ByVal sender As Object, ByVal e As EventArgs) _
            Handles cmdCancel.Click
            returnToList()
        End Sub
        Private Sub returnToList()
            ' Because this page is running in a page viewer
            ' (i.e. in an <IFRAME>), a redirect statement would
            ' display the target URL in the frame, whereas we
            ' want the target page displayed at the top level.
            ' To accomplish this, we'll insert a bit of JavaScript
            ' to perform a window.open().
            Response.Write("<script>window.open('" + hlListUrl.NavigateUrl + _
                "','_top');</script>")
        End Sub
End Class
```

Recipe—C#: Default.aspx (See Project AddComment, Class Default.aspx.cs)

```
using System;
using System.Data;
using System.Configuration;
using System.Web;
using System.Web.Security;
using System.Web.UI;
using System.Web.UI.WebControls;
using System.Web.UI.WebControls.WebParts;
using System.Web.UI.HtmlControls;
using Microsoft.SharePoint;
using Microsoft.SharePoint.WebControls;
public partial class _Default : System.Web.UI.Page
{
    const string COMMENTS_SITE_URL = "http://<yourserver>/<siteurl>";
    const string COMMENTS_WEB_NAME = "<webname>";
    const string COMMENTS_LIST = "DocComments";
    protected void Page_Load(object sender, EventArgs e)
    {
        try
        {
            // Step 2: Get parse querystring for parameters.
            // We are assuming that this page is hosted in
            // a page viewer web part on a web-part page.
            // So get the parameters passed to the web-part
            // page containing this page in a PageViewer
```

```
string[] querystring =
    Server.UrlDecode(
        Request.UrlReferrer.Query).ToLower().Replace("?", "") ➥
            .Split('&');
// Step 3: Display querystring parameters
for (int i = 0; i < querystring.Length; i++)
{
    if (querystring[i].IndexOf("itemid=") != -1)
        lblItemId.Text = querystring[i].Split('=')[1];
    if (querystring[i].IndexOf("itemurl=") != -1)
    {
        hlItemUrl.NavigateUrl = querystring[i].Split('=')[1];
        hlItemUrl.Text = querystring[i].Split('=')[1];
    }
    if (querystring[i].IndexOf("listid=") != -1)
        lblListId.Text = querystring[i].Split('=')[1];
    if (querystring[i].IndexOf("siteurl=") != -1)
    {
        hlSiteUrl.NavigateUrl = querystring[i].Split('=')[1];
        hlSiteUrl.Text = querystring[i].Split('=')[1];
    }
}
// Step 4: Get the list name and URL from its GUID
SPSite site = new SPSite(hlSiteUrl.NavigateUrl);
// Extract the web URL
string webUrl = hlSiteUrl.NavigateUrl.ToLower().Replace(site.Url, "");
if (webUrl.IndexOf("/") == 0) webUrl = webUrl.Substring(1);
SPWeb web = site.OpenWeb(webUrl);
Guid guid = new Guid(lblListId.Text);
SPList origList = web.Lists[guid];
lblListName.Text = origList.Title;
hlListUrl.NavigateUrl = web.Url + "/" + origList.RootFolder.Url;
hlListUrl.Text = web.Url + "/" + origList.RootFolder.Url;
// Step 5: Display existing comments for this document
SPSite siteComments = new SPSite(COMMENTS_SITE_URL);
SPWeb webComments = siteComments.OpenWeb(COMMENTS_WEB_NAME);
SPList docComments = webComments.Lists[COMMENTS_LIST];
DataTable dtComments = docComments.Items.GetDataTable();
dtComments.TableName = "Comments";
DataView dvComments = new DataView(
    dtComments, "ItemUrl='"
        + hlItemUrl.NavigateUrl
        + "'", "Created DESC",
    DataViewRowState.CurrentRows);
GridView1.DataSource = dvComments;
GridView1.DataBind();
web.Dispose();
site.Dispose();
```

```csharp
            webComments.Dispose();
            siteComments.Dispose();
        }
        catch (Exception ex)
        {
        }
    }
    protected void cmdSave_Click(object sender, EventArgs e)
    {
        // Get handle to web
        SPSite siteComments = new SPSite(COMMENTS_SITE_URL);
        SPWeb webComments = siteComments.OpenWeb(COMMENTS_WEB_NAME);
        webComments.AllowUnsafeUpdates = true;
        // Step 6: Write new comment to DOCCOMMENTS list
        SPList docComments = webComments.Lists[COMMENTS_LIST];
        SPListItem item = docComments.Items.Add();
        item["ItemId"] = lblItemId.Text;
        item["ItemUrl"] = hlItemUrl.NavigateUrl;
        item["ListId"] = lblListId.Text;
        item["SiteUrl"] = hlSiteUrl.NavigateUrl;
        item["Comment"] = txtComments.Text;
        item.Update();
        webComments.Dispose();
        siteComments.Dispose();
        // Step 7: Return user to list
        returnToList();
    }
    protected void cmdCancel_Click(object sender, EventArgs e)
    {
        returnToList();
    }
    private void returnToList()
    {
        // Because this page is running in a page viewer
        // (i.e. in an <IFRAME>), a redirect statement would
        // display the target URL in the frame, whereas we
        // want the target page displayed at the top level.
        // To accomplish this, we'll insert a bit of JavaScript
        // to perform a window.open().
        Response.Write(
            "<script>window.open('" + hlListUrl.NavigateUrl + "','_top');</script>"
        );
    }
}
```

Web.config Changes

You will also need to tell ASP.NET to pass the user's credentials through to the AddComment application. You do this by editing the Web.config file in the AddComment application, adding the <identity impersonate="true"/> element just after the <authentication mode="Windows"/> tag.

IIS Configuration

1. Whether you use the VB or C# version of the AddComment application, the application will be accessed from http://<yourserver>/_layouts/ AddComment/Default.aspx (or some similar virtual path under /_layouts). To do this, open the IIS management console, navigate to the web site SharePoint - 80/_layouts, right-click on the _layouts node, and choose the New ➤ Virtual Directory option, as shown in Figure 6-2.

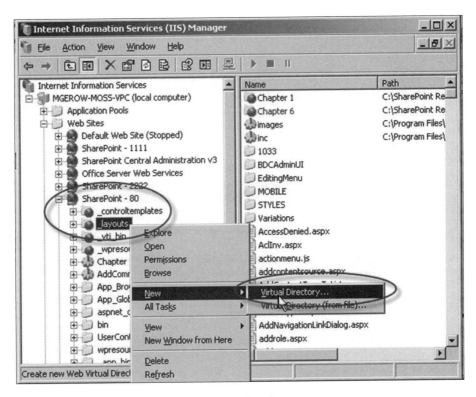

Figure 6-2. *Adding a new virtual directory under _layouts*

2. Click Next, and name the new virtual directory AddComment (Figure 6-3).

3. Enter the path to the physical application and click Next (Figure 6-4).

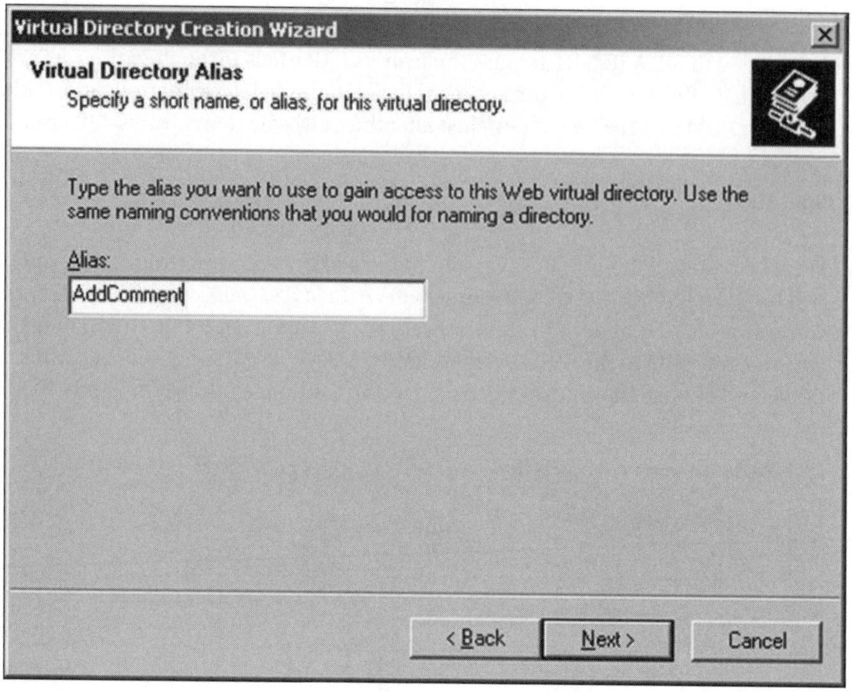

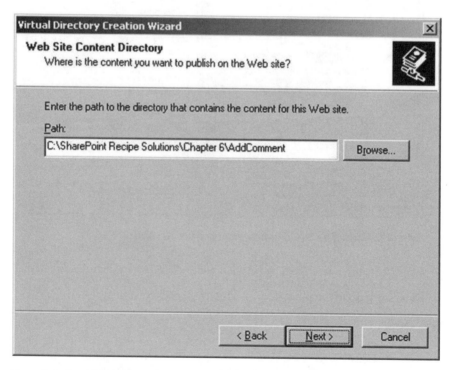

Figure 6-3. *Naming the virtual directory*

Figure 6-4. *Specifying the path to the physical application*

4. Tell IIS to allow scripts to run from this virtual directory, and click Next and then Finish (Figure 6-5). The application will now be accessible from any SharePoint web site as `.../_layouts/AddComment/Default.aspx`.

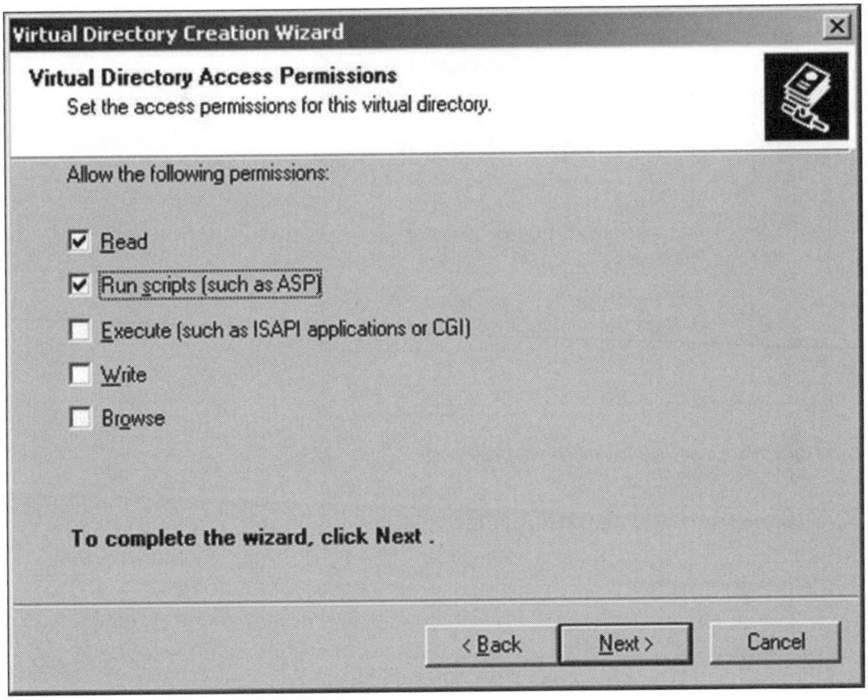

Figure 6-5. *Setting the directory options*

To Run

Before you can use your new custom action, you'll need to create a web-part page to display the `AddComment/Default.aspx` form that you have created:

■**Note** The following instructions assume you have a document library named `Pages` in the site `http://<yourserver>/<yoursite>`. If this is not the case, you should create the `Pages` document library before proceeding.

---

1. Navigate to the http://<yourserver>/<yoursite> (replace <yourserver> and <yoursite> with values you specified in the preceding feature definition), and select Site Actions ➤ Create (Figure 6-6).

Figure 6-6. *Creating a new web-part page*

2. Click the Web Part Page option (Figure 6-7).

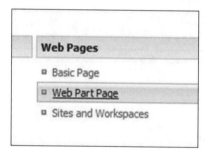

Figure 6-7. *Selecting the Web Part Page option*

3. Create a new page name, Comments.aspx, placing it in the document library named Pages (Figure 6-8).

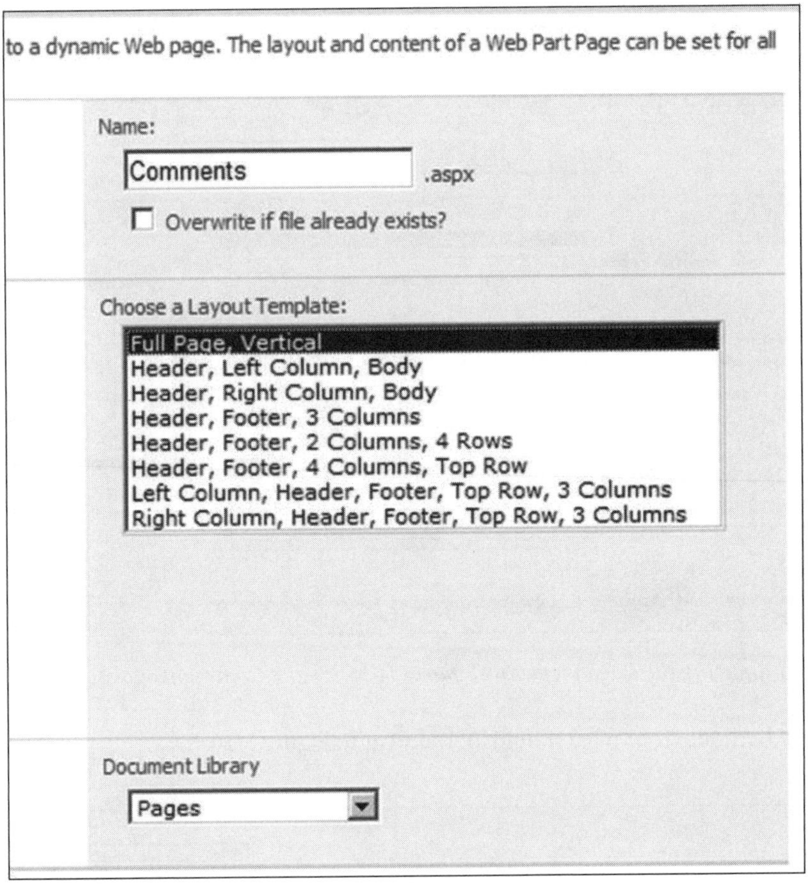

to a dynamic Web page. The layout and content of a Web Part Page can be set for all

Name:

Comments   .aspx

☐ Overwrite if file already exists?

Choose a Layout Template:

Full Page, Vertical
Header, Left Column, Body
Header, Right Column, Body
Header, Footer, 3 Columns
Header, Footer, 2 Columns, 4 Rows
Header, Footer, 4 Columns, Top Row
Left Column, Header, Footer, Top Row, 3 Columns
Right Column, Header, Footer, Top Row, 3 Columns

Document Library

Pages   ▼

Figure 6-8. *Creating the Comments.aspx page*

4. In design mode on the page `Comments.aspx`, add a Page Viewer web part by clicking on the Add a Web Part banner. Set the Page Viewer's link property to `http://<yourserver>/ _layouts/AddComment/Default.aspx`, as shown in Figure 6-9. In addition, set the height of the page to 10 inches.

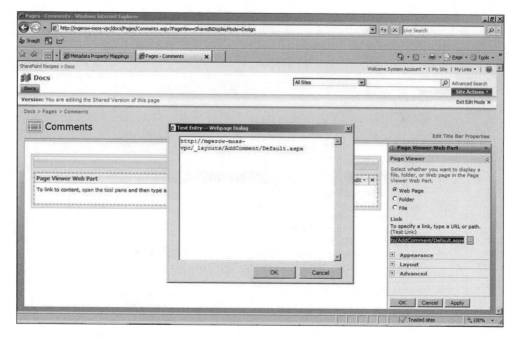

Figure 6-9. *Configuring the Page Viewer web part to display the Comments page*

5. Exit edit mode. Your page should look similar to Figure 6-10.

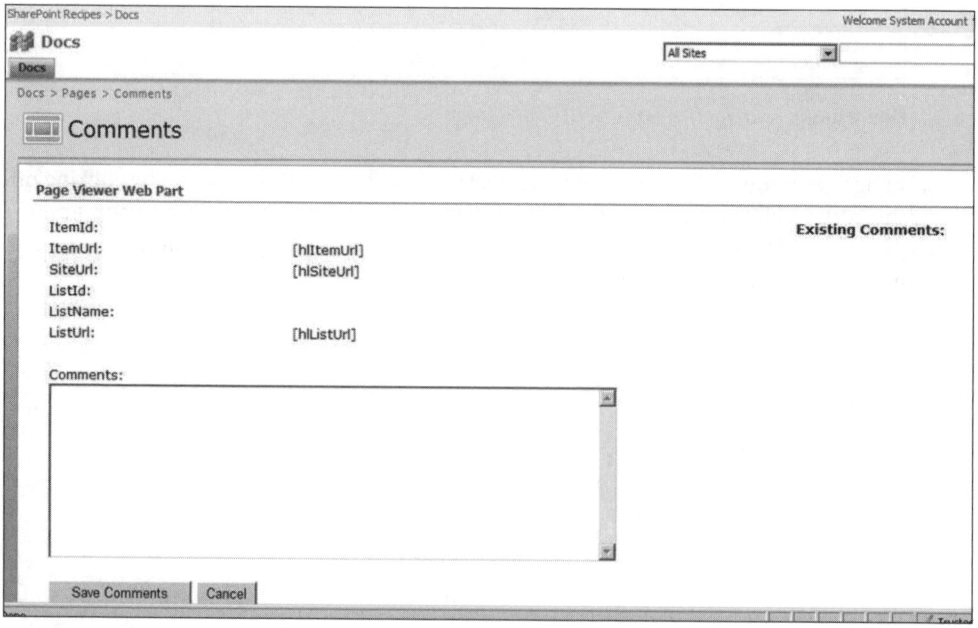

Figure 6-10. *The completed comment-editing page*

You're not quite there yet. You'll need a custom list named DocComments in the same site you placed your web-part page in the preceding steps. This list will hold all user comments. The finished list should have the fields shown in Figure 6-11.

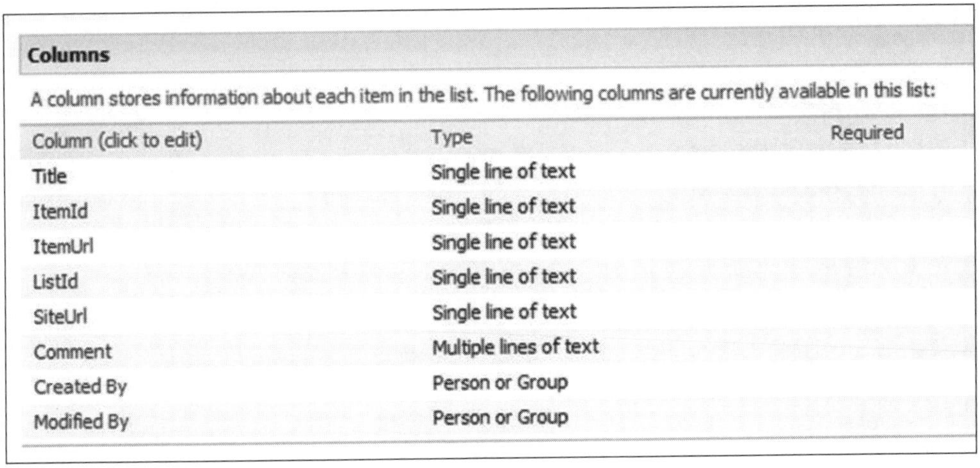

Columns

A column stores information about each item in the list. The following columns are currently available in this list:

Column (click to edit)	Type	Required
Title	Single line of text	
ItemId	Single line of text	
ItemUrl	Single line of text	
ListId	Single line of text	
SiteUrl	Single line of text	
Comment	Multiple lines of text	
Created By	Person or Group	
Modified By	Person or Group	

Figure 6-11. *Structure of the DocComments list*

Now that all the pieces are in place and installed, let's take our comments feature for a spin. First, be sure to run the command script to install the two custom actions. Then navigate to a document library on the web site in which you installed the feature (http://<yourserver>/ <yoursite>), mouse over a document, and display the context menu. You should see a new option titled Add Comment, as shown in Figure 6-12. Click the Add Comment link to display the web-part page containing a reference to the AddComment application Default.aspx page.

The AddComment application will be displayed in the Page Viewer web part, as shown in Figure 6-13.

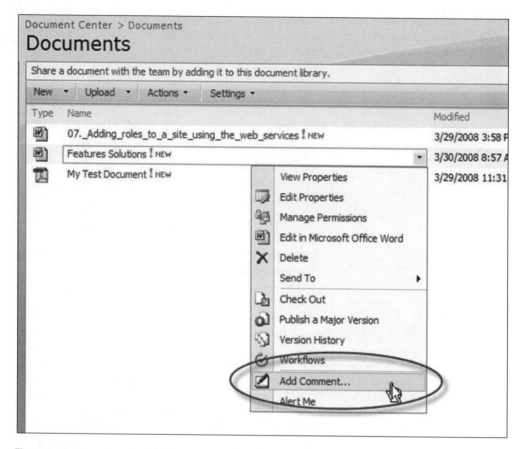

Figure 6-12. *Choosing the Add Comment option for a selected document*

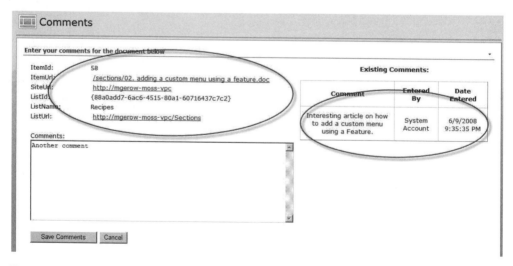

Figure 6-13. *The AddComment application page*

As shown in Figure 6-13, the AddComment application extracts the querystring parameters sent to its containing web-part page and displays them on the web form, along with any preexisting comments for the source document.

You will also find a new option on the Site Actions menu titled View Comments, as shown in Figure 6-14.

Figure 6-14. *Selecting the View Comments site action*

Selecting this option will redirect the browser to the default view of the DocComments list on the Docs web site (Figure 6-15).

■**Caution** Be sure that the DocComments list permissions (and those of the web site containing it) are such that all users who can access the Add Comments or View Comments custom actions can also insert new items and navigate to the view.

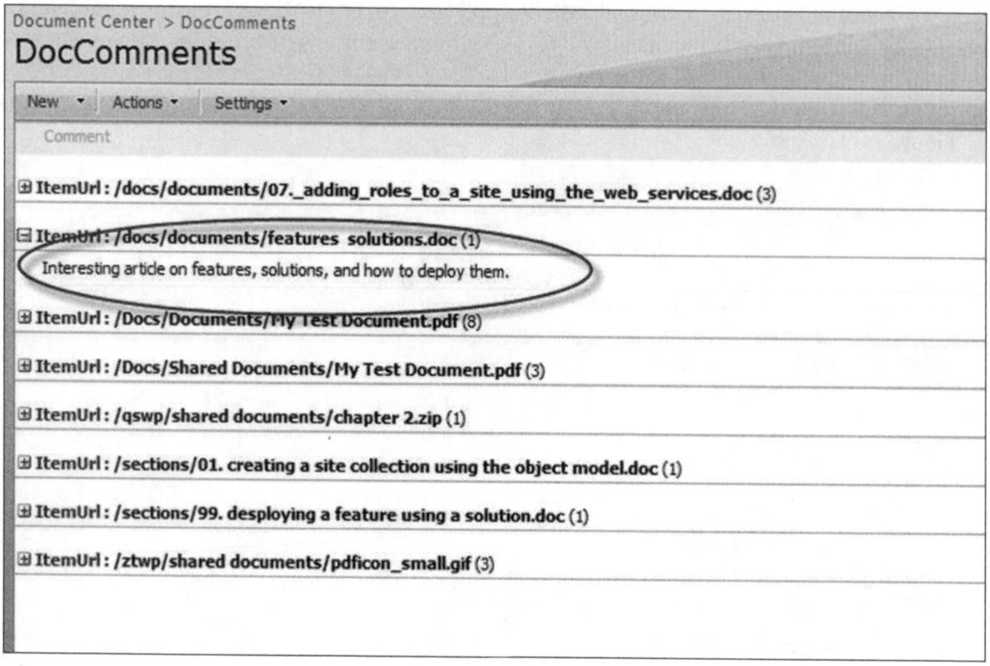

Figure 6-15. *The DocComments list*

Recipe 6-3. Adding Web Parts Through Onet.xml

Onet.xml plays a central role in the process of provisioning new SharePoint sites. When a new site is requested, Onet.xml provides the "punch list" of components to be added. These components include characteristics such as features, lists, and web parts, to name a few. After a site is provisioned, the Onet.xml file has essentially done its job, and will not be read again—which is not the case with other site-definition elements of which Onet.xml is a part.

In this recipe, you'll look at how to edit the Onet.xml file to instruct SharePoint to add specific web parts to specific pages at provision time. You'll add a Page Viewer and a Content Editor web part to the Default.aspx page of a new site, but you can follow this procedure to add any web part that is registered as safe in SharePoint's Web.config file.

Recipe Type: CAML

Ingredients

- A copy of the C:\Program Files\Common Files\Microsoft Shared\Web Server Extensions\ 12\Template\SiteTemplates\sts folder. In this recipe, I copied it to C:\Program Files\ Common Files\Microsoft Shared\Web Server Extensions\12\Template\SiteTemplates\ sts-Mgerow2.

- Web-part definition (.dwp or .webpart) files for the web parts you want to add to the page.

Special Considerations

- Never edit the out-of-the-box site-definition templates that ship with SharePoint. If you introduce errors to some components of those definitions, SharePoint may become inoperable, and Microsoft may not support your installation. You should therefore always make a copy of the out-of-the-box site definition, or another working custom site definition, that most closely matches the definition you are trying to create to serve as the basis for your new definition.

■Caution Microsoft may refuse to support your SharePoint installation if you've made edits to any of the out-of-the-box site-definition templates. For that reason, you should always make your customizations to copies of these templates.

- SharePoint provides scant information about any errors it may find in an `Onet.xml` file during provisioning, so it's best to make your customizations a little bit at a time, testing those changes at each step by provisioning a new site. That way you can back out an erroneous change to the `Onet.xml` file without losing too much work.

- Remember that CAML (the flavor of XML used by SharePoint) is case sensitive—as is all XML—and all element tags must be properly closed.

Preparation

1. Add a Page Viewer and Content Editor web part to a web-part page on your site. Set their properties as desired. For example, specify a URL to display in the Page Viewer and add some text to display in the Content Editor web parts.

2. Export each of the web parts by using the Export option on the web part's menu. You will need the resulting `.dwp` or `.webpart` files later.

3. Create a copy of the folder `C:\Program Files\Common Files\Microsoft Shared\Web Server Extensions\12\Template\SiteTemplates\sts`. I named my copy `sts-MGEROW2`, but you may give your copy any name you wish as long as it's unique.

4. Open the file `C:\Program Files\Common Files\Microsoft Shared\Web Server Extensions\12\Template\SiteTemplates\sts-Mgerow2\XML\Onet.xml` in Visual Studio, Notepad, or whatever text editor you prefer.

5. Find the two following sequences of elements just after the `</Configurations>` closing tag:

```
<Modules>
<Module Name="Default" Url="" Path="">
     <File Url="default.aspx" NavBarHome="True">
```

6. Within the `<File>` element, add the following two child elements:

```
<AllUsersWebPart WebPartZoneID="Left" WebPartOrder="1">
<![CDATA[
]]>
</AllUsersWebPart>
<AllUsersWebPart WebPartZoneID="Right" WebPartOrder="1">
<![CDATA[
]]>
</AllUsersWebPart>
```

7. Open the `.dwp` or `.webpart` file created when you exported the Page Viewer web part, and copy the `<WebPart></WebPart>` element and all of its contents in between the first set of `<![CDATA[` and `]]>` tags (see the following section, "Recipe—Page Viewer Web Part").

8. Open the `.dwp` or `.webpart` file created when you exported the Content Editor web part, and copy the `<WebPart></WebPart>` element and all of its contents in between the second set of `<![CDATA[` and `]]>` tags (see the upcoming section "Recipe—Content Editor Web Part").

9. Create a copy of `C:\Program Files\Common Files\Microsoft Shared\Web Server Extensions\12\Template\1033\XML\Webtemp.xml`. I named my copy `Webtempsts-Mgerow.xml`, but you may choose any name as long as it begins with `Wemtemp`, has an `.xml` extension, and is unique. At startup, SharePoint concatenates the contents of all XML files beginning with `Webtemp` in this folder to build its list of available site definitions.

10. Open the new `Webtemp` file you created in the preceding step, and delete all the `<Template>` elements within the `<Templates>` parent element.

11. Within the `<Templates>` element, create the following child element:

```
<Template Name="STS-MGEROW2" ID="1002">
    <Configuration ID="0"
     Title="Adding web parts directly to ONET.XML"
     Hidden="FALSE"
     ImageUrl="/_layouts/images/stsprev.png"
     Description="A custom site definition based on STS.  ➥
         The only difference is the addition of web-part definitions  ➥
         directly into
         ONET.XML by using the AllUsersWebPart element."
     DisplayCategory="Chapter 6" >

    </Configuration>
</Template>
```

■**Caution** The template ID value must be unique within your SharePoint installation. To avoid collisions with out-of-the-box templates, I typically begin my numbering at 1001. Failure to provide a unique ID will result in an error when you attempt to provision a site with the new template.

---

12. Issue an `IISRESET` console command to force SharePoint to reload its list of site definitions.

Figure 6-16 shows how the `<Configuration>` attributes map to template-selection page elements in SharePoint.

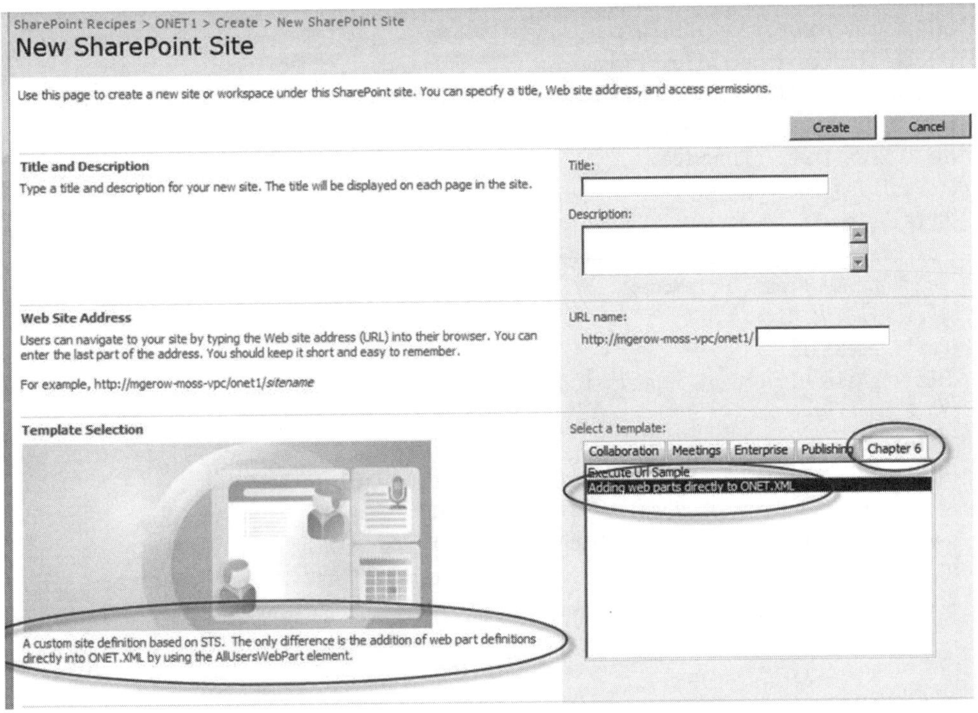

Figure 6-16. *Webtemp <Configuration> attributes as displayed in the New SharePoint Site page*

Recipe—Page Viewer Web Part

The following is the XML that SharePoint creates when I export my Page Viewer web part, without the opening `<?xml…>` tag. This is what you will need to pass between the `<![CDATA[` and `]]>` tags of the first `<AllUsersWebPart>` element. Essentially you are telling SharePoint to automate the process of adding a Page Viewer web part and setting its properties when it provisions a new web site.

```
<WebPart xmlns:xsi="http://www.w3.org/2001/XMLSchema-instance" ➥
    xmlns:xsd="http://www.w3.org/2001/XMLSchema" ➥
    xmlns="http://schemas.microsoft.com/WebPart/v2">
  <Title>And here's my page viewer web part!</Title>
  <FrameType>Default</FrameType>
  <Description>Use to display linked content, such as files, folders, or Web pages. ➥
        The linked content is isolated from other content on the ➥
        Web Part Page.</Description>
```

```
        <IsIncluded>true</IsIncluded>
        <ZoneID>Left</ZoneID>
        <PartOrder>0</PartOrder>
        <FrameState>Normal</FrameState>
        <Height>1000px</Height>
        <Width />
        <AllowRemove>true</AllowRemove>
        <AllowZoneChange>true</AllowZoneChange>
        <AllowMinimize>true</AllowMinimize>
        <AllowConnect>true</AllowConnect>
        <AllowEdit>true</AllowEdit>
        <AllowHide>true</AllowHide>
        <IsVisible>true</IsVisible>
        <DetailLink />
        <HelpLink />
        <HelpMode>Modeless</HelpMode>
        <Dir>Default</Dir>
        <PartImageSmall />
        <MissingAssembly>Cannot import this Web Part.</MissingAssembly>
        <PartImageLarge />
        <IsIncludedFilter />
        <Assembly>Microsoft.SharePoint, Version=12.0.0.0, Culture=neutral, ➥
            PublicKeyToken=71e9bce111e9429c</Assembly>
        <TypeName>Microsoft.SharePoint.WebPartPages.PageViewerWebPart</TypeName>
        <ContentLink xmlns="http://schemas.microsoft.com/WebPart/v2/PageViewer"> ➥
            http://www.apress.com/book/view/1430209615</ContentLink>
        <SourceType xmlns="http://schemas.microsoft.com/WebPart/v2/PageViewer">URL
            </SourceType>
</WebPart>
```

Recipe—Content Editor Web Part

As with the Page Viewer web-part definition in the preceding section, you will paste the following portion of the Content Editor web-part definition file between the <![CDATA[and]]> tags of the second <AllUsersWebPart> element.

```
<WebPart xmlns:xsi="http://www.w3.org/2001/XMLSchema-instance" ➥
        xmlns:xsd="http://www.w3.org/2001/XMLSchema" ➥
        xmlns="http://schemas.microsoft.com/WebPart/v2">
    <Title>Hello World web part</Title>
    <FrameType>Default</FrameType>
    <Description>Use for formatted text, tables, and images.</Description>
    <IsIncluded>true</IsIncluded>
    <ZoneID>Right</ZoneID>
    <PartOrder>0</PartOrder>
    <FrameState>Normal</FrameState>
    <Height />
    <Width />
```

```
<AllowRemove>true</AllowRemove>
<AllowZoneChange>true</AllowZoneChange>
<AllowMinimize>true</AllowMinimize>
<AllowConnect>true</AllowConnect>
<AllowEdit>true</AllowEdit>
<AllowHide>true</AllowHide>
<IsVisible>true</IsVisible>
<DetailLink />
<HelpLink />
<HelpMode>Modeless</HelpMode>
<Dir>Default</Dir>
<PartImageSmall />
<MissingAssembly>Cannot import this Web Part.</MissingAssembly>
<PartImageLarge />
<IsIncludedFilter />
<Assembly>Microsoft.SharePoint, Version=12.0.0.0, Culture=neutral, ➡
        PublicKeyToken=71e9bce111e9429c</Assembly>
<TypeName>Microsoft.SharePoint.WebPartPages.ContentEditorWebPart</TypeName>
<ContentLink xmlns="http://schemas.microsoft.com/WebPart/v2/ContentEditor" />
<Content xmlns="http://schemas.microsoft.com/WebPart/v2/ContentEditor">
        Hello World!
</Content>
<PartStorage xmlns="http://schemas.microsoft.com/WebPart/v2/ContentEditor" />
</WebPart>
```

■**Caution** When SharePoint exports a Content Editor web part, it will place the text contained in the `<Content>` element in a `<![CDATA[ ]]>` element. Because CAML doesn't support nested `<![CDATA[ ]]>` elements, you will need to remove that element before pasting your `<WebPart>` element into `Onet.xml`. For example, the original contents of the `<Content>` element as exported by SharePoint was `<![CDATA[Hello World!]]>`, but was altered to `Hello World` when added to `Onet.xml`.

To Run

At this point, you've created your new site definition, edited the `Onet.xml` file to contain the two web-part definitions, added a new `Webtemp*.xml` file to tell SharePoint about the new site definition, and you've run the `IISRESET` command to force SharePoint to refresh its list of site definitions in memory. You're now ready to provision a site based on the new template.

To test your new site-definition template, follow these steps:

1. Select the Site Actions ➤ Create option from any page on an existing SharePoint web site, and then click Sites and Workspaces.

2. Enter a title and URL for the new site.

3. Click the Chapter 6 tab in the template section and highlight the Adding Web Parts Directly to `Onet.xml` template.

4. Click the Create button. After the new site has been created, you should see a page similar to that shown in Figure 6-17.

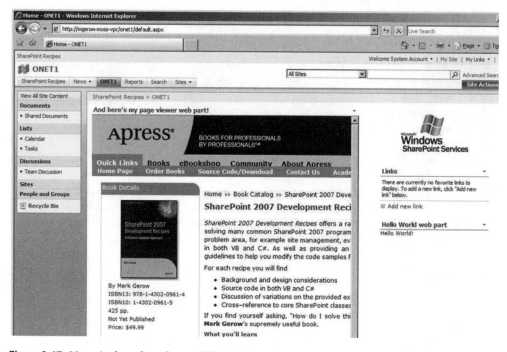

Figure 6-17. *New site based on the modified Onet.xml*

Note that in addition to the standard image and links web parts that are part of the base `sts` template, our two additional web parts are displayed.

Variations

- In this recipe, we left the preexisting web-part definitions. However, we could have easily deleted the preexisting `<AllUsersWebPart>` elements to start with a clean slate.

- The out-of-the-box `sts` `Onet.xml` file references only one page, `Default.aspx`. However, you can easily add more pages at provision time, and assign web parts to each of them in this manner. To do so, simply make a copy of the file `C:\Program Files\Common Files\Microsoft Shared\Web Server Extensions\12\Template\SiteTemplates\sts-MGEROW2\Default.aspx` under a different name (for example, `Default2.aspx`), and add a new `<File>` element under the same `<Module>` element that contains our reference to `Default.aspx`, but with its `Url` attribute changed to reference `Default2.aspx`. Edit or add `<AllUsersWebPart>` elements to this second `<File>` element as needed.

Related Recipes

- Recipe 1-6 in Chapter 1

- Recipe 6-4

Recipe 6-4. Adding an ExecuteUrl Directive to Onet.xml

SharePoint's site-definition template framework is incredibly flexible, providing you a declarative language in the form of CAML (a special variety of XML). Through the use of CAML in Onet.xml combined with the features framework, you can do a great deal. But, as a programmer I really appreciate that Microsoft included a way to plug in whatever code I want to execute at the end of the site-provisioning process. This is done by inserting an <ExecuteUrl> element into the Onet.xml file for a given site-definition template. The <ExecuteUrl> element tells SharePoint what ASP.NET web page to redirect to after the site has been provisioned. That page can gather additional data from the site requestor, perform additional site definition under your control, and optionally redirect the user to any page on the new site.

In this recipe, you'll see how easy it is to incorporate your postprovisioning code into a site-definition template to modify the web parts on the Default.aspx page of a new site before it's presented to the requestor. In this instance, you'll display a page giving the requestor the following three options:

- Delete any preexisting web parts that were part of the site-definition template

- Add a Hello World Content Editor web part

- Add a Page Viewer web part displaying a URL of the requestor's choice

Recipe Type: CAML + ASP.NET

Ingredients

Assembly References

- Windows SharePoint Services .NET assembly

Class Library References

- Microsoft.SharePoint class library

- Microsoft.SharePoint.WebControls class library

- Microsoft.SharePoint.WebParts class library

Other Ingredients

- The `AddContentEditorWebPart()` and `AddWebPart()` methods developed in Recipe 1-6 in Chapter 1

- A copy of the `..\12\Template\SiteTemplates\sts` folder (for example, `..\12\Template\SiteTemplates\Sts-new`)

- A copy of the `..\12\Template\1033\XML\Webtemp.xml` file (for example, `..\12\Template\1033\XML\Webtempsts-new.xml`)

■**Note** The reference to 1033 in the preceding ingredient is specific to the English language version of SharePoint. If you are using a different language version, substitute the appropriate numeric designation.

Special Considerations

- You will want to configure the ASP.NET application hosting the `ExecuteUrl` to be accessible under the virtual `_layouts` path. Rather than physically placing the application files under that path, you can create a virtual directory in IIS under `_layouts` pointing to the physical location of the application on your SharePoint server.

- Create a new site-definition template by copying one of the existing definitions under `..\12\Template\SiteTemplates`. In this recipe, I copied the `sts` folder, which contains the standard team site definition.

■**Caution** You should never edit the out-of-the-box site-definition templates that ship with MOSS or WSS. Instead, always copy one of those templates or a custom definition derived from one of those templates to form the basis for a new custom definition.

- SharePoint doesn't provide much of a safety net when editing `Onet.xml` or `Webtemp*.xml` files, which is one reason never to edit the stock versions. In fact, it's not a bad idea to use configuration-management software such as Microsoft Visual SourceSafe to keep track of prior versions in case you need to roll back edits that render either file unusable.

- Be sure to give your new definition template a unique ID, or SharePoint will balk when you attempt to use it. You do this by assigning a unique value to the ID attribute of the `<Template>` element in your `Webtemp*.xml` file.

Preparation

1. Create a copy of the folder `C:\Program Files\Common Files\Microsoft Shared\ Web Server Extensions\12\Template\SiteTemplates\sts`. I named my copy `sts-Mgerow`, but you may give your copy any name you wish as long as it's unique.

2. Open the file `C:\Program Files\Common Files\Microsoft Shared\Web Server Extensions\ 12\Template\SiteTemplates\sts-MGEROW\xml\Onet.xml` in Visual Studio, Notepad, or whatever text editor you prefer.

3. Find the `<Configuration ID="0" Name="Default">` element, and within this add the following child element:

```
<ExecuteUrl Url="_layouts/SelectWebParts/SelectWebParts.aspx"></ExecuteUrl>
```

Note the use of the _layouts/ virtual path. This is important because we want our SelectWebParts application to be able to detect the context of the SharePoint web site being created.

4. Save your changes to `Onet.xml`.

5. Create a copy of `C:\Program Files\Common Files\Microsoft Shared\ Web Server Extensions\12\Template\1033\XML\Webtemp.xml`. I named my copy `Webtempsts-Mgerow.xml`, but you may choose any name as long as it begins with `Webtemp`, has an `.xml` extension, and is unique. At startup, SharePoint concatenates the contents of all XML files beginning with `Webtemp` in this folder to build its list of available site definitions.

6. Within the `<Templates>` element, remove the existing contents of the file's `<Templates>` element, and create the following child element:

```
<Template Name="STS-MGEROW" ID="1001">
    <Configuration ID="0"
        Title="Execute Url Sample"
        Hidden="FALSE"
        ImageUrl="/_layouts/images/stsprev.png"
        Description="A custom site definition based on STS"
        DisplayCategory="Chapter 6" >
    </Configuration>
</Template>
```

7. Issue an `IISRESET` console command to force SharePoint to reload its list of site definitions.

Figure 6-18 shows how the `<Configuration>` attributes map to template-selection page elements in SharePoint.

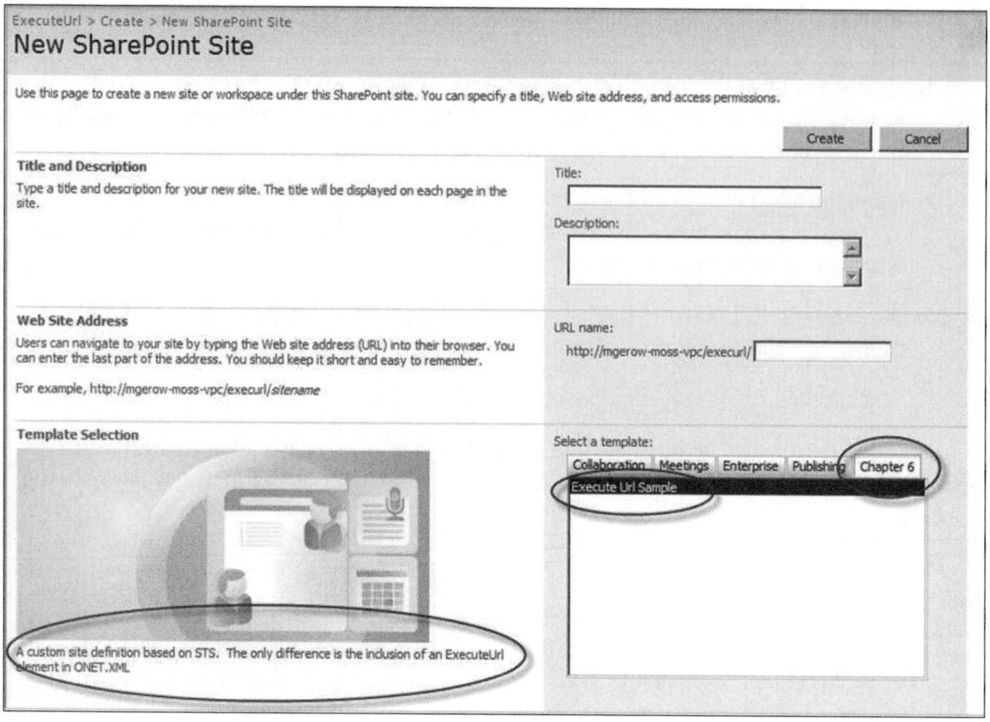

Figure 6-18. *Webtemp <Configuration> attributes as displayed in the New SharePoint Site page*

■**Caution** The `Template ID` attribute must be a unique value within the collection of site-definition templates on your server, or SharePoint will not recognize your template. I typically begin numbering my templates at 1001 to achieve this end.

---

8. Create a new ASP.NET application on your SharePoint. I named my C# application `SelectWebParts-CS`, but you may name it as you wish.

9. Rename `Default.aspx` to `SelectWebParts.aspx` in your new ASP.NET application.

10. Add a reference to the Windows SharePoint Services .NET assembly.

11. Add a `using` (C#) or `Imports` (VB.NET) reference to the `Microsoft.SharePoint` class library.

12. Open up the IIS Manager application (found under Administrative Tools) and create a new virtual directory named `SelectWebParts` under `Web Sites/SharePoint - 80/_layouts` that points to the root folder of your `SelectWebParts-CS` ASP.NET application (Figure 6-19).

■**Note** If you are not using the default `SharePoint-80` web application, please replace references to that web application as appropriate.

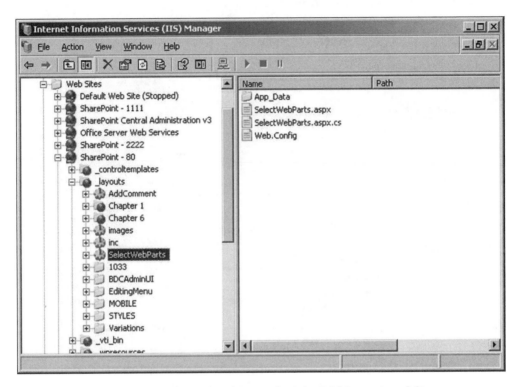

Figure 6-19. *The IIS Manager application showing the SelectWebParts virtual directory*

13. Right-click on the new virtual directory and select the Properties context menu item to open its properties dialog box.

14. Click the Create button to the right of the Application Name field if it's grayed out, to designate this virtual directory as a self-contained ASP.NET application.

15. Select SharePoint—80 from the Application Pool drop-down list to ensure that your application runs in the same security context as SharePoint (Figure 6-20).

■**Note** The SharePoint—80 application pool will exist in a default SharePoint installation. If your installation differs, you should select the same application pool as that being used the SharePoint web application you will be using with this recipe.

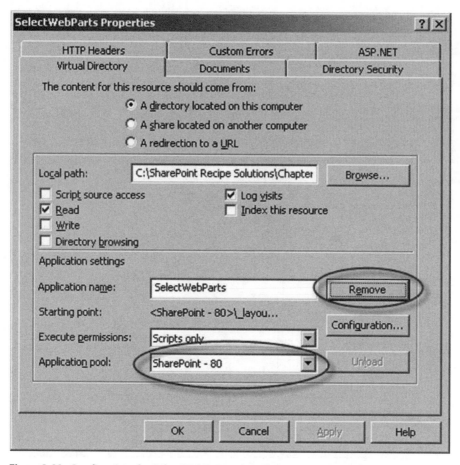

Figure 6-20. *Configuring the SelectWebParts virtual directory properties*

We're now ready to code our SelectWebParts application.

Process Flow: Finish_Click()

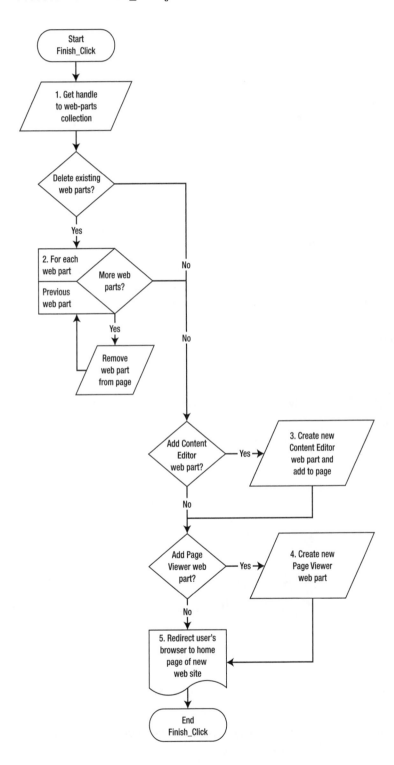

1. Use the `SPControl.GetContextWeb()` method to get a handle to the new web site just provisioned.

2. If the user has selected the checkbox to remove preexisting web parts, iterate through the collection of web parts on the new web site's home page, removing each.

Note As each web part is deleted from the web-part collection, the collection `Count` is decremented, so we must iterate backward through the collection to avoid a runtime error.

---

3. If the user has selected the checkbox to add a new Content Editor web part, call the `AddContentEditorWebPart()` custom method we created in Chapter 1 to add the Hello World web part.

4. If the user has selected the checkbox to add a new Page Viewer web part, call the `AddWebPart()` method we created in Chapter 1 to add a page view of the URL that the user entered into the `SelectWebParts.aspx` web form.

5. When all postprovisioning modifications are complete, redirect the user's browser to the home page (typically `Default.aspx`) of the new web site.

Page Layout: SelectWebParts.aspx

Figure 6-21 shows the page layout for `SelectWebParts.aspx`.

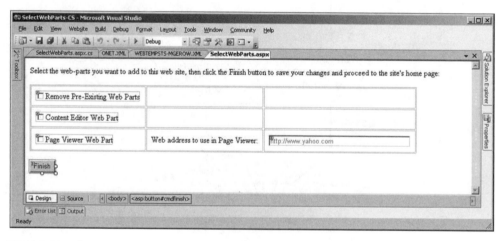

Figure 6-21. *SelectWebParts.aspx page layout*

The following fields are defined on the form:

`cbRemoveExisting`: A checkbox indicating whether existing web parts should be removed from the new web site's `Default.aspx` page·

`cbCEWP`: A checkbox indicating whether a new Hello World Content Editor web part should be added to `Default.aspx` cbPVWP: A checkbox indicating whether a new Page Viewer web part should be added to Default.aspx

txtPVUrl: The source URL to assign to the new Page Viewer web part if added

cmdFinish: A Submit button that calls the Finish_Click() form event handler

Recipe—VB (See Project SelectWebParts-VB, Class SelectWebParts.aspx.vb)

```vb
Imports System
Imports System.Data
Imports System.Configuration
Imports System.Web
Imports System.Web.Security
Imports System.Web.UI
Imports System.Web.UI.WebControls
Imports System.Web.UI.WebControls.WebParts
Imports System.Web.UI.HtmlControls
Imports Microsoft.SharePoint
Imports Microsoft.SharePoint.WebControls
Imports Microsoft.SharePoint.WebPartPages
Imports System.Xml
Partial Public Class _Default
    Inherits System.Web.UI.Page
    Private Shared Function AddContentEditorWebPart(ByVal strContent As String, _
        ByVal strTitle As String, _
        ByVal strSiteUrl As String, _
        ByVal strWebName As String, _
        ByVal strDocLibName As String, _
        ByVal strPage As String, _
        ByVal strZone As String, _
        ByVal numOrder As Integer, _
        ByVal pScope As System.Web.UI.WebControls.WebParts.PersonalizationScope) _
        As Microsoft.SharePoint.WebPartPages.ContentEditorWebPart
        Try
            ' Create an empty Content Editor web part.
            Dim cewp As New Microsoft.SharePoint.WebPartPages.ContentEditorWebPart()
            ' Create an xml element object and transfer the content
            'into the web part.
            Dim xmlDoc As New XmlDocument()
            Dim xmlElem As System.Xml.XmlElement = xmlDoc.CreateElement("xmlElem")
            xmlElem.InnerText = strContent
            cewp.Content = xmlElem
            ' Call generic method to add the web part
            cewp = AddWebPart(cewp, _
                strTitle, _
                strSiteUrl, _
                strWebName, _
```

```vb
                strDocLibName, _
                strPage, _
                strZone, _
                numOrder, _
                System.Web.UI.WebControls.WebParts.PersonalizationScope.[Shared])
            Return cewp
        Catch ex As Exception
            Throw New Exception("AddContentEditorWebPart() error: " + ex.Message)
        End Try
    End Function
    Private Shared Function AddWebPart(_
        ByVal oWebPart As System.Web.UI.WebControls.WebParts.WebPart, _
        ByVal strTitle As String, _
        ByVal strSiteUrl As String, _
        ByVal strWebName As String, _
        ByVal strDocLibName As String, _
        ByVal strPage As String, _
        ByVal strZone As String, _
        ByVal numOrder As Integer, _
        ByVal pScope As System.Web.UI.WebControls.WebParts.PersonalizationScope) _
        As System.Web.UI.WebControls.WebParts.WebPart
        Try
            ' Get handles to site, web, and page to which
            ' web part will be added.
            Dim site As New SPSite(strSiteUrl)
            Dim web As SPWeb = site.OpenWeb(strWebName)
            ' Enable update of page
            web.AllowUnsafeUpdates = True
            Dim webParts As SPLimitedWebPartManager
            If (strDocLibName <> "") Then
                webParts = web.GetLimitedWebPartManager(strDocLibName + "/" _
                    + strPage, pScope)
            Else
                webParts = web.GetLimitedWebPartManager(strPage, pScope)
            End If
            ' If web-part page is in a document library,
            ' disable checkout requirement
            ' for duration of update
            Dim list As SPList = Nothing
            Dim origForceCheckoutValue As Boolean = False
            If (strDocLibName <> "") Then
                list = web.Lists(strDocLibName)
                origForceCheckoutValue = list.ForceCheckout
                list.ForceCheckout = False
                list.Update()
            End If
```

```
                ' Add the web part
                oWebPart.Title = strTitle
                webParts.AddWebPart(oWebPart, strZone, numOrder)
                ' Save changes back to the SharePoint database
                webParts.SaveChanges(oWebPart)
                web.Update()
                ' If necessary, restore ForceCheckout setting
                If (strDocLibName <> "") Then
                    list.ForceCheckout = origForceCheckoutValue
                    list.Update()
                End If
                web.Dispose()
                site.Dispose()
                Return oWebPart
            Catch ex As Exception
                Throw New Exception(("AddWebPart() error: " + ex.Message))
            End Try
        End Function
    Protected Sub Finish_Click(ByVal sender As Object, ByVal e As EventArgs) _
            Handles cmdFinish.Click
            ' Step 1: Get handle to web site being created
            Dim web As SPWeb = SPControl.GetContextWeb(Context)
            web.AllowUnsafeUpdates = True
            ' Step 2: If requested, clear out any existing
            ' web parts
            If cbRemoveExisting.Checked Then
                Dim webparts As SPLimitedWebPartManager _
                    = web.GetLimitedWebPartManager( _
                        "default.aspx", PersonalizationScope.[Shared])
                For i As Integer = webparts.WebParts.Count - 1 To -1 + 1 Step -1
                    webparts.DeleteWebPart(webparts.WebParts(i))
                Next
            End If
            ' Step 3: If requested, add an instance of a SharePoint
            ' "ContentEditorWebPart", which is a descendent of
            ' the generic .NET 2.0 WebPart class
            If cbCEWP.Checked Then
                Dim oCEwp As New _
                    Microsoft.SharePoint.WebPartPages.ContentEditorWebPart()
                oCEwp = AddContentEditorWebPart( _
"Hello World!", _
"Hello World web part", _
web.Site.Url.ToString(), web.ServerRelativeUrl.Substring(1), "", _
"Default.aspx", _
                    "Right", 0, _
```

```vb
System.Web.UI.WebControls.WebParts.PersonalizationScope.[Shared])
        End If
        ' Step 4: If requested, add a PageViewer web part
        If cbPVWP.Checked Then
            Dim oPVwp As New Microsoft.SharePoint.WebPartPages.PageViewerWebPart()
            oPVwp.SourceType = PathPattern.URL
            oPVwp.ContentLink = txtPVUrl.Text
            oPVwp.Height = "1000px"
            oPVwp = AddWebPart(oPVwp, _
"And here's my page viewer web part!", _
web.Site.Url.ToString(), _
web.ServerRelativeUrl.Substring(1), "", _
"Default.aspx", _
                    "Left", 0, _
System.Web.UI.WebControls.WebParts.PersonalizationScope.[Shared])
        End If
        ' Step 5: Now take the user to the home page of the new
        ' web site
        Response.Redirect(web.ServerRelativeUrl)
    End Sub
    ' Determine whether Url text box should
    ' be enabled based on whether
    ' option to add a Page Viewer web part
    ' is checked
    Protected Sub cbPVWP_CheckedChanged( _
            ByVal sender As Object, ByVal e As EventArgs) _
            Handles cbPVWP.CheckedChanged
        txtPVUrl.Enabled = cbPVWP.Checked
    End Sub
End Class
```

Recipe—C# (See Project SelectWebParts-CS, Class SelectWebParts.aspx.cs)

```csharp
using System;
using System.Data;
using System.Configuration;
using System.Web;
using System.Web.Security;
using System.Web.UI;
using System.Web.UI.WebControls;
using System.Web.UI.WebControls.WebParts;
using System.Web.UI.HtmlControls;
using Microsoft.SharePoint;
using Microsoft.SharePoint.WebControls;
using Microsoft.SharePoint.WebPartPages;
using System.Xml;
```

```csharp
public partial class _Default : System.Web.UI.Page
{
    private static Microsoft.SharePoint.WebPartPages.ContentEditorWebPart
    AddContentEditorWebPart(
        string strContent,
        string strTitle,
        string strSiteUrl,
        string strWebName,
        string strDocLibName,
        string strPage,
        string strZone,
        int numOrder,
        System.Web.UI.WebControls.WebParts.PersonalizationScope pScope)
    {
        try
        {
            // Create an empty content editor web part.
            Microsoft.SharePoint.WebPartPages.ContentEditorWebPart cewp
                = new Microsoft.SharePoint.WebPartPages.ContentEditorWebPart();
            // Create an xml element object and transfer the content
            //into the web part.
            XmlDocument xmlDoc = new XmlDocument();
            System.Xml.XmlElement xmlElem = xmlDoc.CreateElement("xmlElem");
            xmlElem.InnerText = strContent;
            cewp.Content = xmlElem;
            // Call generic method to add the web part
            cewp = (Microsoft.SharePoint.WebPartPages.ContentEditorWebPart)
            AddWebPart(
                cewp,
                strTitle,
                strSiteUrl,
                strWebName,
                strDocLibName,
                strPage,
                strZone,
                numOrder,
                System.Web.UI.WebControls.WebParts.PersonalizationScope.Shared);
            return cewp;
        }
        catch (Exception ex)
        {
            throw new Exception(
                "AddContentEditorWebPart() error: " + ex.Message);
        }
    }
```

```
private static System.Web.UI.WebControls.WebParts.WebPart
AddWebPart(
System.Web.UI.WebControls.WebParts.WebPart oWebPart,
string strTitle,
string strSiteUrl,
string strWebName,
string strDocLibName,
string strPage,
string strZone,
int numOrder, System.Web.UI.WebControls.WebParts.PersonalizationScope pScope)
    {
        try
        {
            // Get handles to site, web, and page to which
            // web part will be added.
            SPSite site = new SPSite(strSiteUrl);
            SPWeb web = site.OpenWeb(strWebName);
            // Enable update of page
            web.AllowUnsafeUpdates = true;
            SPLimitedWebPartManager webParts;
            if ((strDocLibName != ""))
            {
                webParts = web.GetLimitedWebPartManager(
                    strDocLibName + "/" + strPage, pScope);
            }
            else
            {
                webParts = web.GetLimitedWebPartManager(strPage, pScope);
            }
            // If web-part page is in a document library,
            // disable checkout requirement
            // for duration of update
            SPList list = null;
            bool origForceCheckoutValue = false;
            if ((strDocLibName != ""))
            {
                list = web.Lists[strDocLibName];
                origForceCheckoutValue = list.ForceCheckout;
                list.ForceCheckout = false;
                list.Update();
            }
            // Add the web part
            oWebPart.Title = strTitle;
            webParts.AddWebPart(oWebPart, strZone, numOrder);
            // Save changes back to the SharePoint database
            webParts.SaveChanges(oWebPart);
            web.Update();
```

```
            // If necessary, restore ForceCheckout setting
            if ((strDocLibName != ""))
            {
                list.ForceCheckout = origForceCheckoutValue;
                list.Update();
            }
            web.Dispose();
            site.Dispose();
            return oWebPart;
        }
        catch (Exception ex)
        {
            throw new Exception((("AddWebPart() error: " + ex.Message)));
        }
    }
protected void Finish_Click(object sender, EventArgs e)
{
    // Step 1: Get handle to web site being created
    SPWeb web = SPControl.GetContextWeb(Context);
    web.AllowUnsafeUpdates = true;
    // Step 2: If requested, clear out any existing
    // web parts
    if (cbRemoveExisting.Checked)
    {
        SPLimitedWebPartManager webparts
            = web.GetLimitedWebPartManager("default.aspx", _
                PersonalizationScope.Shared);
        for (int i = webparts.WebParts.Count - 1; i > -1; i--)
        {
            webparts.DeleteWebPart(webparts.WebParts[i]);
        }
    }
    // Step 3: If requested, add an instance of a SharePoint
    // "ContentEditorWebPart", which is a descendent of
    // the generic .NET 2.0 WebPart class
    if (cbCEWP.Checked)
    {
        Microsoft.SharePoint.WebPartPages.ContentEditorWebPart oCEwp
            = new Microsoft.SharePoint.WebPartPages.ContentEditorWebPart();
        oCEwp = AddContentEditorWebPart(
            "Hello World!",
            "Hello World web part",
            web.Site.Url.ToString(),
            web.ServerRelativeUrl.Substring(1),
            "",
            "Default.aspx",
            "Right",
```

```
                0,
                System.Web.UI.WebControls.WebParts.PersonalizationScope.Shared);
        }
        // Step 4: If requested, add a PageViewer web part
        if (cbPVWP.Checked)
        {
            Microsoft.SharePoint.WebPartPages.PageViewerWebPart oPVwp
                = new Microsoft.SharePoint.WebPartPages.PageViewerWebPart();
            oPVwp.SourceType = PathPattern.URL;
            oPVwp.ContentLink = txtPVUrl.Text;
            oPVwp.Height = "1000px";
            oPVwp = (Microsoft.SharePoint.WebPartPages.PageViewerWebPart)
            AddWebPart(
                    oPVwp,
                    "And here's my page viewer web part!",
                    web.Site.Url.ToString(),
                    web.ServerRelativeUrl.Substring(1),
                    "",
                    "Default.aspx",
                    "Left",
                    0,
                    System.Web.UI.WebControls.WebParts.PersonalizationScope.Shared);
        }
        // Step 5: Now take the user to the home page of the new
        // web site
        Response.Redirect(web.ServerRelativeUrl);
    }
    // Determine whether Url text box should
    // be enabled based on whether
    // option to add a Page Viewer web part
    // is checked
    protected void cbPVWP_CheckedChanged(object sender, EventArgs e)
    {
        txtPVUrl.Enabled = cbPVWP.Checked;
    }
}
```

To Run

1. To test our new recipe, select the Site Actions ➤ Create option from any page on an existing SharePoint web site, and then click Sites and Workspaces.

2. Enter a title and URL for the new site.

3. Click the Chapter 6 tab in the template section and highlight Execute URL Sample.

4. Click the Create button. After the new site has been created and the site-definition template has been applied, your `SelectWebParts.aspx` page will be displayed.

5. Select all checkboxes and enter `http://www.apress.com/book/view/1430209615` in the Page Viewer URL field. The form should appear as shown in Figure 6-22.

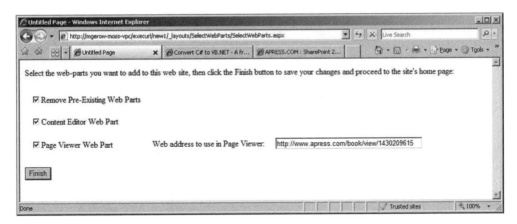

Figure 6-22. *Completed SelectWebParts.aspx form*

6. Click the Finish button. The resulting home page of the new SharePoint web site should appear as shown in Figure 6-23.

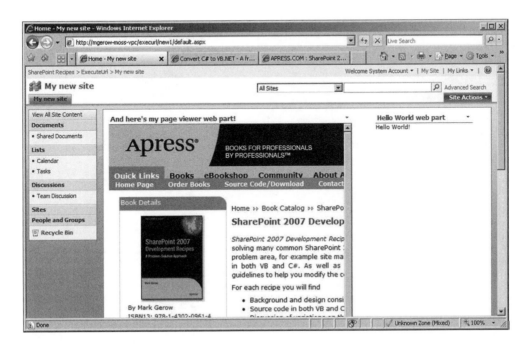

Figure 6-23. *Home page of provisioned SharePoint web site*

Variations

There are so many possible variations when it comes to adding custom postprovisioning code. Here are a few possibilities:

- Log the creation of the new site, along with the requestor, to a SQL database for reporting.

- Send an email to the SharePoint administrator notifying them that a new site was created.

- Provide multiple groups of web parts that will be added together depending on the purpose of the site.

- Give the requestor the option of viewing a tutorial on the purpose and use of the selected template.

Related Recipes

- Recipe 1-6 in Chapter 1
- Recipe 6-3

■ ■ ■

CHAPTER 7

Modifying Pages with JavaScript

One of the surprising techniques available to SharePoint developers is the use of JavaScript to perform *postprocessing* on pages rendered by SharePoint. This gives you a great deal of flexibility, because you can make any modifications that can be programmed by using JavaScript and the browser's Document Object Model (DOM). This approach has several advantages, including the fact that it doesn't require any .NET programming or modification to underlying site-definition templates, does not require the individual making the modifications to be familiar with .NET programming—only JavaScript, and allows for rapid prototyping.

In this chapter, you'll explore two recipes that provide a good example of what's possible: hiding the QuickLaunch menu on a page, and opening links in a new browser window. Both of these are common requests that end users have, and would require modifying site-definition templates or out-of-the-box libraries to accomplish when using traditional SharePoint customization techniques. However, through the use of JavaScript entered into Content Editor web parts, you can quickly make these changes on a page-by-page basis.

Of course, these two recipes barely scratch the surface of what's possible. I've used similar techniques to associate bar graphs with list items based on the value of a field in the item, to cause links to redirect to a page that records link clicks in a SQL database, and many more variations. What you can do with JavaScript in Content Editor web parts is essentially limited only by your knowledge of how SharePoint renders the page in the first place, and of JavaScript in general.

Let's see how this works in practice.

Recipe 7-1. Hiding the QuickLaunch Menu

The QuickLaunch menu is handy most of the time, but it also takes up a great deal of screen real estate, particularly for users who prefer to set their monitors to a low resolution. Wouldn't it be great if you could give your end users the best of both worlds: having the convenience of being able to access the links on the QuickLaunch menu when needed, but being able to hide it when not in use?

In this recipe, you'll see how a little bit of JavaScript can accomplish this, without the need to alter any of the out-of-the-box SharePoint site definitions or applications.

Recipe Type: JavaScript

Ingredients

All that you need to cook up this application is a little bit of JavaScript and some understanding of how Cascading Style Sheets (CSS) works. You'll also need a Content Editor web part to contain your JavaScript.

Special Considerations

- This recipe relies on the browser's implementation of JavaScript. It has been tested with Internet Explorer (IE) 6.0 and above, and Firefox. If you need to support other browsers, be sure to test it thoroughly.

- Even if the browser used is capable of supporting JavaScript, the individual user (or firm policy) may have disabled that feature, in which case the following recipe may not work as expected. On the other hand, so much of SharePoint 2007 relies on JavaScript that it would in any case be almost unusable without JavaScript enabled.

- JavaScript recipes apply only to the page on which they're placed, not throughout a web site, site collection, or farm, as is the case with many of the other recipes described in this book.

■Note Although it was common practice several years ago to disable JavaScript support in browsers for security reasons, this practice is much less common today because of the cost in terms of reduced functionality and because of the availability of less-intrusive ways to ensure security and prevent malicious browser-based viruses.

Preparation

1. In a browser, open a SharePoint web site on which you have at least Design permissions.

2. Add a Content Editor web part to the page.

3. From the Content Editor web part's menu, choose the Modify option.

4. Click the Source Editor button.

5. Enter the JavaScript shown in the following recipe section.

Process Flow

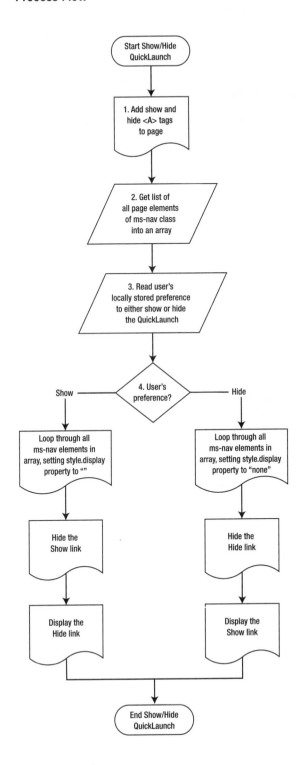

1. Write two <A> elements to the page; one to display the Show link, the other to display the Hide link—only one of the two links will be visible on the page at any one time.

2. Call the getElementsByClass() helper function to fill an array with references to all page elements that are assigned to the ms-nav class.

3. Read the isQuickLaunchHidden browser cookie from the user's local cookie cache to determine the start state for the QuickLaunch.

4. If the user's preference is Show, loop through all elements in the array returned by the getElementsByClass("ms-nav") function call, setting each element's style.display property to an empty string—thus showing that page element. If the preference is Hide, set each element's style.display property to none.

Recipe—JavaScript

```
<script>
// Step 1: Add <a> tags to page to hold Hide/Show options
document.write (' ➡
    <a id="HideOption" href="javascript:Hide()" style="display:none"> ➡
        Hide Quicklaunch menu ➡
    </a>');
document.write (' ➡
    <a id="ShowOption" href="javascript:Show()"> ➡
        Show Quicklaunch menu ➡
    </a>');
// Step 2: Declare an array containing a list
// of all page elements assigned the "ms-nav"
// class
var _NavElements = getElementsByClass("ms-nav");
// Step 3: Read user's current Show/Hide preference
// from local cookie
var isQuickLaunchHidden = readCookie('isQuickLaunchHidden');
// Step 4: Show or hide the QuickLaunch
// depending on user preference
if (isQuickLaunchHidden == 'true')
{
  Hide();
} else {
  Show();
}
// Helper function to save a cookie representing user-specific
// choice to show or hide the QuickLaunch menu
function createCookie(name,value,days) {
    if (days) {
        var date = new Date();
        date.setTime(date.getTime()+(days*24*60*60*1000));
        var expires = "; expires="+date.toGMTString();
    }
```

```
        else var expires = "";
        document.cookie = name+"="+value+expires+"; path=/";
}
// Helper function to read the cookie to determine whether
// the QuickLaunch menu should be displayed
function readCookie(name) {
    var nameEQ = name + "=";
    var ca = document.cookie.split(';');
    for(var i=0;i < ca.length;i++) {
        var c = ca[i];
        while (c.charAt(0)==' ') c = c.substring(1,c.length);
        if (c.indexOf(nameEQ) == 0) return c.substring(nameEQ.length,c.length);
    }
    return null;
}
// Helper function to delete a specified cookie
function eraseCookie(name) {
    createCookie(name,"",-1);
}
// Helper function to return an array of web-
// page elements of the specified class.  This
// function is needed because SharePoint assigns
// the QuickLaunch a class, but not an ID.
// Otherwise, we could use the native
// GetElementById() JavaScript function.
function getElementsByClass(searchClass,node,tag) {
    var classElements = new Array();
    if ( node == null )
        node = document;
    if ( tag == null )
        tag = '*';
    var els = node.getElementsByTagName(tag);
    var elsLen = els.length;
    var pattern = new RegExp('(^|\\s)'+searchClass+'(\\s|$)');
    for (var i = 0, j = 0; i < elsLen; i++) {
        if ( pattern.test(els[i].className) ) {
            classElements[j] = els[i];
            j++;
        }
    }
    return classElements;
}
```

```
// Helper function to hide the QuickLaunch
function Hide()
{
  for (var i=0; i<_NavElements.length; i++)
  {
      _NavElements[i].style.display = "none";
  }
  document.getElementById("HideOption").style.display = "none";
  document.getElementById("ShowOption").style.display = "";
  createCookie ('isQuickLaunchHidden','true',365);
}
// Helper function to display the QuickLaunch
function Show()
{
  for (var i = 0; i<_NavElements.length; i++)
  {
      _NavElements[i].style.display = "";
  }
  document.getElementById("HideOption").style.display = "";
  document.getElementById("ShowOption").style.display = "none";
  createCookie ('isQuickLaunchHidden','false',365);
}
</script>
```

To Run

Deploying the Show/Hide recipe is simply a matter of entering the JavaScript into a Content Editor web part on a web-part page. Figure 7-1 shows the Text Entry dialog box of a Content Editor web part after the JavaScript has been entered. After you click the Save button, the Hide QuickLaunch Menu option will be displayed on the page.

Figure 7-2 shows the content editor containing the Show/Hide JavaScript on the page.

■**Note** You will typically want to set the `Chrome Type` property of the Content Editor web part containing the Show/Hide JavaScript to `none` so that only the `<A>` elements are displayed.

```
Text Entry -- Webpage Dialog                                              [X]

<script>

// Step 1: Add <a> tags to page to hold hide/show options
document.write ('<a id="HideOption" href="javascript:Hide()" style="display:none"> Hide
Quicklaunch menu</a>');
document.write ('<a id="ShowOption" href="javascript:Show()">Show Quicklaunch menu</a>');

// Step 2: Declare an array containing a list
// of all page elements assigned the "ms-nav"
// class
var _NavElements = getElementsByClass("ms-nav");

// Step 3: Read user's current show/hide preference
// from local cookie
var isQuickLaunchHidden = readCookie('isQuickLa[Builder Text Area]);

// Step 4: Show or hide the quicklaunch
// depending on user preference
if (isQuickLaunchHidden == 'true')
{
  Hide();
} else {
  Show();
}

// Helper function to save a cookie representing user-specific
// choice to show or hide the quicklaunch menu
```

```
                                          [ Save ]    [ Cancel ]
```

Figure 7-1. *JavaScript entered into the text box of the Content Editor web part*

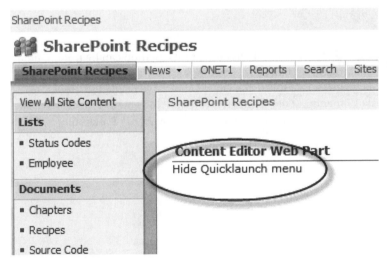

Figure 7-2. *Hide option displayed on page*

Figure 7-3 shows the page after the Hide option has been clicked.

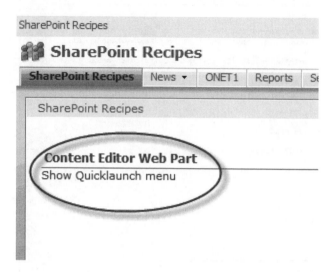

Figure 7-3. *Effect of clicking the Hide option*

Because the user's preference is stored in a local cookie, that preference is "remembered" from session to session, and from page to page. Because of this, if the Show/Hide web part is placed on multiple web-part pages, the user's preference will be used for all instances.

Variations

- In this example, we hid the QuickLaunch menu, but this method can be used to hide any element or elements on a page that can be identified. Because Microsoft's standard templates do not assign an element ID to the QuickLaunch, we needed to use the getElementsByClass() function. If the element(s) you want to show or hide do have an assigned ID, you can use the standard getElementById() JavaScript function.

Related Recipes

- Recipe 7-2

Recipe 7-2. Opening List Items in a New Window

SharePoint opens list items, except for document library items that have an associated application, in the same browser window. There are times when you, or your end users, would prefer these items to be opened in a new window so that that original list display is not lost. This recipe shows you how, with just a bit of JavaScript, to add that feature to any page that displays list items.

To accomplish this bit of magic, we'll use JavaScript to find all the links (that is, <A> elements) on the web page, inspecting the links' href property to decide whether it's associated with a list item, and if so modify the target property to force the target link to open in a new browser window.

One other change we'll need to make to the link is to disable any onclick event handler that may be associated with it, because that handler will fire before the href + target combination, and thus will prevent the target page from opening in a new window despite our changes.

Recipe Type: JavaScript

Ingredients

As with the previous JavaScript recipe, all you really need is a Content Editor web part in which to place the JavaScript. In this recipe, we'll take a slightly different approach, in that the bulk of the JavaScript will be stored outside the web part, and will be included by using a <SCRIPT SRC =...> HTML element. The advantage of this approach is that you don't need to copy the code to each page into which you want to insert it. This makes your code much more maintainable and enables you to scale its use to a large number of pages.

Special Considerations

- This recipe relies on the browser's implementation of JavaScript. It has been tested with IE 6.0 and above, and Firefox. If you need to support other browsers, be sure to test it thoroughly.

- Even if the browser used is capable of supporting JavaScript, the individual user (or firm policy) may have disabled that feature, in which case the following recipe may not work as expected. As noted previously, however, without JavaScript support, SharePoint 2007 becomes unusable.

- JavaScript recipes apply only to the page on which they're placed, not throughout a web site, site collection, or farm, as is the case with many of the other recipes described in this book.

■**Note** Although it was common practice several years ago to disable JavaScript support in browsers for security reasons, this practice is much less common today because of the cost in terms of reduced functionality and because of the availability of less-intrusive ways to ensure security and prevent malicious browser-based viruses.

Preparation

1. In a browser, open a SharePoint web site on which you have at least Design permissions.

2. Add a Content Editor web part to the page.

3. From the Content Editor web part's menu, choose the Modify option.

4. Click the Source Editor button.

5. Enter the JavaScript shown in the following "Recipe—Content Editor" section.

6. Enter the JavaScript shown in the following "Recipe—Library" section and save to a file named something like `OpenInNewWindow.js` to a web-accessible location (for example, a document library).

■**Note** The following recipe source code assumes a specific location for the `OpenInNewWindow.js` file. Please be sure that the URL you specify in your code matches the location you choose for the `.js` file.

Process Flow

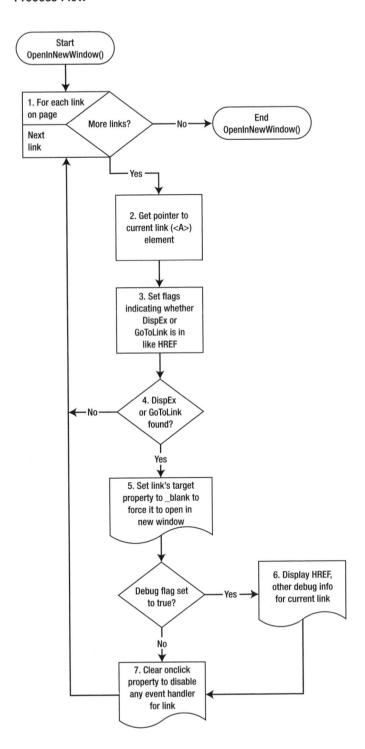

1. Loop through the collection of all `<A>` elements on the current page.

2. Assign a pointer to the current `<A>` element in the collection to a variable for easier reference.

3. Determine whether the `href` property of the current `<A>` element includes a reference to one of the target pages we're interested in.

4. If so ...

5. Set the `target` property to `_blank` to force the page to open in a new browser window.

6. If the calling JavaScript has passed in a value of `true` for the debug flag, write the debug info to the page.

7. Clear out the `onclick` event handler reference, because any existing SharePoint list item JavaScript `onclick` handler will supersede our added `href`/`target` combination, and prevent our change from having any effect.

■Note Clearing out the default JavaScript `onclick` event handler for the page will disable some of the client application integration features that would otherwise be available in document libraries, especially with Office 2007 documents.

Recipe—Content Editor

```
<!-- Include JavaScript source library -->
<script src="http://mgerow-moss-vpc/Source%20Code/OpenInNewWindow.js"></script>
<!-- Call the function to modify <A> page elements -->
<script>
    setOpenInNewWindow(true);
</script>
```

Recipe—Library

```
function setOpenInNewWindow(boolDebug) {
    // handle to current <A> element being processed
    var linkElement;
    // flag, test var for "GoToLink" call
    // used on simple links
    var boolTrapGoToLink = true;
    var boolIsGoToLink = false;
    // flag, test var for "DispEx" call
    // used on links that have associated
    // context menus
    var boolTrapDispEx = true;
    var boolIsDispEx = false;
```

```javascript
// Step 1: Loop through all links on page
for (var i=0; i<document.links.length; i++)
{
    // Step 2: Get handle to current link
    linkElement = document.links[i];
    try {
        // Step 3: Determine whether link has either of the
        // href values sought
        boolIsGoToLink =
                    (linkElement.onclick.toString().indexOf("GoToLink") != -1) &&
                        boolTrapGoToLink;
        boolIsDispEx =
                (linkElement.onclick.toString().indexOf("DispEx") != -1) &&
                    boolTrapDispEx;

        // Step 4: If link requires fix-up
        if ( boolIsGoToLink || boolIsDispEx ) {
            // Step 5: Assign link's target to new window
            linkElement.target = "_blank";
            // Step 6: If debug flag on, print out key information
            // for affected links
            if (boolDebug) {
                document.write("<br/>" +
                    linkElement.Id + ": " +
                    linkElement.innerText + ": " +
                    linkElement.href + ": " +
                    linkElement.target);
                document.write("<br/>     " +
                    linkElement.onclick);
                document.write("<br/>     GoToLink at: " +
                    linkElement.onclick.toString().indexOf("GoToLink"));
                document.write("<br/>     DispEx at: " +
                    linkElement.onclick.toString().indexOf("DispEx"));
            }
            // Step 7: Clear onclick handler so .target
            // parameter will be used to open
            // link
            linkElement.onclick = "";
        }
    } catch (e) {
        //document.write(e);
    }
}
}
```

To Run

After you've uploaded the JavaScript listed in the preceding "Recipe—Library" section, add a new content editor to the bottom of a list page, as shown in Figure 7-4.

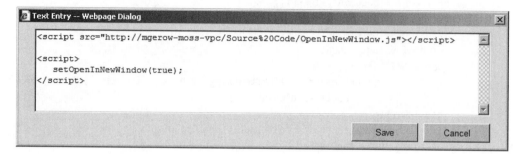

Figure 7-4. *Call to setOpenInNewWindow() JavaScript function in Content Editor web part*

Note that setOpenInNewWindow() is called with a debug flag of true. In general use, you would pass a value of false to avoid displaying the debug information to the page. Save the content and exit page edit mode. Your page should look similar to that shown in Figure 7-5.

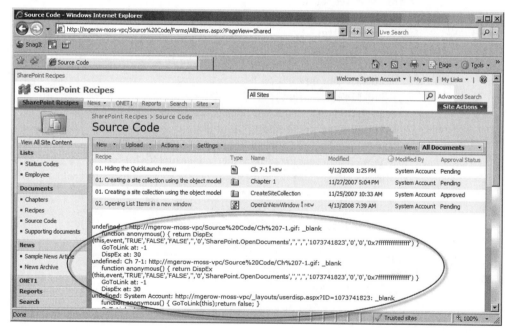

Figure 7-5. *Installed web part showing debug information produced by function call*

Note the debug information shown at the bottom of the page. Finally, you can test your web part by clicking the Name link of a document that would usually open in the same browser window. In my example, I clicked the Ch 7-1 image file. The result is shown in Figure 7-6.

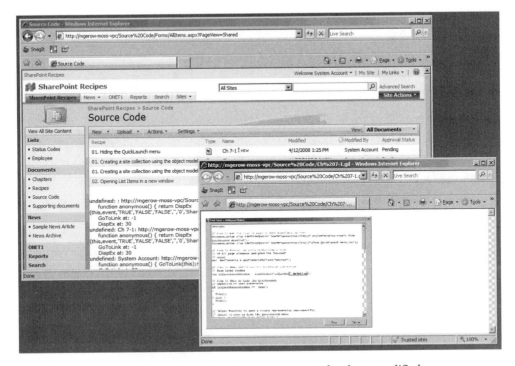

Figure 7-6. *Result of clicking the link after its target property has been modified*

Variations

- This recipe is specifically designed to look for href values containing DispEx calls used for document context menus, or GoToLink calls used for nondocument list items. These two calls are not exhaustive of all the targets SharePoint uses for links, so you will want to experiment to find the right set for your purposes. Of course, you may have your own specific links you'd like to fix by using this technique.

- Use JavaScript in a Content Editor web part placed on a web-part page (such as the home page of a site) to open Links list items in a new window.

- Related to the previous variation, you could modify the setOpenInNewWindow() method to take an additional string parameter containing the string sequence to search for. That way, you don't need to hard-code the href values within the function itself.

Related Recipes

- Recipe 7-1

CHAPTER 8

■ ■ ■

Advanced Dishes

There just never seems to be an end to the ways in which you can customize SharePoint 2007! In this chapter, you'll explore a few more. Specifically, you'll look at how to index a SQL Server database by using the Business Data Catalog (BDC) in MOSS, how to create a custom search page—also in MOSS, and last but not least, how to add your own commands to STSADM (sure to win your SharePoint administrator's heart).

As with all of our recipes, you're sure to find plenty here to spark your imagination and set you on the path to creating your own unique variations. Let's dig in.

Recipe 8-1. Customizing the STSADM Command

You're probably familiar with the STSADM utility that can be used to perform a variety of Share-Point administrative functions from the Windows console. But you may not be aware that you can add your own commands to this utility with just a little bit of coding.

Given that you can perform almost every function that the STSADM utility supports by using the SharePoint Central Administration Website, or through the standard Site Settings pages, why would you want to use STSADM?

There are essentially two reasons. First, this utility may be readily mastered by a system administrator who has a limited understanding of SharePoint. So, if you want to provide your system administrator with quick and simple access to some basic custom utilities, customizing STSADM might be just what you need. And because STSADM provides a consistent interface across all commands, your customizations will be easier for the user to learn and remember.

Second, STSADM commands can be easily scheduled by using the Windows Task Scheduler. Of course, you could simply write a console application, but customizing the STSADM command enforces a consistency and simplicity that promotes not only ease of use but improved maintainability.

In this recipe, you'll add two custom commands to the STSADM utility: one to add a new document library to a site, and the other to add an announcement to the top of a web site's default page. Through these two examples, you'll see how easy it is to extend the STSADM command.

Recipe Type: STSADM Extension

Ingredients

Assembly References

- `System.Web` .NET assembly

- Windows SharePoint Services NET assembly

Special Considerations

- The required `ISPStsadmCommand` interface throws an error when used in VB.NET because it does not recognize the signatures of the required functions `GetHelpMessage()` and `Run()`, so only the C# example is shown here.

Preparation

1. Create an XML document called `stsadmcommands.recipes.xml` in the `C:\Program Files\ Common Files\Microsoft Shared\Web Server Extensions\12\Config` folder of your SharePoint server. See the following "Recipe—XML" section for the contents of this file.

■**Note** The STSADM customization XML file name must take the form `stsadmcommands.<some text>.xml`, where you supply the value for `<some text>`. Microsoft recommends use of your organization's name and some indication of the purpose of the extensions, such as `stsadmcommands.acme.corp.mycommands.xml`, but actual naming is up to you.

---

2. Create a new C# class library.

3. Add references to the Windows SharePoint Services, `System.Web` and `System.Xml` .NET assemblies.

4. Sign the assembly with a strong-name key file.

5. Add the code shown in the following "Recipe—C#" section.

6. Compile the class.

7. Deploy the compiled `.dll` to the GAC.

Process Flow

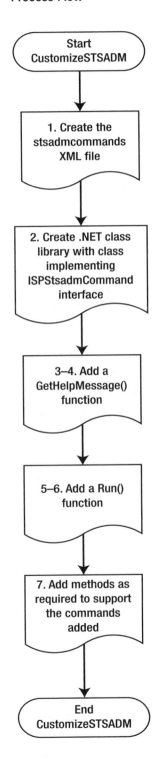

1. Create the `stsadmcommands.recipe.xml` file in the `C:\Program Files\Common Files\ Microsoft Shared\Web Server Extensions\12\Config` folder. This file will be read by the STSADM command at runtime to find our assembly containing the new commands.

2. Create a new C# .NET class library, referencing the Windows SharePoint Services, `System.Web`, and `System.Xml` .NET assemblies. Add `using` statements as shown in the following source code and implement the `ISPStsadmCommand` interface.

3. Add a function called `GetHelpMessage()` per the `ISPStsadmCommand` interface.

4. Add help text for each of the commands referenced in the `stsadmcommands.recipe.xml` file.

5. Add a function called `Run()` per the `ISPStsadmCommand` interface.

6. Add calls to supporting methods for each of the commands referenced in the `stsadmcommands.recipe.xml` file.

7. Write the support methods referenced in step 6.

Recipe—XML (See Project CustomizeSTSADM-CS, File stsadmcommands.recipes.xml)

The `stsadmcommands.recipe.xml` file tells the STSADM command the names of the custom commands we're adding, where to find the assemblies containing the executable code, and the names of the classes containing that executable code.

■**Note** The `class` attribute of the `<command>` element must be formatted correctly, or the STSADM command will throw an error when you try to execute your custom commands. The format is `class="<namespace>. <classname>, <assembly file name without .dll extension>, Version=<version - which will be 1.0.0.0 unless you change it>, Culture=neutral, PublicKeyToken=<strong key name assigned to the assembly>"`.

```xml
<?xml version="1.0" encoding="utf-8"?>
<!-- Step 1: Add references to the commands to be added -->
<commands>
    <command name="adddoclibtosite" class="CustomizeStsAdm.MyCustomizations,
CustomizeSTSADM, Version=1.0.0.0, Culture=neutral,
PublicKeyToken=61edc6796f256444" />
    <command name="addnoticetosite"
        class="CustomizeStsAdm.MyCustomizations, CustomizeSTSADM,
        Version=1.0.0.0, Culture=neutral,
        PublicKeyToken=61edc6796f256444" />
</commands>
```

■**Caution** In the previous XML source, all text within the `<command>` elements should be entered on a single line.

Recipe—C# (See Project CustomizeSTSADM-CS, CustomizeSTSADM-CS.cs)

```csharp
using System;
using System.Collections.Generic;
using System.Collections.Specialized;
using System.Text;
using Microsoft.SharePoint;
using Microsoft.SharePoint.StsAdmin;
using System.Xml;
using Microsoft.SharePoint.WebPartPages;
using System.Web;
using System.Web.UI.WebControls;
namespace CustomizeStsAdm
{
    // Step 2: Class must implement the ISPStsadmCommand
    // interface to allow it to be registered with
    // STSADM command
    public class MyCustomizations : ISPStsadmCommand
    {
        // Step 3: Implement the GetHelpMessage method
        //  to provide a response when user runs the
        //  new command with the -help flag
        public string GetHelpMessage(string command)
        {
            command = command.ToLower();
            // Step 4: Provide as many cases as there are
            // commands supported by this class
            switch (command)
            {
                case "adddoclibtosite":
                    return "\n-site <full url to a site collection "
                        + "in SharePoint>"
                        + "\n-web <web name to add doclib to"
                        + "\n-libname <name to give new doclib>"
                        + "\n-description <description for new "
                        + "doclib>";
                case "addnoticetosite":
                    return "\n-site <full url to a site collection "
                        + "in SharePoint>"
                        + "\n-web <web name to add doclib to"
                        + "\n-text <text of notice to add>";
                default:
                    throw new InvalidOperationException();
            }
        }
    }
```

```
// Step 5: Implement the Run method to
//  actually execute the commands defined in this
//  class
public int Run(string command,
    StringDictionary keyValues, out string output)
{
    command = command.ToLower();
    // Step 6: Provide as many cases as there are
    //  commands supported by this class
    switch (command)
    {
        case "adddoclibtosite":
            return addDoclibToSite(keyValues, out output);
        case "addnoticetosite":
            return addNoticeToSite(keyValues, out output);
        default:
            throw new InvalidOperationException();
    }
}
// Step 7: Add the methods and code that will perform
//  the operations for each command supported
private int addNoticeToSite(StringDictionary keyValues,
    out string output)
{
    // Get handle to target web site
    SPSite site = new SPSite(keyValues["site"]);
    // Get handle to web
    SPWeb web;
    if (keyValues["web"] == null)
    {
        web = site.RootWeb;
    }
    else
    {
        web = site.OpenWeb(keyValues["web"]);
    }
    // Get a handle to the default page of the target web
    // NOTE: we're assuming page called "default.aspx" exists
    web.AllowUnsafeUpdates = true;
    SPLimitedWebPartManager webParts =
        web.GetLimitedWebPartManager("default.aspx",
        System.Web.UI.WebControls.WebParts. ➡
            PersonalizationScope.Shared);
    // Create XML element to hold notice text
    ContentEditorWebPart cewp = new ContentEditorWebPart();
    XmlDocument xmlDoc = new XmlDocument();
    XmlElement xmlElem = xmlDoc.CreateElement("xmlElem");
```

```
        xmlElem.InnerXml =
            "<![CDATA["
            + "<div align='center' "
            + "    style='font-family: Arial; font-size: medium;"
            + "    font-weight: bold; "
            + "    background-color: red; color: white; border:"
            + "    medium solid black; "
            + "    width: 50%; padding: 10px; margin: 10px;'>"
            + keyValues["text"].ToString()
            + "</div>"
            + "]]>";
        // Add the CEWP to the page
        // NOTE: we're assuming a zone called "Left" exists
        cewp.ChromeType =
            System.Web.UI.WebControls.WebParts.PartChromeType.None;
        cewp.Content = xmlElem;
        webParts.AddWebPart(cewp, "Left", 0);
        webParts.SaveChanges(cewp);
        web.Update();
        web.Dispose();
        site.Dispose();
        output = "";
        return 0;
    }
    private int addDoclibToSite(StringDictionary keyValues, out string output)
    {
        // Get handle to target web site
        SPSite site = new SPSite(keyValues["site"]);
        // Get handle to web
        SPWeb web;
        if (keyValues["web"] == null)
        {
            web = site.RootWeb;
        }
        else
        {
            web = site.OpenWeb(keyValues["web"]);
        }
        // Add a list to target site
        web.AllowUnsafeUpdates = true;
        web.Lists.Add(keyValues["listname"],
            keyValues["description"],
            SPListTemplateType.DocumentLibrary);
        SPList list = web.Lists[keyValues["libname"]];
        list.OnQuickLaunch = true;
        list.Update();
        web.Update();
```

```
                web.Dispose();
                site.Dispose();
                output = "";
                return 0;
            }
        }
    }
}
```

To Run

After the `stsadmcommands.recipe.xml` file has been saved to `C:\Program Files\Common Files\ Microsoft Shared\Web Server Extensions\12\Config`, and the class library has been compiled and deployed to the GAC, you're ready to test this recipe. To test the `addnoticetosite` command, do the following:

1. Open a console window.

2. Navigate to the `C:\Program Files\Common Files\Microsoft Shared\Web Server Extensions\12\bin` folder.

3. Type `STSADM` to display a list of all commands. Figure 8-1 shows the `STSADM` command output with the two new commands listed.

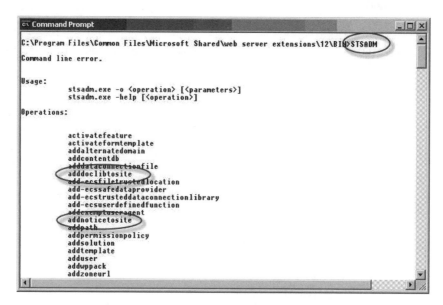

Figure 8-1. *STSADM command output listing new commands*

4. Enter the STSADM addnoticetosite command with the following parameter values, as shown in Figure 8-2:

- site = http://localhost

- web = stsadm

- text = "Now is the time for all good developers to come to the aid of their SharePoint administrator!"

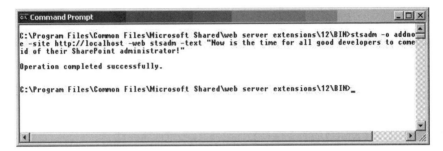

Figure 8-2. *Running the STSADM addnoticetosite command*

Figure 8-3 shows the result of running the addnoticetosite command.

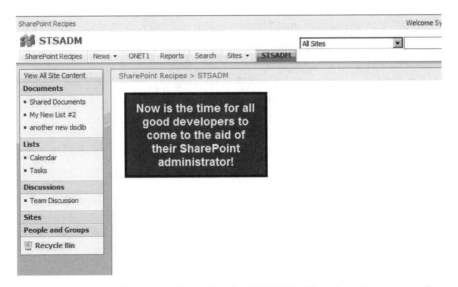

Figure 8-3. *Notice added to page by using the STSADM addnoticetosite command*

▪**Note** You can test the `adddoclibtosite` command in a similar fashion.

Variations

- There are really as many opportunities to extend STSADM as your needs dictate. The key limitation is that the STSADM command must be run from the console so the user interface is very limited. Hence this technique is best suited to operations that take limited inputs and don't need to display much, if any, information back to the end user.

Related Recipes

- Recipe 1-6 in Chapter 1

- Recipe 3-1 in Chapter 3

Recipe 8-2. Crawling a Database Table by Using a BDC Schema

One of the really exciting enhancements to Office SharePoint Server is the inclusion of the BDC. The BDC enables you to define external data sources such as databases or web services to SharePoint, and make those sources available through web parts, list lookup fields, or Search.

This recipe focuses on one specific application of the BDC: configuring Search to index a SQL database. When a database is indexed in this way, your end users can search for database records in the same way as they would documents in document libraries or external web sites.

▪**Note** This recipe requires a version of Microsoft Office SharePoint Server (MOSS) that includes the Business Data Catalog feature. This recipe will not work with Windows SharePoint Services alone.

Recipe Type: BDC Schema

Ingredients

In this recipe, you will crawl a database named MyDatabase, indexing a table named SharePointClasses that contains a list of classes and associated information. You will need the following:

- A database named MyDatabase

- A table in MyDatabase named SharePointClasses

- A user in the MyDatabase database mapped to the SharePoint administration account—in my example, MGEROW-MOSS-VPC\Administrator

---

■**Caution** SharePoint will attempt to crawl the database by logging on with the service account configured for all Search crawls. Whatever account you've configured in SharePoint for that purpose should have at least Select permissions for any tables you want to crawl.

- An XML schema in BDC format defining the database connection and table we want to index

Special Considerations

- The BDC schema we'll create here is fairly limited and has just enough information to allow Search to index the database, but not enough to take full advantage of the BDC web parts that ship with MOSS. For an explanation of how to create a fully featured BDC schema, see the MOSS SDK, which you can download from www.microsoft.com/downloads/details.aspx?familyid=6D94E307-67D9-41AC-B2D6-0074D6286FA9&displaylang=en.

Preparation

First, create the data source:

1. Open the Microsoft SQL Server 2005 Management Studio (or Enterprise Manager if you're using SQL Server 2000) and create a new database named MyDatabase.

2. Add a new table to the database named SharePointClasses with the columns shown in Figure 8-4.

Table - dbo.SharePointClasses	Table - dbo.SharePointClasse	
Column Name	Data Type	Allow Nulls
Class	varchar(50)	☐
Namespace	varchar(MAX)	☑
Comments	text	☑
		☐

Figure 8-4. *SharePointClasses table structure*

The SQL statement to create the preceding table is as follows:

```
CREATE TABLE [dbo].[SharePointClasses](
    [Class] [varchar](50) COLLATE Latin1_General_CI_AI NOT NULL,
    [Namespace] [varchar](max) COLLATE Latin1_General_CI_AI NULL,
    [Comments] [text] COLLATE Latin1_General_CI_AI NULL,
 CONSTRAINT [PK_SharePointClasses] PRIMARY KEY CLUSTERED
(
```

```
    [Class] ASC
)WITH (PAD_INDEX  = OFF, STATISTICS_NORECOMPUTE = OFF,
IGNORE_DUP_KEY = OFF, ALLOW_ROW_LOCKS = ON,
ALLOW_PAGE_LOCKS  = ON) ON [PRIMARY]
) ON [PRIMARY] TEXTIMAGE_ON [PRIMARY]
```

3. Save the table and then enter some sample data as shown in Figure 8-5.

Class	Namespace	Comments
dWebPartManager	Microsoft.SharePoint.WebPartPages	Provides methods and properties to manage a collection of web parts on a web part page
SPList	Microsoft.SharePoint	Provides methods and properties to manage lists
SPSite	Microsoft.SharePoint	Provides methods and properties to manage site collections
SPWeb	Microsoft.SharePoint	Provides methods and properties to manage individual webs
NULL	NULL	NULL

Figure 8-5. *Sample data*

Next, create an XML file that will describe the data source to SharePoint:

4. If you haven't done so already, install the SharePoint Server 2007 SDK and follow the instructions for installing the BDC definition editor.

5. Open the BDC definition editor and choose the option to Add LOB System (*LOB* stands for *line-of-business*).

6. Select the option to Connect to Database, as shown in Figure 8-6. Set the connection type to SqlServer, enter a valid connection string to your new database, and then click the Connect button.

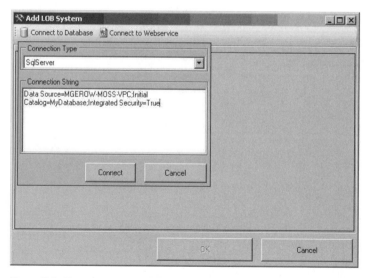

Figure 8-6. *Entering a connection string*

7. Click the Add Table button to add the SharePointClasses table to the design surface, and then click OK (Figure 8-7).

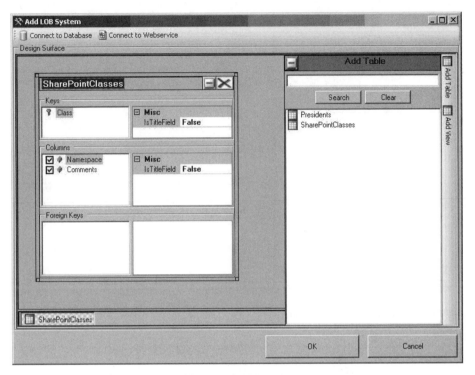

Figure 8-7. *BDC definition editor design surface with SharePointClasses table displayed*

8. Name the new schema MyDatabase and click OK.

9. The BDC schema editor window should look similar to Figure 8-8.

10. Export the schema to an XML file by selecting the top-level node in the object outline (named MyDatabase) and clicking the Export button (Figure 8-9).

11. When prompted, name the schema file MyDatabase.xml. (The XML file source is shown in the "Recipe—BDC Schema XML" section.)

12. Now import the schema into MOSS and define a Search content source by using the schema.

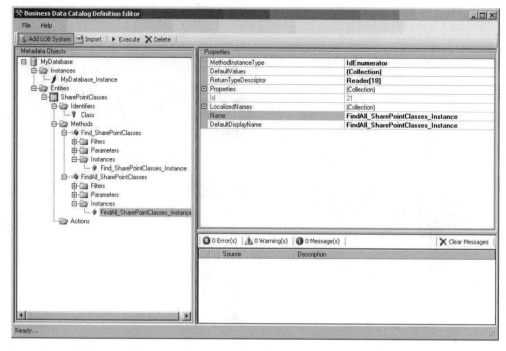

Figure 8-8. *The completed BDC schema*

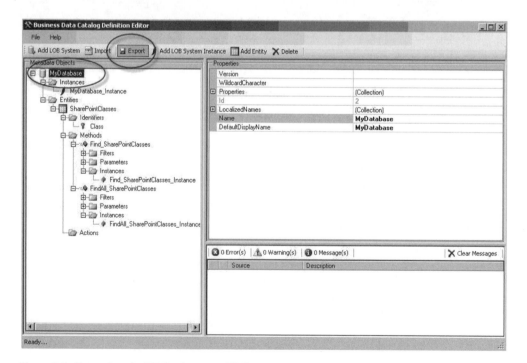

Figure 8-9. *Exporting the BDC schema to XML*

13. Open the SharePoint Central Administration Website (SCAW) and click the Shared Services Administration link as shown in Figure 8-10.

■**Note** By default, SharePoint names the shared services web application `SharedServices1`, but your installation may differ.

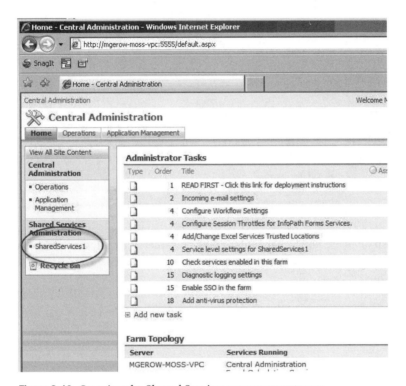

Figure 8-10. *Opening the Shared Services management page*

14. Click the Import Application Definition link under the Business Data Catalog heading (Figure 8-11).

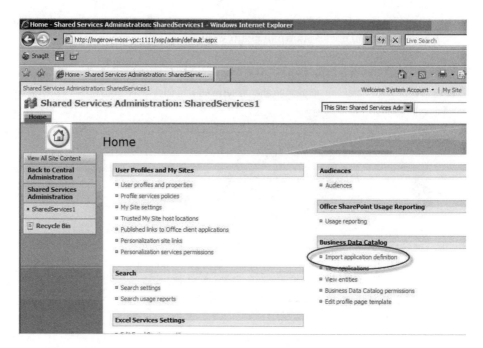

Figure 8-11. *Navigating to the BDC schema import page*

15. Enter the path to the XML schema file you saved earlier, select all the Resources to Import checkboxes, and then click the Import button (Figure 8-12).

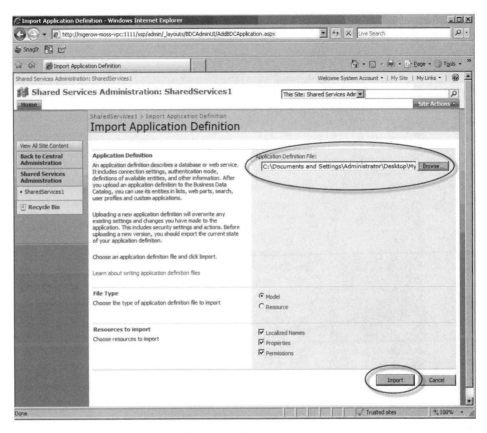

Figure 8-12. *Importing the BDC schema into SharePoint*

16. After the schema has been imported, return to the Shared Services Administration page and select Search Settings to define a new Search content source based on the BDC schema (Figure 8-13).

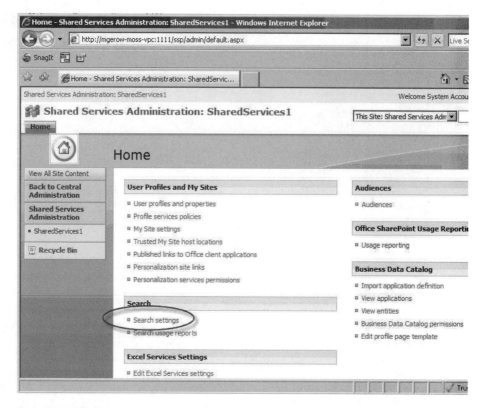

Figure 8-13. *Navigating to the search settings main page*

17. On the Configure Search Settings page, click the Content Sources and Crawl Schedules link (Figure 8-14).

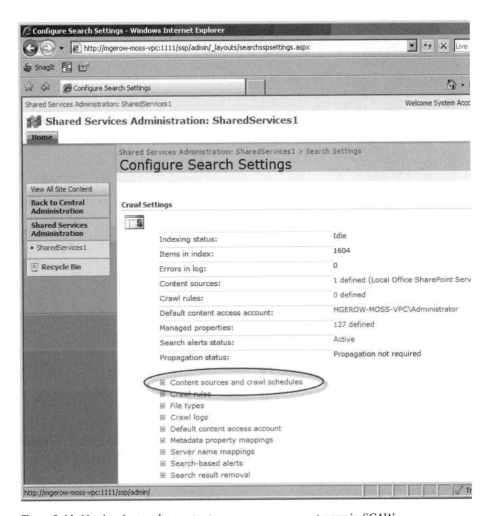

Figure 8-14. *Navigating to the content source management page in SCAW*

18. Click the New Content Source button and name the new content source MyDatabase.
Select Business Data as the Content Source Type, select the Crawl Selected Applications
radio button, and select the MyDatabase_Instance BDC schema checkbox. Then click
OK (Figure 8-15).

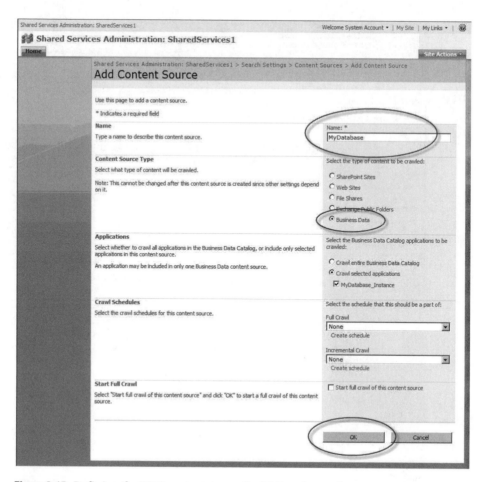

Figure 8-15. *Defining the BDC content source for MyDatabase schema*

19. SharePoint will return you to the Manage Content Sources page. Mouse over the MyDatabase content source and select Start Full Crawl from the context menu (Figure 8-16).

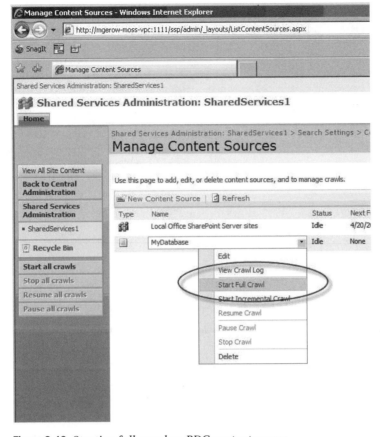

Figure 8-16. *Starting full crawl on BDC content source*

20. You can verify that the database was crawled successfully by choosing the View Crawl Log option from the same context menu (Figure 8-17).

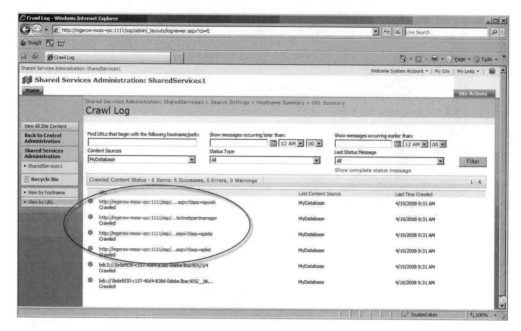

Figure 8-17. *Verifying that Search successfully crawled the BDC content source*

The text of the SharePointClasses table rows is now indexed and ready to search from within SharePoint.

Recipe—BDC Schema XML

The following is the output of the BDC definition editor, which you saved earlier. For the purposes of our recipe, you shouldn't need to edit the schema—it's provided here for your reference.

```xml
<?xml version="1.0" encoding="utf-8" standalone="yes"?>
<LobSystem xmlns:xsi="http://www.w3.org/2001/XMLSchema-instance"
xsi:schemaLocation=
"http://schemas.microsoft.com/office/2006/03/
BusinessDataCatalogBDCMetadata.xsd"
Type="Database" Version="1.0.0.0" Name="MyDatabase"
xmlns="http://schemas.microsoft.com/office/2006/03/
BusinessDataCatalog">
  <LobSystemInstances>
    <LobSystemInstance Name="MyDatabase_Instance">
      <Properties>
        <Property Name="rdbconnection Data Source"
          Type="System.String">MGEROW-MOSS-VPC</Property>
        <Property Name="rdbconnection Initial Catalog"
          Type="System.String">MyDatabase</Property>
        <Property Name="rdbconnection Integrated Security"
          Type="System.String">True</Property>
```

```
      <Property Name="DatabaseAccessProvider"
         Type="Microsoft.Office.Server.ApplicationRegistry. ➥
            SystemSpecific.Db.DbAccessProvider">SqlServer</Property>
      <Property Name="AuthenticationMode"
         Type="Microsoft.Office.Server.ApplicationRegistry. ➥
         SystemSpecific.Db.DbAuthenticationMode"> ➥
         PassThrough</Property>
    </Properties>
  </LobSystemInstance>
</LobSystemInstances>
<Entities>
  <Entity EstimatedInstanceCount="10000" Name="SharePointClasses">
    <Identifiers>
      <Identifier TypeName="System.String" Name="Class" />
    </Identifiers>
    <Methods>
      <Method Name="Find_SharePointClasses">
        <Properties>
          <Property Name="RdbCommandType"
             Type="System.Data.CommandType,
             System.Data,
             Version=2.0.0.0, Culture=neutral,
             PublicKeyToken=b77a5c561934e089">Text</Property>
          <Property Name="RdbCommandText"
             Type="System.String">
                Select "Class","Namespace","Comments" from ➥
                   SharePointClasses where Class=@Class
          </Property>
        </Properties>
        <Parameters>
          <Parameter Direction="In" Name="@Class">
            <TypeDescriptor TypeName="System.String, mscorlib,
               Version=2.0.0.0, Culture=neutral,
               PublicKeyToken=b77a5c561934e089"
               IdentifierName="Class" Name="Class" />
          </Parameter>
          <Parameter Direction="Return" Name="@SharePointClasses">
            <TypeDescriptor TypeName="System.Data.IDataReader,
               System.Data, Version=2.0.0.0, Culture=neutral,
               PublicKeyToken=b77a5c561934e089" IsCollection="true"
               Name="Reader">
              <TypeDescriptors>
                <TypeDescriptor TypeName="System.Data.IDataRecord,
                   System.Data, Version=2.0.0.0, Culture=neutral,
                   PublicKeyToken=b77a5c561934e089" Name="Record">
```

```
                    <TypeDescriptors>
                      <TypeDescriptor TypeName="System.String,
                          mscorlib, Version=2.0.0.0, Culture=neutral,
                          PublicKeyToken=b77a5c561934e089"
                          IdentifierName="Class" Name="Class" />
                      <TypeDescriptor TypeName="System.String,
                          mscorlib, Version=2.0.0.0, Culture=neutral,
                          PublicKeyToken=b77a5c561934e089"
                          Name="Namespace" />
                      <TypeDescriptor TypeName="System.String,
                          mscorlib, Version=2.0.0.0, Culture=neutral,
                          PublicKeyToken=b77a5c561934e089"
                          Name="Comments" />
                    </TypeDescriptors>
                  </TypeDescriptor>
                </TypeDescriptors>
              </TypeDescriptor>
          </Parameter>
        </Parameters>
        <MethodInstances>
```

■**Note** The SpecificFinder method instance tells SharePoint Search how to retrieve one row of the table
in order to include its contents in the index.

```
          <MethodInstance Type="SpecificFinder"
              ReturnParameterName="@SharePointClasses"
              ReturnTypeDescriptorName="Reader"
              ReturnTypeDescriptorLevel="0"
              Name="Find_SharePointClasses_Instance" />
        </MethodInstances>
      </Method>
      <Method Name="FindAll_SharePointClasses">
        <Properties>
          <Property Name="RdbCommandType"
              Type="System.Data.CommandType, System.Data,
              Version=2.0.0.0, Culture=neutral,
              PublicKeyToken=b77a5c561934e089">Text</Property>
          <Property Name="RdbCommandText"
              Type="System.String">Select "Class" from  ➥
                  SharePointClasses
          </Property>
        </Properties>
        <Parameters>
          <Parameter Direction="Return" Name="@SharePointClasses">
```

```
        <TypeDescriptor TypeName="System.Data.IDataReader,
            System.Data, Version=2.0.0.0, Culture=neutral,
            PublicKeyToken=b77a5c561934e089" IsCollection="true"
            Name="Reader">
          <TypeDescriptors>
            <TypeDescriptor TypeName="System.Data.IDataRecord,
                System.Data, Version=2.0.0.0, Culture=neutral,
                PublicKeyToken=b77a5c561934e089" Name="Record">
              <TypeDescriptors>
                <TypeDescriptor TypeName="System.String,
                    mscorlib, Version=2.0.0.0, Culture=neutral,
                    PublicKeyToken=b77a5c561934e089"
                    IdentifierName="Class" Name="Class" />
              </TypeDescriptors>
            </TypeDescriptor>
          </TypeDescriptors>
        </TypeDescriptor>
      </Parameter>
    </Parameters>
    <MethodInstances>
```

■Note The `IdEnumerator()` method instance tells SharePoint Search how to retrieve a list of primary keys for all rows in the source table.

```
        <MethodInstance Type="IdEnumerator"
            ReturnParameterName="@SharePointClasses"
            ReturnTypeDescriptorName="Reader"
            ReturnTypeDescriptorLevel="0"
            Name="FindAll_SharePointClasses_Instance" />
        </MethodInstances>
      </Method>
    </Methods>
  </Entity>
 </Entities>
</LobSystem>
```

To Run

You may search your new BDC content source in the same way you would any SharePoint content. To do so, navigate to your root MOSS page and enter a term that you'd expect to find in your database. In the example shown in Figure 8-18, I entered SPLimitedWebPartManager.

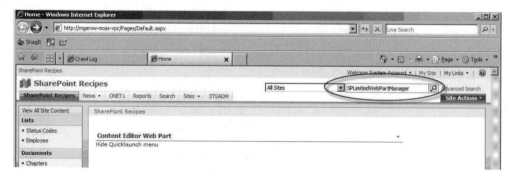

Figure 8-18. *Entering search term*

The resulting page displays all "documents" that include that term (Figure 8-19).

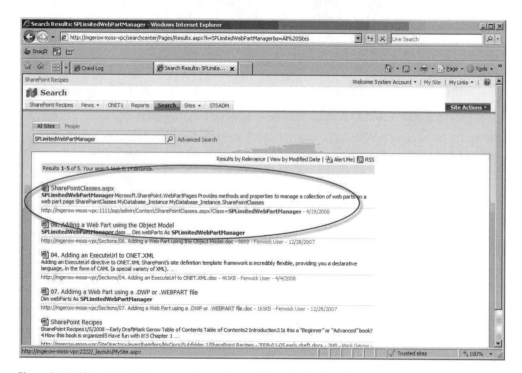

Figure 8-19. *SharePointClasses row found using SharePoint Search*

Note that the first entry is for a page named SharePointClasses.aspx. SharePoint created this page to display data for a given row from our SharePointClasses table. Clicking the link will display the default viewer page for the SharePointClasses table (Figure 8-20).

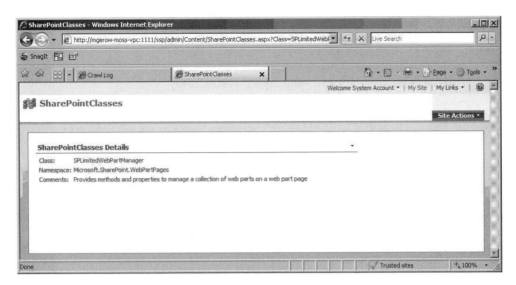

Figure 8-20. *The default SharePointClasses viewer page*

Variations

- As you can see, enabling a search of a database table is fairly easy, although it does entail many steps. But after you've created a schema, creating additional schemas and installing them is pretty straightforward. In this example, we used a simple query from a single table, but you can just as easily query views, multitable Selects, or stored procedures by using the same approach, simply by changing the RdbCommandText property as shown here:

```
<Property Name="RdbCommandText" Type="System.String">
    Select "Class","Namespace","Comments" from
        SharePointClasses where Class=@Class
</Property>
```

- We did not include an instance of a Finder descriptor, but you can add one to allow your BDC schema to be used with the BDC web parts that ship with MOSS. The additional method descriptor for our example would look like the following:

```
<Method Name="Finder">
  <Properties>
```

■**Note** The use of LIKE rather than = in the Select command allows you to perform wildcard searches.

```
        <Property Name="RdbCommandText" Type="System.String">
           Select * from SharePointClasses  where Class LIKE ➡
              @Class</Property>
        <Property Name="RdbCommandType"
           Type="System.Data.CommandType, System.Data,
           Version=2.0.0.0, Culture=neutral,
           PublicKeyToken=b77a5c561934e089">Text</Property>
     </Properties>
```

Note The <FilterDescriptor> element enables you to define prompts that users can enter search strings into via the BDC web parts to query the database.

```
        <FilterDescriptors>
          <FilterDescriptor Type="Comparison" Name="Class">
            <Properties>
              <Property Name="Comparator"
                 Type="System.String">Equals</Property>
            </Properties>
          </FilterDescriptor>
        </FilterDescriptors>
        <Parameters>
          <Parameter Direction="In" Name="@Class">
            <TypeDescriptor TypeName="System.String"
               IdentifierName="Class" AssociatedFilter="Class"
               Name="Class">
              <DefaultValues>
                <DefaultValue MethodInstanceName="Finder"
                   Type="System.String"></DefaultValue>
              </DefaultValues>
            </TypeDescriptor>
          </Parameter>
          <Parameter Direction="Return" Name="@SharePointClasses">
            <TypeDescriptor TypeName="System.Data.IDataReader,
                System.Data, Version=2.0.0.0, Culture=neutral,
                PublicKeyToken=b77a5c561934e089" IsCollection="true"
                Name="Reader">
              <TypeDescriptors>
                <TypeDescriptor TypeName="System.Data.IDataRecord,
                    System.Data, Version=2.0.0.0, Culture=neutral,
                    PublicKeyToken=b77a5c561934e089" Name="Record">
                  <TypeDescriptors>
                    <TypeDescriptor TypeName="System.String"
                        IdentifierName="Class" Name="Class" />
```

```
            <TypeDescriptor TypeName="System.String"
                Name="Namespace" />
            <TypeDescriptor TypeName="System.String"
                Name="Comments" />
          </TypeDescriptors>
        </TypeDescriptor>
      </TypeDescriptors>
    </TypeDescriptor>
  </Parameter>
</Parameters>
<MethodInstances>
  <MethodInstance Type="Finder"
      ReturnParameterName="@SharePointClasses"
      ReturnTypeDescriptorName="Reader"
      ReturnTypeDescriptorLevel="0" Name="Finder" />
</MethodInstances>
</Method>
```

Figure 8-21 shows an example of a BDC List web part for our schema.

Figure 8-21. *SharePointClasses row found using the BDC List web part*

Related Recipes

- Recipe 8-3

Recipe 8-3. Creating a Custom MOSS Search Page

As you've already seen, MOSS Search is a significantly richer product than was available in SharePoint Server 2003. In addition to the ability to index database content through the BDC, its performance and accuracy are much better. With all the potential of Search, it's not surprising that Microsoft has provided developers with access through the object model. By using this, it's possible to create a wide range of customized search solutions, such as the one we'll create here.

In out-of-the-box MOSS implementations, the search results are formatted by using an XSLT transform. This approach is incredibly flexible and requires no programming to perform many slick formatting operations. However, sometimes you'll want to get your hands on the result set to perform more-complex operations than those available via XSLT. In such a situation, it's helpful to load the results into a DataTable object for further manipulation.

In this recipe, you'll create a custom ASP.NET web application to query the Search index and display the results. After the results are obtained, you'll perform some basic formatting and then display your results by using a `GridView` control.

Recipe Type: ASP.NET Application

Ingredients

Assembly References

- `Microsoft.Office.Server` .NET assembly

- `Microsoft.Office.Server.Search` .NET assembly

- `Microsoft.SharePoint.Portal` .NET assembly

■**Note** Most of the recipes in this book do not require MOSS and so use the Windows SharePoint Services .NET assembly. Because here we are performing operations that are available only in MOSS, we substitute that library for its MOSS equivalent.

Special Considerations

- This page should run by using the same application pool as MOSS; typically that is the SharePoint–80 pool (Figure 8-22).

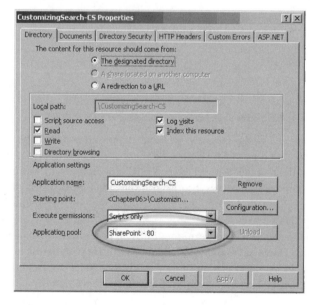

Figure 8-22. *Assigning the application pool in IIS Manager*

Preparation

1. Create a new ASP.NET web application.

2. Add references to the Windows SharePoint Services, `Microsoft.Office.Server`, `Microsoft.Office.Server.Search`, and `Microsoft.Portal.Server` .NET assemblies.

3. Add `using` or `Imports` statements for the `Microsoft.Office.Server`, `Microsoft.Office.Server.Search`, `Microsoft.Office.Server.Search.Query`, and `Microsoft.Office.Server.Search.Administration` namespaces.

4. Add the following web controls to the page:

   `txtSearch`: A text box to hold the search string

   `cmdSearch`: A command button to execute the search

   `gridSearch`: A `GridView` control to display the results

   `blMsg`: A `Label` control to display any messages to the user

   The completed web page will look similar to that shown in Figure 8-23.

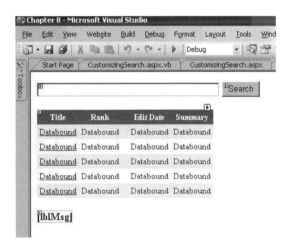

Figure 8-23. *Customized search page layout*

5. Add the source code shown in the appropriate Recipe section.

Process Flow

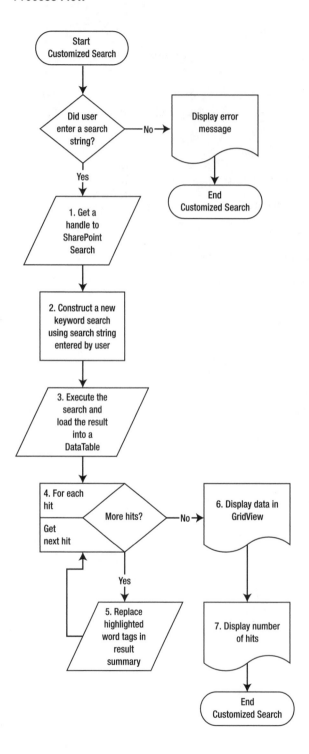

1. If the user entered a search string, get a handle to the Search service on the current MOSS server by using the `ServerContext.GetContext()` method; otherwise, display a message informing the user that a search string is required and exit.

2. Construct a new keyword query using the search text. In addition, set the time-out to 60 seconds, and the row limit to 1,000.

3. Execute the keyword query search, and use the `DataTable.Load()` method to copy the resulting data into a `DataTable` object for simplified processing.

4. Loop through returned rows, finding the `<c0>` through `<c3>` tags embedded in the `HitHighlightedSummary` field.

5. Replace those tags with `<span>` tags to bold and highlight search words in the summary text when output to the page.

6. Load the formatted `DataTable` into a `GridView` web control for display on the page.

7. Write the number of hits (that is, the number of rows in the `DataTable`) to the bottom of the page and then display the results.

Recipe—ASPX (See Project CustomizingSearch-CS, File CustomizingSearch.aspx)

```
<%@ Page Language="C#" AutoEventWireup="true" ➥
CodeFile="CustomizingSearch.aspx.cs" Inherits="_Default" %>
<!DOCTYPE html PUBLIC "-//W3C//DTD XHTML 1.0 Transitional//EN" ➥
"http://www.w3.org/TR/xhtml1/DTD/xhtml1-transitional.dtd">
<html xmlns="http://www.w3.org/1999/xhtml" >
<head runat="server">
    <title>Untitled Page</title>
    <link type="text/css" href="StyleSheet.css" />
</head>
<body>
    <form id="form1" runat="server">
    <div>
        <asp:TextBox ID="txtSearch" runat="server"
            Width="287px"></asp:TextBox>
        <asp:Button ID="cmdSearch" runat="server"
            OnClick="cmdSearch_Click" Text="Search" /><br />
        <br />
        <asp:GridView ID="gridSearch" runat="server"
            AutoGenerateColumns="False" CellPadding="4"
            Font-Size="Smaller" ForeColor="#333333" GridLines="None">
            <FooterStyle BackColor="#5D7B9D" Font-Bold="True"
                ForeColor="White" />
            <RowStyle BackColor="#F7F6F3" ForeColor="#333333" />
            <Columns>
                <asp:HyperLinkField DataNavigateUrlFields="Path"
                    DataTextField="Title" HeaderText="Title"
                    Text="Title" />
```

```
                    <asp:BoundField DataField="Rank" HeaderText="Rank" />
                    <asp:BoundField />
                    <asp:BoundField DataField="Write" HeaderText="Edit
                    Date" />
                    <asp:BoundField DataField="HitHighlightedSummary"
                        HeaderText="Summary" HtmlEncode="False"
                        HtmlEncodeFormatString="False" />
                </Columns>
                <PagerStyle BackColor="#284775" ForeColor="White"
                    HorizontalAlign="Center" />
                <SelectedRowStyle BackColor="#E2DED6" Font-Bold="True"
                    ForeColor="#333333" />
                <HeaderStyle BackColor="#5D7B9D" Font-Bold="True"
                    ForeColor="White" />
                <EditRowStyle BackColor="#999999" />
                <AlternatingRowStyle BackColor="White"
                    ForeColor="#284775" />
            </asp:GridView>
            <br />
            <asp:Label ID="lblMsg" runat="server" Font-Bold="true"></asp:Label></div>
        </form>
    </body>
    </html>
```

Recipe—VB (See Project CustomizingSearch-VB, Class CustomizingSearch.aspx.vb)

```vb
Imports System
Imports System.Data
Imports System.Configuration
Imports System.Web
Imports System.Web.Security
Imports System.Web.UI
Imports System.Web.UI.WebControls
Imports Microsoft.Office.Server
Imports Microsoft.Office.Server.Search
Imports Microsoft.Office.Server.Search.Query
Imports Microsoft.Office.Server.Search.Administration
Partial Public Class _Default
    Inherits System.Web.UI.Page
    Protected Sub cmdSearch_Click(ByVal sender As Object,
        ByVal e As EventArgs) Handles cmdSearch.Click
        If txtSearch.Text <> "" Then
            performSearch()
        Else
            lblMsg.Text = "Please enter a search string"
        End If
    End Sub
```

```
Private Sub performSearch()
    ' Step 1: Get a handle to the Shared Services Search context
    Dim context As ServerContext = ServerContext.GetContext("SharedServices1")
    ' Step 2: Construct a keyword search query
    Dim kwq As New KeywordQuery(context)
    kwq.ResultTypes = ResultType.RelevantResults
    kwq.EnableStemming = True
    kwq.TrimDuplicates = True
    kwq.QueryText = txtSearch.Text
    kwq.Timeout = 60000
    kwq.RowLimit = 1000
    kwq.KeywordInclusion = KeywordInclusion.AllKeywords
    ' Step 3: Get the results to a DataTable
    Dim results As ResultTableCollection = kwq.Execute()
    Dim resultTable As ResultTable = results(ResultType.RelevantResults)
    Dim dtResults As New DataTable()
    dtResults.Load(resultTable)
    ' Step 4: Format summary
    For Each drResult As DataRow In dtResults.Rows
        drResult("HitHighlightedSummary") = ➡
            formatSummary(drResult("HitHighlightedSummary"))
    Next
    ' Step 6: Write out table of results
    gridSearch.DataSource = dtResults
    gridSearch.DataBind()
    ' Step 7: Inform the user how many hits were found
    lblMsg.Text = dtResults.Rows.Count.ToString() + " hits"
End Sub
' Step 5: Highlight first 4 hits
' SharePoint Search places <c[#]> tags around the
' first 10 words in the summary that match
' a keyword search term. Here I just find
' the first four and replace them with
' a <SPAN> element to show the hits in
' bold with a yellow background
Private Function formatSummary(ByVal strSummary As String) As String
    strSummary = strSummary.Replace( _
        "<c0>", _
        "<span style='font-weight:bold; background-color:yellow'>")
    strSummary = strSummary.Replace("</c0>", "</span>")
    strSummary = strSummary.Replace( _
        "<c1>",
        "<span style='font-weight:bold; background-color:yellow'>")
    strSummary = strSummary.Replace("</c1>", "</span>")
    strSummary = strSummary.Replace( _ _
```

```
            "<c2>", "<span style='font-weight:bold; ➥
                background-color:yellow'>")
        strSummary = strSummary.Replace("</c2>", "</span>")
        strSummary = strSummary.Replace( _ _
            "<c3>", "<span style='font-weight:bold; ➥
                background-color:yellow'>")
        strSummary = strSummary.Replace("</c3>", "</span>")
        Return strSummary
    End Function
End Class
```

Recipe—C# (See Project CustomizingSearch-CS, Class CustomizingSearch.aspx.cs)

```csharp
using System;
using System.Data;
using System.Configuration;
using System.Web;
using System.Web.Security;
using System.Web.UI;
using System.Web.UI.WebControls;
using Microsoft.Office.Server;
using Microsoft.Office.Server.Search;
using Microsoft.Office.Server.Search.Query;
using Microsoft.Office.Server.Search.Administration;
public partial class _Default : System.Web.UI.Page
{
    protected void cmdSearch_Click(object sender, EventArgs e)
    {
        if (txtSearch.Text != "")
        {
            performSearch();
        }
        else
        {
            lblMsg.Text = "Please enter a search string";
        }
    }
    private void performSearch()
    {
        // Step 1: Get a handle to the Shared Services Search context
        ServerContext context = ServerContext.GetContext("SharedServices1");
        // Step 2: Construct a keyword search query
        KeywordQuery kwq = new KeywordQuery(context);
        kwq.ResultTypes = ResultType.RelevantResults;
        kwq.EnableStemming = true;
        kwq.TrimDuplicates = true;
        kwq.QueryText = txtSearch.Text;
```

```csharp
        kwq.Timeout = 60000;
        kwq.RowLimit = 1000;
        kwq.KeywordInclusion = KeywordInclusion.AllKeywords;
        // Step 3: Get the results to a DataTable
        ResultTableCollection results = kwq.Execute();
        ResultTable resultTable = results[ResultType.RelevantResults];
        DataTable dtResults = new DataTable();
        dtResults.Load(resultTable);
        // Step 4: Format summary
        foreach (DataRow drResult in dtResults.Rows)
        {
            drResult["HitHighlightedSummary"] =
                formatSummary(
                drResult["HitHighlightedSummary"].ToString());
        }
        // Step 6: Write out table of results
        gridSearch.DataSource = dtResults;
        gridSearch.DataBind();
        // Step 7: Inform the user how many hits were found
        lblMsg.Text = dtResults.Rows.Count.ToString() + " hits";
}
// Step 5: Highlight first 4 hits
//   SharePoint Search places <c[#]> tags around the
//   first 10 words in the summary that match
//   a keyword search term.  Here I just find
//   the first four and replace them with
//   a <SPAN> element to show the hits in
//   bold with a yellow background
string formatSummary(string strSummary)
{
    strSummary = strSummary.Replace(
        "<c0>",
        "<span style='font-weight:bold; ➥
            background-color:yellow'>");
    strSummary = strSummary.Replace("</c0>","</span>");
    strSummary = strSummary.Replace(
        "<c1>",
        "<span style='font-weight:bold; ➥
            background-color:yellow'>");
    strSummary = strSummary.Replace("</c1>", "</span>");

    strSummary = strSummary.Replace(
        "<c2>",
        "<span style='font-weight:bold; ➥
            background-color:yellow'>");
    strSummary = strSummary.Replace("</c2>", "</span>");
```

```
        strSummary = strSummary.Replace(
          "<c3>",
          "<span style='font-weight:bold; ➡
              background-color:yellow'>");
        strSummary = strSummary.Replace("</c3>", "</span>");

        return strSummary;
    }
}
```

To Run

After you've created the ASP.NET web application and entered the code as shown, you're ready to run your application. In Visual Studio, click the Run button. Enter a search string and click the Search button; you should see a web page similar to that shown in Figure 8-24.

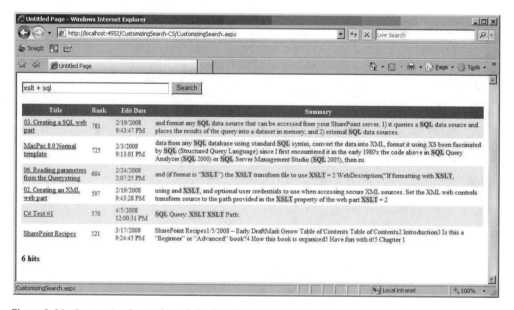

Figure 8-24. *Customized search with hit highlighting displayed*

This page will respond to the same search syntax you can use on a standard MOSS search page.

Variations

- In this recipe, we are returning only the default managed properties; however, you can return any managed property defined on your search server. For example, if you want to include the ContentSource managed property in your result, you can use the KeywordQuery. SelectedProperties.Add() method prior to executing your query. The following code snippet shows the lines that need to be added:

```
// Add the specific managed properties to output
kwq.SelectProperties.Add("Title");
kwq.SelectProperties.Add("Rank");
kwq.SelectProperties.Add("Size");
kwq.SelectProperties.Add("Write");
kwq.SelectProperties.Add("Path");
kwq.SelectProperties.Add("HitHighlightedSummary");
kwq.SelectProperties.Add("ContentSource");
```

Note If you use this method, you will need to specify all properties you want included in the result table.

And Figure 8-25 shows the resulting output, including the ContentSource property.

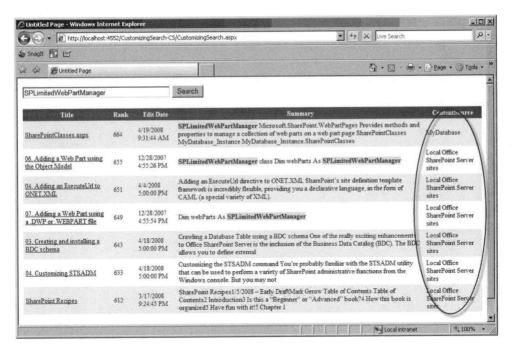

Figure 8-25. *Customized search page with ContentSource property displayed*

Related Recipes

- Recipe 8-2

Index

■Symbols

& (ampersand), 284

? (question mark), 284

■A

Active Directory (AD), 79

 adding users to, 132–143

 connection strings in, 133

AddComment application, 382–401

AddContentEditorWebPart() method, 410, 416

AddGroupOM application, 105–111

addnoticetosite command, 451

AddRoleOM application, 112–121

AddRoleWS application, 121–132

AddUserOM application, 90–96

AddUserToADService application, 132–143

AddUserWS application, 97–105

AddWebPart() method, 52, 410, 416

AddWebPartDWP application, 63–75

AddWebPartOM application, 52–62

ADO.NET DataTable, 276

ADO.NET DataView object, 276

Alerts, email, 349–356

AllowUnsafeUpdates, 52

<AllUsersWebPart> element, 408

ampersand (&), 284

application pool, assigning, 472

ASP.NET 2.0, web-part framework, 207, 209

ASP.NET applications

 for adding and modifying properties, 44–52

 for adding documents to document library, 191–197

 for adding roles to web sites, 121–132

 for list creation, 145–167

 for list updates, 167–191

 to query Search index, 471–481

 for site collection creation, 13–24

 for site creation, 24–44

 for site user information, 79–90

 for uploading documents to document library, 197–205

 security restrictions on, 2, 13

ASP.NET web service, for adding users to Active Directory, 132–143

assembly references, 2

asynchronous events, 338

authentication, with web services, 14

authentication modes, web part, 251

■B

base permissions, 112, 124

batch operations, 180, 191

browsers, support for JavaScript in, 428, 435

btn_Click() event handler, 317, 320

built-in security model, 79

Business Data Catalog (BDC), 452

Business Data Catalog (BDC) content source, 461–463, 467

Business Data Catalog (BDC) schema

   crawling database table using, 452–471

   exporting to XML file, 455

   importing into SharePoint, 457–459

■C

C#

   AddComment application, 390–393

   AddGroupOM application, 109–111

   AddRoleOM application, 116–119

   AddRoleWS application, 128–130

   AddUserOM application, 94–96

   AddUserToADService application, 108–141

   AddUserWS application, 102–105

   AddWebPartDWP application, 69

   AddWebPartOM application, 58–62

   ConnectablePageViewer application, 268–271

   CreateListOM application, 151–154

   CreateListService application, 162–167

   CreateSiteCollectionConsole application, 7–13

   CreateSiteCollectionWebService application, 19–24

   CreateSiteConsole application, 27–32

   CreateWeb application, 42–44

   CreateWebService application, 38–42

   CustomizesSTSADM application, 446–450

   CustomizingSearch application, 478–480

   EditSiteProperties application, 50–52

   FileUploadOM application, 195–196

   FileUploadServive application, 201–204

   InstallPreventDeletion application, 362–364

   InstallSendEmail application, 355–356

   InstallSetDocumentFields application, 346–349

   InstallUpdateFieldsEventHandler application, 373–376

   ObtainAllUsersInSite application, 85–89

   PageViewerWebPart application, 256–259

   PreventDeletion application, 361–362

   QuerystringWebPart application, 279–283

   RSSWebPart application, 214–217

   SelectWebParts application, 420–424

   SendEmail application, 353–355

   SetDocumentFields application, 344

   SmartPartStatusWebPart application, 293–297

   SQLWebPart application, 243–246

   UpdateFieldsEventHandler application, 370–373

   UpdateListOM application, 174–179

   UpdateListWS application, 186–190

   WebPropertiesWebPart application, 328–334

   XMLWebPart application, 227–232

   ZoneTabWebPart application, 308–314

calculations, in list fields, using event handler, 364–376

<![CDATA[.]]> element, 407

Chrome Type property, 432

Clients.xslt, 283

client-side validation, 24

Code Access Security (CAS), 208

Collaborative Application Markup Language (CAML), 156, 403, 409

<command> element, 446

Commands, batching, 180, 191

<Configuration> attributes, 405, 411

configuration-management software, 410

ConnectablePageViewer application, 261–272

connection strings, in Active Directory, 133

ConnectionConsumer() method, 264, 267, 271

ConnectionProvider() method, 264, 266, 270

console applications, 2

Content Editor web parts, 403–407, 427–441

ContentSource property, 480

Create GUID utility, 385

CreateChildControls() method, 264–270, 298, 300, 318

CreateListOM application, 145–155

CreateListService application, 156–167

CreateSiteCollectionConsole application, 13

CreateSiteCollectionWebService application, 13–24

CreateSiteConsole application, 24–32

CreateWebService application, 33–44

credentials, passing, 262

custom menus, adding, using Feature interface, 381–401

custom roles, 112

custom web parts, 63–62

CustomizingSearch application, 471–481

■ D

Data property, 356

database, configuring Search to index, 452–471

DataGrid object, 276

DataGrid web control, 219, 240

DataSet object, 219, 222

DataTable.Load() method, 475

debugging, event handlers, 340, 357

Default.aspx, 52

delbtn_Click() event handler, 317, 322

DirectoryServices library, 132

displayClientData() method, 274

Dispose() method, 7

Docicon. Xml, adding PDF image to, 377–380

document libraries
    adding documents to, 191–205
    updating list fields when adding documents to, 339–349

DocumentComments.xml, 385–387

documents
    adding to document library, using object model, 191–197
    adding to document library, using web services, 197–205

.dwp file, adding web parts using, 63–75

■ E

EditControlBlock action, 387

EditProperties application, 44–52

ElementManifests, 385–387

email
    formatting, 356
    sending upon task completion, 349–356

event handlers
    creating calculated fields with, 364–376
    debugging, 340, 357
    exception handling, 365
    to generate email, 349–356
    performance issues and, 365
    to prevent deletion of list items, 357–364
    reasons to create, 337
    SharePoint 2007 enhancements, 338–339
    updating list fields, 339–349
    workflows vs., 337–338

EventHandler Explorer, 347

events
asynchronous, 338
synchronous, 338
exception handling, with event handlers, 365
ExecuteUrl directive
adding to Onet.xml, 409–426
provided in Onet.xml, 24, 33
<ExecuteUrl> element, 409
explicit authentication mode, 251
Extensible Stylesheet Language Transformation (XSLT), 76, 233–236, 246–247, 274

■F

Feature interface, adding custom menus using, 381–401
features
activating, 387
components of, 385
deactivating, 387
ElementManifests, 385–387
installer script, 387
installing/deinstalling, 387
scope of, 382, 385
storage of, 384
FileUploadOM application, 191–197
FileUploadService application, 197–205
<FilterDescriptor> element, 470
Finder descriptor, 469
format property, 240

■G

getElementById() function, 434
getElementsByClass() function, 430, 434
GetHelpMessage() function, 446
GetPermissionFlags() method, 121, 124
GetProfileStatus() method, 287

Global Assembly Cache (GAC), 207, 208
GridView control, 472, 475
groups
adding, using object model, 105–111
adding, using web services, 97–105
GUID features, 385

■H

href property, 438
HTML, web parts, 251

■I

.ico files, 286
IdEnumerator() method, 467
<IFRAME> tag, 261, 262
IIS. See Internet Information Services
IIS Manager application, 412
IISRESET command, 378, 380, 405, 411
Impersonate web-part property, 222
impersonation authentication mode, 251
index, database, 452–471
InstallPreventDeletion application, 360–364
InstallSendEmail application, 353–356
InstallSetDocumentFields application, 343, 346–349
InstallUpdateFieldsEventHandler application, 369, 373–376
Internet Information Services (IIS)
configuration, for AddComment application, 393–401
web servers, 33
invoke() method, 135
ISPStsadmCommand interface, 444, 446
isQuickLaunchHidden cookie, 430
ItemAdded event, 356
ItemUpdating event, 364

■J

JavaScript

    hiding QuickLaunch menu with, 427–435

    for opening list items in new window, 435–441

    page modification with, 427–441

■K

KeywordQuery.SelectedProperties.Add() method, 480

■L

layouts directory, 384

_layouts/virtual path, 410, 411

list fields

    creating calculated, with event handler, 364–376

    updating, when adding document to document library, 339–349

list items

    opening in new window, 435–441

    preventing deletion of, 357–364

lists

    creating, using object model, 145–155

    creating, using web services, 156–167

    updating, using object model, 167–179

    updating, using web services, 180–191

Lists.asmx web service, 180

Lists.GetListItems() method, 180

Lists.UpdateListItems() method, 180

■M

Manage Event Handlers, 347

maximum file size, 198

Microsoft Office SharePoint Server (MOSS)

    creating custom search page, 471–481

    RSS Feed web part, 219

Microsoft Visual SourceSafe, 410

Microsoft.SharePoint class library, 2, 382, 412

Microsoft.SharePoint namespace, 287, 316

Microsoft.SharePoint.WebControls namespace, 287

■N

.NET console applications

    for adding groups, 105–111

    for adding roles to web sites, 112–121

    for adding users and groups, 97–105

    for adding users, 90–96

    for adding web parts, 52–75

    for site collection creation, 13

    for site creation, 24–32

.NET interface, 264

.NET user control, using SmartPart to expose, 285–297

.NET Windows application, 13

■O

-O CREATESITE command, 13, 14, 24

object model

    adding documents to document library using, 191–197

    adding groups using, 105–111

    adding roles using, 112–121

    adding users with, 90–96

    adding web parts using, 52–62

    list creation using, 145–155

    list updates using, 167–179

    SharePoint, 209

    site collection creation using, 13

    site creation using, 24–32

ObtainAllUsersInSite application, 79–90

onclick event handler, 435, 438

Onet.xml, 24, 33, 381

    adding ExecuteUrl directive to, 409–426

    adding web parts through, 402–408

organizational units, AD, 135

■P

page layout, SelectWebParts application, 416–417

Page Viewer web part, 403–406, 261–272

PageViewerWebPart application, 250–261

parameters, web-part, 273–285

passwords, setting to never expire, 133–135

PDF file icon, adding to Docicon.xml, 377–380

permissions

    base, 112, 124

    configuration, web parts and, 208

    inheritance of, 112

    to prevent deletion of list items, 357–364

    verifying new, 119

portability, 13

postprocessing, 427

PreventDeletion application, 359–364

properties, site

    adding and modifiying, 44–52

    web part for editing, 304–335

property bag, 44

property collections, 316

public method, web part, 264

■Q

queries, 238

Querystring web part, 273–285

QuerystringWebPart application, 273–285

question mark (?), 284

QuickLaunch menu, hiding, 427–435

■R

RdbCommandText property, 469

Reflector, 217

relative references, 262

RenderContents() method, 261, 267, 270, 274, 299, 317

Response.Redirect() method, 384

role definitions. *See* roles

roles

    adding, using object model, 112–121

    adding, using web services, 121–132

    defined, 112

root web, 24

RSS feeds, creating simple web part for, 208–219

RSSWebPart application, 208–219

Run() function, 446

■S

<SafeControl> element, 207, 217

scope, feature, 382, 385

<SCRIPT SRC=...> element, 435

security configurations, web parts and, 208

SelectWebParts application, 414–426

SendEmail application, 351–355

ServerContext.GetContext() method, 475

SetDocumentFields application, 342–344

setOpenInNewWindow() function, 435–441

Shared Services Administration, 457

SharePoint 2007

    event handler enhancements in, 338–339

    security restrictions, 2, 13

    site collection creation and, 2

SharePoint Central Administration Website (SCAW), 198, 382

SharePoint Search

configuring, to index SQL database, 452–471

creating custom search page, 471–481

SharePoint web-part classes, 207

ShowHideWebParts() method, 299, 301–302, 317

Simple Mail Transfer Protocol (SMTP), 350

Site Actions menu, 105

site collections

creating, using object model, 13

creating, using web services, 13–24

site creation

using a web service, 33–44

using the object model, 24–32

site management

adding and modifying properties, 44–52

adding web parts, 52–75

introduction to, 1

site properties

adding and modifying, 44–52

web part for editing, 304–335

site-definition templates

adding ExecuteUrl directive to, 409–426

editing, 403, 410

new, 402–408

sites

adding groups to, using object model, 105–111

adding groups to, using web services, 97–105

adding roles, using object model, 112–121

adding roles, using web services, 121–132

adding users to, using object model, 90–96

adding users to, using web services, 97–105

adding web parts to, 1

SmartPart, 285–297

SmartPartStatusWebPart application, 289–297

SMTP (Simple Mail Transfer Protocol), 350

SN.exe command, 217, 340, 350, 358

SPBasePermissions enum type, 122, 124

SPControl.getContextWeb() method, 416

SpecificFinder method, 466

SPItemEventReceiver, 339

SPList object, 287

SPList.GetItems(SPQuery), 342

SPListEventReceiver, 339

SPListItem object, 342, 351, 359

SPListItem.Update() method, 170

SPListItemCollection.Add() method, 170

SPListItems.GetDataTable() method, 276

SPRoleDefinition class, 114

SPRoleDefinitionCollection class, 114

SPSecurity.RunWithElevatedPrivileges() method, 33

SPSite class, 24

SPSite objectss, 7, 287

SPSite.AllWebs.Add() method, 24, 33

SPSite.RootWeb property, 24

SPSiteCollection object, 4

SPSiteCollection.Add() method, 4

SPUser object, 359

SPUser.Email property, 356

SPUser.Roles collection, 80

SPWeb objects, 7, 276, 287, 359

SPWeb.AllowUnsafeUpdates property, 44, 168

SPWeb.CurrentUser.IsSiteAdmin property, 316

SPWeb.Groups collection, 106

SPWeb.Properties collection, 44

SPWeb.Properties.Update() method, 44

SPWeb.Roles collection, 106

SPWeb.SiteGroups collection, 106

SPWeb.SiteUsers collection, 106

SPWeb.Users collection, 106

SPWeb.UsersIsWebAdmin, 316

SPWebEventReceiver, 339

SQL database, configuring Search to index, 452–471

SQL web part, 238–250

SQLWebPart application, 238–250

_statusList variable, 289, 293

_statusListSiteUrl variable, 289, 293

_statusListWeb variable, 289, 293

STSADM command, 381, 387

    addnoticetosite command, 451

    backing up with, 1

    customizing, 443–452

    -O CREATESITE command, 13, 24

stsadmcommands.recipes.xml, 444–446

synchronous events, 338

System.Drawing assembly, 298

System.Net.CredentialCache.DefaultCredentials property, 14

System.Net.Mail.MailMessage object, 351

System.Net.NetworkCredential() method, 14, 209

System.Net.WebRequest class, 262

System.Web assembly, 274, 298, 316

System.Web.UI.WebControls class library, 220, 238, 251, 262

System.Web.UI.WebControls.WebParts class library, 220, 238, 251, 262

System.Xml, 122

SystemUpdate() method, 367

■T

tabs, ZoneTab web part for, 298–315

target property, 435, 438

Template ID attribute, 412

template ID values, 404

<Templates> element, 411

TransformSource property, 240

Trffc10a.ico, 286

Trffc10b.ico, 286

Trffc10c.ico, 286

Try/Catch statements, 208

■U

Update() method, 148

UpdateFieldsEventHandler application, 367–376

UpdateList() method, 158

UpdateListItems() method, 180

UpdateListOM application, 167–179

UpdateListWS application, 182–191

UpdateStatus() method, 288

Url custom property, 210

Url() read-only property, 265

UrlAction, 387

UrlConsumer() method, 267, 271

user controls, using SmartPart to expose, 285–297

user credentials, 14

user interface (UI), site management through, 1

user security, 33

UserGroup.GetRoleCollectionFromWeb()
method, 132

users

adding, to Active Directory, 132–143

adding, using object model, 90–96

adding, using web services, 97–105

obtaining and displaying, 79–90

■V

versioning, 76

virtual directory, 33

creating, 412–414

in layouts path, 410–411

Visual Basic (VB)

AddComment application, 387

AddGroupOM application, 108

AddRoleOM application, 114

AddRoleWS application, 126

AddUserOM application, 93

AddUserToADService application, 135

AddUserWS application, 99

AddWebPartDWP application, 65–69

AddWebPartOM application, 52–59

ConnectablePageViewer application, 264

CreateListOM application, 148

CreateListService application, 158

CreateSiteCollectionConsole application, 4–7

CreateSiteCollectionWebService application, 16–19

CreateSiteConsole application, 25–27

CreateWeb application, 35–37

CreateWebService application, 33–35

CustomizingSearch application, 476

EditProperties application, 45–49

FileUploadOM application, 194

FileUploadServe application, 200

InstallPreventDeletion application, 360

InstallSendEmail application, 353

InstallSetDocumentFields application, 343

InstallUpdateFieldsEventHandler application, 369

ObtainAllUsersInSite application, 82

PageViewerWebPart application, 253

PreventDeletion application, 359

QuerystringWebPart application, 276

RSSWebPart application, 211

SelectWebParts application, 417

SendEmail application, 351

SetDocumentFields application, 342

SmartPartStatusWebPart application, 289–293

SQLWebPart application, 240

UpdateFieldsEventHandler application, 367

UpdateListOM application, 170

UpdateListWS application, 182

WebPropertiesWebPart application, 322

XMLWebPart application, 222

ZoneTabWebPart application, 302

■W

W3wp.exe, 340, 357

web controls, 264

web creation, using a web service, 33–44

web parts

adding, through Onet.xml, 402–408

adding, to sites, 1

adding, using .dwp or .webpart file, 63–75

adding, using object model, 52–62

authentication modes, 251

connectable Page Viewer, 261–272

Content Editor, 403–407

creating simple RSS feed, 208–219

custom, 63–62

deploying, 207, 208, 209

exporting, 403

introduction to, 207–208

manipulating HTML of, 251

Page Viewer, 250–272, 403–406

Querystring, 273–285

reading parameters from querystring, 273–285

reading programmatically, 209

signed, 208

SmartPart, 285–297

SQL, 238–250

Web Properties, 316–335

XML, 219–232, 235–237

ZoneTab, 298–315

.webpart file, adding web parts using, 63–75

Web Properties web part, 316–335

web services

adding documents to document library using, 197–205

adding roles using, 121–132

adding users and groups using, 97–105

authentication, 14

for adding users to Active Directory, 132–143

list creation with, 156–167

list updates using, 180–191

portability of, 13

site collection creation using, 13–24

site creation using, 33–44

web services references, 14, 33

web sites. *See* sites

Web.config file, editing in AddComment application, 393

web pages, postprocessing of, 427

web-part classes, 209

consumer, 264, 267, 270

provider, 264, 265, 268

web-part page, creating for AddComment application, 395–397

WebPropertiesWebPart application, 304–335

Webtemp.xml, 404

wildcard searches, 469

window.open() JavaScript command, 384

Windows SharePoint Services 3.0 Tools: Visual Studios 2005 Extensions, Version 1.1, 207

Windows SharePoint Services library, 382

Windows Task Scheduler, 2

Windows.SharePoint.Services .NET assembly, 274, 286, 316

workflows, event handlers vs., 337–338

■X

XML files, 232–233

Docicon. xml, 377–380

exporting BDC schema to, 455

modifications to, 377

Onet.xml, 402–408

for STSADM customization, 444–446

XML transformations (XSLT), 76, 233–237, 246–247, 274

XML web part, 219–237

XmlReader, 63

XMLWebPart application, 219–232

■Z

ZoneTab web part, 298–315

ZoneTabWebPart application, 298–315

You Need the Companion eBook

Your purchase of this book entitles you to buy the companion PDF-version eBook for only $10. Take the weightless companion with you anywhere.

We believe this Apress title will prove so indispensable that you'll want to carry it with you everywhere, which is why we are offering the companion eBook (in PDF format) for $10 to customers who purchase this book now. Convenient and fully searchable, the PDF version of any content-rich, page-heavy Apress book makes a valuable addition to your programming library. You can easily find and copy code—or perform examples by quickly toggling between instructions and the application. Even simultaneously tackling a donut, diet soda, and complex code becomes simplified with hands-free eBooks!

Once you purchase your book, getting the $10 companion eBook is simple:

❶ Visit **www.apress.com/promo/tendollars/**.

❷ Complete a basic registration form to receive a randomly generated question about this title.

❸ Answer the question correctly in 60 seconds, and you will receive a promotional code to redeem for the $10.00 eBook.

THE EXPERT'S VOICE™

2855 TELEGRAPH AVENUE | SUITE 600 | BERKELEY, CA 94705

All Apress eBooks subject to copyright protection. No part may be reproduced or transmitted in any form or by any means, electronic or mechanical, including photocopying, recording, or by any information storage or retrieval system, without the prior written permission of the copyright owner and the publisher. The purchaser may print the work in full or in part for their own noncommercial use. The purchaser may place the eBook title on any of their personal computers for their own personal reading and reference.

Offer valid through 12/3/08.